Chicagoland at 45 RPM

Chicagoland at 45 RPM
The Mid–1960s Midwest Music Mecca

George Plasketes

McFarland & Company, Inc., Publishers
Jefferson, North Carolina

LIBRARY OF CONGRESS CATALOGUING-IN-PUBLICATION DATA

Names: Plasketes, George, author.
Title: Chicagoland at 45 RPM : the mid-1960s Midwest music mecca / George Plasketes.
Description: Jefferson, North Carolina : McFarland & Company, Inc., Publishers, 2024. | Includes bibliographical references and index.
Identifiers: LCCN 2024026029 | ISBN 9781476669823 (paperback : acid free paper) ∞ ISBN 9781476653723 (ebook)
Subjects: LCSH: Popular music—Illinois—Chicago—1961-1970—History and criticism. | Popular music—Illinois—Chicago—1971-1980—History and criticism. | Rock groups—Illinois—Chicago—History. | Music radio stations—Illinois—Chicago—History. | BISAC: MUSIC / Genres & Styles / Rock
Classification: LCC ML3477.7.I3 P53 2024 | DDC 782.4216409773—dc23/eng/20240617
LC record available at https://lccn.loc.gov/2024026029

BRITISH LIBRARY CATALOGUING DATA ARE AVAILABLE

ISBN (print) 978-1-4766-6982-3
ISBN (ebook) 978-1-4766-5372-3

© 2024 George Plasketes. All rights reserved

No part of this book may be reproduced or transmitted in any form or by any means, electronic or mechanical, including photocopying or recording, or by any information storage and retrieval system, without permission in writing from the publisher.

Front cover images © 2024 Shutterstock

McFarland & Company, Inc., Publishers
Box 611, Jefferson, North Carolina 28640
www.mcfarlandpub.com

Table of Contents

*Acknowledgments and Appreciation:
   A Chicagoland Comeback*   vii

*Prelude—Make It in the Midwest: Once Upon a Time
   in Chicagoland*   1

*Introduction—45 RPM (Revolutions Per Midwest):
   A Regional Rotation and Prolific Pop Rock Garage Pocket*   13

1. AM Radio Reformation: WLS, Middle America's
   Bright New Sound   31

2. Breakthrough and Colonization   55

3. Oh Yeah '66: From "Gloria" to Glorious Train Wreck   74

4. It's Dunwich Man   93

5. Hey Baby, They're Playing Our Songs: The Buckinghams'
   Smashing '67   132

6. It's a Cryan' Shame   153

7. Ba Da Ba Ba Dah: Brass and the Bungalows of Berwyn   182

8. Cornerstone Coda: In One Ear and Gone Tomorrow   206

*Selected and Annotated Discography: The Sounds
   of Mid–1960s Chicagoland*   215

Chapter Notes   225

Bibliography   233

Index   237

Acknowledgments and Appreciation
A Chicagoland Comeback

AI (as is). All content in this book was produced by a human. I am not a robot.

Infinitude. The soundtrack, spirit and seeds of this project's origins were sown and cultivated—innocently, innately, irresistibly—in the Once Upon a Way Back When of my youthful daze in the western suburbs of Chicago, circa the 1960s and into the 1970s. Fast forward or slow turning, to the more recent sphere of adulthood and the AARProvince.... The research and writing that produced these pages has been a prolonged process, a six-plus year run-on sentence, give or take. Ironically, that span coincided with the approximate length of the period that I was documenting.

Speaking of sentences—in POW (Prisoner of Writer/Writing) terms—my wife, Julie, of Chicagoland (Oak Park) origin, could undoubtedly provide a more specific calendar count of just how long it took me to chronicle how the Midwest was won. As I was easing precariously closer toward completion of the manuscript marathon, Julie casually handed me a small rectangular box, conspicuously compatible with jewelry, and wrapped in last-ditch incentive. "You can give this to me when you are finished," she said casually, with hopeful end-in-sight, "are we there yet?" expectancy. I opened the container for a peek. Resting inside, a bracelet with the infinity symbol centered, connecting two strands. The sideway eight, our number. A simultaneous pledge and playful push across the finish line, and a wink to perseverance and purpose, paragraphs and pages, project and partnership. "You have arrived at your destination."

To loosely adapt the renowned Lennonism to authorship, life is what happens while you're busy writing another chapter. A pandemic, personal passages, scenarios, plot and episode twists and turns, and cross-country boomerangs and relocations, have been among the conditions and circumstances that have coincided with the course of this book. In short, and long, life happening.

Fullness was a factor as well. I may have initially managed to miscalculate the magnitude of the Chicagoland mid–1960s music scene that I have been devoted to documenting. I initially figured that the primary focus of the critical chronicle was largely going to focus on a cluster of 1960s suburban bands. Seven bands in an approximate seven-year span, from 1965 to 1972-ish. Seven and seven is a seemingly simple enough equation of equivalency. Lucky seven. And there was the legendary WLS AM, the 50,000-watt radio station in the room. The Suburbs Seven, as I have unofficially branded these suburbands, are certainly a foundational framework and fixation of the work; a core, or in this case, as proclaimed, a cornerstone. As is The Big 89, WLS. Not to mention its watt-worthy rival WCFL.

Yet, the Midwest vicinity where I had spent my first 16 years before heading to the Deep South in 1973 to attend college (or "study in Oxford" as I have learned to mildly mislead) was a vista, more vast and more vibrant in reality and romantic retrospect. In my comeback chronicle, reaching way beyond my formative years of familiarity and recollections, my research and ruminations, which were compelled by a commitment to comprehensiveness and contextualization, resulted in revelation, rediscovery, and ricochets. Lots of them.

Beyond the Suburbs Seven and their songs, singles and albums in a seven-year span, there were many more bands. Some I overlooked, others I forgot about; a few I was not familiar with at all. And there were local record labels with packed rosters. Record producers and studios with high profile engineers. Teen clubs and magazines. A discount department store with a spectacular vinyl record inventory. Television stations, broadcasting shows and live performances, B.C. (Before Cable). Iconic, innovative instruments, from the combo organ to drum kits to guitars. And more garage bands to uncover in the surroundings, to documenting the broader domestic scene and the boom beyond with the Beatles and British Invasion. Oh, yes, those two high-wattage radio stations also featured a charismatic cast of disc jockeys who infused personality into the programs, popular playlists and hit parade. Particles proliferating, many which I didn't initially see or hear coming. All part of the wonder of exploration, discovery, connecting the dots, and locating buried treasure, resounded with relevance. That also helps frame, explain, or rationalize the overwhelming nature, the drawn-outness and the infinitude of this geo-music map of the Midwest.

Multitudes. There is an abundance of goodness, grace and gratitude to go around, with my boundless admiration and appreciation to scatter…

Chicagoland to McFarLand. Up front and in Upper Case with favorite fonts forward (Papyrus or MV Boli), my endless thanks to everyone at McFarland—in every department and at every stage—for the opportunity be a part of your esteemed Press. I really appreciate your unwavering faith in me and the subject, persisting from project proposal through the protracted process toward completion and publication. Professionalism and editorial excellence abound. Not to mention the alliteration lenience. Thanks to Senior Editor Gary Mitchem for the ticket to write. Sophia Lyons has been the Guiding Force. Sophia's supervision, direction and project presence has been super heroic, saintly and more sensational than Siri. Calm, comprehensive and considerate, Sophia thoughtfully chaperoned this manuscript (and the accompanying author angst) through the production phase maze. Along the way,

Acknowledgments and Appreciation

Sophia was attentive, reassuring and indulgent, among other splendid qualities. Her direction was masterful, mindful, and merit badge worthy. Thanks also to Dré Person for manuscript maintenance; to Lisa Camp and Whitney Wallace for editorial finishing touches and con-genie-ality of granting me more than three wishes for late revisions. Color kudos to Mark Durr for design detail, fine tuning and tinting, and to the merry marketeers Karl-Heinz Roseman, Lori Tedder, Kristal Hamby; and Stephanie Nichols in Sales & Publicity.

A chorus and cast of crowd-pleasing characters. Hail to the dynamic cast presented in this chronicle: each and every mid–1960s/early–1970s Chicagoland band that plugged in an amp in the garage, a basement, in a studio or on a stage during the glorious time and place. (All apologies if I overlooked, neglected or failed to mention any groups or personnel.) And to all the local radio disc jockeys—personalities plus, on air and off, and favorite uncles to us transistor listeners; to the visionary producers, record label owners, sound engineers, club owners, and the teens of the times. Basically, anyone and everyone who made the scene happen, made these pages happen. Thank you. And, an unforgettable five-finger 45 footnote, from 7th grade to this day and forward, a citation for the compassion of the hometown North Riverside E.J. Korvette store security officer circa '67.

It was an honor (and slightly surreal) for me to engage in conversations and correspondences with a Fab Five of suburband members—the Buckinghams' Carl Giammarese, Cryan' Shames' hooke, Jim Pilster, New Colony Sixer Ray Graffia and Bob Bergland and Chuck Soumar of the Ides of March—all who graciously took the time to share their thoughts with me. At WLS Radio in Chicago, Cumulus Media personable professionals Marv Nyren and Victoria Jarrett kindly assisted with securing licensing for the Personality Radio images.

Box Set Bibliography. Routinely cited throughout these chapters, a bibliographic ensemble of Chicagoland music scene critics, chroniclers, curators, colorists, commentators and liner note legends have informed and enhanced this narrative: Mike Baker (*Forgottten 45s*), Clark Besch, Mike Dugo (*Lance Monthly*), Jeff Jarema, Kent Kotal (*Forgotten Hits*), Steve Krakow (aka Plastic Crimewave) *Secret History of Chicago Music,* Adam Langer (*The Chicago Reader*), Dave Traut (*Classic Garage Library*), Dean Milano, Jerry Schollenberger, and radiohead WLS whizzes Stew Salowitz and Jeff Roteman, among the Informants. Supreme sourcerers and archivists all, I genuinely admire and appreciate your passion for the period, and your perspectives that enhance these pages.

Affection for the people and things that went before...

Old Cool/School Spirit. Here's to Mater Christi Catholic School elementary primer, Komarek junior high class of '69; Riverside-Brookfield High School Class of '73. ["Nobody beats the zoo!" (Well, except, on occasion, most of our West Suburban Conference rivals and some non-conference opponents.)] With teacher appreciation and coaching commendations, for so many who instilled qualities early on that eventually came to fruition in some form or fashion along the way. The lengthy lineage of coaches extends from Robert P. "Bob" Lang at Komarek through the RBHS tandem, "Vandy" (Bill Vande Merkt) and Otto (Zeman) among revered ranks. At the head of my earliest instructional Influencers was the recently departed JoAnne (Glimco) Kosey, my 4th grade teacher with a penchant for singing and for writing. I'm pretty certain that the longtime Riverside resident and local columnist would have been genuinely delighted that this Chicagoland music tale was eventually told by one of the crew-cut kids in her classroom.

Glory Daze: Chicagoland Idol. Time traveling with this text invoked corresponding cameos of boyhood inspiration that coincided with the music scene. Prolific pairings were a pattern in the locale. The era co-starred dynamic duos beyond the media magnets, WLS and WCFL, and the major metropolitan newspapers, the *Chicago Tribune* and the *Sun Times.* Among the most notable: the toothless wonders on ice, Chicago Blackhawks' Stan Mikita and Bobby Hull, "The Golden Jet"; and gridiron greats, running back Gale Sayers and linebacker Dick Butkus, both first round draft choices in 1965. The dynamic duality remains the only time an NFL team has selected two (eventual) Hall of Famers in the first round of the same draft. As for Chicago baseball—the Cubs and White Sox, Wrigley Field and Comiskey Park—I won't comment on Ernie Banks and Ron Santo et al. since I was raised a St. Louis Cardinals fan. Numerologically, there were two formative number "14"s who made an early imprint: Cardinals' captain and All Star third baseman, Ken Boyer; and more tangibly, hometown hero, Jim Cannataro, a standout quarterback who drove a Shelby GT and eventually became a Nintendo executive vice president.

"*All these places have their moments.*" The sense of place has been a contemplative backdrop, wistful thread and a meditative murmuring presence during this writing. My journey through The Past to the Midwest motherland has been poignant. The expressive experience summons a scene from Mattew Weiner's superb series *Mad Men* (AMC), also set in the 1960s. In a first season (2007) episode entitled "The Wheel," ad executive Don Draper (Jon Hamm) adroitly positions "nostalgia" at the core of his pitch for the Kodak slide carousel. His sentimental soliloquy gently depicts "the twinge in your heart more powerful than memory," and the time machine that allows us backwards and forwards, around and around, and back home again.

My memory carousel turn, turn, turns to coming of age hangouts, haunts, suburban stomping grounds and adolescent activities: paper routes and spitballs; Winter, snow days and frozen ponds; the Hill, a slick sledding slope; curbside leaf burning in the autumn; following behind the cloud of DDT fog sprayed by mosquito abatement trucks on summer evenings (before being banned in 1972); amusement parks Kiddieland (stylized KiDDieLAND) on North Avenue for starters, advancing to Riverview; E.J. Korvettes' record department; Miller Meadow, the Des Plaines River, Salt Creek and the bike trail winding alongside; the 6th Avenue ball fields; the Brookfield Zoo; stops along Cermak Road (22nd) in North Riverside, between 8th and 11th Avenues—Vesuvio's Bakery, A&W Root Beer, Val Mar's shop, which always was first to get the latest series of Topps baseball cards, with a stick of bubble gum for a nickel a pack; and Bart's Hobby Shop, the den of cool; Novi's in Berwyn for Italian beef and/or sausage and a Chicago dog; pizza, from nearby Barone's and Salerno's to the deep-dish domain downtown. And, when we advanced from the banana seats and high handlebars of our bikes to drivers' licenses, gasoline was priced around 30 cents a gallon.

Maximizing, Materializing the Muse. More abstractly and artifactually, with commendation of creative cosmicity and compositional costuming, there are notable objects and stuff that emanated good thoughts, steady word flow, color, energy, and vibe: my Zevonian gray wool cap, worn out charcoal grey writing shirts (with old paint splatters, drips of expression and holes for ventilation); specific settings and seating spots, the primary one a vintage Kroehler cushioned square chair with a set of sizeable smooth stones placed on the arm rest, laminated memorial holy cards within reach, a traditional Lithuanian wedding weave folk sash (PIRSLIUI) that was a Gluhman gift, draped across the back; a window with a view of Julie's studio, and her art coloring the walls and spirit of our home sweet home, surrounding every seating, setting and line of sight. And in recognition of other spaces of pulse, peace, and writing process: from early mornings at Max Fitness to the serene surroundings of our homestead, the woods, yarden, and the Corona-Harper Rustone Sculpture and Meditation Garden, just out our door. Arranging rocks and rust; paragraphs, passages and pages. Location and inspiration.

Permanent playlist. Always in the meaningful mix: George Lewis, Jim Dees, Remy Miller, Greg Metcalf, John Fortenberry, Emmett Winn, Dave Engen, Virg Kolar. Also, a gentle nod to the local color and kindness of our inimitable, occasionally idiosyncratic Auburn Arts Association ally, gallery guru, patron, artist and friend, Margaret Gluhman; who has uniquely enriched Julie's and my life.

A requisite riff of reverence to my friend, mentor, teacher and prolific media culture critic, Gary Edgerton, an incomparable inspiration and yonder star to follow. And Gary Burns, a longtime colleague and eminent journal editor of *Popular Music & Society* and *Rock Music Studies,* (with Tom Kitts), has been a standard-setting shadow over this project. As a Midwesterner, with a distinguished academic career spanning Northwestern to Northern Illinois University, Gary lived the mid–1960s Chicagoland music scene. The American Breed played at his high school's post-prom party! (Our RBHS class could only manage the Lettermen.) Gary mentioned the band playing "Old Man River," though he doesn't recall with certainty that they played their hit, "Bend Me Shape Me." Must have been the potent punch. Gary and Janet Novak routinely attend the Cornerstones of Rock Concert series. Throughout the course of this project, I have hoped that my account of Chicagoland's mid–1960s scene corroborates Gary's experience and his critical recollection. And a bold byline to Will Norton for his enduring piloting presence of the Journalism Mentor Ship.

Home Schooling: In my current home room School of Communication and Journalism at Auburn University, our directors, present and past, Debra Worthington and Jennifer Wood Adams, have been continually resourceful, encouraging and accommodating in support of all our faculty pursuits. Including my music related shindigs such as this. Such backing means a lot. The Bronczek funds are a generous allowance that sure comes in handy with those pesky permissions and image licensing fees that a bake sale or mowing the dean of liberal arts' lawn just would not cover. I greatly appreciate the sponsorship. Situated in the same School space, I'm very fortunate to be affiliated with a diverse, engaging, collegial company of the finest fellow faculty and a dynamic duo of indispensable administrative marvels, Kathy Klick and Shannon Solomon. Go! Team.

IT (Conquered the World). I genuinely value the rapport and rhythm with my trusty International Harvester PC (an IH sticker homage to my father; the Harvester company never diversified from farm equipment to computers). Out of laptop loyalty, I have turned down several rounds of new device faculty upgrades so I could complete this book with this computer companion. On the human front and center, it's always reassuring to know that the Keepers of the Keyboards in the tech-know of the College of Liberal Arts—Darrell Crutchley, Lisa Whitmore, Matthew Warren, Stacey Powell—keep me (and everyone in the College) plugged in and running on IT. With continual gratitude and praise to these Unsung Heroes.

Questions 67 and 68. While I have genuinely appreciated the occasional random interest of the casual query—"how's the book coming?," I usually prefer *not* to engage in that dialogue, no matter how well intentioned, sincere or obligatory. Providing a writing progress report has always induced mild unease within. That said, South Side Chicago native and distinguished professor, Craig Darch, courteously, routinely asked me for a manuscript update at the gym; as did faithful 4th avenue figure Mike Laczynski via intermittent e-mail dispatches. And my thoughtful sister, Lynette. Thank you very much for the kindness of your curiosity along the way.

Buried treasure. A ghost is born. There were several profoundly personal passings that marked the ponderous pace of this project with heartache. Among the dearest departures, my proud Polish mother, Rita Plasketes—diligent, devout and distinctive for having never driven a car in her 94 years; and my caring, conversational father-in-law, Rodger F. Williams. The losses of my treasured friends—boyhood best Bill Kolar; Oxford, Mississippi, legendary Kool, Ronzo Shapiro; and his singular cinema-centric sidekick, Barton Segal—has left a void in my soul. I carry their spirits with me most days. And Bill and Ronzo still conjure, charm, make me think, and most importantly, make me laugh from the Great Beyond, without a séance or Ouija board.

Bring the family. In recognition of my west suburban sisters, Laura Plasketes in Westchester; and Lynette in Bolingbrook, and the Piekarskis, Tyler and Amy, Alexa and Chan. And, situated Down South, Materfamilias Joan and the Williams dynasty, spanning Mississippi, Alabama, Kentucky, Georgia and parts unknown.

Catalyst. And here's to our Caspurr, for your sweet and soulful kitty companionship and for sharing your scratch pad of a chair with me, settling across my lap and laptop and in flanking spaces. So grateful that you found us, a prodigious gift of grace on that clammy day Aprils ago. Your Spirit resides. With one eye on Heaven, and one Eye on earth.

Love Letters. At the risk of channeling Hallmark…. Lastingly, first, foremost, forever and always—to, for and with Julie, Anaïs and Rivers. My Heartbeat, my Muses, my Wholly Trinity. There simply is no wellspring of words or expressions— never has been, never will be—adequate enough to articulate the collective meaning, place and daily inspiration that you all infuse in my life. Or the depth of my limitless love and adoration for you. Everything I write is essentially a love letter, a love song, a postcard to Julie Grace, who wears her middle name well. Decades and counting, I have been captivated by the sm*art*istic and boundless beauty of her Being. And, as a father, I continue to savor with wonder the glow and the growth, personally and professionally, of our favorite daughter and son, Anaïs and Rivers. During the arc of this project, they have charted separate courses from Los Angeles (and Palm Springs) to New Orleans and back, with Stanley and Betty merrily along for the ride; and from Brooklyn to Miami.

Deadicated. I know that my "Dedicated to" go-to's—Julie, Anaïs, Rivers—won't mind sharing that perennial prelude pedestal this writing go 'round with a Chicagoland Trio of Late Greats and Indelibles on my (and our) Time Line—my low-key Lithuanian father, Charles Plasketes, an International Harvester and St. Louis Cardinal lifer and record collector who steered me toward and along a sound track; my father-in-law, Dr. Rodger F. Williams, DDS, with Chicagoland rounds in Oak Park, Elmhurst and at Loyola; and my Life/Afterlife Long Best, Bill Kolar. Your perpetual lights shine on brightly, with permeating presence.

The Acknowledgment Page Orchestra is meandering into the grand finale melody in my head, signaling time to wrap this up….

Every second (and word) counts. During the abbreviated span of sketching out the initial draft of these liner notes, Julie—with her new infinity bracelet gracing her wrist—and I fittingly finished the finale of Season Two of *The Bear,* the "Original Beef of Chicagoland" kitchen culture FX series on Hulu. A day or so later, "windy" (as in City) happened to be the Wordle word. Both the season ending episode and the four guesses to green glimmered in a grin, serendipitously synchronized as affirmation of continuity and completion, conclusion and comeback. Confirmation of the overarching privilege and reverential revisitation of my Midwest, Illi*noise,* Chicagoland, North Riverside roots. Backwards and forwards, around and around, and back home again…

gp

Prelude

Make It in the Midwest: Once Upon a Time in Chicagoland

> [Mick] Jagger told me that we were going to be big because we were from Chicago. And he said, you make it in New York and you can spread in about one-third of the country. You make it in L.A. and you can spread out another third. But, when you make it from Chicago and you go a third each way you've got two-thirds of the country. He said if you make it in the Midwest you're really going to make it.[1]
>
> I've never lived in Chicago proper. I've always been from the suburbs. When you're in a small suburb like Prospect Heights, Illinois, where I grew up, you always say "Chicago" so you seem like you're part of something bigger and more important.[2]
>
> —Jimy Sohns, Shadows of Knight

Nearest Far Out Light Years Away: A Prologue of P*rock*simity

> *It was a glorious time.*
> —Gene Lubin, the Knaves[3]

> *It was magic. We were in our own little bubble.*
> —Jim Pilster (J.C. Hooke), the Cryan' Shames[4]

"Once upon a time, in a far-out land called Chicago...." So begins the handwritten, storybook-style liner note essay that occupies the entire back cover sleeve space of the Cryan' Shames' ambitious second album, *A Scratch in the Sky*, released on Columbia Records a few weeks before Christmas in December 1967. The two-column cursive composition overlays a corresponding black-and-white illustration, which adroitly alludes to the album's 11 tracks in a pen-and-ink waterside townscape sketch. The tale, set in the band's hometown—Hinsdale, a suburb 22 miles west of downtown Chicago—was crafted by Gloria Stavers, credited as "Official Fairy Godmother, *16 Magazine*."[5]

The whimsical byline conjures waving a wonder wand weaving words into a fable. That should not diminish or detract from the noteworthy source of authorship.

As another resonant "G-l-o-r-i-a" of the era, "Fairy Godmother" Gloria was a torchbearer, renowned for a pioneering publishing presence positioned at the forefront of rock music and popular culture journalism between the late–1950s and into the mid–1970s. Stavers's ascent was meteoric, a trajectory launched from the fashion field that arrived prominently in print on pages as a writer, glamour photographer, and unparalleled editor-in-chief with a flair for shaping music careers of the era. The visionary, enigmatic editor was committed to a publication with youthful appeal that specifically targeted the preteen and teenage female audience.

The premiere issue of *16 Magazine* in May 1957 featured Elvis Presley on its cover. The publication's initial emphasis on 1950s teen idols progressed into highlighting selective 1960s television, rock and roll, and pop act "fave raves." *A Scratch in the Sky*'s back cover composition carried considerable cachet, cataloging the Cryan' Shames and the Chicago area in Stavers's rich writing résumé of rock profiles, interviews, and features that included the Beatles, Jim Morrison and the Doors, Paul Revere & the Raiders, and Herman's Hermits, among a countless chorus. The magazine's daring format swerve from general interest and cinema to personality prominence was initially accompanied by misperceptions of "rag readership." The transition summoned strands of gender-based backlash and elicited slights from star scoffers who discredited the magazine content as trivial and juvenile, while tagging Stavers with the belittling brand "Mother Superior of the Inferior." Stavers persevered, presiding for 11 years over the bi-monthly pop publication, which during her tenure became known as "America's most imitated magazine."

Columbia Records enlisted prominent, pioneering music journalist and editor of *16 Magazine* Gloria Stavers to contribute a liner note essay for the Cryan' Shames' second album, *A Scratch in the Sky*, released in December 1967 (Karen Steele, gloriastavers.typepad.com).

Stavers's liner note lead on *A Scratch in the Sky* fancifully fuses fairy tale formula with jazz speak and '60 psychedelic slang to evoke a vicinity vibe. The "once upon a time…" hook is a distant antecedent that ricochets from the Cryan' Shames' 1967 album in a timeless trail across the cultural landscape. Among other contemporary destinations, the locution relocates five decades down the road, in Quentin Tarantino's cinematic application in the 1960s setting of *Once Upon a Time in Hollywood* in 2019. Stavers's application in the back cover sleeve's prologue passage convenes in closer contiguity with its era of origin. The expression situates abstractly and inconspicuously. Smack dab in the '67 midway that bridges hallmarks that are spaced in two-year intervals within the four-year frame between 1965 and 1969. On the front side of the sixties symmetrical span lies the profound punch of the hallowed "once upon a time" recitation that kick-starts the Bob Dylan touchstone "Like a Rolling Stone" in 1965. And resounding ever since.

At the other margin, the trippy "far-out land" of the phrase augurs a Southern California surf echo that washes Pacifica ripples shimmering onto Lake Michigan's shoreline skyline from the nostalgic notion in the Beach Boys' "The Nearest Faraway Place," a lovely instrumental track from their *20/20* album in 1969.[6] In an ensuing two-year evocation in 1971, the Ides of March, a Berwyn-based band a few suburbs away from the Cryan' Shames' hometown of Hinsdale, further supplement Stavers's setting in suburb sentimentality. Lead singer and songwriter Jim Peterik strikes a "Somewhere Over the Sunset Strip" pose in the yearning homeward gaze of the wistful "L.A. Goodbye" lyric, "and now I feel light years away from the West Side of Chicago."[7]

Via Chicagoland: How the Midwest Was Won

This land has a name today and is marked on maps.
—Opening narration, *How the West Was Won* (MGM, 1962)
Dir: John Ford, Henry Hathaway, George Marshall[8]

From Mick's "Jaggerography" cross-country calculation in thirds to Beat phrasing, Beach Boys lyrics, Berwyn bohemia; beyond and between a "far-out land" and a "nearest far away place" to "light years away," these varied voices, visions, and vistas in Midwest musings and measures murmur and mingle with the traditional tenacity of "toddling town" tags such as "Chi-Town"; "Windy City"; the improvisation troupe and New York City rivalry inspired, "Second City"; "City of Big Shoulders," from the lead line of a Carl Sandburg poem; and the blues standard "Sweet Home Chicago." The accumulation of these abounding appellations expand and contract, advance and recede, ebb, and flow, arriving at and settling in and around the poetic pop rock garage p*rocks*imity known as "Chicagoland."

Formally and flexibly, the city's Chamber of Commerce demarcates the "Chicagoland" sector and its capacity as the collective of connected counties Cook, DuPage, Kane, Kendall, Lake, McHenry, and Will. The approximation of the contiguous seven-county consolidation sprawls from south of Milwaukee, Wisconsin, west of DeKalb in Northern Illinois, south past Joliet, and into Northwest Indiana. The term was introduced in the first half of the 1900s by Robert "Colonel" McCormick, the owner of the major metro daily newspaper, *The Chicago Tribune*. When the Colonel coined "Chicagoland," the purpose of the designation was to describe the city scope and its various domains, such as grain, timber, and livestock, which spread across the Midwest region from Illinois to Indiana, Wisconsin, Michigan, and Iowa. Despite its presence, music was not recognized or included among the commodities at the time.

The inclusive colloquia*local* label "Chicagoland"—with an intrinsic, alluring amusement park air and frontier tenor, not to mention a catchy convenience for branding and businesses—encompasses and extends from the municipality downtown to the surrounding sprawl of suburbs, in neighborhoods, villages, towns, townships, districts, and communities. And occasionally making inroads and crossroads across adjacent state lines in the Great Lakes region. The city-state, metro-suburban signification that converges via the "greater Chicagoland area" marque simultaneously and subtly suggests a concurrent identity and an identity crisis. With frequent, friendly residency reminders of the stark divide between city proper and surrounding suburbs, that "you don't really live *in* Chicago."[9] Loosely translated, and applying the localized logic of the Shadows of Knight lead Jimy Sohns, the "Chicagoland" designation seems and sounds like "a part of something bigger and more important."

The notion of scale, significance, and setting circulated in appreciable undercurrents. When the Cryan' Shames released "Mr. Unreliable" as a 45 overture to *A Scratch in the Sky* in 1967 and bridge from their *Sugar and Spice* debut LP the year before, a *Billboard* magazine ad (March 18, 1967) framed "the smash single that's now

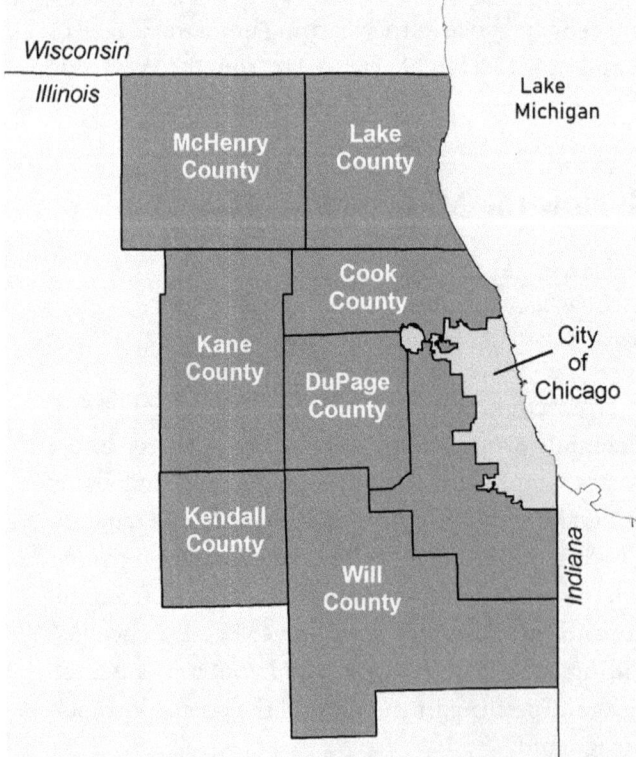

The seven-county mosaic that outlines the suburban sprawl of the Windy City periphery is commonly identified as "Greater Chicagoland" (Adapted from *UIC Today*, "Real Time Talks," February 19, 2014).

spreading out in all directions" and its "'All America' album bestseller" with the banner "How the Midwest Was Won." The full-page proclamation in the foremost music industry trade publication is presumably paraphrased from *How the West Was Won*, the Academy Award–nominated Western epic from five years earlier in 1962. The Cinerama spectacle is a creative collaboration between a triumvirate of directors: John Ford, Henry Hathaway, and George Marshall. The trinity constructs the film's narrative into chapters that are narrated by Spencer Tracy, with John Wayne, Jimmy Stewart, Debbie Reynolds, Gregory Peck, Karl Malden, Henry Fonda, Eli Wallach, and Richard Widmark among the film's notable cast of cowboys, homesteaders, and frontier folk.

The retitled regional reference that shifts from "West" to "Midwest" in the ad for the Cryan' Shames' single was not only convenient and clever, but also a relevant redirection that aligns with Mick Jagger's sectional supposition. While the *How the West Was Won* film is true to its era and genre conventions such as pioneers and prospectors, ranches and railroads, wagon trains across the rivers and plains, the mid–1960s midwestern music scene modification modernizes to a suburban settlement not limited to banjo and harmonica campfire sing-alongs. Each of these kindred spirit westward expansions was, in part, driven by a gold rush and *Goldmine* (magazine), whether sifting scenic shallow streams or the city-suburban soundscape scene for nuggets, gems, and buried treasure shimmering with solid gold reward.

Chicagoland was the gateway to how the Midwest was won. During the period spanning the mid–1960s into the early 1970s, the Chicagoland music experience embodied, exuded, and embraced a once-upon-a-time aura. The "Aire of Good Feeling" of the Ides of March 1970 song delightfully amplified into an *"era* of good feeling." The setting and its ardent activity were commonly colored in magical shades tinted glowing and glorious and comfortably characterized as "our own little bubble" by its musicians, participants, bystanders, and chroniclers. The Midwest region was a center of gravity, a distinct music mecca marked by a multitude of bands situated within a happening locality stretching from city to suburbs and surrounding scope including out of state. The spirited scene was bursting and bountiful, its pulse propelled by a resourceful range of conditions, complementary collaborators, and cohorts, both creative and commercial. The framework was anchored by a pair of powerhouse AM radio stations, with musical single-air-it-y that was infused with a cast of dynamic disc jockeys and a network of savvy promoters, programmers, and producers. The hyperactivity of the surrounding support system featured local record labels, recording studios, and a flourishing teen club circuit.

My Back Pages:
The Town I'd Like to Go Back To

Gloria Stavers's familiar folksy phrasing and fairytale tone that playfully preface the musical attributes of *A Scratch in the Sky* provide précis that remains wistfully fitting and flowing with enduring enchantment and resonance for anyone, including myself, whose west suburban *Wonder Years* coming of age coincided with that captivating period. "The Town I'd Like to Go Back To," the deep track dreamscape that closes side one of the Cryan' Shames' unsung '67 album, trances a fitting nostalgic ambiance and theme that evoke the "places I'll remember" of the Beatles' *Rubber Soul* reminiscence, "In My Life," from two years prior in 1965. That retro vibe eases forward into contemporary correspondence with current Chicagolanders, Wilco, and their enigmatic "Via Chicago" in 1999, with its solemn, mesmerizing mantra, "I'm coming home, I'm coming home."[10]

My resident résumé reads "raised in North Riverside," a suburb, 12 miles and 20 minutes west of Chicago. The "village," as the zone is commonly identified, is outlined by 26th Street, with a forest preserve and Salt Creek on its south side, 22nd (Cermak Road) on the north, and 17th to Harlem Avenue on the east and west edges. The Des Plaines River meanders as a mildly murky midway marker between both sides of town. The westerly streets are labeled numerically, from First Avenue to 17th, the easterly with names Keystone, Forest, Park, Westover, Burr Oak, Hainsworth, and Northgate among its avenue arrangement. Bordering North Riverside are predominantly white neighborhoods and townships that include the B-sides Brookfield, Broadview, and Berwyn and historic Riverside, a landmark locale established in 1869 as one of the first planned model communities. Designed by landscape architect Frederick Law Olmstead and Calvert Vaux in 1869, the setting's unique layout features curvilinear streets, pastoral parkways, and green spaces, accentuated with the splendid architecture of Frank Lloyd Wright and skyscraper innovator William Le Baron Jenney. An architectural aside or addendum: the families of two of my high school classmates lived in Wright's prairie style designed homes in Riverside—the Frederick F. Tomek and Avery Coonley Houses.

The splendid settings of the National Historic Landmark homes were occasionally enriched with youthful ingenuity that commonly coincided with parents being away. At the Coonley estate, when the swimming pool was drained for the off-season, the resourceful resident Riverside teenagers adapted the pool parameters into a screening space, projecting Super 8 mm movies onto the 10-foot wall of the deep end, with a seating setup arranged within the dry blue-green concrete confines.

Also adjacent to "the village, the quiet village" of North Riverside lies the renowned Brookfield Zoo, with approximately 2,000-plus inhabitants occupying the vast preserve cornered by 31st Street and First Avenue. The high school I attended, Riverside-Brookfield (Class of '73), is located next to (and occasionally mistaken for) the zoo. The animal house juxtaposition inspired school spirit that was expressed in a triumphant, albeit overstated, pep rally chant, "Nobody beats the zoo!" If students were somehow stranded after school and/or extracurricular activities without a ride home in the pre–Uber/Lyft era, the contiguous Animal Kingdom and its 216 acres provided a uniquely convenient cut-through route, in an era when walking home was a common and secure school-age option, with minimal parental fear of their kid's image being posted "missing" alongside pets on a utility pole (before the milk carton method and homogenized Amber Alert [circa 2002]). Back in the Day, suburban settings were relatively safe. The casual (wimo)way from high school homeward bound took 30–40 minutes, depending on how much time was spent lingering at the polar bear outdoor exhibit or dispensing pocket change into one of the cool Mold-A-Rama 3-D souvenir machines. The direction home coursed from R-B's rear entrance past the accommodating gatekeeper granting permission to pass through the zoological society entrance; strolling the sanctuary and gardens, down the tunnel under 31st street, up to the parking lot, and through a fence (hopefully with its gate unlocked), to a path preceding the slope of the winter sledding hill overlooking the Stephen King–like institution Scottish Home for the aging; navigating the knee-high prairie grass (often the flammable brush stoked by our juvenile pyro-compulsions) in a diagonal direction through a field and woodsy boundary; looking both ways before crossing 26th Street to 5th Avenue, to the 2400 block, right side of the street, five doors down. 2437. Home.

A noteworthy fun fact and foot(loose) note of relevance and romanticism (overlooked by our imaginary class historian and yet to surface as a lost episode of *The Dating Game*): Ides of March front Jim Peterik, who, with his Berwyn bandmates, attended nearby cross-conference rival Morton West High School, first met his future wife, Karen, at a Turtles concert that was booked in our RBHS gym in April 1968. Peterik later proposed to Karen at the same love-at-first-site near the school entrance.

In another verse of so "Happy Together," my wife, Julie Grace, was suburborn in nearby Oak Park, 13 minutes and a mere four miles away from my hometown of North Riverside. For a long time, we were the proverbial pair of "ships passing in the night," our paths not crossing until a few preordained decades later in 1980 in Oxford, Mississippi, 625 miles south of Chicagoland. In my personal unofficial Oak Park resident rankings, a trinity of distinguished runners-up to Julie Grace Williams includes architect Frank Lloyd Wright, fast food founder Ray Kroc of the McDonald's Golden Arches empire, and literary icon Ernest Hemingway, who purportedly pronounced his hometown as a place of "wide lawns and narrow minds," though there has never been any written or spoken documentation of the mythical sentiment.

Being rooted in the mid–1960s music scene's west suburban setting was a privilege of place and presence, of participation, perspective, and point of view. And a baptism, a sacred soundtrack, sacrament, and rite of passage to a lifetime of music appreciation and fulfillment. The Thunderclap Newman mid-summer '69 stamp, "Something in the Air," instigated by John "Speedy" Keen, certainly reverberated, with or without revolution, figuratively and literally. The "something" in the AM radio air waves teeming with music and effervescent disc jockeys, emanating from the downtown towers of the legendary station, WLS, and its worthy competitor,

WCFL, was a transistor siren song of sensations and satis-fact-ion, with Eighth Wonder of the World status.

Our neighborhood, like most others across the vicinity during the era, was dotted with dreamers and wannabes in basement bands and garage groups in various stages of formation, floundering, and an occasional low-fi 45 rpm pressing. Among the most promising and popular, the Things to Come (a common band name across the country) featured a flamboyant out-of-town lead singer named Pierre, with local Chuck Fister banging out backbeat on his drums. Another, the Freedom Five, a group of Riverside residents and RBHSers (before my freshman arrival, wary of the of notorious "elevator pass" scam perpetrated by upper-class ilk)—Guy Gangi, Cary Babinec, Robert Miller—cut a punkish D.I.Y. single, "We Aren't Free"/ "To Save My Soul," issued in 1966 on the SRI label, located on north Harlem Avenue in Oak Park. Both local bands were among the music multitude who remained memorable momentary mid–1960s garage anonymities.

Attending live shows to catch performances by the myriad of bands from the area, including several whose songs were receiving radio airplay and/or released on records, was routine. If you could find a ride. Access and affordability were automatic, with inviting, informal stage settings that were distant performance precursors to *MTV Unplugged* and National Public Radio's *Tiny Desk Concerts*, from high school gymnasiums and youth and community centers to civic halls and teen clubs to the claustrophobic confines of the adjoining activity building at St. Mary's Church in Riverside. The cramped space's low ceiling acoustics certainly did not inhibit the high note horns of the Ides of March's Impressions-istic soulful suburban rendition of fellow Chicagoan Curtis Mayfield's 1965 gospel-influenced civil rights anthem, "People Get Ready."

The local heroes were also visible off stage. The casual chorus of suburband citizens were commonly, sporadically sighted in passing as familiar faces in the crowd. In one such happenstance, while hanging out at the Oak Brook outdoor shopping center circa late 1960s/early 1970s, I recognized Jim Peterik entering the Crate & Barrel home décor store. The Ides front was charismatically conspicuous and pretty easy to spot in any crowd: tall, shag cut, McGuinn mod granny glasses, long coat. Someone else across the concourse also noticed the Ides icon Peterik's stylish presence and Liverpudlian look-alikeness, as a voice resounded from another direction: "Hey, look! It's John Lennon!" True story. A case of mistaken *Ides*dentity.

The E.J. Korvette Record Department Disaster 1967 (and Other Off-Key Misadventures)

Another central component, if not pillar, within the suburban setting and music scene infrastructure was the E.J. Korvette department store. There was one conveniently located a half-mile away at the Harlem and Cermak Plaza on the North Riverside–Berwyn boundary. The pioneering discount chain was an essential record resource and ritual—and for me, a frequent destination with my dad. An escalator provided a "stairway to heaven" ascent, and a post-purchase "satisfaction" descent, an escort to and from a second-floor quadrant stocked with a vast vinyl inventory. The extraordinarily enticing, abundant arrangement of records magnificently displayed in a Wall of Sound was enhanced by routine rotating sale pricing (usually according to record labels), which efficiently fostered and fulfilled formative 45 rpm and long play 33⅓ record affinities and audio artifact accumulation into a collection, in mono and stereo, father and son, in tune across the generational divide.

Fortunately for one budding record collector, North Riverside's E.J. Korvette had a store detective who was much more compassionate than the penance piling parish priest presiding over heaven or hell hearing for a notorious Komarek School seventh grader of Lithuanian-Polish descent's misappropriation of a 45 rpm. The object of aural attraction in the early onset kleptos caper was the pre-disco Bee Gees Beatlesque 1967 single "New York Mining Disaster 1941." Priced under one dollar, the inventory indiscretion seemed pretty petty, the pilfering principle notwithstanding. By most catechismal, soul-smudging standards on the sinful scale, clearly a "venial" rather than "mortal" transgression in the hell or holy water hierarchy. As benevolent as he was observant, the 45-single swipe sleuth graciously granted me a reprieve, which spared me a prolonged grounded sentence administered from the parental front. A week or so later, the voice from the shadow posed like a Wizard of God(zilla?) behind the sliding screen in the Mater Christi confessional booth—or "penalty box" as we referred to it in Blackhawks hockey homage—dished out a disproportionate volume of Hail Marys for a run around the rosary beads for the 99-cent music misdemeanor.[11]

The brothers Gibb botched blunder was not the lone record-related reprimand and off-key music mishap that marked my mid–1960s adolescence. In middle school, I chose the Hollies' hit song "Look Through Any Window" to recite in class for a poetry assignment. A rather precocious selection for fifth grade. As I stood in front of the classroom, fearlessly delivering the first four lines flawlessly from memory, classmate James Oles, acting like a fervent *Name That Tune* contestant, blurted out, "Hey! That's a song on the radio!" The vinyl record-scratch sound effect cued "Uh-oh" in my mind. Our homeroom nun stood in silent scowl momentarily before intervening. Her Holiness—or in this case "Hollie"ness—in black and white halted the pop-rock rendition. Sister sternly pointed her handy wooden ruler that appeared to be surgically and spiritually attached, exiling me back to my seat before I could get to the "movin' on their way" chorus and the song's remaining verses. And clearly neither "Bus Stop" nor "On Carousel" would do for an encore reading. The open mic moment turned out not to be very open-minded. In my poet perp walk down the row of desks, I hip checked and hissed "Rat Fink" when passing The Tattler. The proverbial note to my parents from the strict sister was mysteriously "lost" somewhere along the five-block walk home, though the details were recounted during parent teacher conferences at the next school open house. The incident signaled my Scorpio sign, which surfaced seeking playful pop reprisal. From that incident forward, I frequently borrowed other Hollies song titles to discreetly, irreverently refer to nuns: Sister Jennifer Eccles, Sister Carrie Anne, Sister Eloise, and, of course, "Long *Cold* Woman in a Black Dress."

The peculiar prohibition of the Hollies Hell was precedent that foreshadowed other minor pop poetic injustices that continued to capriciously mark my presence and playlist in west suburban scholastic settings. Among the further adventures along the way, a high school English teacher unplugged another pop rock poetry project proposal, this one featuring budding Los Angeles singer-songwriter Jackson Browne. It was 1972, and Browne's auspicious self-titled debut album (often referred to as *Saturate Before Using* [or *confusing?*]) struck a chord. The impressive set of songs, which included charting singles "Doctor My Eyes" and "Rock Me on the Water," was apparently not persuasive or poetic enough to make my fresh-face literary case for the promising troubadour. Nor did it seem to matter that the gifted Browne, at age 16, wrote "These Days," a song of remembrance that was recorded by pop artist Andy Warhol protégé Nico on her *Chelsea Girl* album in 1967. In compromise or consolation, the teacher graciously suggested Bob Dylan or Joan Baez as more suitable songwriter subjects for the assignment.

When there happened to be a rare instance of pop permission in a school setting, the outcome turned out to be more underwhelming than it was gleeful. In another middle school music moment, circa '66 in an exclusive booking in the Mater Christi Marine Room, a quintet of classmates (Rat Fink Oles *not* among them) assembled to perform a makeshift "air instrument" rendition of the Dave Clark Five's "Over and Over," one of the British band's many hits during the decade. As a resourceful replicate of drummer Dave Clark, I utilized #2 pencils as drumsticks, percussing on a metal two-shelf office cart. My dexterous display of lead licks had been honed home alone in front of a mirror in Charlie Watts pose pounding "Paint It Black" in thin air. The DC5 enactment would be the closest I ever got to sitting behind some semblance of a drum kit and playing, as that boyhood musical instrument wish was never granted, rather annually stiffed by Santa for years. Our pre-karaoke clunky Clark wind-up toy manner rapidly unwound when one of our impersonating troupe missed the bridge cue, forcing me into multi-instrumental mode, with a futile rescue attempt by mouth mimicking a harmonica.

Maps and Local Legends: Timeless Timbre

On the surface, the partners in crime and the classroom calamities were conspicuously London– and Los Angeles–based, rather than rooted with Chicagoland origins. The suburban collective's absenteeism in the series of unfortunate events was misleading. Their company was implicit as culpable co-conspirators: shadow accomplices, accessories, and instigators in the last temptation of the Bee Gees, the Hollies any window reading, the Dave Clark Five imposture, and the Jackson Browne pitch.

The homegrown groups, whether live, on record, or on the radio, personified the sound and spirit of the times, nationally or internationally, no matter the sphere or circumference. Their prevalent presence in the "little bubble" resonated on a different plane. Within our youthful community confines, suburban circumstance, and accommodating infrastructure, the local bands registered the happening cultural climate, verifying its validity, volume, and vibe. These groups were "ours." They rendered the broader pop rock panorama of music—from the Byrds, Box Tops, Turtles, and Raiders to the Beatles, Rolling Stones, Who, and British Invasion—more personal and tangible, more lucid and accessible, more meaningful and quintessential.

The Midwest regionalism situated the swinging sound and style of England and of stateside sites throughout Chicagoland. The imports and influences integrated from London and Liverpool, Manchester and Tottenham, the Carnaby Street crowd and Mersey River beat; and the West Coast boulevards and canyon echoes from Topanga and Laurel, reciprocating in North Riverside, Riverside, and Berwyn to Oak Park, Hinsdale, Mt. Prospect, and all across the surrounding suburban sprawl.

Routinely and precariously positioned early on within a series of idiosyncratic antecedent *Schoolhouse Rock!* episodes may be conveniently categorized and construed as adolescent antics and juvenile hijinks, and easily dismissed with a shrug in the name of pure ploy, playful posturing, or boyhood boat rocking. However, the elementary escapades were in no way a ruse, nor were they a revolt. Rather, just a school-age soul taking shape whose intentions were good, even if maybe mildly misunderstood. The vignettes were a vanguard of genuine music appreciation and emergent expressions, with indelible impressions, settling in and along the formative stages of my chronology, a percolating preface of a nascent passion and pursuit that would continue to accumulate meaning on multifarious levels, evolving effusively into pleasant permanence, profound preoccupation and occupation.

The nearest faraway narrative portrayed and presented via the passages and perspectives in the chapters, verses, and chorus that follow is a regional rendering of residence and relevance, reverence and romanticism, in riffs and recordings; recollections, reveries, and reflections; ruminations and ricochets. The geomusiculture chronicle combines critical cartography, collage, and homage, with a connect-the-dots demeanor that is accentuated with abundant alliteration, coming-of-age undercurrents, and Back Pages of personal *procks*imity within the west suburban panorama during the prolific period. Mapping and meaningful meandering, a medley of meditation, musing, and memoir in methodological mix and measures to frame how the Midwest was won. And wonder filled. This period piece is a suburban suite that arranges and compiles, colors and contextualizes the catalog, contours, and cornerstones of the "little bubble," and the era, the aura, the "aire of good feeling" that was the mid–1960s-into-early-1970s Chicagoland music mecca. The tale traces and tracks the timeless timbre of the evolution/revolution and reverberation into being "a part of something bigger and more important." Musically, geographically, socially, culturally, historically, biographically. A musical manifest destiny. Making it in the Midwest.

Once upon a glorious time and place….

Introduction

45 RPM (Revolutions Per Midwest): A Regional Rotation and Prolific Pop Rock Garage Pocket

> *It was a fun period. It was exciting. At that point, there weren't a lot of bands who were making it out of Chicago. We were breaking new ground. The bands back then were groundbreakers for the bands today. In the early 60s, it was very difficult to get anything going. But it was exciting because you felt that things were starting to happen.*
> —music producer Bob Monaco, MG Productions[1]

Chicagoland was well represented in the profuse pop rock playlist of the mid–1960s. In an approximately seven-year span between late 1965 into 1972, the prolific pocket produced a significant soundtrack that reverberated from the Midwest throughout the country's high-volume singles-rich rotation. The vicinity's vibrant suburban scene contributed a notable catalog of music highlighted by a striking sum of nearly 40 singles that reached the record charts locally and regionally. Several of the 45s placed on the national listings in the music industry trade publications *Billboard* and *Cashbox*, with a few reaching the Top 10 registered as hits. More than 30 of those record releases from the Midwest mix clustered into a particularly plentiful parenthesis between 1966 and 1968. A small sampling of the Chicagoland hit parade from the period includes "Kind of a Drag"; "Don't You Care"; "Vehicle"; "Bend Me, Shape Me"; "Sugar and Spice"; "It Could Be We're in Love"; "Things I'd Like to Say"; and "Gloria." The source of those popular singles was a swatch of suburbands—the Buckinghams, Ides of March, American Breed, Cryan' Shames, New Colony Six, and Shadows of Knight.

Surf's Up!: "They're Out There A-Havin' Fun…"

While "I Confess" by the New Colony Six and the Shadows of Knight's cover version of Them's "Gloria" are commonly credited with being the singles that initiated Chicagoland's homegrown regional rock revolution in late 1965, there was a curious interloping ripple of rhythm from 95 miles away that set the tuneful tone a year earlier. The Rivieras, a garage group from South Bend, Indiana, recorded and released "California Sun" as a surf cover in 1963. The pulsating single entered the charts in January 1964. On the surfless surface, the sound seemed somewhat of a Midwest misnomer in search of a sandy shoreline around the bend from the St. Joseph River. "California Sun" was first recorded by R&B singer Joe Jones in 1961, with composition credits to Henry Glover and Roulette Records owner Morris Levy. The Rivieras' Hoosier state beach party rendition replaces the original's saxophone with Otto Nuss's punchy organ in duet with Joe Pennell's surf guitar riffs, buoyed by Marty Fortson's vocals.

Musically, the Rivieras were at the leading edge of American bands, among them the Doors, who used the iconic Vox Continental transistor-based organ. The "Connie" was the combo keyboard of choice with the British Invasion groups. Among the English Vox virtuosos were Alan Price, originally the keyboardist for the Animals (and featured in a scene in D.A. Pennebaker's groundbreaking cinema verité documentary of Bob Dylan's 1965 European concert tour, *Don't Look Back* [1967]), and classically trained pianist Mike Smith of the Dave Clark Five. John Lennon is portrayed pounding a Vox Continental in footage of the historic Beatles Shea Stadium Concert in New York in 1965. While the organ's unmistakable oscillating sound stood out on many Animals and Dave Clark Five recordings, among them "House of the Rising Sun" and the DC-5's B-side "Because," one of the signature Vox songs, the 1966 garage classic kiss off "96 Tears," also has Midwest origins with the Saginaw, Michigan, based band, ? and the Mysterians (a.k.a. Question Mark and the Mysterians).

The swingin' sum of the Rivieras' instrumentation in "California Sun" shimmies sensations, good vibrations, and a crest of West Coast Watusi waves from the Midwest. Jim Golden, owner of the independent Chicago record labels U.S.A. and Destination, was among the many who noticed. "Along the way I started going around listening to groups and heard the Rivieras singing a song called 'California Sun,'" said Golden. "I said 'That's a hit.' I remember it costing like $164. And it sold a whole lot of records."[2] Distributed by U.S.A. Records, the South Bend surf single crested at #5 on the *Billboard* Hot 100, and remained on the charts for 10 weeks in 1964. The Rivieras' popular record encompasses a distinctive duality as both prelude and punctuation, as the 45 lies at the forefront as Chicagoland's first rock and roll hit, while also being considered the last American smash tune before the British Invasion.

The British Are Coming: Talkin' 'bout a Music Explosion

Every block there was a group. I lived in the northwest suburbs and you can drive down any block any given night and hear some band rehearsing in the basement. And I've heard some great bands that never made it out of the basement.

—Jerry Smith, The Flock[3]

Introduction   15

The new music was just bursting out all over.
—Gene Lubin, The Knaves[4]

By mid-decade, budding bands across Chicagoland were bouncing to the English beat of the British Invasion, borrowing hooks and harmonies, riffs and rhythms, presence and posture that were imported by the Yardbirds, Rolling Stones, Kinks, Hollies, and, most markedly, Beatlemania, which landed stateside on February 7, 1964. Local groups were taking shape in initial incarnations such as the Pulsations, Centuries, Patsmen Knight Lites, Shadows, Travelers, and Shondels, among others, rehearsing, rooting, and making noise throughout the region's high energy, burgeoning youth culture.

Gene Lubin, the drummer for the edgy proto-punk north suburban Chicagoland band the Knaves, ruminates on the garagedom experience and spirit during the era, his perspective fixated with fascination from the first time he heard the Who's "My Generation" and its assimilation in the aftermath:

> Back in 1964 or '65 you'd hear this song and you'd think, "Wow! How can they do that!?" It was like underground code or something ... right under everybody's noses.... Man.... I thought all hell had broken loose and the FBI would be out to shut down the radio station in a matter of hours.... As a matter of fact, the song was banned from most Chicago radio stations within the week, and the Who did have trouble getting into the country for their first US tour. Of course every garage band in the world just had to perform it on stage after that.... When people came to see us [the Knaves] there was no doubt in my mind that they were coming out to see what it was all about! We were more than just a surrogate for these English rock groups. To these suburban high school kids we weren't just a cover band ... we were the Who and the Kinks and the Stones![5]

There were simpler conveyances of the initiation, innocence, and imprints of influences to supplement Lubin's emphatic exposition of the scene's essence. "Once in a while, we would get together and have parties and play a couple of Ventures songs," recounts Nick Fortuna of his pre–Buckinghams primer.[6] Signs and sounds of the times vibrated across neighborhoods, from garages, carports, and basements to teen clubs, high school gyms, restaurants, weekend parties, and sock hops, and on AM airwaves, transistor radios, and television teen dance shows. "It was the time of garage bands," said the Cryan' Shames' Jim Pilster. "When you had a party at home, you'd have a band. Back in those days, you'd set up and play in your living room."[7] Which may provide some context for why many of the teen bands were initially managed by their parents, the adult supervision in the room.

While most of those parentages may have preferred the accordion and its polka party popularity, there was a new instrumental infatuation at the cultural forefront. Fender Stratocaster, Gibson, and ringing Rickenbacker guitars that plugged into Sears Silvertone and other brand amplifiers were in abundance. Steady backbeats banged out on Ludwig, Rogers, Slingerland, or Gretsch sparkling drum kits, equipped with snappy snares, smooth cymbals, and tight tom toms. The common criteria for band membership included three chords competence and riff samplings from standard songs of the day such as "Hey Joe," "Day Tripper," "(I Can't Get No) Satisfaction," and "You Really Got Me" for a guitarist advancing from strumming acoustic to plugging into electric. While any drummer had to dexterously solo the sequence from the Surfaris' surf classic "Wipe Out," with Charlie Watts, Ringo Starr, Keith Moon, and Ginger Baker among those setting the sticks standard.

Rock formations avalanched, igniting and emerging from the garage group gatherings and bands in basements and living rooms on Every Block across Chicagoland's neighborhoods. The vast array of local groups included the Flock, the Rovin' Kind, the Knaves, H.P. Lovecraft, Aorta, Huns, Trolls, Saturday's Children, Banshees, Exceptions, One Eyed Jacks, Riddles, Baby Huey and the Babysitters, the Del-Vetts, Rotary Connection, Daughters of Eve, among many, many others.

The happening hullabaloo also crossed the tri-state lines, extending the bandwidth into neighboring Indiana, Wisconsin, and Michigan. In addition to the aforementioned Rivieras, the Luv'd Ones, Sheffields, Cherry Slush, Ricochettes, Robbs, Trafalgar Square, Idle Few, and Jokers were among a jammed lineup of out-of-staters commonly and comfortably linked with the Chicagoland scene. Their association was based in part on proximity, but also familiarity fostered by frequent teen club scene bookings across the suburban circuit. Many of the bands were signed to local independent record labels, among them U.S.A. Records, Destination, Dunwich, and Freeport, where they released recordings, mostly singles. Among the notable 45s was the Five Emprees' infectious cover of the Addrisi Brothers' "Little Miss Sad," which became a regional hit for the Benton Harbor, Michigan, band, located across Lake Michigan looping 100 miles east of Chicago.[8]

Jim Fairs of the Cryan' Shames places the "anything goes" abundance of the period and the region within a socioeconomic context:

> The times at that particular time were different. I think it was the effect of the largest generation in the history of the world being born in poverty and coming of age in incredible wealth and prosperity. There was an amazing amount of energy because everybody had money to try things and there were a lot of people trying them. Just about anything went. There were so many people trying so many things that all you could sense was an explosion rather than any one particular direction.[9]

The Suburbs Seven

Amidst the energetic eruption of the vast music milieu, there was a seven-band bedrock that anchored the flourishing Chicagoland scene. Alphabetically, the aforementioned American Breed, Buckinghams, Cryan' Shames, Ides of March, Mauds, New Colony Six, and Shadows of Knight composed a prevalent suburban syndicate of sound that personified the period and place during the seven-year span. Seven and seven is…

Seven appeared to be a common if not "auspicious" numerical draw in the area.

Though the musical septet centerpiece did not officially adopt "Suburbs Seven" as an encompassing title or band bundle brand, the designation coincided with other odd numbered indigenous assemblages, most notably the Chicago Seven. The counterculture coalition of renowned revolutionaries and antiwar activists—Jerry Rubin, Abbie Hoffman, Tom Hayden, Rennie Davis, David Dellinger, John Froines, and Lee Weiner—were central figures during the 1968 Democratic National Convention held in the Chicago, one of the era's turbulent touchstone events. The group subtracted from the original Chicago/Conspiracy Eight into a minus one after the case against defendant Bobby Seale was declared a mistrial. And, outside the city's sociopolitical sphere, at WLS-AM radio, "Swinging Seven" was the marque adopted by the celebrated cast of radio personalities, led by luminary Dick Biondi, with shifts along the station's popular programming schedule.

Musically, another significant seven—the band Chicago—was also forming within this time frame and locale. The seven-piece group was initially known as The Big Thing in 1967, before evolving into the Chicago Transit Authority the following year, en route to being an even bigger thing as "Chicago" in 1969. By the decade's cusp, their brassy horn style, influenced by the hometown rock and rhythm and blues show band The MOB, progressed into a signature sound in the namesake city.

Outside of Chicago's steady band ascendancy to an autonomous super status sphere, the "Suburbs Seven" embodied the Chicagoland mid–1960s music core. As cornerstones—which the collective was christened decades later—the bands lived up to the *Billboard* billing for the Cryan' Shames' 1967 single, "Mr. Unreliable," that spiritedly stated in the headline of the full-page ad: "How the Midwest Was Won." The set of seven pronounced the presence of a noteworthy regional roster and rotation that transcended their prominence on the local and midwestern live music scene and radio's Top 40 rotation. The bands delivered a steady series of singles that broke through on a national scale to distinguish Chicago in the striking mid-to-late-1960s playlist. The cluster of suburbands also established a Long Play presence, as they generated the bulk of album length recordings within the single-centric mid-decade Midwest scene.

Measuring the music accumulation across the singles soundscape, the New Colony Six were the leaders of the local pack, totaling 10 charting 45s, primarily pleasant love songs and ballads composed by Ronnie Rice. The Buckinghams followed with seven, while the Cryan' Shames and three of the other bands had five songs each. The Mauds managed a pair. The lone national #1 hit among the groups' singles was the Buckinghams' "Kind of a Drag" in 1966, which was potent enough to knock the telegenic Monkees' borrowed Neil Diamond tune, "I'm a Believer," out of the top spot. The following year, the Buckinghams' "Mercy, Mercy, Mercy" reached #5 and "Don't You Care" #6, while three of their other songs settled just outside the Top 10.

While the Buckinghams' chart saturation for that period may have approached a Beatles benchmark, their second-tier status aligned more closely with one of the underappreciated bands of the British Invasion—the Dave Clark Five—who produced a striking 16 top 30 hits in a three-year span from 1964 to 1967. As a result of their five successful singles, the Buckinghams were anointed *Billboard*'s "Most Listened to Band America" in 1967. Other Chicagoland Top 10s in the period included the American Breed's "Bend Me, Shape Me," which topped the local charts and reached #5 nationally in 1967; the Shadows of Knight, who made it to #10 with "Gloria" in 1966; and the Ides of March's "Vehicle," which peaked at #2 in 1970, unable to unseat the Guess Who's "American Woman" from the top spot. The Berwyn-based band's huge horn hit had the distinction of being the fastest selling single in the history of the Warner Bros. record label at the time.

The overlooked Spanky and Our Gang, their name derived from Hal Roach's 1930s comedies, was a conspicuous 135-mile outlier of the Chicagoland circumference and its suburband brand. Conveniently classified as Twin City Peoria-Bloomington based more than they were associated with the Old Town folk scene where they were regulars, the group's notable chart presence, not to mention their local roots, stock, and identity, were seemingly lost in translation, their sunshine pop sound eclipsed by the Suburbs Seven's long shadow. More geographically and generically, the group's pleasant harmony style was commonly crisscrossed with the cross-country West Coast canyon Mamas and Papas sound. Fronted by Peoria-born Elaine McFarlane, by way of the New Wine Singers and their Irish folk and jug band protest songs, McFarlane and Our Gang contributed a noteworthy set of Top 40 sunshine pop hits in 1967–68 that were released on the Mercury Records label. Their succession of successful singles featured the Top 10 "Sunday Will Never Be the Same" (#9), "Making Every Minute Count" (#31), and "Lazy Day" (#14) in 1967, with "Sunday Mornin'" (#30) and "Like to Get to Know You" (#17) the following year. Beyond their sequence of charting 45s that continued into 1969, Spanky and Our Gang distinguished themselves for being one of the few area bands outside of the Suburbs Seven core with a 33⅓ identity. The group generated enough material to record four albums for Mercury between 1967 and 1970.

Most of the popular singles produced by the Chicagoland groups exhibited respectable staying power on the music charts, with several songs sustaining occupancies that extended into double-digit weeks. The longest singles stay was the New Colony Six's "Things I'd Like to Say," which lingered lightly for an impressive 16 weeks in 1968, with a matching chart position peak at #16. "Bend Me, Shape Me" endured for 14 weeks, while "Gloria" lasted 12. Five of the seven Buckingham singles that charted remained in the rotation between 10 and 14 weeks.

As a midwestern microcosm of the broader national and international music scenes, the steady stream of singles produced by the Chicagoland suburbands mirrored many of the productive, high-profile hitmakers of the time, from Gary Lewis & the Playboys, the Box Tops, the Beau Brummels, Three Dog Night, the Lovin' Spoonful, the Grass Roots, the Turtles, the Association, Gary Puckett & The Union Gap, and the Classics IV to the English Beat British Invaders such as Herman's Hermits, the Hollies, and Freddie and the Dreamers. The most popular of the Chicagoland bands were larger than local, though smaller than sensations on a grander scope and scale across the country. While a few may have blinked from a single into obscurity, the typical trajectory of the majority of the groups was a two- to four-year arc. This compact course was common despite a few of the bands being signed to major labels such as Columbia and Warner Bros., their music being well received critically, and their production of a number of hits comparable to many of the national and international groups with whom they shared the charts.

Sixties Suburbia:
Sound, Style, Social Consciousness

Everybody really had their individual distinct sound, it was all part of Chicago, and the way their lives were, what sort of music they felt.
—Jimy Rogers, the Mauds.[10]

The origins of the multitude of suburbands were spread across Chicagoland in all directions except easterly, of course, which was water, where one of the Great Lakes (Lake Michigan) lies. The collective musical styles of the bands did not naturally coalesce into or generate a signature "suburban sound" or forge a groundbreaking genre that redefined the region's musical map the way that the blues and jazz had. "As for creating our 'own sound of Chicago,' we were all pretty different from each other," said Buckingham Carl Giammarese, echoing Jimy Rogers's view. "We were influenced by what we heard on the radio—British groups, American bands, R&B, soul. It all turned our key."[11]

Aside from the coincidental, if not quirky, commonality of four of the bands featuring fronts with the first name "Jim"—Peterik, Pilster, Rogers, Sohns—the closest to a shared sound may be the horns that were mainstreamed by the group Chicago and utilized by the American Breed, Buckinghams, and Ides of March. Each band incorporated the instrumentation differently: the Buckinghams punchy soul, the American Breed polished bubblegum garage, and the Ides of March a blend of folk, rock, and jazz. The Ides of March's use of the brassy sound in trumpet solos, intros, bridges, and extensive arrangements was a pop precursor to (more so than a widely misperceived imitation of) bands such as Blood, Sweat & Tears; Lighthouse; Chase; and local contemporaries Chicago Transit Authority/Chicago, which wore the brass badge as a horn of plenty.

In addition to some inventive integration of trumpets and saxophones, the musical styles represented in the predominant suburbands incorporated the popular American hooks and British roots of the era. Giammarese considered the influences reciprocating, with the Buckinghams essentially "buying into" the Beatles' boomerang or "bounce back" effect:

What was going on was that the British groups and musicians were listening to American music; that's what they were into. The Beatles were big fans of the Everly Brothers, Buddy

Holly, Elvis, Chuck Berry, Carl Perkins, and listened to some of the soul, R&B, and girl groups. So they were trying to emulate that kind of music. *Our* music. And then it just kind of bounced back here from them. And when they stepped in here and recorded it, it just came out different when they did it. So it was really us buying into our own music, but it was coming from England."[12]

The Buckinghams' music blended Dennis Tufano and Carl Giammarese vocals of Jim Holvay compositions with rock, soul, and stray psychedelia ("Susan"). The New Colony Six sound started out with exuberant garage rock employing Farfisa organ and the unique Lesley guitar before evolving into pop/rock softness and harmonizing balladry that included strings. The Ides of March incorporated horns with hippie hints, combining complex jazz, rock, soul, and folk stylings with occasional sprawling jam arrangements. The edgy Shadows of Knight sound, self-described as an English version of the blues with a Chicago touch, commonly draws comparisons to a tri-amalgam of the Rolling Stones, Animals, and Yardbirds. The Mauds' single "Soul Drippin'" perhaps best characterized the band's gritty R&B, blue-eyed soul sound. They, along with the Buckinghams, preceded the Rolling Stones as white bands to record at Chicago's renowned Chess Records. The Cryan' Shames, who fashioned the grungiest garage presence of the local lineup, were a musical melting pot with a Byrdsian emphasis of jingle jangling guitars, tambourine, and multiple vocals. "We opened for the Byrds when they came through the first time," said Jim Pilster. "We would have opened for them for free. We would have paid to open for the Byrds."[13] Their group built upon the imprint of Byrds basics, blending Beatlesque arrangements, Rolling Stones–style riffs, occasional Yardbirds fuzz, and layered harmonies reminiscent of the Beach Boys, the Hollies, and the Association with baroque and roll accents of the Left Banke.

The totality of the resourceful sound styles of the suburbands was inventively and deftly derivative, cleverly concomitant, and notably diverse. To their credit, the bands' borrowings were more blended than blatant; their derivations, interpretations, and adoptions of devices avoided insensitive imitation and failed disguises of acquainted musical manners. True to the standard music mode of many pop rock apprenticeships and formative garage gatherings, the Chicagoland groups were inspired by and borrowed from not only familiar sounds and styles but from specific songs. Cover versions were prevalent parts of the bands' live performance sets, as recordings as album tracks, and released as both A- and B-sides of singles. Before "Kind of a Drag" became a national hit, the Buckinghams' regional releases were a range of versions that included James Brown's "I'll Go Crazy," the Beatles' "I Call Your Name," and the Hollies' "I've Been Wrong Before." They followed with Lloyd Price's "Lawdy Miss Clawdy" and Cannonball Adderley's "Mercy Mercy, Mercy," both which charted. The American Breed's most popular song, "Bend Me, Shape Me," was actually a castoff from the Outsiders, best known for their hit "Time Won't Let Me." They also charted with Chip Taylor's "Step Outside Your Mind" and recorded numerous Brill Building tunes, among them the Carole King/Gerry

Goffin gems "I Don't Think You Know Me," "Don't Forget About Me" (also recorded by Barbara Lewis and Dusty Springfield), and "Sometime in the Morning" (also recorded by the Monkees), and Barry Mann/Cynthia Weil's Animals' hit "We Gotta Get Outta This Place." In addition, the American Breed covered "Hi-Heel Sneakers," Eddie Floyd's "Knock on Wood," and songs written by Paul Williams and Van McCoy.

R&B and soul tunes were commonly in the interpretive queue, particularly by the Shadows of Knight. In addition to their top-10 hit with Van Morrison/Them's "Gloria," they charted with a version of Muddy Waters's "Oh Yeah" and recorded songs by Willie Dixon, John Lee Hooker, Chuck Berry, and Carole Bayer Sager. Bo Diddley's "Cadillac" was a B-side for the New Colony Six's "Long Time to Be Alone." The Mauds also recorded "Knock on Wood" and Sam & Dave's classic "Hold On," in a radio-friendly version that contained a chorus edit from the original.[14] The Ides of March, whose 1970 debut LP *Vehicle* featured jazzy extended Beatles ("Symphony for Eleanor [Eleanor Rigby]") and Crosby, Stills & Nash variations ("Wooden Ships/Dharma for One"), also performed songs by James Brown, Arthur Conley, and Curtis Mayfield ("People Get Ready") in their regular set lists during live shows.

Between their successful singles and carrying significant album appeal among the "Suburbs Seven," the Cryan' Shames may have leaned on cover versions more than most of their colleagues. Their three albums, all released on the Columbia major label, were well stocked with compositions from various songbooks. As the Travelers, they recorded "If I Needed Someone" intent on the familiar Beatles song being their inaugural single for the Destination label. Its composer, George Harrison, had other ideas. Apparently displeased with the Hollies' rendition of his song, despite its Top 20 placement in England, the "quiet and cool" Beatle refused to license his song stateside. The Travelers' version was never released as a single but was subsequently included on the Cryan' Shames' debut album, *Sugar and Spice*, in 1966. The album resembled a contemporary tribute/cover compilation, leading off with the single "Sugar and Spice," a Tony Hatch (as Fred Nightingale) composition popularized by the English group the Searchers in 1964. An array of interpretations of the 1960s playlist followed—Harrison's "If I Needed Someone"; Martha and the Vandellas' "Heat Wave"; the popular "We Gotta Get Out of This Place"; Gene Clark's Byrds' B-side gem, "She Don't Care About Time"; and a requisite version of the Leaves and Jimi Hendrix's "Hey Joe."[15] The Cryan' Shames' two subsequent albums featured another Brill Building cornerstone, King and Goffin's "Up on the Roof," Hoagy Carmichael's "Baltimore Oriole," and the oft-covered anthem "Get Together." The band's final 45 single in 1969 was also a cover, the relatively obscure "Rainmaker," the B-side to Harry Nilsson's "Everybody's Talkin'," written by Fred Neil in 1967 and featured in the soundtrack of the film *Midnight Cowboy* (1969).

Individual group identities, styles, images, and attitudes emerged in conjunction with each suburband's musical sounds within the context of the era's sociocultural conditions. Amidst the overarching white suburban manner, boots-and-bell-bottoms fashion, and long hair leanings of the times that occasionally violated high school dress codes and grooming standards, the bands for the most part adopted a tidy, presentable posture, with a style spectrum that was uniformly continental and colonial more than singularly choirboy or counterculture. "We were all supposed to look pretty clean-cut," said Ronnie Rice.[16]

There were modest exceptions within the mod. By fashion standards, the Cryan' Shames were the grubbiest of the garage groups when it came to grooming, largely due to lengthy laundering lapses with their clothes, particularly and proudly, Pilster. And the Shadows of Knight, billed as "Chicago's Rolling Stones," exhibited a self-described and admittedly "justified … bad-boy, steal your daughter image," highlighted by in the cross-the-line shirtless stage swagger of front Jimy Sohns.[17]

The English influence among the bands was discernible and a thread throughout. New Colony Six fashioned an anti–Brit style, adopting colonial costuming comparable to Paul Revere & the Raiders. The Buckinghams, who evolved out of the Pulsations and the Centuries, changed their original name in order to reflect a continental Englander image following a failed audition for a WGN-TV variety show. Producers said they "weren't British enough." "We morphed into a more English-looking group," said Carl Giammarese. "At first we were a bunch of greasers. Nice suits, wearing our hair five inches on the top of our heads. Little by little, one guy at a time, we started looking more like the Beatles, dressing differently with a more Carnaby Street London look."[18]

Fortuna seconds that notion of his bandmate, attributing the seismic stylistic shift and stimulus to the Fab Four.

> The players and musicians really got touched by the Beatles. And that whole English scene. That little country really did a lot of damage here, and it was a change of life … of thinking … of attitude—everything. Everyone that used to be wearing motorcycle boots and the jeans and hanging out on the street corner and getting into trouble, all of the sudden all of these guys I knew from back then were wearing these bell-bottom pants and growing long hair and walking around with flowers a few years later…. It was like everyone went to this place someplace else and came back different. It was a way of life. Everybody changed their thinking.[19]

Inspired suburbands aside, not everyone was enamored with the exuberant twist and shout, mop top Liverpudlian presence. In *Joy and Fear: The Beatles, Chicago and the 1960s* (2021), historian John F. Lyons suggests that resistance to Beatlemania, its unsettling music, counterculture values and accompanying hysteria, was more widespread and more deeply rooted in Chicago than in in any other major American city during the era. The hostility extended beyond the parental province and generational divide to authoritative figures within the Midwest establishment. A *Chicago Tribune* editor and the iconic big city boss, Mayor Richard J. Daley, were among the alarmists and unyielding antagonists who deemed the Beatles a menace and a threat to the well-being of their city.

Within the context of the turbulent times a-changin', youthful rebellion, and a widening chasm of the g-g-generation gap and social movements from civil rights to anti-war, the Chicagoland bands generally displayed a middle-of-the-road neutrality, with a trace of a midwestern conservative undercurrent counter to prevalent counterculture ideals. "If they found out you were involved with drugs or anything like that, the radio station wouldn't play your records," said New Colony Sixer Ronnie Rice. "The underground stations thought it was hip, but we weren't doing music for the underground stations. So we were pretty clean. We were the Pat Boones of rock music."[20]

While Pat Boone wholesomeness may be an overstatement, the Chicagoland bands were generally safe. They did not wear nonconformity and anti-establishment on their sleeves, whether outfit or recordings, and were not overtly political in their viewpoints, voices, or verses. Activist anthems and protest songs were not blowin' in the Windy City, nor were there urgent (Graham) Nashian echoes lyrically petitioning to "please come to Chicago" to "change and rearrange the world" ringing with local origination and suburban stamp.[21] Among the sparse sociopolitical perspective on the Chicagoland soundtrack is the Buckinghams' "Foreign Policy" in 1967, written by producer James William Guercio. Released as the B-side to the group's Columbia single "Susan" and sequenced as the closing track on their *Time and Changes* (1967) LP, the song is highlighted by a sample from a John F. Kennedy speech.[22] Also among the mindful, H.P. Lovecraft (1967) and the Cryan' Shames' (1969) dually duplicated "Get Together" (also "Let's Get Together"), Chet Powers's mid-decade impassioned plea for peace that became a frequently covered tune, most notably by the Youngbloods in 1967.

The void in ideological themes and socially relevant expressions in song was not necessarily an indication of lack of awareness on the part of the Chicagoland musicians. While the bands generally remained above the fray, they were inescapably tuned into the times. Case in point: as a multiracial group, with Black bassist Chuck Colbert among its membership, the American Breed experienced discrimination directly. While touring across regions outside the Midwest, band members were subject to "back of the bus" biases, color barriers, and segregation in restaurants, restrooms, and hotels, particularly and stereotypically in the South. "There was lot of prejudice that I was unaware of down there," said lead singer Gary Loizzo. "We played colleges and college kids didn't have any bias. It was the older people who frowned upon having a Black person in the band. I had never thought that we [the American Breed] were 'integrated.' It never crossed my mind."[23]

Vehicles, Baby:
"Take You Anywhere You Want to Go...."

Things happened so fast in those days. One time we recorded a song in an afternoon, and we heard it on the radio on the way back from the studio. And I'm not kidding. That's how quick things got done in the city at the time. You didn't have to get Top 40 before they actually played you.
—Jim Pilster (a.k.a. J.C. Hooke), the Cryan' Shames[24]

The speed of sound in singles traveled swiftly throughout Chicagoland during the era. New songs produced by the locals charted a precipitous path of striking immediacy, from production to prompt promotion, playlist, and airplay, a course from studio to station to radio rotation and across nearby neighborhoods, the city, suburbs, and Midwest region. Jim Pilster's ready recount of the accelerated advance of a Cryan' Shames single conveys a wondrous, wide-eyed tale of delivering a recording studio take on acetate to a deejay down the street at WLS and then, as if magic, hearing their new tune blaring from the car radio on the ride home.

The legend and local lore were not hyperbole or happenstance, rather common occurrence. That was the norm and standard music modus operandi in the period and place. Record release radio recollections are detailed and vivid imprints among suburband members. Ray Graffia of the New Colony Six recalls driving in his 1959 Triumph on the Kennedy Expressway in December 1965 when their debut single, "I Confess," hit the AM airwaves. "I took the sidecar and I said 'I'm on the radio! Turn up WLS!' It was about 11:00 at night. It was one of those request things."[25] The Ides of March front Jim Peterik's account of listening to "You Wouldn't Listen" is similarly lucid and gushing. He and his bandmates were riding in a 1970 black Cadillac when the familiar voice of deejay Art Roberts sounded through the oval dashboard speaker. Delivering words that the band of Berwyners had been waiting to hear their whole lives, Roberts's "pick to click" selection declared "a new one from a new band on the scene ... the Ides of March"—"You Wouldn't Listen." On cue, Peterik's crisp Jazzmaster Kinks-inspired lead riff ensued, announcing the Ides' single and its radio arrival on the Chicagoland soundscape. Their car ride shifted into celebratory overdrive, with the exuberant passengers rolling down the windows and shouting in radio recognition, "That's us! That's us!" Cruising down Cermak Road—characterized by Peterik as "kind of the Rodeo Drive of Berwyn and Cicero"—the Cadillac's hit parade route passed local landmarks and Czech points along the neighborhood's main strip: movie theaters (the Olympic and the Berwyn); savings and loans and banks on every block, among them Lincoln Federal Savings and Loan (where my frugal father had an account); Vesecky's Bakery; and the Troy Department Store. "I experienced a feeling like no other," writes Peterik in his memoir. "I was born for this moment.... And there's something about that night that lives forever in me."[26]

Jimy Sohns is similarly specific in his recollection of the debut of "Gloria"—the time, date, and place. The Shadows of Knight lead was not behind the wheel of a car, rather behind a double cheeseburger at McDonald's when his band's song premiered over the airwaves. "We recorded 'Gloria' and three days later, before there were any records pressed, they played it on the radio, on WLS at 3:10 in the afternoon," said Sohns. "All of a sudden. I thought I was hearing things. I had my radio on and I thought I heard 'Gloria,' so I turned it up a little bit ... and I thought, 'Oh my God, they're playing my song on the radio.'"[27]

The Buckinghams' Nick Fortuna was also among the myriad who affirmed the perspectives on skyrocketing singles and the scene's swift succession. "One day, everything is basically normal and you're living this normal everyday situation, and one day you wake up and you walk into a store and you open the door and it's like walking into a new world. It wasn't a slow process. It wasn't an overnight situation, but it sure seemed like it. It happened very quickly."[28]

The efficient course progressed from bands playing live in a living room, basement, or garage to laying down a recording studio take on acetate and often hand delivering a copy down the avenue to a deejay at WLS and then miraculously hearing their song premiere on the radio on the ride home, the single in full promotional course on its way to the charts, record retailers, and an awaiting youth audience.

The steadily activating, accumulating assemblage of bands across the Chicagoland area were concurrently contributing constituents of the scene as well as beneficiaries of a well-established, inimitable music infrastructure. The system was founded on a lively web of facilitating exposure vehicles and venues located within the city and its suburban surroundings, with a reach that resonated well beyond regional boundaries.

The groundwork of the vibrant, voluminous vortex of the Midwest's specific "star making machinery" and its promising path of possibility was secured and propelled by two powerhouse AM radio stations, the legendary 50,000-watt WLS, and its subsequent cross-town competitor, WCFL. Each station vied to launch the latest singles recorded by the locals, circulating and highlighting their respective rotations through the weekly *Silver Dollar Survey* and *Sound 10 Survey*, among other catchy playlist and programming devices.

The intrinsic exposure of expedient airplay was further enhanced by the two radio station rosters brimming with dynamic disc jockeys, a celebrity cast that included Dick Biondi, Dex Card, Ron Riley, Clark Weber, Bernie Allen, Don Phillips, Barney Pip, Art Roberts, Larry Lujack, Ron Britain, and Jim Stagg, among others. From their on-air radio show shifts to headliners hosting dance shows and emceeing live music events throughout the area, the popular personalities were charismatic co-stars and catalysts, maestros and magneteers, within the music scene on multiple platforms, acting as ardent advocates for the Chicagoland bands, as well as national and international recording artists and their music. Among the prototypical trendy deejay-driven vehicles was *Swingin' Majority*, hosted by Art Roberts and originating from the WLS studio located at the top floor of the Chicago Board of Trade and airing on a UHF channel on Saturdays at 11 a.m. The familiar format showcased local bands performing in live lip synch in a studio packed with dancing preteens and teenagers. National appearances ensued as Chicagoland bands made the rounds with bookings on prominent national network television variety and dance presentations, among the notable *The Ed Sullivan Show, American Bandstand*, Lloyd Thaxton's *Showcase '68, The Smothers Brothers Comedy Hour*, and the touring concert *Dick Clark's Caravan of Stars*.

The band/disc jockey symbiosis was a vital dynamic that triangulated with the

TUNE IN YOUR FAVORITE WLS PERSONALITY
They make Listening Great Entertainment all through the
DAY and NIGHT

THE CLARK WEBER SHOW
Monday thru Saturday 6 am-10 am

THE BERNIE ALLEN SHOW
Monday thru Friday 11 am-2 pm
Saturday 10 am-2 pm   Sunday 12 noon-2 pm

THE DEX CARD SHOW
With The Silver Dollar Survey
Monday thru Sunday 2 pm-6 pm

THE RON RILEY SHOW
Monday thru Friday 7 pm-9 pm
Saturday 6:30 pm-9 pm   Sunday 6:30 pm-8:30 pm

THE ART ROBERTS SHOW
Monday thru Saturday 9 pm-12 midnight
Sunday 10 pm-12 midnight
Adventures of Peter Fugitive—Monday thru Friday 10:15 pm

EAST of MIDNIGHT with DON PHILLIPS
Monday thru Saturday 12 midnight-5 am

Radio 890 **WLS** The Station with Personality

Chicago's Only 24 Hour-A-Day Popular Music Station

WLS radio's dynamic and varied personality program lineup, airing seven days a week and rocking around the clock day and night, underscores the renowned radio station's branding savvy (Local print advertisement, personal collection, circa 1967).

local teen audience. "There were personal relationships with radio stations and the people there," said music promoter/record producer Paul Gallis. "And the fact that there were local groups made the DJs want to help them more. The big thing to promote records then was for all the big jocks would do record hops and they would get the group for nothing. The group would go from place to place, playing for nothing, and the DJs would play their records on the air and say 'The Buckinghams are going to be here…. The Cryan' Shames are going to be there.' It was kind of a 'You help me, I'll help you scene.'"[29]

The spirited setting, particularly in the suburbs, was sustained by music activities that progressed from home-based spaces of garages, living rooms, and basements to a thriving circuit of suburban teen clubs with blacklights, graffiti walls, and concrete acoustics. Among the local hot spots were the Cellar, the Blue Village, Green Gorilla, and Wild Goose; city sites included Like Young in Old Town, The Cheetah, and Kinetic Playground.[30] Other popular outlets for live music from the homegrown groups included church and community youth recreation centers, VFW halls and dance ballrooms, skating rinks, ski lodges, high school gymnasiums, and record sock hops. "I don't know what we had going on was different from other cities," said Carl Giammarese of the exuberant suburban scene. "What we had was a lot of dances and teen clubs. We were able to work every week on such a big circuit."[31]

On a larger stage scale, the Arie Crown Theater, a 5,000-seat venue named in honor of a local Lithuanian immigrant industrialist, philanthropic family, opened in 1960 as part of the McCormick Place lakefront complex. Despite accumulating credentials that included some major label support, swift ascension and consistent chart presence, critical favor and recognition beyond the region, the local garage groups and suburbands generally were not the concert headliners at the convention center on South Lake Shore Drive. They frequently performed, however, as the opening acts for touring national bands that were booked big in larger locations such as the Arie Crown and civic auditoriums, arenas, and stadiums.

Local record production and distribution were also integral infrastructural components of the Chicagoland music scene. Recording studios, with the legendary R&B soul stop at 2120 South Michigan Avenue, Chess, and Ter-Mar (named after Chess founders Phil and Leonard's sons, Terry and Marshall) among the most notable, were part of the foundational framework along with savvy producers, executives, and music managers such as Jim Golden, Bob Monaco, Bill Traut, and James Guercio. There were also numerous renowned local record labels/companies that included Vee-Jay, U.S.A., Destination, and Dunwich, some which were subsidiaries of national record companies such as the Atlantic Records Group and Dot. As exposure broadened and the Chicagoland bands' singles continued to receive airplay and achieve respectable chart positions, major labels took notice and lured several of the Chicagoland locals and signed them from their independent labels. The breakthrough came with Columbia Records signing the Cryan' Shames following their 1966 debut on Destination. The Buckinghams followed, also joining Columbia in 1967 from Chicago's U.S.A. Records (1966–1967). The Ides of March began on their own label, Epitome, then went to Parrot (1966), which also had the Zombies on its roster; and eventually recorded two albums each for Warner Bros. (1970–1971) and RCA (1972–1973). In between two successful singles on Sentar (initially Centaur) and their final two 45s on Sunlight, the New Colony Six recorded on Mercury, which also had signed the Mauds. The Shadows of Knight were on the Atlantic Record Group's

Chicago-based Dunwich label, while the American Breed rostered on Acta, a subsidiary of Dot Records.

With record sales surging for 45 rpm singles and record companies primed to expand to 33⅓ long play albums pressed in both monaural and stereo sound formats, the music marketplace naturally expanded. Vinyl's distribution and supply were not limited to record store retailers in the region. Product circulated throughout well-stocked outlets such as Polk Brothers, a major home appliance and electronics dealer, and the pioneering discount department chain, E.J. Korvette, with its spectacular "all label sale," distinguishing itself as "the world's largest record department."

Music Mania: Midwest Music-teers?

There were hundreds of groups coming out of Chicago, all kinds of 'em. There was room for everybody.
—Chicago music promoter/producer Paul Gallis[32]

It was kind of like Wrestlemania. We were all real friendly, but there was always that edge. Everybody felt that they were the best and we all went out to prove it.
—Tom Doody, the Cryan' Shames[33]

The accommodating music infrastructure and atmosphere within the Chicagoland setting fostered a mutuality of awareness, appreciation, and respect among the suburbands. There was prevailing sense of common cause and occupational co-op consciousness. Within the fraternal sense of alliance, a mention, discussion, or interview that focused on one group routinely ricocheted in reference to their contemporaries in the enclave of suburbands. The convenient, conscientious, communal manner of concentrated locality and identity was a Midwest Musketeerian (or Music-teerian) "all for one and one for all" assumption that was generally positive, though with some parameters as their popularity proliferated. Bookings, airplay, chart placements, performances, and audience sizes and enthusiasm did not go unnoticed between the bands and their members. "We didn't hang out together.... We'd just work different jobs together," said Rice of the New Colony Six. "We were friends, but you'd hope the other guys didn't do quite as well as you. Everybody was watching each other. You'd see the Cryan' Shames and say, 'What're they doin' in *Billboard* this week?' When we had a hit record we were happy as hell and we all thought we'd hit the big time."[34]

The increasing exposure and energized environment cultivated a naturally competitive spirit that generally, though not entirely, tended to be more constructive than cruel. "Band relationships in the '60s were fairly cutthroat to be honest," confessed New Colony Six's Ray Graffia. "We didn't wish each other bodily harm, but we all vied to be the number one group in Chicago, from record sales to stage performances. When booked at the same venues, we were civil but not cuddly."[35] The intrinsic blend of unsettling inspiration, one-upmanship, and any measure of professional jealousy between bands translated into musical motivation. "We would go out and hear other bands who were our competition," said Giammarese. "We were all influenced by each other. You'd hear one group do a song and say, 'That's really cool, we gotta do that. We gotta top that.' I remember hearing the New Colony Six play at the club Like Young in Old Town. They played 'I Confess.' It was like, 'God, we gotta get going here.'"[36]

And they did. The Buckinghams took the competitive cue, capturing the crown and the local lead, and separating slightly from the pack with their string of hit singles that was initiated by the chart-topping "Kind of a Drag" in 1967, resulting in national recognition and relevance for the Midwest. "Before 'Kind of Drag' came out, we all played basically the same circuit and we were all striving for the top rung on the ladder," said Fortuna. "After 'Kind of a Drag,' it was like we [the Buckinghams] weren't in their league anymore. We went to the majors and they were still in the minors. The competition and resentment was left back with them. We didn't really look it at it that way anymore. When we went on the road and we did interviews, we would talk about a lot of the local groups."[37]

The Buckinghams' achievement became a benchmark for the Chicagoland suburbands, simultaneously stirring a mindful measure of inevitable intergroup positioning and awareness, and upholding the competitive yet courteous kinship code that, musically, the Midwest was one for all, and all for one—with room for everybody.

Chapter 1

AM Radio Reformation

WLS, Middle America's Bright New Sound

So, it was a great station. It was the best. It was almost like taking candy from a kid. That's how important WLS was in those days. It was unbelievable.
—Jim Golden, producer/president, U.S.A./Destination Records, Chicago[1]

I'm your vehicle baby / I'll take you anywhere you want to go
—Jim Peterik, Ides of March, "Vehicle"[2]

To be on the Big 89 was a big deal. You could hear a song over and over again on a record, but when you heard it on the radio it was like nothing else. Pure magic.
—Carl Giammarese, the Buckinghams[3]

But there will be nothing like WLS again.
—WLS disc jockey Dex Card[4]

Alley (L)oop: From Prairie to Pop

On Monday morning, May 2, 1960, many midwestern radio listeners began their day, the new week, and the new month as they had for the past 36 years, awakening to sound of the familiar 6:00 a.m. farm report on WLS, featuring the familiar futures and commodities quotes and corn, grains, dairy, and livestock headlines. What followed 30 minutes later signaled a momentous shift in the region's radio routine. The Anita Kerr Singers harmoniously announced "the bright new swingin' sound of 8-9-0 in Chicago," with elongated enunciation—"double-youuu-ellll-essss, in Chi-caah-goh." The smooth station identification immediately segued into the Hollywood Argyles' rendition of "Alley Oop," a tumbling term tune composed and recorded by country musician Dallas Frazier in 1957. The song was inspired by the lead character in the V.T. Hamlin syndicated comic strip of the same name, a fantasy adventure set in the prehistoric kingdom of Moo. The Hollywood Argyles single was produced for the Lute label by the eccentric Los Angeles music figure Kim Fowley, whose production signature colored a series of novelty and cult pop rock songs during the era. Fowley eventually managed the Runaways in the 1970s after introducing group founders Joan Jett and Sandy West to each other.

The Hollywood Argyles' novelty single, "Alley Oop," pronounced WLS radio's programming format transition from prairie to pop in 1960. The Wham Records picture sleeve edition, with a Phil Flowers B-side, "C. C. Rider," followed the initial pressing of the single on the Lute label (Wham Records 7037, circa 1962).

The evanescent Hollywood Argyles were riding "Alley Oop" to the top of the *Billboard* Hot 100, and to #3 on the US R&B charts. They were unknowingly launching a pop lineage for the catchy song. Several other artists would subsequently record "Alley Oop" during the decade, among them the Beach Boys; Dave Van Ronk with his early ensemble the Hudson Dusters; and British bands the Bonzo Dog Doo-Dah Band, a satirical art rock/pop group, and the Tremeloes, known for their hits "Silence Is Golden" and "Here Come My Baby," a Cat Stevens composition. In the decades to follow, Danté and The Evergreens, Darlene Love, George Thorogood and the Destroyers, and country pop comedian Ray Stevens were among others who also recorded versions of "Alley Oop."

Following the Hollywood Argyles' playful prelude on the radio, Jim Dunbar commenced his morning shift by greeting listeners and welcoming them to the new WLS era. The conversion was complete; "the bright new swingin' sound" of WLS Chicago had alley ooped across the Chicago Loop into arrival over the airwaves, on its way to becoming one of the country's great radio stations.

Upon This Rock: Rural, Retail, Religion: World's Largest Store

WLS's exuberant music makeover from prairie programming to Top 40 ignited a radio revolution in Chicagoland that resounded through the hub of its music scene during the era. The shift was foundational. From "the bright new sound" of the 1960s to "the Big 89" and "the Rock of Chicago" in the early 1970s, WLS at 890 in the middle of the AM dial defined music radio and Top 40 in the region, with reverberations well beyond Midwest markers. Being located in the central United States with a contiguous expanse of flat terrain enhanced the station's nighttime sky wave coverage, in latitudes, longitudes, and *loud*itudes that crisscrossed the country, from the Rocky Mountains to the East Coast, and a north-south span from Canada to the Gulf Coast. The station's mighty 50,000-watt non-directional signal—referred to by radio industrialists and aficionados as a "blow torch"—transmitted from facilities 30 miles south of the city in Crete, Illinois, consistently, clearly, commandingly reached between 38 and 42 of the 50 states.

Before the station rocked into the 1960s, WLS's radio roots were rural and retail. In the early 1920s, with radio increasingly sounding in the commercial and public sphere, the corporate executives at Sears, Roebuck and Company were among those who took notice and were interested in utilizing the medium. Recognizing the efficient and mass means to simultaneously advance the Sears-Roebuck Agricultural Foundation and reach the midwestern farm community and a substantial rural audience that relied on the popular Sears catalog for mail order merchandise, the company bought program time on several Chicago and national radio stations. In 1923, Sears-Roebuck applied for a broadcast license and announced plans to construct its own radio station that would serve the rural community. The following year, after a lengthy testing period, promotion and marketing, experimental transmissions, and station identification deliberations, Sears-Roebuck's new station, WLS, debuted on April 12, 1924, its call letters an appropriate acronym signifying the "World's Largest Store." The fledgling station operated from a small studio next to the Agricultural Foundation offices on the 11th floor of Sears-Roebuck's 14-story headquarters complex towering on Chicago's West Side.[5]

WLSears was a short-lived signal. Two years after its inauguration, the Sears-Roebuck station transformed into *The Prairie Farmer* station when WLS was sold to Burridge D. Butler's prominent farm publication. In the aftermath of the transaction, WLS's main studios relocated from the Sears complex on Homan Avenue to the Prairie Farmer publishing headquarters on Chicago's Near West Side at 1230 West

Washington Boulevard. Butler's vision of WLS was similar to Sears-Roebuck's. He expected the widespread media exposure to benefit the *Prairie Farmer* publication just as it had the Sears Company and its catalog, and was committed to the prairie station's rural reach that primarily targeted, informed, and entertained the farming population in the hundreds of miles of heartland south and west from Chicago. Butler steered WLS to the national stage by providing an appealing pool of programs, personalities, and talented performers beyond the barnyard basics of livestock reports and weather updates. Andy Williams, George Goebel, "the Singing Cowboy" Gene Autry, Red Foley, Patsy Montana, and comedian Pat Buttram were among the cast of popular performers who rose through the WLS ranks on their way to successful entertainment careers in music, television, and film. The live weekend music/comedy variety roundup, *The National Barn Dance*, became the Prairie Farmer station's signature show and a precursor to Nashville's legendary *The Grand Ole Opry*.[6]

During the mid-to-late 1950s, significant sociocultural and technological shifts resonated through radio, in large part propelled by the appealing visual presence of television as a primary medium within broadcast airwaves, along with film, which had already established itself as a cultural centerpiece in the expanding media marketplace. America was steadily progressing from a rural to an urban society. As Chicago was becoming more cosmopolitan, and its postwar suburban sprawl steadily expanding north and west of the city, WLS's popularity began to decline. The daily programming schedule featuring farm reports, country and western music, and religious shows was losing ground and receiving less airtime in favor of local news, weather, and recorded music with deejay shows. Even the station's Saturday night staple, *The National Barn Dance*, was showing signs of diminishing appeal after 36 years.

The Prairie Farmer folks fully recognized that the farm format was fading, if not facing foreclosure. They appeared ready and willing to sell. The American Broadcasting Company (ABC), which evolved out of the NBC Blue Network, emerged as the leading potential purchaser. The network, intrigued with the Midwest station location and its abundant wattage, had earlier purchased Paramount Theatres, Inc., which had been a share time operation with WLS through the 1950s. ABC controlled WENR, a television property in Chicago, and was considering pursuing a license for the forthcoming frequency modulated (FM) radio band. Preparations to buy WLS began in November 1959, and by March 18, 1960, The Prairie Farmer Publishing Company and WLS Radio became a wholly owned subsidiary of ABC.

In shaping its new Midwest station, ABC took cultural and corporate cues from its AM affiliates in Pittsburgh (KVQ-AM) and New York (WABC), where contemporary formats were flourishing. They assigned a pair of programming pros from Pittsburgh's KVQ—general manager Ralph Beaudin and program director Sam Holman—to supervise the ambitious transition at WLS from polite rural and religion radio to pop and rock. In the Chicago market, contemporary music was being programmed primarily during the nighttime daypart, and featured on stations WIND (560) and WJJD (1160). Most radio programmers were not convinced that a music format, particularly rock and roll, could anchor a schedule, and they worried—maybe even hoped—that the music genre was merely a passing fad that was unable to support itself. Reflecting ABC's corporate view, Beaudin and Holman believed otherwise, and were committed to proving the prevalent (mis)perception wrong. Their focus was on the emerging demographic of young age listeners, the first Baby Boomers whose "g-g-generation" was birthed January 1, 1946, which made the target group 14 years old at the time of WLS's music mediamorphosis in 1960.

Despite the skepticism and resistance, WLS's roll into rock seemed to be a sound decision, literally and figuratively, on multiple levels. Mort Crowley, who was among the new crew of young announcer recruits, recalls the state of the station:

> Here you had a big, fifty-thousand watt station that had absolutely no audience, none at all. They could hear this thing all over the middle West, virtually in three-quarters of the United States at night, and there was nobody listening to it. They cleaned up the signal, they put in new equipment. It was unheard of that a radio station that big was going to go rock 'n' roll. This was some kind of anathema to purists, but it is what the general public wanted.[7]

WLS's transformation and subsequent ascent to national prominence was not sudden, nor was it seamless or smooth. Long-time WLS listeners and loyalists naturally lamented the loss of their Prairie Farmer programming after nearly four decades. According to Beaudin, the audience's adverse reaction was more religion related than it was agriculturally rooted: "The station was carrying 40 hours of commercial religion a week. We received ten thousand letters protesting the dropping of religious programming. And we answered all of those letters."[8] The "losing my religion" disappointment, combined with stiff competition from Chicago stations WGN and WIND, contributed to the new WLS initially stalling in third place in the Windy City's radio ratings. Not only was promotion for the fresh format minimal, the ABC network stunted the schedule with requisite news and programming such Don McNeill's *Breakfast Club*, which were incompatible with the new youth-targeted music format.

Station location was also becoming a concern. The nearby neighborhood within blocks of the Washington Boulevard building that WLS shared with *Prairie Farmer* magazine was deteriorating; Madison Street was commonly referred to as "skid row." According to WLS lore, there were ripples that reached its own building foundation. When the hefty pallets of paper were dropped on the basement floor of the printing plant, the vibration literally shook the structure, frequently causing records that were being played on the air to skip. The station relocated to 360 N. Michigan Avenue the following year in 1961.[9]

"The Swingin' Seven": Personality Radio

Amidst the varied challenges, Beaudin and Holman remained steadfast and focused on their vision for WLS as reflected in the station's "bright new sound" slogan that was routinely proclaimed and packaged during station breaks and promo spots. One of their first steps was to cast the net for on-air talent and the best personalities to suit the format, the schedule, and the station signal. "The idea was to bring in bright young guys, preferably from out of town, who didn't know it wouldn't work," said Beaudin.[10] More than 350 disc jockeys submitted audition tapes in response to the station's solicitation. From that pool of personalities and possibilities, seven deejays were selected for the initial slate, including Holman, who would supervise the collective, and short-termer Ed Grennan, a misfit as a holdover from the Prairie Farm staff. The representation of the recruits for WLS's on-air radio roster had conspicuous roots east of the Mississippi: Mort Crowley (New York City), Jim Dunbar (New Orleans), and midwesterners Bob Hale (Peoria, Illinois) and Gene Taylor, who had been broadcasting as "Happy O'Day" (Milwaukee). Taylor's steady climb at WLS over the next several years would make him program director in 1961, station manager in 1965, and general manager the following year, a position he held for five years.

The most boisterous of the bunch, Dick Biondi from Buffalo, New York, was a rebel, ranter, and raver who was assigned to the important nighttime shift from 9:00 p.m. to midnight. Biondi's brand of bravado, as the self-styled "Wild I-tralian," stood out within WLS's swinging sound proclaimed as "The Big Beat." Biondi emerged as the station supernova, the out-front guy, the most popular and flagship carrier of the inaugural unit of WLS personalities. Described varyingly by his colleagues as anti-authority, anti-establishment, pizzazz and noise, charismatic and uniquely talented, Biondi as a disc jockey "owned everyone under 30" and could relate to 12–15-year-old girl and guy demographic with a Pied Piper presence. "He was emotionally and psychologically stuck forever in that crack between 17 and 17½ years old," said Jim Dunbar. "He got to be a monster, and the rest of us just kind of circled around that orbit … we benefitted from the luster of Biondi."[11]

Through addition and subtraction, the original "Swinging Seven," frequently pronounced "The Magnificent Seven," a designation conveniently appropriated from the popular 1960 film Western starring Steve McQueen, Eli Wallach, James Coburn, Robert Vaughn, and Charles Bronson, morphed into replacements that became a celebrated cast of household names that sustained across WLS's exclusive 24-hour schedule over the course of the decade. Beyond Biondi and the initial cluster of deejays, the station lineup continuity amidst steady departures, defections, and promotions was further amplified and anchored by a sequel staff that included "Mother's Weber's oldest son" Clark Weber, who eventually became program director; Bernie Allen; Dex Card, known as "the crew cut fellow in the first row"; Art Roberts; "Ringo" Ron Riley; and Don Phillips on the "East of Midnight" late shift.

The station's popularity and national notoriety continued to attract top talents throughout the decade and into the 1970s. Larry Lujack, Chuck Buell, Kris

Erik Stevens, Joel Sebastian, Fred Winston, Gary Gears, Jerry Kay, Bob Sirott, John Records Landecker, Scotty Brink, "The First Lady of Chicago radio" Yvonne Daniels, Steve Dahl (who instigated the infamous and ill-fated "Disco Demolition Night" at Comiskey Park on July 12, 1979), Garry Meier, Brant Miller, Tom Kent, Steve King, Jeff Davis, and Tommy Edwards were among those joining the parade of personalities in WLS's legendary lineage. Many of the disc jockeys eventually earned radio Hall of Fame distinctions at various levels.

As part of WLS's 1960 format change, the deejays themselves chose the music for their weekly rotations from a list of 60 to 65 songs that were approved by the program director. Playlists highlighted the hottest records, gold records, and the Top 40, though were not always limited to the newest releases. Well-established records of older songs and artists going back between five and seven years also made the rounds. In Beaudin's view, the formula was pretty straightforward and simple: "We hit the market rather quickly and we were consistent in our formatting.... And we had it heavily day-parted across morning, midday, afternoon drive, and evening. The format is what really carried it, and we had just was had damn good guys that executed and worked damn hard."[12]

In stylistic contrast to the bombast and reverb of the Top 40 tone of its sister station, WABC in New York, WLS's music programming, approach, and its personalities reflected an overall milder midwestern demeanor that was decidedly spirited yet simple, occasionally nutty, with usual deejay chatter and fast-paced patter without being excessively noisy, heavily processed, or overproduced. Biondi was perhaps the most noticeable and frequent exception.

"The people that ran the station had the insight to leave us alone and let us do what we thought was right. We developed our own character within the format, but we were pretty free. If we saw a trend, we could jump on it, and they would back us," said Ron Riley.[13]

"We had a good sound, a good working group ... and we could fill in for each other, but it wasn't the same when we did that," said Bob Hale. "We got a rhythm going that we could play off each other and had a lot of respect for each other, and each one was distinctive. Nobody really sounded like the other guy."[14]

Silver Dollar Survey

Beyond the inherent energetic, alluring triplet of the music, the artists, and the disc jockeys, the WLS station management resourcefully promoted its song playlists and on-air personalities and their schedules. On October 14, 1960, five months following its music makeover, WLS premiered its "Silver Dollar Survey." The city's "only authentic" and "official record survey," based on sales figures gathered from local record outlets, provided a listing or scorecard of the week's Top 40 songs, the artist, record label, and previous week's place on the chart. The bottom-third of the slender slip included "featured albums of the week" and a show promo, frequently with a headshot of one of its personalities and their schedule. The back-side space was devoted to advertisements. The colorful 3½-by-8½-inch triple sheets, printed varyingly in light blue, green, pink, yellow, and an occasional orange hue, were issued weekly and distributed for free throughout Chicagoland record departments of retail stores, music shops, and other hip locales. Among the first flyer highlights were "Shortnin' Bread" by Paul Chaplain, which held the #1 spot; Elvis Presley, the Everly Brothers, Ray Charles, Bobby Vee, Bobby Rydell, Sam Cooke, Connie Francis, Brenda Lee, Paul Anka, The Ventures, The Chiffons, and The Fleetwoods among the chart notables; Fats Domino's *A Lot of Dominos* highlighted as the "feature album of the week"; and an invitation to "Swing along with the Gene Taylor Show." WLS program director Sam Holman coined the survey's "silver dollar" heading, adapting the title from the popular collectible coin of the era and its "value over time" implication. The signature survey was swiftly incorporated into a popular countdown program in the afternoon block between 3:30 and 6:00, with a history of hosts beginning with Holman and including Hale, Taylor, Card, and Larry Lujack, who had back and forth stints between rival WCFL (1967; 1972–76) and WLS (1967–72; 1976–87). Card's tenure presiding over the signature show was the longest, a three-year run that began with his arrival at WLS in 1964 and continued through 1967 when he left the station.

The weekly paper slip survey sustained for nearly three decades, with numerous reconfigurations along the way. Among the notable design makeovers and modifications were adding the station subheading "Personality Radio in Chicago" by mid-decade; a retitled "Silver Beatle Survey" in February 1964 during the Beatlemania frenzy, with the Fab Four's multiple singles on multiple record labels (Capitol, Swan, Vee-Jay) on the charts, including "I Want to Hold Your Hand" and "She Loves Me" in the top two spots, and the WLS jockeys, many of them balding, pictured coiffed in Beatle haircuts posing as the "New Beatles"; an alliterative "Super Summer Survey in 1967"; a retitle into "Hit Parade" by the end of the 1960s; and eventual FM editions that emphasized popular albums as well as hit singles. The WLS-AM version of the Silver Doll Survey lasted until August 10, 1985. Five years later and nearly 30 years after its inception, the acclaimed WLS Top 40 register reached the end of its weekly run on May 5, 1990, with Irish singer Sinéad O'Connor's cover version of The Artist Formerly Known as Prince's "Nothing Compares 2 U" holding the #1 spot on Volume 30, Number 29, the station's final published playlist.[15]

Opposite: The weekly WLS Silver Dollar Survey was compiled into a Top 40 based on sales reports from Chicagoland record outlets. The colorful circulating slips complemented an on-air countdown of "WLS's official playlist" every afternoon. The Suburbs Seven regularly occupied spots, holding their own in a crowded field of 45s. In the mid–April 1967 edition of the Survey, the Buckinghams, Cryan' Shames, and New Colony Six placed their singles at #6, #7, and #17 (WLS AM Radio, personal collection).

WLS

PERSONALITY RADIO IN CHICAGO

SILVER DOLLAR SURVEY

WLS' OFFICIAL PLAY LIST

THIS WEEK	APRIL 14, 1967		WEEKS PLAYED
* 1.	Little Bit Of Me, Little Bit Of You	Monkees — Colgems	7
* 2.	Happy Together	Turtles — White Whale	14
* 3.	Say Something Stupid	Frank & Nancy Sinatra — Reprise	7
* 4.	On A Carousel	Hollies — Imperial	10
* 5.	For What It's Worth	Buffalo Springfield — Atco	13
* 6.	Don't You Care	Buckinghams — Columbia	7
* 7.	Mr. Unreliable	Cryan' Shames — Columbia	9
8.	Penny Lane	Beatles — Capitol	11
* 9.	Walk Tall	2 Of Clubs — Fraternity	13
*10.	Dedicated To The One I Love	Mama's & Papa's — Dunhill	10
*11.	This Is My Song	Pet Clark — W.B.	10
*12.	Western Union	5 Americans — Abnak	11
*13.	California Nights	Leslie Gore — Mercury	13
*14.	You Got What It Takes	Dave Clark 5 — Epic	5
*15.	Jimmy Mack	Martha & Vandellas — Gordy	7
*16.	At The Zoo	Simon & Garfunkle — Columbia	5
*17.	You're Gonna Be Mine	New Colony 6 — Sentar	6
*18.	Happening	Supremes — Motown	5
*19.	Here Comes My Baby	Tremelos — Epic	5
*20.	Midnight Hour	Messengers — U.S.A.	7
*21.	Hippy-Dippy Weatherman	George Carlin — RCA	8
*22.	59th Street Bridge Song	Harpers Bizarre — W.B.	11
*23.	Love Eyes	Nancy Sinatra — Reprise	6
24.	Bernadette	4 Tops — Motown	9
*25.	Somebody To Love	Jefferson Airplane — RCA	5
*26.	Sunday For Tea	Peter & Gordon — Capitol	6
27.	Beggin'	4 Seasons — Philips	8
*28.	I'm A Man	Spencer Davis — U.A.	6
*29.	Girl, You'll Be A Woman Soon	Neil Diamond — Bang	5
*30.	Music To Watch Girls By	Andy Williams — Columbia	6
*31.	Detroit City	Tom Jones — Parrot	9
*32.	Sweets For My Sweet	Riddles — Mercury	10
*33.	Tell It To My Face	Keith — Mercury	8
*34.	Buy For Me	Nitty Gritty Dirt Band — Liberty	5
*35.	Can't Seem To Make You Mine	Seeds — Cresendo	5
*36.	Close Your Eyes	Peaches & Herb — Date	3
*37.	Travlin' Man	Stevie Wonder — Tamla	4
*38.	Dry Your Eyes	Brenda & Tabulations — Dion	5
*39.	Shake Hands	Lou Christie — Columbia	4
*40.	Sweet Soul Music	Arthur Conley — Atco	4

FEATURED ALBUM
IN THE ARMS OF LOVE — ANDY WILLIAMS — COLUMBIA

FINAL WEEKS!
LIMITED SUPPLY AVAILABLE

WLS Personality Magazine!
On Newsstands Now...

64 pages and over 200 photos of WLS music personalities at the studio, at home, and with recording stars.

WLS/890 • AN ABC OWNED STATION

This list is selected each week by WLS/Chicago from reports of all record sales gathered from leading record outlets in the Chicagoland area and other sources available to WLS/Chicago. Hear Dex Card play all the SILVER DOLLAR SURVEY hits daily from 2:00 to 6:00 P.M. *Denotes record first heard in Chicago on WLS.

Radio Resourcefulness:
Programs and Personas, Gags and Gimmicks

In addition to "The Silver Dollar Survey," there were other programs, gimmicks, personas, and routines that complemented the music playlist and further endeared the on-air radio personalities to their listeners. Among the highlights of the programming accents was Dick Biondi's off-key rendition of "The Pizza Song," adapted from the melody of the traditional folk tune "On Top of Old Smoky." Popularized by the Weavers in 1951, the song became a standard that was re-recorded by numerous artists, including Burl Ives, Pete Seeger, Gene Autry, Bing Crosby and Perry Como. When "The Pizza Song" was released as a 45 single in 1961, with its

Dick Biondi, "the Wild I-tralian," emerged as a star figure among Chicagoland's dynamic disc jockey force, with screamer stints at both WLS and WCFL. His novelty single, "The Pizza Song," with a "Knock-Knock" joke nod and wink on the flip side, was a local hit in 1961 (International Recording Co. 6904, Popimages/Alamy Stock Photo).

flip side, "Knock-Knock" in reference to Biondi's frequent on-air joke deliveries, the novelty tune sold a respectable 11,000 copies.

Riley and Weber ingeniously fabricated a convincing on-air feud into a long running gag that resulted in the fan factions "Riley's Raiders" and "Weber's Commandos." The playful, plausible rift actually contained some authenticity that had its origins in musical taste preferences. Riley was the big Beatles backer on the staff, earning him the nickname "Ringo Ron," which Weber conveniently, cleverly, comically customized to "Ringworm Ron" during their dramatic disputes. Weber took "the other side," countering the mythical, mandatory Beatles adulation with his ardent advocacy of non–Beatle British bands such as the Dave Clark Five.

In the name of "Holy cross-promotion, Batman!" between ABC's radio and television entities, Riley tapped into the popularity of the kitschy *Batman* television series, starring Adam West. The synergy-savvy inventive disc jockey began providing on-air updates of the caped crusader's adventures fighting crime against notorious and colorful villains such as the Penguin, Joker, Riddler, and Catwoman, among others. The clever routine evolved into a thriving Batman base, complete with fan club cards, bumper stickers, and a Batman costume that Riley would occasionally wear. Riley eventually landed a cameo on the popular prime-time series as an ice rink usher in the episode "Ice Spy" (a wordplay reference to another mid-decade, partners-in-crime prime-time television series, *I Spy* [NBC, 1965–68], starring Robert Culp and Bill Cosby as undercover agents) in which he delivers the line, "Mr. Wayne, you have a phone call."

The erudite Art Roberts, known for his triumphant signature sign-off "Excelsior!" (the loose Latin translation meaning "ever upward"), fit the "classic definition of a disc jockey." In the view of his colleague Bernie Allen, Roberts would "work pretty hard on breaking new records and getting information."[16] Well informed about the broader music scene, Roberts had the distinction of introducing some of the biggest British bands in Chicago, among them, the Rolling Stones and the Dave Clark Five. He was also slightly ahead of the Beatles curve locally, having founded Chicago's Beatles Fan Club Number One, which registered a modest membership of 150 Fab followers before Beatlemania burst onto the US scene.[17]

Roberts's radio show was rich with resources beyond music. His popular on-air bedtime stories were compiled and released into an album, *Hip Fables* (1967). The show also featured *The Adventures of Peter Fugitive*, a serial created and produced by unsung WLS production director Ray Van Steen. Roberts's skills and presence translated across media. Recognizing Roberts's flair at WLS and his rapport with the youth audience, Jack Mulqueen, a puppeteer and pioneering producer of the children's show *The Mulqueens*, which he hosted with his wife Elaine on Chicago's WGN-TV in 1963, approached Roberts about emceeing a Saturday night teen show for television. The timing for such a production was fitting as the genre was trending positively, or, in more era-specific lingo, was a mid–1960s "happening." Beyond Dick Clark's iconic *American Bandstand* (ABC), which aired from 1952 to 1983 in slight variations, music variety shows targeting teens and the energetic youth audience were scattered across television's schedule, from after-school and afternoons through prime-time evening slots. Among the popular shows were *Shindig!* (ABC, 1964–1966), *Hullabaloo* (NBC 1965–1966), *Where the Action Is* (ABC, 1965–1967), and *Happening '68* (ABC), which continued into 1969 as *Happening*. The show also featured a weekday spinoff, *It's Happening*, that aired Monday through Friday from mid–July through late October 1969.[18]

Mulqueen did not hesitate to hop aboard the bandwagon. As "the Dick Clark of the sandbox set," he fashioned Chicago's own pint-sized version of *American Bandstand* called *Mulqueen's Kiddie A-Go-Go* (later minus the "Mulqueen's" from the title). Though the show's debut in 1966 on WGN-TV was a smash, there was an accompanying undercurrent of backlash from anti-rock crusaders. Some considered the dance format to be age inappropriate, and were uncomfortable with its title that evoked the renowned Los Angeles Sunset Strip nightclub, Whisky a Go Go, which helped popularize go-go dancing. WLS-TV station manager Dick O'Leary conceded to the *Go-Go* no-nos and canceled the show the same week that the major department store Carson Pirie Scott happened to begin selling *Kiddie A-Go-Go* "Swinging Sweatshirts."

The showbiz-savvy Mulqueens didn't miss a beat, relocating their dance show to a small studio space in the Board of Trade Building, where the fledgling UHF station, WCIU, operated. For the next four years, *Kiddie A-Go-Go* was a daily staple of Channel 26's programming schedule, alongside a black-and-white menu of offerings that included bullfighting, foreign language programming, NBA basketball, and a 15-minute sports show hosted by Olympic great Jesse Owens. In 1970, the same year *Kiddie A-Go-Go*'s run concluded, WCIU introduced the groundbreaking African American music dance program *Soul Train*, hosted by its creator, Don Cornelius, who was the WCIU news and sports reporter at the time. When the *Train* pulled into the national syndication station and moved production to Los Angeles the following year, WCIU continued to produce a local version of *Soul Train* exclusively for the Chicago market until 1976.

As a joyful juvenile dance show, *Kiddie A-Go-Go* was predictably innocent, yet mildly idiosyncratic with psychedelic undercurrents. The production was a kooky kaleidoscope that included a cramped studio dance floor, framed by children's programming conventions and tone and low tech commercial inserts. Featured characters included "Record Picker," an eccentric figure in robe and sun god mask, who gobbled up records the kids didn't like, and the peculiar and perky, pixie-like hostess, Pandora (Elaine Mulqueen), whose dress varied between a mini skirt and a Harlequin clown costume, appearing out of a special effect box superimposed over a camera pan of parents in the studio audience.

The highlight of every show was an appearance by the era's hottest musical guests sheepishly lip syncing their hit tunes, with grade schoolers from five to 12 years old in the foreground, gyrating, bobbing, and busting their best dance

Harlequin hostess Pandora (Elaine Mulqueen) presides with pixie-like presence over the mid–1960s local television (WBKB-Chicago) tween-age dance show, *Kiddie A-Go-Go*, created by her husband, Jack Mulqueen, a puppeteer and pioneering children's television producer (WBKB-TV, Chicago; The Jack Mulqueen Papers; Loyola University Chicago, Archives and Special Collections).

moves—the frug, pony, jerk, swim, and the fad "Freddie," the signature jumping jack–like hop of the popular British band Freddie and the Dreamers—with cool and clueless awkward abandon on a cluttered dance floor. Of note, Mulqueen's memoir-like *The Golden Age of Chicago Children's Television* (2004, with Ted Okuda) features a letter of appreciation from the ageless teenager Dick Clark to Mulqueen, revealing that *Kiddie A-Go-Go* was the first show Clark ever actually danced on.[19] The dance program was not only a fan favorite, but appealed to record companies, who were attracted to the television exposure for their artists. "John Sipple, a promoter for Mercury Records, was in constant contact with me, and was happy to let us have anyone who was in town," said Mulqueen.[20] The steady stream of stars guesting on *Kiddie A-Go-Go* ranged from locals the New Colony Six to national figures such as Glen Campbell, Lesley Gore, Roger Miller, Frankie Valli and the Four Seasons, the Left Banke, and the Cowsills.

The Swingin' Majority, as titled by Roberts, had a similar format as *Kiddie A-Go-Go*, though with a more mature audience and sophisticated approach and content. Shot in the same small studio as *Kiddie A-Go-Go*, Roberts's swinging show was not as a much a dance party as it was a music showcase, with live lip sync performances from a small stage and interviews. Roberts demonstrated his continued commitment to homegrown music by devoting one segment of every show to local groups. "There was always an influx of artists in Chicago, and we could always find three or four who would be appearing somewhere, so it wasn't hard to get talent," said Roberts.[21] The Buckinghams, the Mauds, the Rovin' Kind/Illinois Speed Press, and the Ides of March were among the profusion of suburbands groups booked on *The Swingin' Majority*. The Ides' guest spot, which predated their smash 1970 single "Vehicle," was notable for being the same show that a then-unknown outfit from Gary, Indiana, the Jackson Five, made their national television debut singing their local Steeltown Records single "Big Boy," featuring Michael Jackson's premiere vocal. The show's regional recruiting reach extended 90 to 120 miles into Wisconsin, with the Oconomowoc brother-based sunshine psych band the Robbs, who assumed Traveling Wilburys–like precursor pseudonyms, and the Destinations from nearby Milwaukee. *The Swingin' Majority*'s ample guest register also included Tommy James & the Shondells, Stevie Wonder, Sonny & Cher, the Byrds, Gladys Knight & the Pips, Smokey Robinson, Jay and the Americans, Jerry Butler, Martha and the Vandellas, the Grass Roots, Boyce and Hart, and one-hit husband-and-wife folk duo Jim and Cathy Post, as Friend and Lover, with their groovy get-together "Reach Out of the Darkness." According to Roberts, "we had everybody on that program except Elvis Presley and the Beatles."[22]

The Swingin' Majority's successful two-year run that began in 1967 was eventually undermined by a Van Morrison appearance. According to producer Mulqueen's account, Morrison, like many of the show's guests, showed up late, and in haste went directly to the stage and on camera where he was introduced by host Roberts. As Morrison sang his hit "Brown Eyed Girl," the control room switchboard began lighting up with phone calls, all from teenage viewers asking "what kind of drugs Van Morrison was on." Mulqueen said he couldn't tell "one way or the other" about Morrison's condition, though the studio crew "had no doubts he was under the influence."[23] Clean-cut, Catholic, and committed to kid-quality content, Mulqueen took the moral high ground (pun always intended, despite disclaimers) and decreed that for subsequent shows, any scheduled guest who arrived late would not be allowed on the air. Roberts acquiesced, though his loyalties remained entrenched with the artists. Mulqueen's reflection on the Morrison episode was shaded with religious conviction, rock-star lifestyle wariness, and generational paranoia that reflected the times:

> To me, however, no program was worth sacrificing my religious convictions for. And don't forget, our show was going out live. In my wild imagination, I thought the authorities would see this guy strung out in drugs and think we were operating some kind of opium den. I had visions of getting raided by the police when we were on the air.[24]

A few shows later, Roberts circumvented their delicate punctuality pact and introduced a late arrival recording artist who appeared on the air before Mulqueen could intervene. Mulqueen reacted with relief and stern parental-like principle, saying, "Thank God he wasn't on drugs, but Art knew how I still felt about this."[25] Roberts reportedly exited quickly after the show. There was never a follow-up discussion between Roberts and Mulqueen. Shortly thereafter, the two simply parted ways, and with their split *The Swingin' Majority* ended.

WLS Deejays and Vee-Jay: The Beatles' American Debutune

Gimmicks, novelties, and program accents aside, WLS's charismatic personalities were at their most influential and impactful when introducing new music and recording artists—particularly the locals, as well as national and internationalists—to their vast listenership, whether on-air, on television shows, at record hops, or at Chicago's major concert sites such as McCormick Place or home team baseball sites, Comiskey Park and Wrigley Field. The deejay collective's considerable cachet, which had swiftly accrued, was further magnified into full display in a historic two-minute spin of a song titled "Please Please Me," courtesy of Dick Biondi during his February 8, 1963, show on WLS. The moment marked the first US radio airplay of a record by a relatively unknown British band named the Beatles. Despite a range of intriguing introduction counter claims that stretch from "Murray the K" Kauffman at WINS New York to WWDC in Washington, D.C., to George Harrison's sister's involvement with WFRX in West Frankfort, Illinois, Chicago music historian Kent Kotal's single-minded, comprehensive chronicle at *ForgottenHits.com* provides a convincing, if not conclusive, case for Biondi's Beatles' baptism stateside on the WLS radio airwaves.[26]

The Fab Four's first single, "Love Me Do," written by John Lennon and Paul McCartney in 1958, with its B-side, "P.S. I Love You," had been released in the UK months earlier, in October 1962, charting at #17. That record was not released in the US until 1964. The band's US single "Please Please Me"/"Ask Me Why" was a pop prelude, with Biondi's introduction inserting WLS into the forefront of the British band's music chronicle that carved a curious, conflicted course between multiple American and UK record labels. The Beatles' US debutune, a Lennon/McCartney composition, with George Martin production input and inspired by Roy Orbison and Bing Crosby, was released on the Chicago R&B label Vee-Jay Records, one year before the group landed in New York City on their inaugural visit as a band to America. The Fab Four arrival baptized Beatlemania and the British Invasion, along with the American garage band era, ahead of the Liverpudlians' historic live television debut on *The Ed Sullivan Show* on CBS on Sunday evening, February 9, 1964.

Vee-Jay, one of the earliest and, for a time, most successful independent African American–owned record companies, was founded in 1953 by the husband and wife team of Vivian Carter and James Bracken. Their first initials merged to form the Vee-Jay label designation. (Chess Records founders Phil and Leonard Chess also used the initialization technique when naming Ter Mar Studios after their sons Terry and Marshall.) The couple borrowed $500 from pawnbroker Maurice Tepper to record a group they discovered in Gary, Indiana, where they owned a record store. The borrowed sum was not even enough to cover costs beyond local distribution. The label's inaugural recording, "Baby It's You" by the R&B doo-wop group the Spaniels, reached the R&B Top 10, followed by their "Goodnite, Sweetheart, Goodnite." Signings and recordings ensued at the emerging label, from the El Dorados to Mississippian Jimmy Reed, who was working in the Chicago stockyards at the time and had been turned down by the renowned Chess Records. Riding early chart successes that included Reed's "High Lonesome," the Brackens moved their record operation 30 miles to Chicago. The savvy Vivian Carter recruited her brother Calvin as the A&R rep and landed Ewart Abner, one of the Chicago music scene's top promotors. Abner, who eventually followed Berry Gordy as head of Motown Records, had been associated with Art Sheridan's Chance Records, another Chicago-based label, which specialized in jazz, blues, doo-wop, and gospel, with the Flamingos and Moonglows among its groups. Chance also handled distribution of the early Vee-Jay recordings.[27]

Musical talent was teeming in the city, plentiful enough to sustain several record labels. Many of the companies were located on Michigan Avenue in the city's South Loop, a 12-block stretch that became known as "Record Row." The mythical Chess Records, the blues beacon founded in 1950 by Polish émigré brothers Phil and Leonard Chess, may have been the most distinguishable, though it did not monopolize the music market. Vee-Jay recognized there were other soulful strands and sounds happening beyond Chess's blues-based roster that included giants Sonny Boy Williamson, Howlin' Wolf, and Muddy Waters. Two early Vee-Jay recordings (distributed across subsidiary labels Falcon, Abner, and Cadet) eventually reached the ranks of *Rolling Stone* magazine's list of "The 500 Greatest Songs of All Time," published in December 2004: in 1956 soul forerunner quintet the Dells' Top 10 hit "Oh What a Night" (# 263) and in 1958 "For Your Precious Love" (# 335) by Jerry Butler and the Impressions, a group that included Curtis Mayfield.

By the early 1960s, Vee-Jay had established itself as one of America's top R&B labels, with four million-sellers among a roster that included its first star, Reed, Butler, top gospel groups, the pre–Stax Staple Singers, John Lee Hooker, and Betty Everett ("You're No Good," "The Shoop Shoop Song [It's in His Kiss]"). Vee-Jay also had a solid jazz catalog and maintained its crossover appeal as home to enduring doo-wop records, notably "Duke of Earl" by Gene Chandler in 1961. In an unprecedented move for a Black-owned record label, Vee-Jay ventured into enlisting white acts, with the Four Seasons, featuring the "sound of Frankie Valli," and folk singer-songwriter Hoyt Axton among their more notable signings. The unconventional, if not daring, deviation resulted in Vee-Jay's biggest hit, the Four Seasons' "Sherry," which reached the #1 spot on the charts, where it stayed for five weeks in 1962. Another #1 million-seller followed from the quartet, "Big Girls Don't Cry."

The Beatles' presence on Vee-Jay was oddly incidental and contractually complex. In the early 1960s, US airplay for British recording artists was limited. Among the welcome imports was Frank Ifield, whose falsetto vocal style blended easy listening and country with an occasional yodel. His song "I Remember You" was huge hit in England and worldwide. At the time, Capitol Records, an EMI company, was issuing Ifield material without much backing, much to the chagrin of Ifield's manager. The singer's contract was offered to Vee-Jay, which, despite its small label status, was attractive as an aggressive promoter of its artists. As another part of the proposed package, EMI insisted that if Vee-Jay wanted Ifield and his coveted hit, they would have to agree to also take a group that had been turned down by the major Capitol. That group happened to be the Beatles. The band and distributorship, which were repeatedly offered to Capitol and other record companies, drew little or no interest, in part because no British rock band had yet achieved significant success in the United States. As inconceivable as it sounds in retrospect, Calvin Carter's view of the five-year Vee-Jay contract affirms that the Beatles were merely a "throw in, … a pickup" on the Ifield contract.[28]

According to most accounts, both casual and detailed, of the Beatles' radio debut over American airwaves on WLS, Vee-Jay's shrewd promoter Abner brought a copy of "Please Please Me" along with Beatles stories and teen magazine pictures of the quartet from England. The artifacts were part of his pitch to the WLS studio, his friend Biondi, and to Roberts, who was the station's music director at the time. Envisioning the possibility of the group becoming as popular in the United States as they were burgeoning abroad across England and Europe, Roberts readily added the Beatles' song to the WLS playlist.

On WLS, "Please Please Me" peaked at #35 in mid–March during the second of its two weeks on the WLS Silver Dollar Survey. However, the song did not chart on any other major national American listing until 1964. One year following the Biondi Beatle debut, the re-release of "Please Please Me" became a widespread hit, eventually peaking at #3 on the *Billboard* Hot 100 chart in March 1964, trailing only a pair of the band's other singles, "I Want to Hold Your Hand" and "She Loves You." "Please Please Me," which also became the title of the Beatles' debut LP on the UK label Parlophone, was one of the five Beatles records that occupied the top five spots on the *Billboard* Hot 100 of April 4, 1964.

Further contributing to the song's curious chronology was a typographical error on the first pressings of the Vee-Jay single, which was assigned the catalog number 498. The band's name was spelled incorrectly—as "The Beattles"—on the record's inner label. The misspelling also appeared on WLS's Silver Dollar Surveys in 1963 before the error was corrected on subsequent pressings of the record. In addition, the composers on the Vee-Jay edition were credited on both sides as "J. Lennon—P. McCartney," unlike on the UK Parlophone edition, which listed the names in the reverse order. Existing copies of the Vee-Jay 498 edition, with the correct or incorrect spelling of "The Beatles" on the 45's inner label, predictably became valuable collector's items.

Despite doing its best to be the little label that could, Vee-Jay was improbably overwhelmed by its ascendancy between 1962 and 1964. The label's inability to fund more pressings of the Four Seasons' smash "Sherry" foreshadowed the company's struggles to manage hit records and the necessary mass production and distribution. The problem persisted. Ironically, the Beatles deal made matters worse. When the British Invasion soared early in 1964, Vee-Jay sold 2.5 million Beatles records in one month, but they could not keep the records pressed and on the shelves to meet demands or to pay the artist royalties. Multiple pressing plants spread across the country, subcontracts, subsidiaries, and intermediaries added more layers of production, distribution, legal, and financial complexity. Prolonged legal entanglements and royalty disputes ensued, exacerbating Vee-Jay's mounting financial troubles largely due to mismanagement. Despite the explosion of several million-sellers and trendsetting artists, the company was still being run like it had been when it was a small business. In the liner notes of the four-record box set *Vee-Jay: The Definitive Collection* (2007), Michael Ribas, who compiled the collection for the Shout Factory label, cites Abner's "unusual practices," "crazy, crazy schemes [and] stunts," and gambling as counterproductive, if not damaging, factors that contributed to the company's escalating calamities.[29]

In 1964, the Four Seasons left the label for Philips Records, and EMI's Capitol Records legally secured the rights to Frank Ifield and the Vee-Jay Beatles catalog that consisted of 14 songs that were somewhat resourcefully stretched into five albums, six singles, four reissue singles, and an EP that sold more than one million copies. Calvin Carter summarized Vee-Jay's disarray:

> We were selling so many Beatle records we just couldn't afford to fight for the five-year rights. At that point, we had even got a 10-year moratorium from our creditors on our outstanding bills, that we'd just keep them coming. There was a lot of pressure on us. We sold in one month's time about 2.6 million Beatle singles on Vee Jay and Tollie. Those were fantastic times. And right in the middle of this, we moved from Chicago to California. What a mess, what a mess.[30]

Vee-Jay descended toward its demise. The cash-strapped record company was forced to temporarily cease operations late in 1963; it shut its doors in 1964 before finally declaring bankruptcy with $3 million in debt in 1966. One of Vee-Jay's last singles provided prominent punctuation for the pioneering label, with Little Richard in full gospel mode on "I Don't Know What You've Got (But It's Got Me)," backed by a young unknown named Jimi Hendrix on guitar. For the independent record label that had once been ahead of its time and even eclipsed mythical Motown for a period, the 13-year run was over. Though its success was relatively short term, Vee-Jay Records' impact was irrefutable, with a rich legacy that contained a conspicuous Dick Biondi and Beatles footnote.

WCFL: Cross-River Radio Rival

With its personalities and programming settled into place, the WLS music format makeover clicked big time, particularly with the teen audience coming of age, and more broadly, the under-30 demographic. By 1965, WLS was leading the ratings for young adults in Chicago and was #1 in the midday, afternoon, and evening dayparts. As programming shares and ratings steadily rose, so did the high-wattage station's national recognition.

WLS's impactful identity sounded across the country and Chicagoland radio, which had been dominated by the rivalry between AM giants WGN and WIND, whose competitive spirit and adult demographic appeal was best personified in the stations' morning show match between Wally Phillips and Howard Miller. WLS established itself as a national music force and enjoyed an unchallenged place in the Windy City music market for nearly five years, until mid-decade, when the neighboring Chicago Federation of Labor radio flagship, WCFL, under the direction of programmer Ken Draper from Cleveland, abandoned its labor and broker intensive programming. Mirroring the WLS transformation from prairie to pop, WCFL converted its "Voice of Labor" identity into a Top 40 face, joining its predecessor WLS and bringing another 50,000 watts to Chicago's hit music mix sounding across the mid–1960s radio airwaves.

While the intercity, cross-river radio rivalry and the respective listener loyalties may not have reached the unattainable magnitude of the one-or-the-other-neverboth dichotomy that defined Chicago's longtime baseball binary between the fervent fans of the North Side Cubs versus the South Side White Sox, WLS and WCFL were unrelenting competitors as purveyors of the playlist of popular tunes of the times.

The "Big 10 CFL" or "Super CFL"—1000 on the AM dial—mirrored WLS beyond its commanding wattage, contemporary music format and a corresponding compilation, the Sound 10 Survey, a 3" × 5" trifold design that matched WLS's weekly playlist promotion, Silver Dollar Survey. Inspired by the WLS on-air talent template, WCFL also assembled a compelling roster of disc jockeys, among them Jim Runyon, Larry Lujack, Jim Stagg, Ron Britain, Barney Pip, Joel Sebastian, Dick Williamson, and eventually Biondi. The popular "Wild I-tralian" left WLS in 1963 after three years following a fallout that included alleged fisticuffs with station management and hurled ashtrays over what Biondi considered an excessive amount of commercials (approximately 21 minutes) during his show, which took away time from playing records and talking. Other radio urban legend versions that circulated suggest that Biondi's departure was due to an obscene joke he told on-air. In between WLS and his return to Chicago radio and WCFL in October 1967, Biondi worked at KRLA-Los Angeles with notables Casey Kasem and Bob Eubanks (host of one of the era's popular television game shows, *The Newlywed Game*). Biondi also hosted a nationally syndicated show, *Dick Biondi's Young America*, for the Mutual Broadcasting System. In similar back-and-forth fashion, rising star Lujack defected from

WCFL to WLS early on in 1967, then regularly ricocheted between the competing stations for several years.

WCFL's schedule also featured several niche programs that supplemented its prevailing music format. Ron Britain, billed as "America's First Psychedelic Disk Johnny," hosted *Subterranean Circus* on Sunday nights. The show, which featured "underground" album-oriented music, was an AM radio rarity and programming precursor to the prevalent FM music formats in the 1970s. The station schedule also included two weekly countdown shows, one British and the other Chicago-centric, with each showcasing recordings of the respective region's bands. One of WCFL's most popular programs, *Chickenman*, was not music related. Inspired by the kitschy *Batman* live action television series that aired 120 episodes on ABC from 1966 to 1968, Dick Orkin's 1966 comic book superhero radio satire featured a shoe salesman turned fantastic feathered fowl crime fighter. Echoing its frantic "he's everywhere, he's everywhere!" tagline, the serial became widely syndicated nationally, including on Armed Forces Radio during the Vietnam War. Following the 273 episodes of *Chickenman* that he wrote and produced, Orkin joined the ranks of the station crossovers when he created a similar series, *The Tooth Fairy*, which aired on WLS in 1971.

Let's Go to the Hop

The WLS disc jockeys, and, in their swell and to a slightly lesser degree, their cross-river colleagues at WCFL, were not merely faceless voices echoing over a combined 100,000 watts. Beyond the basics of pitting and promoting prolific pop playlists, they were personalities, both on air and off, with an impactful presence and outreach. And, like the bands whose songs they plugged in their time slot rotations, the deejays, individually and collectively, were accessible, recognizable celebrities with front row tangibility inside and outside the WLS Michigan Avenue studio throughout Chicagoland's vigorous teenscape.

The listener connection with the WLS disc jockeys was enhanced and personalized by the station's studio viewing room, which was open on Saturday afternoons from 1:00 to 3:00, allowing fans to catch a glimpse of their favorite radio personalities, recording artists, and popular groups such as the Monkees, Chad and Jeremy, Gary Lewis & the Playboys, the Hollies, Herman's Hermits, and others who happened to be doing on-air interviews while in town for performances. Most of the bands of the era—including the Rolling Stones (but not the Beatles who, according to Art Roberts, "just couldn't move around safely [so] you had to go to them")—dropped in at the studio regularly to visit various deejay shows as their "record guys" were eager for the excellent exposure a WLS interview or appearance would bring to their artist and label.[31] Similarly, WCFL's station, located on the 16th floor of the landmark Marina City towers located on State Street and overlooking the Chicago

River, had a "VIP Room" on the fifth floor where the disc jockeys hosted various events such as record parties and autograph sessions for listeners who were members of the WCFL VIP Club.

The WLS personalities' communal commitment to the station and their industrious music vocation extended beyond their studio shows. According to Beaudin, his team of "hard-working guys" were "out doing sock hops and speaking at high schools; they were out all the time doing something. ...they all got wrapped up in our program.... Hell, those guys would drive 200 miles to do a hop."[32]

"Hop," the abridged expression referencing "record hop" or "sock hop," is the label pinned to the popular 1950s and 1960s ritual in which teenagers attending a social music event, removed their shoes, and danced in their stocking feet. The trendy shoelessness at the gatherings was usually compulsory more than it was voluntary, the directive for those activities originating from school and athletic administrators and designed to protect the home court's varnished wooden floors from shoe sole scuff marks. The dances, featuring live or recorded music, were commonly held at local schools, mainly in gymnasiums, and in churches, civic and community centers, and VFW halls. In addition, teen clubs emerged across the suburban setting as Friday and Saturday night hotspots and hosted special occasion non-weekend "No School Next Day" events. Along with concerts and record launches, which were frequent department store and shopping center parking lot happenings, these cross-community activities were primary outreach/reach out means and moments for the WLS radio personalities, enabling them as event emcees to connect with the youth audience and bond with the bands.

Beaudin's characterization of his WLS staff's zeal and their frenetic schedules was not exaggerated. "I can remember weekends where I did five record hops," confirmed Bob Hale. "When I was doing the afternoon show, I'd buzz off at 6:30 or 7 o'clock, go out to a Friday night dance. I'd go to a Saturday afternoon appearance, come back to Chicago and do a Saturday night, go up to Wisconsin on Sunday afternoon, and come back to do a Sunday night gig."[33] Weber and Phillips were both licensed pilots and would frequently fly to multiple record hops in the course of an evening, including locations outside Chicago. Among the common out-of-town dance destinations were Benton Harbor, Michigan, and Lake Geneva, Wisconsin, each between 80 and 100 miles away. When Dex Card left WLS after three years, he went into the nightclub business, opening Dex Card's Wild Goose, a chain of popular suburb clubs in Waukegan, Schererville, Elmhurst, and Joliet. The popular radio figure also produced concerts at college venues across the Midwest.

Right People, Right Place, Right Time

"Personality" was WLS's distinguishing trait, as integral and central to the station identity as its sound and the music that its disc jockeys and programs disseminated throughout Chicagoland and across the country. As testament, WLS further fortified and demonstrated its media magnet brand when the company issued a magazine, *WLS Radio Personality Album*, in 1967. The exclusive print edition was available for 50 cents per copy, through mail and at newsstands, where it was displayed alongside the prevalent teenzines of the era such as *16 Magazine*, *Tiger Beat* and *Teen Beat*. Faithful to that fanzine format, the WLS publication's colorful front cover featured a boat-rocking image depicting the WLS personalities playfully staged with three standing and three sitting in a row boat with record albums and 45s strewn overboard across the floor. The back cover featured a suitable-for-framing autographed pose of the smiling suit-and-tie collective holding an album—Weber, Card, Roberts, Phillips, Riley, and Allen. Inside, the 65 pages contained "behind the scenes" profiles of each "fun-loving personality" of WLS Radio, a Zodiac quiz and star birthdays, and an informative industry article by station manager Gene Taylor explaining how top tunes get rolling toward being a "smash or a bomb." The pages were packed with more than 200 select photos of the radio personalities in-studio, emceeing record hops, at concerts, backstage with stars, and off-mike at home with family. In addition to the in-house, on-air publicity, the magazine was widely promoted across other Chicagoland television and newspaper media outlets and at music events. The initial printing of 50,000 copies, which presumably coincidentally reflected the station's wattage, sold out on newsstands days after its January 10 release. By mid–May 1967, sales doubled, reaching an impressive 100,000 copies sold.[34]

Within rock radio's iconic soundscape of the period, the midwestern radio crew at WLS represented an undeniably unique troupe with a knack for launching local bands and making the music even more prominent than it already was. Their legacy is documented, among other places, in *Chicago's Personality Radio* (1993), an insightful oral history featuring interviews with the early 1960s WLS disc jockeys conducted and compiled by Stew Salowitz. A radio aficionado who came of age in the Chicagoland area during the era, Salowitz is impartial in his acknowledgment that the hip WLS announcers "didn't invent their jobs as top disc jockeys any more than they invented rock 'n' roll music."[35] Nor were the WLS wonder boys necessarily any more popular than other huge deejay favorites of the period in their respective big cities: Alan Freed in Cleveland, New Yorkers "Cousin Brucie" Morrow and "The Fifth Beatle" Murray "the K" Kaufman, Baltimore's soulful Paul "Fat Daddy" Johnson, famous Philly figures Joe "Butterball" Tamburro and Jerry "The Geator with the Heater" Blavat. Yet, Salowitz makes a convincing case for the prominent place of the Chicago legends, offering a romanticized and reverent recollection of the WLS personalities' presence and profound connection with the youth audience:

> The WLS disc jockeys belonged to us in Chicago and the Midwest, giving us an identity all our own. The personalities of the period were able to touch their young listeners in ways that went beyond mere announcing—they were counselors, confidants, social advisers, heroes and influences in career planning. They were friends at times in our lives, when occasionally, no one else would listen or talk to us at our level.

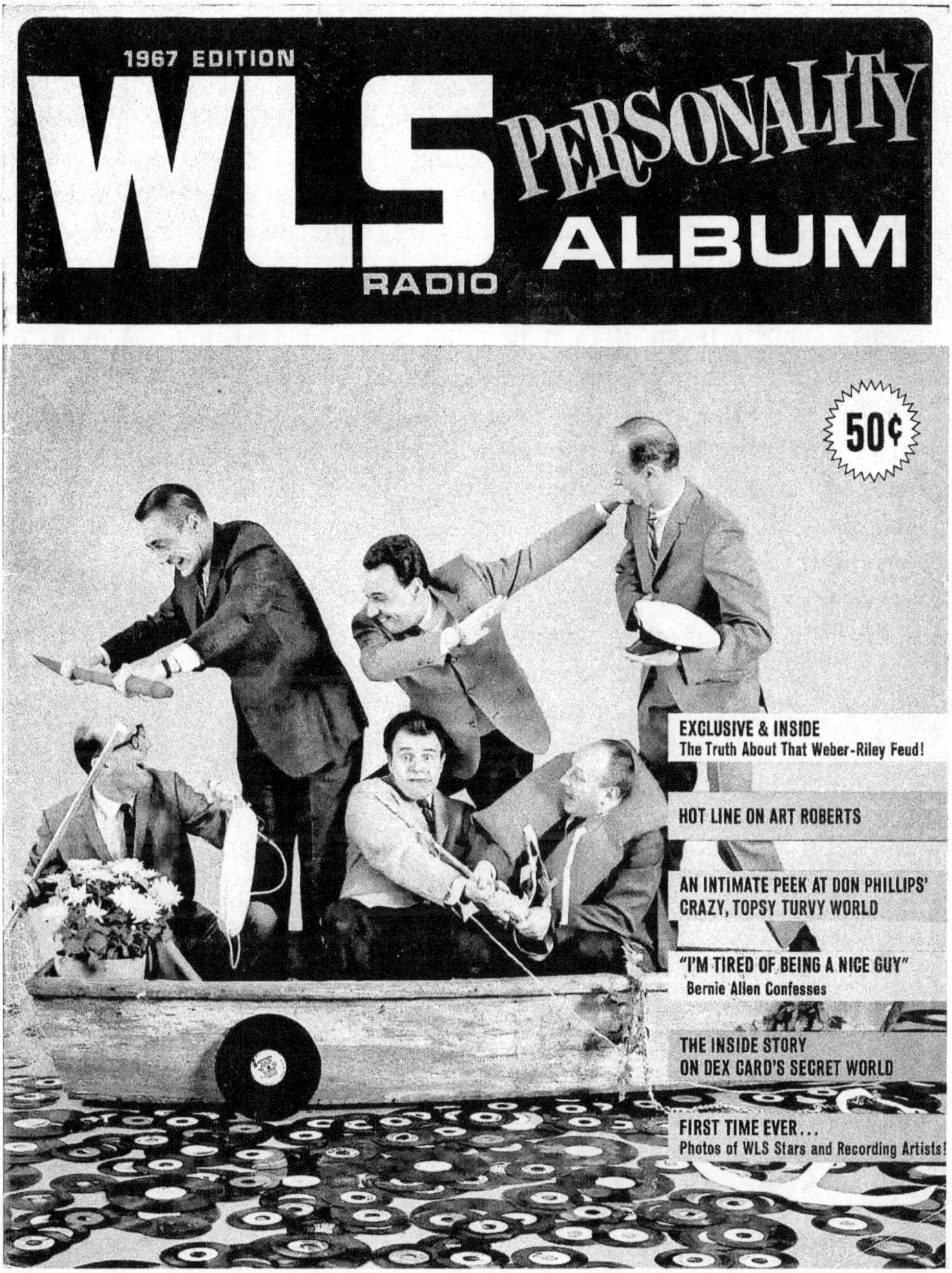

The premiere issue of *WLS Radio Personality Album* in 1967, a 65-page publication priced at a mere 50 cents, was packed with in-studio and off-mike pictures and profiles of the station's popular personalities. The boat rockers, seated (left to right): Clark Weber, Art Roberts, Bernie Allen. Standing (left to right): Dex Card, Ron Riley, Don Phillips (Courtesy of WLS Radio Chicago).

It was an era when disc jockeys, being advocates for music and, subsequently, a lifestyle that teenagers could really identify with, were more than mere automatons or human juke boxes. They could set the mood of a song and lead listeners into a record. Deejays like Dick Biondi and Ron Riley actually sounded like the music, with an energy and movement that sped along at a staccato pace, producing happiness and excitement that was indigenous to the times. Life seemed to move at the pace of music.[36]

Just as local band members were keenly aware and appreciative of the ride in their radio vehicle, the disc jockeys themselves were cognizant of their impact, with a strong sense of time and place. A sampling of their reflections on their shared 1960s Radio 890, WLS experience reveals a unanimity that echoes with script-like sameness and sincerity and is rich with recurring superlatives: "once in a lifetime," "greatest time of my life," "high point of my career," "luckiest guy to have been part of the hottest years." "We were really very influential," said Ron Riley, whose glories include introducing the Beatles and the Rolling Stones at big stadium events in Chicago. "And we were the right guys at the right time."[37]

Riley's "right time" observation was mutual among his colleagues, notably Dex Card and Mort Crowley, who also spoke to the station's singularity. "It was just a phenomenal experience because it was a very exciting time of the British Invasion … and radio was significantly more important to people than it is now," said Card. "I don't think that station will ever be duplicated because during my first year there, we were the only station playing contemporary music."[38] Beyond the minimal competition and numerous other factors and forces that aligned in WLS's favor during the era, the essence of the station's success and spirit, in Card's view, was simply that WLS "was just a great sounding radio station, there was no question about it."[39]

Having the vantage point as one of WLS's original "Swingin' Seven" disc jockeys who steered the station's striking music makeover in 1960, Mort Crowley offers retrospective ruminations on WLS that arrive at radio rarity: "I don't think anything like that will happen again, because of the fact that the mix of music and personalities and everything else … it all came together—the right people at the right place at the right time. It's one of those rare things that happens and why people are still talking about the station."[40]

Chapter 2

Breakthrough and Colonization

In November 1965, a snare shot echoed through Chicagoland's AM radio airwaves, activating a hypnotic lyrical declaration of lifelong desire and devotion, willingness and wanting, emanating from the New Colony Six single "I Confess." The song's distinctive sound was an enticing two minutes and 37 seconds. A trancelike delivery of the opening verses ascends into cascading vocal harmonies, threaded with intriguing instrumentation featuring Farfisa organ undercurrents accented with eruptions of wobbly ripples from a Lesley-fied guitar, an amplifier channeling technique that was novel at the time.

The drumstick snap that initiates "I Confess" may have been slightly subdued compared to similar snare strikes echoing from the intros of some of the era's significant singles. Among them were the shot that ignited the Doors' "Light My Fire" into keyboardist Ray Manzarek's Vox Continental organ in April 1967. In the same year, the series of crisp pats deliver the Box Tops' "The Letter" via Alex Chilton's gruff vocal. And, preceding the New Colony Six's premiere single by a few months, there was the hollow and hallowed kick start to the six-minute magnitude in Bob Dylan's "Like a Rolling Stone" in the summer of '65. "That snare shot sounded like somebody'd kicked open the door to your mind," stated Bruce Springsteen when inducting Dylan into the Rock & Roll Hall of Fame in 1988.

Though less dramatic, the standard snappy drumstick start of the New Colony confession proved a prelude pop that propelled into a ricochet that reverberated with regional resonance. A Chicagolanding. New Colony Six founder Ray Graffia Jr., who co-wrote "I Confess" with Gerry Von Kollenberg, proudly proclaims, with chronological correctness, that "Chicago's rock revolution" launched during the week of Thanksgiving 1965 after the New Colony Six "broke down the radio station walls" when "I Confess" gained airplay across the mighty WLS-AM radio.[1] After climbing to #2 locally on the WLS Silver Dollar Survey, the Six's single reached #80 nationally two months later in February 1966.

"Making Noise in Chi-Town"

Breakthrough, the title of the New Colony Six debut album that followed in 1966, served as a celebratory acknowledgment of radio airplay and the group's inaugural chart entry with "I Confess." The album cover photo depicts the band uniformly outfitted in their signature colonial costume, a fitting fashionable reflection of the revolution underway that Graffia had accurately asserted. The "breakthrough" pronouncement swelled, a signal as coincidentally comprehensive as it was calculated, with reach, relevance, and representation beyond New Colony exclusivity.

The year 1966 marked an arrival for Chicagoland bands as they began to chart a collective course through the increasingly crowded mid-decade songscape. As the Midwest's *Billboard* baptism, "I Confess" was the vanguard of a stream of 10 singles from five bands with Windy City signatures that accumulated on the national charts, clustered in a 10-month sound span between February and December 1966. Shortly after the colonization commenced with the smash "I Confess," the Shadows of Knight turned up the volume on the regional radio representation with their rendition of "Gloria." Released in late January, the striking single reached #1 on the local charts and entered the Top 10 nationally. The group's subsequent sequence of singles in '66—"Oh Yeah," "Bad Little Woman," "I'm Gonna Make You Mine"—placed on playlists from May to November. In the spring, WLS's Art Roberts's routine showcase of "a new song by a new band on the scene" singled out "You Wouldn't Listen" by the Ides of March. Roberts's prestigious "pick to click" plug proved prophetic. The local song received what may have been the era's optimum coast-to-coast coverage when Roberts's fellow Chicago deejay, Ron Riley (at WCFL at the time), told Dick Clark, host of the popular television teen dance show *American Bandstand*, during on on-air phone call that "You Wouldn't Listen" was "making noise in Chi-Town." Responding to Riley's recommendation, Clark cued the Ides' song for *Bandstand*'s "Spotlight Dance," one of the show's weekly centerpiece segments (along with "Rate a Record" and Clearasil commercials) in which teen couples displayed their dance moves to a current smash song. Later in the year, a second Ides' song, "Roller Coaster," briefly charted. Another emerging west suburban band, the Cryan' Shames, delivered a jangly, sunshine pop version of "Sugar and Spice" that settled in mid-chart for nine weeks in the summer and a succeeding "two-sided winner," "I Wanna Meet You"/"We Could Be Happy," which landed lower on *Billboard* in November. The Midwest's 10-song-10 month regional ascent culminated in December with the Buckinghams' "Kind of a Drag" crowning at #1. The hit song's prolonged 13-week stay on the charts was the longest run among Chicago's 10-tune cluster that placed nationally on the *Billboard* charts. The song was simultaneously an exclamation point punctuating Chicagoland's prolific playlist of 1966 and a preface to the Buckinghams' noteworthy string of successful singles that ensued the following year.

A Patsmen Prelude

The New Colony Six were one of Chicagoland's preeminent bands of the mid–1960s era. The group's local and national singles chart incidence was comparable to the Buckinghams, and the Six's four albums, released in a four-year span between 1966 and 1969, further augmented their impressive inventory of music. The group took shape in the spring of 1964 after the collective's impromptu rendition of the Beatles' "I Want to Hold Your Hand" was well received during a school talent show. Among the promising responses was an invitation to an encore performance at a sock hop at a neighboring girls high school. The band of high school seniors was led by dual vocalists, Ray Graffia Jr., tenor and tambourine, and Patrick McBride, baritone and harmonica, and backed by Gerald Von Kollenberg on lead guitar, bassist Walter Kemp, and his cousin Craig Kemp (*née* Gregory Kempinski) on organ and accordion, and Chic James (*née* James Chitkowski) on drums. The outfit initially called themselves The Patsmen, the name derived from the St. Patrick's High School they attended, a historic all-male Catholic school founded in the 1861 and located in the Belmont Cragin neighborhood on the city's Northwest side. As the Patsmen's sock hop and party performances swiftly evolved from skits to song sets, the group "settled on a goal to actually become a real band, one that got paid to play in clubs and at school functions." Graffia admitted that there were clichéd youthful incentives beyond making music. "We really did want to perform—to make music—but I guess if you really got down to the essence of what drove that desire, it was probably the improved opportunity to meet girls."[2]

The members also agreed that the "Patsmen" name languished somewhere between lame and a drag. They proceeded to develop a theme with a bold musical mission statement to "bring rock and roll back to America" alongside the prevailing British Invasion sound. Inspired by England referring to America as the "new

Post Patsmen, New Colony Six founder and lead singer Ray Graffia designed the band's first "calling card" (Courtesy Ray Graffia, New Colony Six).

colonies" and that the freshly formed band was a sextet, the elements in the equation added up to the "New Colony Six" as the group's new name.

Small-scale colonization was gradually underway as the likeable band established a sizable following in the local orbit. In addition to playing teen dances, the group had two venues in the vicinity with varying levels of patronage—Like Young, a teen nightclub in the Old Town district, and Wine and Roses, a cocktail lounge in suburban Schiller Park, 13 miles west of the Chicago Loop. The group considered both spots "sort of home bases" where they honed their performance proficiencies and explored and practiced their material in house band fashion.

"Go West, Young Men, Go West...": The Revere Raider Residency

The mythical phrase "Go West, Young Man" has unverifiable origins commonly attributed to the American author and newspaper editor Horace Greeley. The expression was referencing America's westward expansion and the then-popular concept of manifest destiny, which encouraged people to turn westward and colonize the public lands. Those words echoed as a siren song Midwest way from 1865 to the mid–1960s.

While the majority of mid-decade Chicagoland bands appeared content situated in the Midwest region when starting out, the New Colony Six were restless natives. Despite the best booking efforts of their same-age manager, Tony Terissi, a good friend of Pat McBride's, the New Colony Six was unsettled with their progress and profile and anxious about getting airplay at the time. "Go West" whispered and California dreaming set in. "We went to Hollywood figuring that's where the real action was," said McBride.[3]

The band members' parents consented, rather than contested, the youthful yearning, figuring that the summertime quest would either enrich or end the rock-and-roll dream for their sons. "We felt that landing a recording contract required going West," said Graffia. "And while we never expected parental permission to be granted, when it was, the adventure began."[4]

The hopeful Chicagoans moved into a two-story flat on Sunset Boulevard that they shared with Paul Revere & the Raiders, Portlandians who arrived in Los Angeles around the same time in pursuit of the same rock-and-roll dream. "The only difference was that they had an audition with Dick Clark, which they took good advantage of," said New Colony Sixer Walt Kemp. "We cursed them daily as they went to work while we sat around the pool unemployed."[5]

The opportune Revere and his Raiders landed a big gig as the house band for the Dick Clark production *Where the Action Is*, an *American Bandstand* "so neat to meet your baby" spinoff that aired weekday afternoons on ABC. The teen-targeted television music variety show's black and white production mode could not diminish the youthful exuberance from performers and audience within its predominantly Southern California settings, with the spirited, slapstick Raiders g-g-generating *Action*'s primary pulse. The band's showmanship was always front and center, whether using a comb kazoo while performing their version of Stevie Wonder's "Uptight (Everything's Alright)" or dressed as cavemen at the Los Angles Zoo for a zany lip sync of their "Ballad of a Useless Man." The Raiders' early 1960s origins were rooted in the Pacific Northwest, between Idaho and Oregon. Initially formed as the Boise band the Downbeats, named after a jazz magazine, they relocated to Portland, where they became the Raiders. The common misperception was that "Paul Revere" was an alias, a convenient appropriation of a historical figure for showbiz purposes. Fortunately, when choosing between his memorable surnames, the Idaho-born band founder, Paul Revere Dick, prudently selected the historical hook over the one susceptible to adolescent anatomical humor. Columbia signed the Raiders on the strength of their unique garage, pop rock and R&B sound, or, more simply put by lead singer Mark Lindsay, "a bunch of white bread kids doing their best to sound Black." "The Legend of Paul Revere," provides a compact three-minute tale, beginning with burger-frying Revere recruiting friend Lindsay from being "bun boy" at a bakery to start a band, to Dick Clark making them big stars on TV and in Hollywood. The tune's good-time innocence overshadows the self-promotion: "all the youth stations across the nation please play our records/for your congregations."[6]

The New Colony Six residence with the Raiders was a curious, coincidental criss-cross. The boulevard tenants were kindred spirits of 1776. The "revolutionary" twins mirrored each other conceptually, yet acted independently without reciprocating influence or intentional imitation. Graffia's thematic vision of the New Colony Six in shades of white and blue was an echo of Revere's earlier anointing of himself and the Raiders as "America's answer to the British Invasion." The bands' common threads were perhaps more visual than auditory, more stylistic than musical. Both groups chose autonomously to be outfitted in colonial costume—knee-high black boots, white tights, ruffled white shirts, and color coordinated jackets. There was some differentiation within the duplication. The Raiders wore powder blue jackets, while the New Colony Six dressed in red. Revere's troupe also donned angled tri-corner hats to enhance historical authenticity. Graffia liked the colonial look. "Our initial jackets were purchased at a uniform store where we found the short red jackets," said Graffia. "Boots seemed apropos, as did some ruffling at the neck, whether jabots or otherwise and white shirts/pants between the red and black felt good and, we thought, looked good."[7]

The fashion facsimile, statement, or faux paus invited a range of readings and responses. The "weird threads," as Raider Mark Lindsay called them, were as gimmicky a guise as they were thematic, as derivative as they were novel. Raiders' album titles such as *Midnight Ride* (1966), *Spirit of '67* (1966), and *Revolution!* (1967) certainly reinforced the motif, as did the New Colony Six's second album, *Colonization* (1967). The 1776 attire adopted by the Raiders and New Colony Six may have been a look that appeared more contrived and costumed than other band uniform apparel of the day, at least pre–*Sgt. Pepper*. The Monkees dressed in double-breasted shirts, while the Beatles, Kinks, Gary Lewis's Playboys, Association, Dave Clark Five, and Mersey beaters Gerry and the Pacemakers were among the many popular groups who wore matching slacks, suits, ties, and turtlenecks. In some cases cool coifs were part of the costume, most notably the Beatles with mop-top hairstyles. Ironically, the standardized styles and uniformity in the name of rock and revolution could have been construed as conformist and thus (counter)culturally incongruent. It is notable that despite the Raiders' patriotic posturing, Revere was a conscientious objector when drafted for military service, working instead as a cook at a mental institution as deferment and perhaps a sly source of his "madman" moniker.

Personality and shtick were undeniable aspects of the Raiders' presence, more so than for Graffia and his band of Chicagoland revolutionaries, though music journalist Richie Unterberger did characterize the midwesterners' act as displaying "cabaret-ish qualities."[8] Revere enthusiastically embraced the "madman of rock and roll" persona, a moniker of harmless hype derived from his roadhouse style and keyboard clowning. Every Raider had a nickname except lead singer Lindsay. Bassist Phil "Fang" Volk and lead guitarist Drake "The Kid" Levin together were called "The Twins" for their synchronized steps on stage. When Levin enlisted in the National Guard, his replacement, Jim Valley, became "Harpo" due to his Marx Brother resemblance, while drummer Mike Smith was simply "Smitty." Lindsay, an Oregon native who had relocated to Idaho where he met Revere, didn't need a nickname. He was the emblematic front person with teen idol appeal—handsome, he had a ponytail and a good voice and even played saxophone, notably as an intro on the Raiders' rendition of "Louie, Louie." Curiously, the Raiders and the Kingsmen recorded versions of the Richard Berry 1957 original in the same Portland, Oregon, studio. Both versions were released around the same time, with the Kingsmen's eclipsing the Raiders' in popularity, due in large part to Columbia A&R command Mitch Miller controlling the cover course by pulling the plug on promotion for the Raiders' version.

Their advantageous association with Clark began with an appearance on *American Bandstand* performing their early instrumental single "Like, Long Hair," continued with a one-year engagement as *Action*'s house band (they were replaced by the Robbs from Wisconsin), and led to Revere and Lindsay hosting Clark's *Happening '68* (the '68 was naturally dropped in 1969) that aired after *Bandstand* on Saturdays. The Raiders were highly visible, accruing television credits that included the era's familiar showcases—*The Tonight Show*, *The Ed Sullivan Show*, and *Hullabaloo*—and a kitschy cameo on the popular *Batman* series, where they performed a campaign song for the archvillain Penguin to the tune of "Yankee Doodle."

Clark may have been the biggest business influence behind the Raiders' breakthrough, providing exposure and enriching, if not exploiting, their red, white, and blue image, but it was Terry Melcher who shaped their music. Melcher, son of actress Doris Day, was Columbia's in-house producer, assigned to foster the label's fledgling bands, among them the Byrds and Raiders. On a darker historical note, Melcher was believed to be the central target of the murderous Charles Manson "family" cult at the Cielo Drive residence in Los Angeles in August 1969, after the influential producer refused to sign aspiring rock star Manson to a record contract. The very best and enduring songs in the Raiders' catalog are validated by Melcher's producer imprint. He expanded and strengthened the group's sound with complex, state-of-the-art production, vocal arrangements (including Melcher's voice as the second vocal on "Him or Me"), catchy choruses, and layered harmonies. Much to the dismay of some of the Raiders, Melcher frequently utilized studio musicians, often bringing in Lindsay from touring to lay down vocal tracks with session players for Raiders songs. Beyond Melcher's studio supervision and songwriting contributions, he also solicited songs from the Brill Building writing duo Barry Mann and Cynthia Weil that became two of the Raiders biggest hits: "Hungry" and the anti-drug song "Kicks," reportedly written for the Animals to record and allegedly about fellow Brill writer Gerry Goffin, who was married to Carole King at the time. Melcher became known as the "sixth Raider," with "Terry's Tune" the band's B-side homage on their single "Indian Reservation." His production presence delivered substance to the Raiders' showy style, assuring that they would not dead-end or dissolve into a colorful and costumed novelty act.[9]

Between the fall of 1965 and the winter of 1967, a parallel productive period for the New Colony Six, the Raiders recorded and released an impressive string of songs that charted, with four making the Top 10: the Animals-like "Steppin' Out" (#46); "Just Like Me" (#11), notable for its multi-track guitar; "Kicks" (#4); "Hungry" (#6); "The Great Airplane Strike" (#20); "Good Thing" (#4); "Ups and Downs"(#22); and "Him or Me—What's It Gonna Be?" (#5). During that period, they also recorded the Tommy Boyce and Bobby Hart tune, "(I'm Not Your) Stepping Stone," before it was a hit for the Monkees. Add to that inventory earlier singles "Like, Long Hair" (#38); "Louie, Louie" and its sequel, "Louie Go Home"; and late-decade singles such as "Don't Take It So Hard"(#27) and "Too Much Talk"(#19) that were more modest hits. Of note, the Raiders' *Greatest Hits* album in 1967, along with Bob Dylan's *Greatest Hits*, was designated by music business mogul Clive Davis to test higher record retail pricing.

The Raiders' biggest hit did not come until 1971 on the backside of their best pocket of productivity. Their version of John Loudermilk's "Indian Reservation (The Lament of the Cherokee Reservation Indian)," also a hit for Don Fardon in 1968, reached #1. The Raiders' run was significant, especially when considering their continuous lineup changes, many occurring at the group's peak popularity. The roster of former members is a conspicuously lengthy list. As the band's leader, Revere demonstrated resilience surviving the continuous defections, the most glaring being the entire rhythm section splitting following the group's *Ed Sullivan* appearance in 1967. By 1968, Revere and Lindsay were the only original Raiders remaining. And Lindsay was pursuing a parallel solo career, which yielded popular songs such as "Arizona" and "Silver Bird." Rather than conveniently and trendily disband, Revere displayed a knack for keeping countless Raiders renditions intact as a polished act that maintained his original vision built on warmth and spontaneity.

As impressive as Paul Revere & the Raiders' accomplishments were, proportionally they were probably no better or no worse than most of the bands, whether British, American, or Chicagoland—particularly the New Colony Six and Buckinghams—that sounded in the period's record grooves, crowded airwaves, and charts. Consider the saturation of the Dave Clark Five, who had 16 top 30 hits from 1964 to 1967. Or that the Buckinghams had six charting songs between 1966 and 1968, including "Kind of a Drag" at #1. The Raiders respectfully settle into the prolific era's subjective secondary song stratum—beneath the national/international top-tier Beatles, Byrds and Rolling Stones, and perhaps the Kinks and Who—where the Hollies, Doors, Turtles, Troggs, Association, Gary Lewis & the Playboys, Tommy James & the Shondells, Herman's Hermits, Freddie and the Dreamers (who gimmicked a companion windmill motion do-the-dance, "The Freddie"), and others dwell melodically and memorably. Each group presented a sound and style, image and identity, and similar short-term arcs from success to splintering band member attrition on their way to efficiently compiling enough hits for a compilation to brand the era's soundscape.

Paul Revere & the Raiders did just that. They made their mark (Lindsay pun intended), and they did it with style. The Raiders were—to borrow their song title—a good thing, and, they were a good time. Further, they recorded some really good songs. Their legacy may be as visual as it is musical. Paul Revere & the Raiders' costumed antics and lively stage presence contributed to the increasing visualization of music in the wake of the Beatles' mid–1960s films *A Hard Day's Night* (1964) and *Help!* (1965), and their kitschy Saturday morning cartoon series. The Raiders bridged the Fab Four frolics across mid-decade mass media screens, silver to small, with the Monkees madcap adventures on NBC (1966–68).

Despite his animated aura that at once balanced being a fine organist and keyboard clown, the showman Revere was not one to overstate the Raiders' nature, their accomplishments, or place in the 1960s rock chronology. During a 2002 interview, he modestly stated, "From day one, we've always been a party band that accidentally had some hit records and accidentally got on a hit television series. We were visual and fun and crazy [and] just happened to be at the right time and had the right name and the right gimmick."[10]

Centaur/Sentar: The Parent Company

The New Colony Six returned to their Midwest home base from their wishful West Coast wander and Revered Raider Residency in the fall of 1965 without a record contract. They were undeniably disappointed, in debt, and draft deferred, but the band members had grown up and they remained hopeful. "Our dreams were pretty much shattered by the lack of success, but at least we got to polish our writing skills," recalled Graffia. "So we came back to Chicago quite down, but with some pretty cool music in hand."[11]

The band did not retreat, but was resilient, routinely rehearsing, refining material, and performing. They were also the beneficiaries of unwavering parental support and resourcefulness. Upon hearing the band's latest "pretty cool music," Graffia's father was so impressed that he approached the fellow parents of the band members and suggested that they collectively form a record company that would allow their sons an opportunity to record. With Graffia Sr. fronting costs and the five other Colony parents backing, the family-financed and operated Centaur Records materialized. The company was retitled briefly to the letter-substituted "Sentaur" before settling on the same-sounding "Sentar" following a legal dispute in 1967. The record label logo featured a large white "S" and centaur silhouette, adapted from Greek mythology. The mom-and-pop enterprise included a pair of record promo pros as part of its organization, Howard Bedino and Pete Wright. "They were strong, as in powerful, business-wise guys," recalls Graffia. "I'm not sure we would have had the breakthrough (pun intended) with the Six had not they been involved in management when we were trying to get airplay for 'I Confess.'"[12]

Following a mid-decade West Coast residency with Paul Revere & the Raiders, the New Colony Six, uniformly colonial fashionable, began recording on the "parent label" Centaur (eventually Sentar). Top row (L-R): Craig Kemp, Gerry Van Kollenburg, Wally Kemp, Ray Graffia, Farfisa compact organ. Bottom row (L-R): Chic James, Pat McBride (Courtesy Ray Graffia, New Colony Six; Jerry Schollenberger Archives).

By November 1965, the New Colony Six began mapping its own Chicagoland music course with "I Confess" leading the way. The debut's ascent toward local hit status at the #2 spot on WLS was topped only by Lou Christie's "Lightning Strikes." The band's start-up Centaur/Sentar catalog that accrued during the next two years contained 10 notable singles, the majority concisely under 2:30, with many of the 45s packaged as two-sided releases that were backed by an appealing B-side. In many cases, the flip flipped again, upturning into the A-side that received the primary airplay. The band also recorded and released its initial two albums, *Breakthrough* (1966) and *Colonization* (1967), on the exclusive parent label. Distribution of their music was handled primarily by Chicago's U.S.A. Records and Cameo-Parkway, the fabled Philadelphia independent record company.

The majority of the New Colony Six material was original, with the songwriting credits collaborative and fairly evenly distributed across the band, with Graffia as the core composer.

Their limited cover song selections were a range of recordings that included a non-album single, a romping spelling of Bo Diddley's "Cadillac," backed with "Sunshine," a 45 that was unable to chart in the crowded chorus of the summer of '66. The band's second album, *Colonization* (1967), includes a version of John Sebastian's Lovin' Spoonful folk blues tune "Warm Baby" and an extended rendition of the Yardbirds' "Mister You're a Better Man Than I" that stretches nearly seven minutes, twice the length of the original. (The song's running time is mistakenly listed at 7:55 on the album credits.) In addition, the LP's 12-song set uncovers "I'm Just Waiting Anticipating for Her to Show Up," (also identified as [Anticipatin' For Her to Show Up]), a tune drawn from an intriguing songwriting source, Tony Orlando, and co-writer John Estanislau. Orlando's extensive career résumé features an array of associations that include Cameo-Parkway as a record rep; New York's Brill Building songwriting community; music industry figures producer/publisher/manager/songwriter Don Kirshner, Clive Davis and Columbia Records, and singer-songwriter and soft pop pianist Barry Manilow of "Mandy" fame in 1974. Orlando is best known for fronting the 1970s pop group Dawn, composed of Motown/Stax backing vocalists Telma Hopkins and Joyce Vincent Wilson. The trio generated multiple Top 40 hits in the early 1970s, among them "Candida," "Knock Three Times," and "Tie a Yellow Ribbon Round the Ole Oak Tree," which reached #1 in 1973. Tony Orlando and Dawn also had their own weekly prime-time television variety show that aired for four years on CBS in the mid–1970s.

As a single, the New Colony Six's version of "I'm Just Waiting Anticipating for Her to Show Up" reached #14 locally and #128 on *Billboard* mid–1967. Recorded at Chess Studios in Chicago, the mid-tempo melody with the Rice vocal stood out not only as an Orlando obscurity with an elongated title, but for its production qualities. The song marked the first time the New Colony Six utilized horns, with the arrangement laid down by the Chess studio sessionists, among them, Maurice White, eventual founder of the Chicago-based group Earth, Wind & Fire.

Farfisa: Foundation and Fascination

Brassy instrumentation was steadily gravitating toward being an integral part of the "Chicago sound." Though the New Colony Six may have momentarily veered toward the middle of the road, they did not stay in that lane. As natural as the horns blended with the vocal harmonies on "I'm Just Waiting Anticipating for Her to Show Up," the band was—at least initially—first and foremost organ- and guitar-driven, with a Farfisa and Leslie dual trademark. Kemp's key organics combined with weirdly wonderful currents emanating from Von Kollenberg's guitar being channeled through a Leslie speaker. The instrumentation mingled into unique eerie threads and wobbling reverberations throughout the New Colony Six's early catalog. The chilling vibe was evident from the very start, from front to back of the group's first 45, "I Confess," and its B-side, "Dawn Is Breaking," which pleads: "Why did you leave me ... won't you come home to me?" The bursts of cool tones combined with dual vocals and harmonies ripple throughout the debut LP *Breakthrough*'s song sequence in "Don't You Think It's Time You Stopped Your Cryin'"; the existential "The Time of the Year is Sunset"; and "I and You," which foreshadows the group's subsequent shift into mellow. "Some People Think I'm a Playboy" may not have been as obvious a nod to provocative publisher Hugh Hefner as much as it was a wry recognition of contemporary colleagues Gary Lewis & the Playboys, who produced an impressive string of hits in 1965 and 1966, beginning with the chart topper "This Diamond Ring." As comedian Jerry Lewis's son, front Gary was part of a pocket of pop progeny recording at the time that included Frank Sinatra's son, Frank Jr., and daughter Nancy, who hit big in 1966 with Lee Hazlewood's "These Boots Are Made for Walkin'." The trio Dino, Desi, and Billy featured the sons of Dean Martin and Desi Arnaz and Lucille Ball. The band's third wheel, Billy Hinsche, became a session player who later toured with the Beach Boys. His sister Annie was married to Beach Boy Carl Wilson.

The Farfisa organ sound suited the Six, its freshness an echo of the vibe from the Vox Continental transistor-based combo organ introduced in 1962 by the British enterprise, Jennings Musical Industries. Two years later, the Farfisa Company, located in Osimo, Italy, began manufacturing electric organs. Distribution in the US was handled by the Chicago Musical Instrument Company, which also owned Gibson Guitar from 1944 to 1969. Thus, the keyboard instruments were initialed as "CMI organs" when introduced. Farfisa organs were compact and designed with integrated legs, which could be folded up and stored inside the base. The first models produced were the Compact series of organs between 1964 and 1968. Production continued until the late 1970s when synthesizers became more commonplace in the instrumental keyboard queue.

The Farfisa Compact and Vox Continental were kindred portables that frequently stirred sound-alike deciphering, discussion and debate within the musicologial mythologies surrounding some of the most piercing and popular 1960s garage and psychedelic classics. Among the most popular of the playlist are "96 Tears" by ? and the Mysterians, the Seeds' "Pushin' Too Hard," and the Strawberry Alarm Clock's "Incense and Peppermints." The Vox "Connie" was prevalent in the music and signature songs of the Animals (Alan Price), Doors (Ray Manzarek), Monkees (Peter Tork), Dave Clark Five (Mike Smith), Sir Douglas Quintet (Augie Meyers) with "She's About a Mover," and locally in the Midwest, the Rivieras (Otto Nuss) on "California Sun," among other 1960s groups. The Vox organ was a popular preference among British Invasion bands, including the Beatles. According to Lennon lore and legacy, Beatle John wore out a Vox Continental during the Fab mid–August, mid–1960s New York City performances on *The Ed Sullivan Show* and at the historic Shea Stadium concert. In front of a crowd of 55,600, Lennon closed the legendary 1965 outdoor event wildly pounding the keyboard, elbows and all, with a frenzied rendition of "I'm Down," which resulted in the organ not working properly for their next concert two days later on August 17 in Toronto.

Among the notable pop rock organists to showcase the Farfisa was Domingo Samudio, who, as the turbaned showman "Sam the Sham," was backed by his campy group, The Pharaohs, who had their first hit, "Wooly Bully," in the summer of 1965. Spooner Oldham, the house organist of the legendary chicken-fried swamp Muscle Shoals recording studio in northern Alabama, Farfisa-ed across the southern soul recordings of the 1960s, outstandingly the Percy Sledge classic "When a Man Loves a Woman," among many others.

The Farfisa fascination emitting from "I Confess" was not a one-and-done novelty for the New Colony Six. Their '66 solidified with the February follow-up "I Lie Awake," a Von Kollenberg/McBride/Graffia collaboration. "I Lie Awake" sounded like a continuation of "I Confess," a seamless sequel or sibling song, with both sharing an obsessive possessive entrancing undercurrent. The composition was subtly sophisticated, with traces of Gershwin's classical "Rhapsody in Blue" in the arrangement. The pair of captivating companion songs anchored *Breakthrough*, with each leading off the separate sides of the debut album. The release established the New Colony knack for double-sided singles that attracted radio airplay. "I Lie Awake" was the little 2:00-minute B-side that charted (#20 WLS; #111 *Billboard*) opposite "At the River's Edge," Wally Kemp's yeah, yeah, yeah Yardbirds-style wailing harmonica punk rave-up; a gloom and doom "walk(ing) in the rain" with a "heart full of pain."

The New Colony Six performed "I Lie Awake" on the locally produced (in black and white) kids television show, *Mulqueen's Kiddie A-Go-Go*. Following hostess Pandora's invoking Clark Weber and WLS, and an introduction of "Chicago's own," the camera cuts to the New Colony Six, confined to a small area where they began their lip sync performance. The shot transitions to the studio floor foreground filled with innocence and motion, the pre-teen/tween audience in close to colliding clusters, loosely positioned across from partners, flapping and flailing, springing and gyrating, improvising their best and worst loose-limbed dance moves. Perhaps the most recognizable was a rendering of the "The Freddie," the signature novelty dance of the pop group the Dreamers. The scene was sweetly surreal. And slightly strange. Despite the exposure, the television moment was not a memorable experience for the band. "We were completely embarrassed by the opportunity," recalls Graffia. "Ticked off that they made us the last bit on the show, aggravated that they made us stand in one place, limiting movement to bouncing mildly, and enraged that they didn't even let the tune ... go to its natural end point ... they cut us off late record."[13] The chaotic cameo did not deter the band from future television appearances. During the next two years, the New Colony Six's increased popularity resulted in performances on several other regional and syndicated TV talk, talent, and variety shows with more teen and young adult audience appeal, including *The Mike Douglas Show*, Lloyd Thaxton's *Showcase '68*, and *Upbeat*.

A September 1966 single—"(The Ballad of the) Wingbat Marmaduke"—with a typically strong B-Side, "The Power of Love," was released in advance of *Colonization* in 1967. (On the album, the song title is listed as "Elf Song [Ballad of the Wingbat Marmaduke].")" The adventurous merry fairy tale, loosely based on, adapted from, inspired by J. R. R. Tolkien's literary works *The Hobbit* and *The Lord of the Rings*, failed to chart at any level or locale, even in Chicago. Two months later, the November release, "Love You So Much"/"Let Me Love You," was unequivocally the band's most vibrant two-sided single, an either/or flip for deejays and listeners. Typically fleeting at 1:55 and 2:14, both concise compositions were the collaborative work of the Graffia/McBride/Von Kollenberg songwriting trio. "Love You So Much," which made it all the way to #2 on WLS and peaked at #61 nationally, was a Graffia love note to his then girlfriend and eventual wife. Aptly characterized by New Colony Six archivist Jerry Schollenberger as a "sublime slice of power pop,"[14] the era gem is brimming with ringing rhythm guitar cascades and Hollies-like harmonies over rolling snare flutters from Chic James. On the flip side, "Let Me Love You" delivered an intriguing blend that begins with straightforward garage and psych sound through the bridge and chorus one minute in, where it then melts into a dreamy interlude for the next minute, before awakening to return to a racing guitar fade out. The technique was a softer, surreal variation of the psychedelic "freak out" in the middle of the Buckinghams' "Susan."

Both sides of the Six's striking late '66 single were the one-two lead tracks of the *Colonization* LP. Symmetrical to side one, the first two songs on side two of the album are the band's final two Sentar singles, the aforementioned "I'm Just Waiting Anticipating for Her to Show Up," released in June 1967, and "You're Gonna Be Mine," a catchy, cascading tune from earlier in February that reached the WLS Top 10 and landed just inside the Hot 100 nationally. The song's jangling, strolling infatuation is rhythmic and rife with hormones, handclaps, and textured harmonies that include a "she's so fine" echo layered in between verses and an idiosyncratic, though playfully pleasant, high-pitched calliope-like "di-di-do-do-do-do-do-do" vocal bridge. The simple rhyme scheme gazes with fixation, "swaying easy" from the triplet "street/sweet/meet" into "outta my mind/just the right kind."

Mercury Rice-ing

Ray Graffia co-wrote "You're Gonna Be Mine" with Ronnie Rice, who joined the New Colony Six in the summer 1966, following the departure of the band's skilled keyboardist Craig Kemp. Rice, from nearby Evanston just north of the city, had a solo recording career since 1961, with singles released on the IRC, MGM, Limelight, and Quill labels. Graffia and McBride recruited Rice to fill the significant musical void in the band left by Kemp's absence, reasoning that Rice as a replacement "played keys well enough, dabbled on guitar, and had a great voice."[15] Their personnel decision was a modest miscalculation. In Graffia's view, Rice may have been a "strong writer," but he was "so-so on rhythm guitar and less than what we thought we were getting on keys."[16] The evidence early on that Rice's musical skills were "less than stellar" impacted the band's decision to carry another sideman, Chuck Jobes, to cover keyboards. The accomplished Jobes, initially an allowance from the local group the Revelles, eventually became an official member of the group of Six, though the expansion did not pose a mathematical issue for band branding. "We elected to not change the name to 'New Colony 7' since we feared that folks might think that we were some rip-off band trying to steal the New Colony 6's thunder," said Graffia.[17]

Rice's arrival with the New Colony Six was at the forefront of a band transformation during the following year. The multifarious transition included a further personnel change with Les Kummel, another enlistee from the local Revelles, replacing bassist Walt Kemp, who left to concentrate on college, and a conspicuous shift in the group's music style that coincided with a new record label. In September 1967, the New Colony Six signed with the Chicago-based Mercury Records, hoping for a better shot at national distribution. The company, formed in 1945, handled many music genres, from jazz and classical to country, rock, and pop. With pressing plants in Chicago and St. Louis and mechanization that provided 24-hour turnaround with recordings, Mercury positioned itself as a viable competitor with major record labels such as Columbia, Decca, Capitol, and RCA Victor.

The New Colony Six initially pitched their new label two demos, "Treat Her Groovy" and "I Will Always Think About You," composed by its newest members, Rice and Kummel. According to Rice, Mercury "hated" "I Will Always Think About You," his collaboration with Kummel, and they heard a "hit" in Rice's "Treat Her Groovy." The tune's perky pop "dat-dat-dat" echoes across the bubblegum waters of "Indian Lake" by the Cowsills to the Buddah label singles of the 1910 Fruitgum Company. The sprightly delivery offers relationship advice that is also part pledge, enfolded in a catchy couplet of courtship and innocence: "Treat her groovy/ take her to a movie." Coincidentally, the poetic partnership persisted, with the "groovy/ movie" good time rhyme subsequently surfacing in lyrics in the Buckinghams' "Hey Baby (They're Playing Our Song)" and in the Turtles' "Elenore." Though well received locally, climbing to #12 on WLS, "Treat Her Groovy" failed to chart beyond the Midwest despite Mercury's promotion.

Fortunately, the less than groovy new label inauguration was not a countrywide chart performance precedent, rather a marker of passage to wider recognition. The New Colony Six subsequently delivered a numerically fitting and salient sequence of six singles that placed on the national charts over the next two years, beginning in January 1968 with the tender "I Will Always Think About You" (#22) and concluding with "Barbara I Love You" (#78) in November 1969. Filling the in between from 1968 were "Can't You See Me Cry" (#52) in May and the group's biggest hit, "Things I'd Like to Say" (#2 WLS; #16 *Billboard*; #13 *Cashbox*), in October and into 1969, "I Could Never Lie to You" (#50) in April and "I Want You to Know" (#65) in July. Not only did the Six's six singles peak at respectable positions, they exhibited solid staying power, remaining on the charts for 13, 8, 16, 8, 6, and 5 weeks, respectively. The songs were dispersed equally, with three tracks placed across each of their two Mercury albums, *Revelations* (1968) and *Attacking a Straw Man* (1969).

The set of soothing songs marked a discernible shift in style and sound for the New Colony Six. Though their first two albums included songs titled "A Heart Is Made of Many Things," "Accept My Ring," and "My Dreams Depend on You," the disparity between their Centaur/Sentar recordings from '66–67 and those released on Mercury in '68–69 was nonetheless notable. The group went from the garage to the prom and wedding reception. Their early edges softened significantly, transitioning from tough to tender, politely punkish to polished, easing into becoming a mainstream ballad band, a style that was compatible with their wholesome demeanor.

The familiar romantic themes—longing and love, from true and everlasting to lost and unrequited—transferred efficiently and emotionally though the lyrics were delivered in a notably different tone and tempo. The rave-ups, eerie organ, and guitar bursts that characterized the Sentar songs ebbed into low-light, slow-dance sentimentality via lush arrangements, with horns and strings adding atmospheric textures, interludes, and crescendos that added orchestral sheen to the group's signature dual vocal harmonies. Respected jazz pianist and composer Hoyt Jones was an unsung instrumental source behind many of the elegant touches that textured the arrangements.

Lyrically, the Colony compositions tiptoe across the tenderness tightrope, occasionally tilting into maudlin moments and weepy "you said you'd be mine" self-pity: the lost love lament in "Things I'd Like to Say" ("I was hoping with our love we would get married someday"); the voyeuristic heartache in "Can't You See Me Cry" ("spend my hours looking at your window ... watch you draw your shade when night is falling"); "The nights, the lights, were yours and mine, It's true" in "I Will Always Think About You." "Ronnie Rice wrote great songs that made 14-year-old girls happy," said New Colony Six manager Pete Wright. "And they identified with it."[18]

The New Colony Six's delicate, melodious Mercury singles settled naturally within the plentiful poignant playlist of the mid-1960s between the Beatles' "Love Me Do" and the Beach Boys' "God Only Knows" in tune with the charm of Herman's Hermits' hits, the Association's touchstone "Cherish," the beautiful baroque and roll of the Left Banke's "Walk Away Renee" and "Pretty Ballerina," and "Red Rubber Ball" (co-composed by Paul Simon and Seekers' Bruce Woodley) and "Turn Down Day" by the Cyrkle, among many other groups and songs in the romantic rotation.

The musical transformation for the New Colony Six was not necessarily a Mercury mandate or a random reinvention. Rice's presence certainly shaped the more polished pop direction the band veered toward, while Graffia's songwriting seemed to recede slightly in the transition. Radio disc jockeys also played a role, almost assuring that the "ballad band" identity stuck following the appeal of "I Will Always Think About You." When selecting New Colony Six cuts, deejays routinely chose the Six's softer songs over those with garage psych strands. The subsequent chart success of the ballads validated their preferences. The most discernible example involved the band's biggest hit, "Things I'd Like to Say," the emotive composition by Rice and Kummel that was "rescued from B-side oblivion" by WLS deejay Larry Lujack. The circumstance was similar to the earlier flip-flop with "I Lie Awake"/"At the River's Edge." The 45's intended A-side turned B-side, "Come and Give Your Love to Me," co-written by Graffia, Von Kollenberg, and Jobes, was standard Centaur-Sentar-sounding garage—driving guitar and drums laced with harmonica, a superior version to the album cut. The unsung song's exile lingered as it was a disappointing omission from the New Colony Six collections compiled and reissued in 1993 by archival labels Rhino and Sundazed.

With their successful singles stretch in '68–'69 the New Colony Six inherited the Chicagoland crown that was worn well by the Buckinghams during their 1967 record reign. For two consecutive years, the New Colony Six was named "Best Chicago Area Group," an award voted on by WLS radio listeners. And, as hoped, the Mercury move enhanced the Chicagoland band's national profile during the prolific period, which included multiple national television show appearances, a photo spread in the Montgomery Ward retail catalog, and touring with major acts such as the Beach Boys.

Decolonization: Sunlight Setting

Late decade was the peak period for the New Colony Six. As the 1960s waned, so did the Six. Personnel shifts were in motion, with an influx of replacements from other local groups. Guitarist Bruce Gordon reconnected with his former bandmates, Jobes and Kummel, briefly expanding the Revelles recolonization to half the New Colony sextet's membership. Bill Herman of Aorta replaced drummer Chic James.

The most pronounced change came in August 1969 when the group founder, Ray Graffia, left the Colony. His departure was in part a "blood is thicker than water" circumstance, as Graffia feared that imminent decisions and legal issues within the band might strain his relationship with his father. He respectfully chose to avoid any potential family contention. Graffia also sensed an occupational zenith, prudently acknowledging that the New Colony Six's "best shot at stardom was already past us and it was time to get on with life outside rock and roll."[19] Despite the admirable intentions, acceptance of such a post-rock career transition may have been easier said than carried out in a fulfilling manner. The allure of the stage and spotlight persisted. Graffia recruited former Colonists Chic James and Craig Kemp, rounded out with guitarist Greg Nashan and bass player Terry Stone, and assembled them into the Raymond John Michael Band. The three-part Colony reunion was short-term, resulting in a few recordings—a ballad, "Let There Be Love," and rocker "Rich Kid Blues"—that lingered in legal limbo between the local label Ivanhoe and London Records. In one appearance that Graffia characterized as "a bit sticky and uncomfortable," Raymond John Michael was booked as the opening act for their former band in its fading reconfigurations.

The New Colony Six original member subtraction continued into the new decade. Les Kummel and Pat McBride were the next to move on, with McBride transitioning into production. In the spring of 1971, the reconstituted group signed with the local label Sunlight Records. Though they did not record an album, the late model Colonists released three solid singles that demonstrated some chart life. "Roll On" hit WLS's Top 10 and #56 nationally on *Billboard*; the absorbing parting "Long Time to Be Alone," a Rice, McBride, and Von Kollenberg collaboration, reached #93 on *Billboard*; and the New Colony Six's final record to run the charts nationally, "Someone, Sometime," hit WLS at #13 and *Billboard* #109 in January 1972.

The Sunlight set was a setting sun on the group. Rice exited, returning to solo pursuits, leaving Von Kollenberg the lone remaining original member. Von Kollenberg kept the residual unit active primarily with live performances and a few stray singles on MCA until 1974, the official end of the New Colony Six.

New Colony Contrast: Six-cess and the Battle of the Brands

The New Colony Six's Chicagoland legacy is commonly, critically, and conveniently delineated between the Centaur/Sentar and the Mercury sets of singles and their accompanying pairs of albums on each label. The musical distinctions were patently sharp: the initial raw and edgy suburban garage sound from 1966 to 1967 in punkish-to-polished juxtaposition with the ballads and love songs of 1968–69.

The emblematic early/late music dichotomy within the New Colony Six body of work prompted prolonged critical contemplation and subjective skirmishes. Reconciling such incendiary inclinations was a chronic cultural condition, particularly in Chicagoland, with its rich local tradition of uncompromising argumentative allegiance rooted in notable crosstown crossfires between the North Side and South Side, Cubs and White Sox baseball fans, and radio rotation rivals WLS and WCFL. The New Colony Six labels Centaur/Sentar and Mercury squared off and joined the fray.

The popular perception that the New Colony Six's early recordings are relatively underappreciated contextualizes more broadly beyond the band's internal battle between their own brands. Despite being the groundbreaking single for the group and the emerging regional rotation, "I Confess" remains relatively unsung, a less familiar Farfisa footnote and somewhat subordinate smash to other enduring Chicagoland hit standards of the era such as "Gloria," "Bend Me, Shape Me," "Kind of a Drag," "Sugar and Spice," and "Vehicle."

The New Colony Six's later softer sound may not have been as popular in critical circles as the chart success of those singles suggested they were in the mainstream. Richie Unterberger was among a significant critical cross section with a resounding preference for the New Colony Six's early works. Unterberger proclaimed the group's 1966 debut LP, *Breakthrough*, "one of the finest obscure rock albums of the '60s," citing the blend of American pop hooks and vocal harmonies with tough, organ-dominated British R&B and customary comparisons to the spirit of Them and the Yardbirds. Conversely, he expressed a symmetrical disappointment across the Colony's career divide when the garage rockers "devolved into a cabaret-ish band ... a pedestrian mainstream pop rock outfit that owed more to Gary Puckett [& the Union Gap] than the gritty British Invasion roots."[20] Echoing Unterberger's advocacy, Chicagoland music authority Jeff Jarema provides a detailed discourse on the superiority of the New Colony Six's unsung Centaur/Sentar recordings that the Mercury set "couldn't hold a candle to," in his retrospective liner note treatise, "Why the New Colony Six Rule!," in the Sundazed Records reissue, *At the River's Edge* (1993).[21] The volume compiles 22 tracks from the New Colony Six's first two albums, *Breakthrough* and *Colonization*, and includes non-album cuts as appealing archival extras.

Preferences and popularity aside, the divergent music that marks the New Colony Six's mid-to-late 1960s songbook was not indicative of a haphazard, hit-or-miss approach, dabbling, or experimentation by the band. Their catalog is more cohesive than it is collaged or chaotic. While the sets of singles released on each of the New Colony Six's record labels accentuate and compartmentalize the contrasts, the band's four albums over four years, despite so-so sales, reveal consistent competency and masterful musicianship within the stylistic scope and sequencing of their songs. To their collective credit as songwriters and musicians, the New Colony Six played garage, psychedelic, jangle, soft ballads, and power pop with parallel proficiencies. They also managed to capably and harmoniously pull off two-and-a-half and three-minute instances of fairy tale pop, folk, blues and soul, measures of Merseybeat, and traces of country and bubblegum. And, no matter the genre or subgenre, their songs were predominantly original material.

Reflecting upon the New Colony Six's split stylistic signatures, and the band's evolution and influence as a mid-to-late-1960s Chicagoland music scene centerpiece, Ray Graffia's point of view is pragmatic when recognizing the band's "softie stigma" and the status derived in large part from their Mercury recordings. Graffia concedes that the Six's success resulting from the mainstreamed musical direction of their ballads and love songs may have superseded the significance of the group's innovative, energetic revolution starter set on Centaur/Sentar. "If I had my druthers, we'd have stayed edgy, with stuff like 'At the River's Edge,' and more adventuresome, like 'Let Me Love You' and later 'Sun Within You,'" said the Colony founder. "But how can you argue with success? And who knows if our 'garage band' stuff would have made the impact that the pop music did."[22]

Chapter 3

Oh Yeah '66

From "Gloria" to Glorious Train Wreck

It was a really happening period, the whole British Invasion taken back over by us Americans.
—Jimy Sohns, lead singer, Shadows of Knight[1]

1966 is one of the longest years I can remember. The year never seemed to end.
—Jerry McGeorge, Shadows of Knight guitarist[2]

"The American Rolling Stones"

The Shadows of Knight amplified the Chicagoland regional infiltration and chart presence in '66, generating the most volume, in sound level, sum, and swagger. Launching loudly in late 1965, shortly after the New Colony Six's "I Confess" hit the airwaves, the Shadows of Knight snarled four singles onto the *Billboard* Hot 100 during the year. Their introduction was impactful, beginning with an emphatic adaptive spelling—"Gee-elll-ohh-are-iii-ayy"—a borrowed tune from the Belfast-born soul troubadour Van Morrison and his band Them. Following the single's late January release, reaction to the raucous regional rendition of "Gloria" was swift, as the #1 song in Chicago soared into the *Billboard* national Top 10 by March, with 12 weeks staying power. The song placed a few notches higher at #7 on the record register of the secondary music industry trade publication, *Cashbox*. A few months later, in May, the band followed their striking debut single with another R&B rendition—Bo Diddley's "Oh Yeah," from 1959. The song cracked the Top 40 at #39 before the briefly and barely charting. "Bad Little Woman" (#91) and "I'm Gonna Make You Mine" (#90) rounded out the band's foursome of '66 singles in the Fall.

Punkish and popular, the Shadows of Knight were quintessential garage rockers, the figurative middle finger of the most prevalent suburbands. Their edge was sharpened by fearless front Jimy Sohns, who established himself as the Chicagoland scene's flagrant figure, unabashed in acknowledging that he "burned the candle in the middle and at both ends and upside down."[3] "Oh, we were a garage band alright," verifies the unruly lead singer Sohns, who was 16 when the band kicked off in 1964.

"I was managing a gas station, and when the owner went home, we'd pull into the bay and rehearse there."[4] It was in that DX gas station where the band learned to play "Gloria." "Now if that's not a garage band, I don't know what is," insists Sohns.[5]

The group was composed of high school classmates in Mt. Prospect, a suburb located 25 miles northwest of Chicago. Their formation was a fairly familiar, if not formulaic, fledgling band narrative that included multiple makeovers due to revolving personnel and turnover that was a sign of the times. With origins as a surf-based combo and initially known as the Shadows, the group's original lineup included lead singer Sohns, Warren Rogers on lead guitar, rhythm guitarist Norm Gotsch, Wayne Pursell on bass and guitar, and drummer Tom Schiffour. The lineup continually shifted. Within a span of less than two years, Pursell was replaced by Joe Kelley, who became the band's musical backbone playing lead and bass, while Jerry McGeorge and sessionist Dave "The Hawk" Wolinski took over for Gotsch and Rogers when they were drafted into the US military.

Perhaps as testament to the proliferation of garage groups and band formations in the US, Canada, and the UK, cases of "mistaken identity" were a contagious condition among the suburban bands of the day. Just as fellow locals the Cryan' Shames and the Ides of March initially inadvertently claimed names of already existing bands—the Travelers and the Shondels—the Shadows, after signing a record deal and shortly before the release of their debut album, discovered that they, too, had unknowingly appropriated the name of a highly successful and influential instrumental British band. The Shadows were at the forefront of the UK pre–Beatles beat group boom. As Cliff Richard's backing band, they were one of the UK's most successful singles-generating acts, beginning with the instrumental hit "Apache," which topped the charts for five weeks in 1960. The moniker mistakenly borrowed by northwest Chicago's Shadows while they were making a name for themselves playing live at parties and dances in the suburban vicinity required abrupt amending. "The Tyme" was among the alternatives worn briefly by the band before it was sharply rejected as sounding "really stupid."[6] A more obvious option, "The American Shadows," may have been so seamless that everyone overlooked that name as a possibility. Shortly before their first recording, Sohns and the band inventively, and with minimal alteration and confusion for their Chicago base of followers, dubbed themselves the "Shadows of Knight." In their view, the title retained an English accent. And, coincidence or not, the "Knights" was the name of the Prospect High athletic teams.

The inevitable British Invasion influence was progressively imbedding throughout the Chicagoland bands, with the Beatles borrowing being the most prevalent, along with Kinks riffs, Hollies harmonies, and others providing identifiable styles and strands of Merseybeat. The Shadows of Knight were also enamored with the imports, though they were drawn to the harder, raw, more muscular sonic elements of British Invasion acts, along with their hometown urban blues. "The harder-edged English bands were into the blues a lot sooner than other people were," said Sohns. "And here we were, a band from Chicago doing the Blues. That helped us quite a bit."[7] The Shadows of Knight became commonly referred to as "the American Rolling Stones," and with good reason—beyond Kelley's sheepdog haircut and dead ringer resemblance to Rolling Stones guitarist Brian Jones. Members of the Shadows of Knight related a statement-like ancestral synopsis explaining how they arrived at their brash bluesy blend: "The [Rolling] Stones, Animals, and Yardbirds took the Chicago blues and gave it an English interpretation. We've taken the English version of the Blues and re-added a Chicago touch."[8]

The Teen Club Circuit

Before its initial radio resistance, "Gloria" tracked unswervingly from the band's gas station garage rehearsal to a live rendition on a local club stage. True to the modus operandi of Chicagoland bands in the lively suburban scene, the Shadows of Knight were front and center in the area teen music clubs, a significant secondary source and in-person means of exposure beyond the region's far-reaching AM radio waves.

The colorfully named clubs were hotspots, literally and figuratively, crammed with teens hanging out, dancing, and listening to live music. The lively locales were dutiful showcases for area bands, from those that were discovered and had fan followings to the swarm of smaller, obscure groups. And the venues routinely attracted a striking slate of national and international acts during their early US touring routes, among them Three Dog Night; the Lovin' Spoonful; Blood, Sweat & Tears; the Beau Brummels; the Byrds; Buffalo Springfield; Cream; the Yardbirds; and the Who.

The smaller outlets were commonly located in civic buildings, church basements, VFW halls, and YMCAs, while the larger, more trendy places were independently owned, often operating out of renovated spaces such as grocery stores, warehouses, and barns. The hangouts were nothing fancy, with practicality the primary purpose. They were basically big rooms, merely an open space with a stage set up at one end. The structures did not lend themselves to echoless acoustics; loud was the solitary sound standard in the predominantly concrete and brick surroundings. Décor was minimal, tables and chairs scarce, the lights low, and ventilation poor, all of which conspired to make mingling almost mandatory within the steamy setting. Walls were routinely painted black, some accented with graffiti expressions. The floors were commonly concrete, with chicken wire and netting a frequent garnish suspended from the low ceilings. Neon and black lighting were popular, simulating psychedelia and a fashionable, far-out feeling into the club atmosphere. Though, according to Cryan' Shames' front Jim Pilster, "the black lighting made it so hard to see, we literally had to feel our way down the hall to the stage."[9]

The clubs were not bars; alcohol was not served, and refreshments were nominal beyond a scant snack setup and warm soft drinks. Admission usually cost between one dollar and five dollars. Some clubs had memberships that were restricted to residents and students within the particular township, suburb, or school. It was not uncommon for club membership cards to specify house rules: "No drinking. No necking." The cost-efficient enrollment, with some as low as five cents, was a worthwhile investment as the ID cards carried cool cachet and status in school and social circles. The places were always packed, with attendance regularly exceeding club capacities and safety codes, a range from 500 to 1000-plus occupants, depending on the venue size. On-air promotion of the club music lineups by WLS and WCFL deejays contributed to the inflated crowd numbers. Bob Chiappano, who worked as a security guard at the Blue Village, one of the area's larger locales, claimed that "there were times we had close to 3,400 kids there," which was double its approximate 1,700 suggested occupancy. "We used to joke it was so crowded in there, if someone did pass out, at least they wouldn't hit the floor," said Pilster.[10] Disturbances and incidents inside and out were negligible, escalating no farther than an occasional fight. Such non-events were notable considering the large turnouts, the amount of inevitable illegal substances being circulated, and the diverse makeup of the carefree crowds, an assortment of types that included "outsiders" from nearby suburbs, hippies, greasers, straights, and squares.

Despite the minimal disorder and reported disturbances, undercurrents of the generational divide surfaced among some locals in the conservative communities who were unavoidably annoyed by the scene's vigorous activity. A delegation of discontent residents within the venue vicinities routinely expressed their frustrations to village officials, suggesting the clubs were more harm than good, citing noise levels, speeding cars, and an influx of outsiders, among other nuisances. "We were the scourge of Arlington Heights," recalls Jeff Platt, a patron of the suburb's club The Cellar. "There was the myth that all this evilness was going on."[11] As town commission meetings and licensing discussions escalated, club owners grew weary of the ongoing hassle. In the long and short run, and factoring in swift changes in the music market at the time, the pushback was among factors that likely took a toll on club longevity. "It was almost a constant battle," said Platt. "It probably would have lasted longer if the town would have embraced it."[12] The Cellar managed to hang on for six years, closing in 1970, while the duration of most of the clubs coincided with the relatively short-term, three-year arcs of the era's bands.

While the metropolitan locality had its share of music venues such as the Pink Fink and the Kinetic Playground uptown, the area's best-known clubs weaved a web throughout the suburbs. The music myriad dotted an approximately 50-mile span that arced from the northernmost point in Waukegan, 40 miles north of Chicago, where WLS's Dex Card's Wild Goose club was located; southwesterly 30 miles just north of Algonquin in an unincorporated stretch between Cary and Crystal Lake on Route 31 in a renovated barn called the New Place; further south 10 miles to the Blue Moon Ballroom in Elgin; and 10 more miles to the Jaguar Club in St. Charles, which was the westernmost point of the tour at 40 miles due west of Chicago; then bent back southeast 27 miles toward the city and lake but still well in the western suburbs in Westmont and the Blue Village, housed in a former grocery store along the railroad tracks on Cass Avenue, and featuring the Cryan' Shames as the house band.

On the local live music map, the most distant outlier of Chicagoland suburb affiliation stretched 83 miles northwest into the Lake Geneva, Wisconsin, resort region. The Majestic Hills Bandstand was not a club, rather a popular seasonal music amphitheater in the ski lodge setting on the south shore between Fontana Beach and Black Point and north of the town Linn. The outdoor concert facility, which featured at tree growing through the stage, was standing room only with no seating, with a 2,000-person capacity. Shows were scheduled exclusively in summertime and early fall. The venue naturally drew the nearby Chicagoland bands and was a regular stop for a cross section of major

MAJESTIC July 1969 Schedule

July 2, Wed.—	CLOSED
July 3, Thurs.—	CANNED HEAT-$4.00 4 Days & Nites Lyte Brigade
July 4, Fri.—	BUCKINGHAMS-$3.00 AMERICAN BREED
July 5, Sat.—	STEVIE WONDER-$5.00 SPENCER DAVIS Geneva Convention
July 9, Wed.—	MAUDS-$2.50
July 12, Sat.—	VANILLA FUDGE-$5.00 Dontays
July 16, Wed.—	R.E.O. SPEEDWAGON-$2.00
July 19, Sat.—	MONKEES-$5.50 Circus (This is the last time in the Chicagoland area that you will be able to ever see the Monkees. A GREAT NIGHT YOU WON'T WANT TO MISS!)
July 23, Wed.—	GUILD-$2.00
July 26, Sat.—	CRYAN' SHAMES-$3.00 Back Street Majority
July 30, Wed.—	SLY & THE FAMILY STONE $5.00 Stone Souls

Chicagoland bands and an impressive array of major national and international groups and artists routinely resorted to the outdoor concert setting of the Majestic Hills Bandstand in Lake Geneva, Wisconsin (1969 promo poster; Steve Marovich, Kenosha.com; Joe McMichael/Stu Rosenberg collection).

national and international acts. Among the bandstand bookings were the Who, Three Dog Night, Vanilla Fudge, Janis Joplin, the Association, Byrds, Beach Boys, Buffalo Springfield, Monkees, Herman's Hermits, Canned Heat, Iron Butterfly, Jethro Tull, Stevie Wonder, Spencer Davis Group, and Sly and the Family Stone.[13]

Cellar Dwellers

Geomusically, the biggest concentration of teen clubs was situated in Chicago's north by northwest pocket. On the northerly corridor 20 to 22 miles from the city and half way to Waukegan were the Pit in Glenview and six miles away in

Winnetka, Rolling Stone, which was sited in a renovated garage. The northwest cluster included the Deep End in Park Ridge, 16 miles from Chicago; across the river to Des Plaines and the Green Gorilla; and up the road seven miles to the legendary Cellar in Arlington Heights.

The Cellar was at the forefront of the suburban teen club proliferation. Its founder, Paul Sampson, was a local postal employee who also ran a record store in downtown Arlington Heights. The twenty-something Sampson was a small-scale, scene-setting visionary, sensing that the teen sphere circa '64 was ripe for a soda pop hangout that would feature live music from local bands. "He didn't know a lot about the music business, but he sure knew a lot about teenagers," said producer Bill Traut, who worked closely with Sampson, scouting and securing talent for his Dunwich Records roster.[14]

Sampson, the catalyst, initially rented the local VFW hall for a few Saturday night stands, calling the temporary music quarters The Blast. Despite an instant attraction and the-place-to-be vibe, youth culture and the traditionalist VFWers were mostly a mismatch. Sampson remained resolute in his pursuit of a permanent place for the teen club, relocating numerous times, renting available spaces for a month or two at a time. Among the locations were a country club in Mt. Prospect, an empty Jewel Food Store, and the basement of the former Saint Peter's School, its low-ceiling underground setting providing inspiration for the lasting name, "the Cellar," before Sampson and the club finally settled in a brick factory building it would share with a Firestone tire shop west of downtown at the corner of Salem and Davis.

As the most renowned Chicago suburban scene spot, the Cellar invited comparison to the Cavern Club, birthplace of the Liverpudlian lads who became the Beatles. Ides of March front Jim Peterik's star-struck recollection of his band's beginnings is vivid affirmation. "The first time we auditioned for the Cellar in Arlington Heights, it was as if we'd gone to Liverpool," said Peterik. "What a cool vibe—outside the club was [blues guitarist] Joe Kelley, who was leaning against the wall in a long scarf, smoking a cigarette next to his guitar case. Inside, Saturday's Children, the Mauds, and the Shadows of Knight were all rehearsing. It was like we'd died and gone to heaven."[15]

The Who heightened the club's Brit aura. Their Cellar stop on June 15, 1967, was a guitar-smashing prelude to their mainstream emergence during West Coast performances in the three days that followed. The Who played two nights at the renowned Fillmore Auditorium in San Francisco before an appearance at the first Monterey International Pop Festival on Sunday, June 18. The three-day (June 16–18) event celebrated the beginning of the fabled "Summer of Love." The counterculture concert was marked by musical introductions and the first major American appearances by the Who, the Jimi Hendrix Experience, Ravi Shankar, Janis Joplin with Big Brother and the Holding Company and Otis Redding, backed by Booker T. & the MG's. D. A. Pennebaker's documentary film *Monterey Pop* (1967) was at the forefront of several meaningful concert documentaries of the era: Pennebaker's cinema verité Dylan document *Don't Look Back* (1967); Michael Wadleigh's *Woodstock* (1970), capturing 500,000 youth gathered in mid–August 1969 for "three days of peace and music" at Max Yasgur's dairy farm near Bethel, New York; and brothers Albert and David Maysles' *Gimme Shelter* (1970), a chronicle of the Rolling Stones' ill-fated free concert with Hell's Angels as stage security at Altamont Speedway outside San Francisco on December 6, 1969.

In 1965, before they were "Knighted," the Shadows landed a steady gig at Sampson's Cellar, which was conveniently located just a few miles from their hometown of Mt. Prospect. The band became a huge draw, routinely playing before audiences between 500 and 600 on weekends, sometimes two shows a night, during what Sohns referred to as "the screaming era." "The kids would charge the stage, grab you and that kind of thing when we ended … where it disrupted the headliner coming on after us, and it would mess up the show," said Sohns.[16] The group's regularity at the club resulted in the designation "house band." According to Sohns, they played the Cellar "for about six months straight." The grungy sound and spirit of those early Shadows of Knight sets at the Cellar are compiled by the rarity record archivists Sundazed into a representative 13-song sampler with satisfactory sound quality, *Raw 'N Alive at the Cellar, Chicago 1966!* (1992). Once the band got "big enough to go out on the road"—which meant making regional rounds from Rockford, Illinois, to Valparaiso, Indiana, 55 miles east—the Cellar "actually had to shut down for a while until they could find bands to fill in while we were gone."[17] Music manager/producer Bill Traut was among the adults who noticed the talent on stage. Traut swooped, signing Sohns and company to a record deal as the first artists on the newly founded independent local label and subsidiary of Atlantic Records, Dunwich, which became a centerpiece of the Chicagoland scene.

The Grunge and Glory of "G-l-o-r-i-a"

In the midst of fluctuations, from the band name to personnel changes, the soon to be Shadows of Knight promptly entered the Universal Recording Studios to lay down songs. "Gloria" was the preordained single, with its moody B-side, "Dark Side." Sohns, though appreciative of the prodigious local radio support, resists the notion that WLS, particularly its program director Clark Weber, was the impetus behind recording the single. "We had been playing 'Gloria' for a year, so nobody had to ask us to go out and learn that song in order to put a record out," stressed Sohns.[18] "Six months before we recorded 'Gloria,' we knew it was going to be a smash hit."[19]

A seemingly obvious choice to cover, "Gloria" was actually a B-side to Them's British hit version of Muddy Waters's "Baby Please Don't Go." The song was among "a whole bunch of records" sent to Sohns by his cousin, who was in the army and stationed in Germany. In the translation from Northern Ireland to northwest Chicago, the Shadows of Knight's "Gloria" diverged somewhat from the original. Despite the two groups' commonalities as white teenagers bashing American Black blues and soul sound, Sohns and the Shadows moderately modified the music from Morrison's approach. Their shortened version expanded the three-chord E, D, A, adding a fourth with an open strum that made the opening less hesitant than the Them intro. The result was less choppy overall, and a more rhythmic, danceable track in just over two-and-a-half minutes.

The lyric alterations of "Gloria," though similarly slight, presented a more notable circumstance. The song's lurking "just about midnight" scenario found itself situated in a provocative '66 midway between the Kingsmen's controversial cover of Richard Berry's "Louie, Louie" in 1963, which incited an FBI investigation, and the widely misheard lyrics of the English group Free's pickup hit in 1970, "All Right Now," featuring a Paul Rodgers vocal before he joined Badfinger. Songwriter responses to the turbulent mid–1960s political and sociocultural climate increasingly unsettled radio's gatekeepers, who, in their commitment to keeping the airwaves clean, were circumspect of encroaching objectionable content that might invite an FCC inquiry or result in listener repercussions, particularly from concerned parents.

The paranoia of the times did not strike deep among radio programmers, though they naturally became more prudent with song selections. Incendiary incidents were intermittent and carried cultish cachet. In 1965, Barry McGuire's most popular rendition of P. F. Sloan's protest song "Eve of Destruction" was a #1 hit that was also banned and restricted in many markets in the name of anti–Americanism. In 1966, the novelty breakup-to-crack-up song "They're Coming to Take Me Away, Ha-Haaa!" by Napoleon XIV (Jerry Samuels) on Warner Bros. charted a curious course, peaking at #3 before falling off the charts completely when a predominance of radio programmers and stations, notably the New York City market, removed the song from their rotations due to its irreverent references to mental health. The idiosyncratic psychiatric saga of post-relationship unraveling contains phrases such as "funny farm," "happy home," and "those nice young men in their clean white coats." The song's ban drew opposition that triggered counter-protests.

Radio edits and re-recordings were a common, more compromising response to provocative content. Lou Christie followed his 1965 hit "Lightnin' Strikes" with another weather-related hit on MGM, "Rhapsody in the Rain." The song's suggestive lyrics—"makin' out in the rain" and "in this car … went much too far"—were re-recorded into a cleaner couplet: "fell in love in the rain" and "in this car, love came like a falling star."

Beyond Christie's controversial content, the proximate precedent of a Zombies song compelled producer Bill Traut and the Shadows of Knight to follow the re-recording route in order to be heard. In his *Rock and Roll Radio* memoir published in 2008, Clark Weber recounts his routine as WLS program director, listening to an (unspecified) new release by the Zombies, the British group whose "She's

Not There" and "Tell Her No" were Top 10 tunes in 1964. Weber's wisdom, experienced ear, and programming instincts told him that their new song had similar hit potential. At the same time, the wary Weber recognized that the song's adoption into the WLS playlist could be undercut by the lyrics "I knocked on her bedroom door and she let me in." Traut happened to be hustling by Weber's office at the time of the audition and asked if Weber would play the Zombies' song if it didn't contain the suggestive sequence. Weber said emphatically, "Sure."[20]

The savvy producer Traut, fully aware that his Dunwich label's launch depended on a Shadows of Knight single debut, returned to WLS the following morning to hand deliver a test pressing of a song that had been revised, rehearsed, and recorded overnight on a reel-to-reel tape by the band of unknown Shadows he had recruited to his fledgling record label that he managed with George Badonsky and Eddie Higgins. Taking note of Weber's professional programmer sensitivity to clean airwaves and FCC licensing, Traut dropped the "Gloria" lyric—"She come up to my room and we roll around." "That's all," said Traut. "It was a minor line, but in its day it was shocking."[21]

Traut's commitment to the single status of "Gloria" may have been grounded more in his dedication to Dunwich than it was aesthetic appeal and music appreciation. "To me, it wasn't even a song … it wasn't even music … it was just a bunch of noise," said Traut. "I could understand it. I knew it was commercial and I knew it would sell records, but I was a jazz guy and I hated that shit. I was not a rock fan at all in those days."[22]

Nonetheless, Traut administered noteworthy production touches when cutting the record. "We changed the ending slightly by double-timing it, and I tripled the voices on the yelling of the line 'Gloria,'" said Traut. "I always believed in hitting the chorus hard. Almost like a college yell. Like cheerleaders."[23] Despite yielding what Traut and the production team thought was a great record, the recording session took its toll. The engineers were burned out and the music director quit. Amidst the fatigue and departures, Traut immediately took the recording to the pressing plant on Chicagoland's South Side.

The revisionist release of "Gloria," altered to a more teen-clean "she call out my name," was placed on the WLS playlist and Art Roberts's highly rated request show on its way to million-seller status, #1 in Chicago in March. Two months later, the single reached *Billboard*'s Top 10 nationally. The airplay was an edifying echo of the song's familiarity from the live club and concert circuit. The band's avid followers from the Cellar slyly organized a massive phone-in that flooded the WLS station switchboard with requests for their local "Gloria." The teen zeal and call-in tactic, though a common, well intentioned ritual that accompanied many band beginnings, among them, the Beach Boys', aroused some suspicions among Roberts and the WLS staffers about how widespread the popularity of "Gloria" actually was. Despite the single selling more than 100,000 copies in 10 days, the record was not initially treated as a hit by WLS. There was a hint of antagonism in the air, with "us versus them" paranoia and conspiracy theories circulating among the band. "It seemed like WLS was against us from the beginning. Even when 'Gloria' was first released and began getting incredible numbers of requests, they also held back playing it for a week or so," observed Jerry McGeorge. "Roberts, Riley, and some other Chicago DJs had been professionally roughed up in the summer of '65 by the Byrds, who wouldn't cooperate with their 'sock hop' bull. I think they saw us as an extension of the whole new trend in music and lifestyles, which it was their self-appointed duty to stop."[24]

When "Gloria" exceeded gold record status, the skepticism redirected to the record's sales being understated. Because Dunwich was a local label, the single was released on a staggered sequence throughout the country. The distribution may have diluted the consistency of the song's weekly chart placement, showing peaks in certain markets and not registering in others where the song had yet to be released. Perhaps more significantly, the song was receiving little radio airplay in some major markets in Florida and California, places where Morrison's "Gloria" had charted the previous year. Atlantic stepped in to strengthen the circulation of its Dunwich subsidiary's "Gloria" to supplement Traut's advocacy and tireless marketing.

As the Shadows of Knight signature song, "Gloria" had a swaggering superiority that secured a prominent place in Chicagoland's mid–1960s—if not its all-time—playlist. Their delivery endures as one of the definitive takes of the oft-covered garage anthem. In many critical views, the Shadows of Knight version equals, if not eclipses, not only the Them original, which features a pre–Yardbirds/Led Zeppelin guitar solo by sessionist Jimmy Page, but also the song's most notable interpretations, among them two extended versions—a six-minute live by the Doors and an eight-minute Jimi Hendrix ad lib—and Patti Smith's almost unrecognizable radical rewrite, which incorporates her poem "Oath" in the opening and appears as a track on the album *Horses* (1975).

No matter the version, the lustful legacy of "Gloria" is solidly situated in the rock canon. Sales of the single subsequent to '66 have been estimated to be approximately eight million, with more copies sold during the past 25 years than the song's first 25. The glories of "Gloria" include a Grammy Hall of Fame Award in 1999 and placements in a range of rock lists. In the "500 Songs that Shaped Rock and Roll," an honor roll compiled by Rock & Roll Hall of Fame curator James Henke with input from music critics and writers, "Gloria," specifically the Shadows of Knight version, ranks at #100. Other positions include #69 on critic Dave Marsh's list of *The Heart of Rock & Soul: The 1001 Greatest Singles Ever Made*, published in 1989; #81 on the cable television music network VH1's list of "The 100 Greatest Rock Songs of All Time" in 2001; and #208 on *Rolling Stone*'s list of "The 500 Greatest Songs of All Time."

The release of "Gloria" further validated the Shadows of Knight's arrival after they had jump-started their rise as a rowdy live R&B group with a punk presence that attracted a fervent following. Television appearances and incessant touring ensued, as the band ventured outside their home stage Cellar to open for national groups such as the Byrds, the Lovin' Spoonful, Paul Revere & the Raiders, and the

Beach Boys, among others. The band was also recruited for *Dick Clark's Caravan of Stars*, a road show that had been rocking and rolling since 1959. With "Gloria" as their ticket to ride, the Shadows of Knight joined other popular groups packaged into Clark's cross-country cavalcade with a music *road*-tation that highlighted each group's mid-1960s Top 40 singles. The lineup featured the Outsiders with "Time Won't Let Me," ? and the Mysterians and their classic kiss-off "96 Tears," which was one of the final hits for the Cameo-Parkway label, and the Los Angeles proto-punk, psychedelic Seeds, starring iconic front man Sky Saxon, with "Pushin' Too Hard."

The Shadows of Knight followed "Gloria" with another R&B interpretation, this one of Bo Diddley's "Oh Yeah." Like its hit predecessor, the song accumulated a noteworthy narrative that included inevitable comparisons to the original. The Shadows of Knight version relied on the classic Muddy Waters riff from "I'm a Man," also a Bo Diddley song that was popularized by the Yardbirds' rave-up recorded at Chess studios in Chicago in 1965. The British "I'm a Man" peaked at #17 on the US charts and is considered a signature song, both live and studio, in the Yardbirds' Jeff Beck/Eric Clapton membership catalog. The Shadows of Knight arrangement of "Oh Yeah" features a descending "yeah, yeah, yeah" refrain that perhaps winks as an irreverent blues rock reference to Beatlemania, which, in the view of music journalist Mark Paytress, "gave the brooding, woman chasing song a murkier, pre-psychedelic feel."[25] Strangely, that particular rearrangement of the song had previously appeared on a single in 1964 by West London beat combo The Others. Sohns vaguely recalls producer Traut "saying something about that," but insists the Shadows of Knight recorded "Oh Yeah" for their *Gloria* album without reference to that particular British version. In another studio turn, "Oh Yeah" was re-recorded for the 45 release because Joe Kelley had switched to lead guitar, which provided a tighter, tougher sound for the song.[26]

Kelley's elevation to lead resulted in Rogers being reassigned to bass. Musically, the instrumental interchange was warranted, though it triggered an undertow of proverbial creative consequences. In the firsthand view of fellow group guitarist McGeorge, Kelley's more proficient guitar skills unquestionably belonged front and center in the lineup. While McGeorge regarded Rogers as a "good guitarist and musician with a clear idea of what he wanted," he also characterized him as "unfortunately … a true wacko," who was prone to "long weird periods of brooding silence" and "screaming fits, even on stage, when he wasn't getting his way." The decision to relegate Rogers to bass "obviously led to a lot of resentment," according to McGeorge. "In the end it left the band leaderless. We never again worked together very productively."[27]

Initially, "Oh Yeah" appeared destined to be the band's debut single, emerging as a preference among many band members and its producers. Fans were so familiar with "Gloria" and energized by the band's raucous renditions during live sets for nearly a year and a half, however, that radio's response to the zeal was a consensus "Gloria" as the lead single. "Oh Yeah" was sidelined, suspended into subsequent sequel. In hindsight, Sohns second-guessed the singles strategy, saying, "If we would have put out 'Oh Yeah' first and sell half a million copies and then 'Gloria' be the blockbuster it was, we would've really been huge."[28]

When released in May '66, "Oh Yeah" was saddled with inescapable second-single expectations that were further heightened by the long shadow of success cast by its sibling "Gloria." The follow-up reached #39, a relatively respectable chart position that was nonetheless devalued. By comparison, placement in the Top 40 was obviously not the same as the Top 10. Despite the perceived inconsequence in '66 and "Gloria" subservience, "Oh Yeah" is abiding. The song's frequent inclusion in garage classic compilations and routine referencing in critical considerations persist. As an example, in the January 2017 issue of the UK music magazine *Mojo*, the retrospective page, "What Goes On: Nuggets Unearthed," features a Mark Paytress piece devoted to the garage legacy of "Oh Yeah" 50 years after its recording and launch.

The chart exposure generated by the dynamic duo "Gloria" and "Oh Yeah" provoked a sense of album anticipation with an accompanying urgent undercurrent. The Shadows of Knight recorded and released two albums on Dunwich in a six-month span. *Gloria*, the LP, was rushed into release following its namesake single; a second album, *Back Door Men*, featuring two more singles, was issued in the fall of '66.

Both albums, patchy and with a blues thread, tried to be true to the band's live energies and presence. R&B covers were predictably prevalent, along with the assimilation of the sonic vocabularies of the Rolling Stones and Yardbirds in particular. In addition to the Van Morrison and Bo Diddley compositions that became Top 40 singles, *Gloria*'s nine other tracks feature versions of John Lee Hooker's "Boom Boom," Chuck Berry's "Let it Rock," Muddy Waters's "I Got My Mojo Working," and three Willie Dixon standards that count down to the album's closing: "You Can't Judge a Book (By the Cover)," "(I'm Your) Hoochie Coochie Man," and "I Just Want to Make Love to You." The three originals are Sohns collaborations with Rogers on "It Always Happens That Way" and the B-side of "Gloria," a Rolling Stones–style ballad "Dark Side," and Sohns joining McGeorge on the howling "Light Bulb Blues." In his concise carport catalog of "10 wild LPs" of the '66 fervor, *Rolling Stone* critic Colin Fleming regards the Shadows of Knight's debut album "as apt a garage-rock tutorial as you'll find.... Snotty, strangely charming, earnest and sounding not as old as they wished themselves to be ... but when the chops weren't there, the attitude was."[29]

The fast follow-up, *Back Door Men*, was similarly sneering and defiant, with punk posture aplenty. Yet, the record demonstrated musical growth that advanced beyond being a mere duplication of the debut LP or its delayed double-disc companion. The record contained original compositions, B-sides, a range of covers, and two instrumentals intermingled within the 11-song sequence. The album was rife with raunch, romps, and raves that showcased Kelley's guitar knack, from the Bo Diddley–style slapping syncopation on Schiffour's "Gospel Zone" to Kelley's spiteful "I'll Make You Sorry," both tracks B-sides. Not surprisingly, the Shadows of

"Oh Yeah," the Shadows of Knight's second single in 1966, was a relatively solid follow-up in the long shadow of success cast from their huge hit sibling predecessor, "Gloria," on the local label Dunwich Records. Left panel: Top: Tom Schiffour, Bottom: Jimy Sohns, Center: Jerry McGeorge; Right Panel: Top: Warren Rogers; Bottom: Joe Kelley (*Cashbox* magazine ad/poster, 1966).

Knight paid homage to their Mississippi-via-Chicago blues base with renditions of "Peepin' and Hidin'" by Jimmy Reed and Willie Dixon's "Spoonful." They also drew from early rockin' Little Richard R&B with a version of Huey "Piano" Smith and His Clown's "High Blood Pressure" from 1958. The album's instrumental tracks presented a stylistic spectrum stretched between the smoky blues of "New York Bullseye" and the Eastern rāga and roll of another B-side, "The Behemoth," underscored with Indian instrumentation and psych allusions to the Byrds' *Fifth Dimension*, particularly "Eight Miles High." Recording the Tommy Boyce tune "Tomorrow's Gonna be Another Day" was a curious cover choice for *Back Door Men*, considering that the Monkees' sprightly tambourine-tapping folk-pop version of the song from their debut album in 1966 received airplay on radio and on their madcap musical television series.

The Kelley original "Three for Love" may be even more conspicuous. The B-side song's jangle and harmonies echoed a prevalent folk rock sound of the era that did not quite register in the Shadows of Knight R&B punk rock repertoire. The delivery was also distinct, marking Jerry McGeorge's maiden vocal voyage. What McGeorge himself characterized as "a crummy vocal" was perhaps excusable. It was the "first time [the guitarist] ever sang anything solo in a session," and he admitted to being "scared to death." Renowned garage rock chronicler Jeff Jarema was critically candid of the performance, writing in the liner notes of *Dark Sides: The Best of the Shadows of Knight* collection on Rhino Records (1994) that "Three for Love" is "a gem of a folk rocker … flawed by a hilariously weak vocal from Jerry McGeorge."[30] Whether self-effacing or straightforward, the views on McGeorge as the saboteur singer may be somewhat overstated. The song's prevailing harmonies chime in as a pleasant diversion that conveys a shared, rather than solo, vocal sound.

With the inclusion of "Hey Joe (Where You Gonna Go)," the Shadows of Knight joined a multitude of bands, including fellow locals the Cryan' Shames, who recorded versions of the Leaves' original from the previous year. In addition to the Leaves themselves rerecording their own song in 1966, the Standells, Surfaris, Love, Music Machine, Byrds, and Jimi Hendrix Experience produced variations of the garage rock standard as a single or an album cut the same year. Not to mention that "Hey Joe" was mandatory for any band formation in a garage or basement across the country. The Shadows of Knight's lengthy (5:42) rendition was the centerpiece of *Back Door Men*, though the mid–1960s classic may have already been too widely interpreted for it to stand out and carry the album toward hit standing and sales.

Though the Shadows of Knight maintained their stage status as an all-the-rage live attraction, their commercial appeal, both single and album, summarily sagged following "Gloria" reaching the Top 10. If the ranking of "Oh Yeah" just inside the Top 40 was considered a disappointment, then their subsequent singles were flat-out flops. "Bad Little Woman" (#91) and "I'm Gonna Make You Mine" (#90) barely squeezed into the national 100, where they stalled with fleeting staying power, lasting a mere two weeks. The poor showing may have been, in part, self-inflicted, with the band's uncompromising, expanding sound and lingering issues with suggestive lyrics contributing hindrances. "Bad Little Woman" probably deserved better as a single. The aggressive "I'm Gonna Make You Mine" served as the band's "ultimate musical statement" packed with power chords and a fierce delivery that attempted to recreate the band's live dynamic on record. The non-album single initially sold strong in its first two weeks, until the lines "you're gonna give, I'm gonna make you" rattled the radio establishment, leading to widespread banning. The record was pulled from the playlists of all ABC Drake affiliates, which at the time accounted for nearly three-quarters of all the radio stations playing a rock format.

The Shadows of Knight's daring that dead-ended in radio indifference late in '66 foreshadowed the band's fate. Their final Dunwich singles that followed in 1967 contained even less commercial value, with minimal appeal for the teen-oriented AM audience. The band's sound veered farther from its garage roots, which simultaneously suggested musical growth, betrayal, and/or an identity crisis. In February, the melancholy folk ballad "Willie Jean" (B-side "The Behemoth") featured a world-weary lead vocal by Schiffour. The August release, "Someone Like Me" (B-side "Three for Love"), borrowed a brassy horn arrangement that was a prevalent 1960s suburban sound. The brassiness was pioneered locally by The MOB and brought to the forefront by such bands as the Buckinghams and American Breed before becoming a signature of the Ides of March and the mega-group Chicago.

By mid–1967, the Shadows of Knight splintered, with Schiffour, McGeorge, Wolinski, and Kelley scattering across the varied local music sphere into other transitory groups—the psychedelic H.P. Lovecraft, progressive Bangor Flying Circus, and Joe Kelley Blues Band. Wolinski also eventually joined Ask Rufus and Chaka Khan. The disintegration, which some accounts suggest was prompted by Sohns, left the lead vocalist the lone remaining original member standing in the Shadows of Knight.

The Shadows of Knight Dunwich deal deteriorated. In Sohns's view, the band's relationship with the record label was never dynamic to begin with. "We happened like a hot potato and the next thing they do was sign like up like 20 other bands around Chicago and say, 'Look what we did for the Shadows, and really they didn't do anything,'" said Sohns.[31] One of the songs Traut and Dunwich passed on for the Shadows of Knight was "(I'm Not Your) Steppin' Stone," a Tommy Boyce and Bobby Hart composition that was recorded by Paul Revere & the Raiders in May 1966, before the Monkees' version reached #20 in November as the B-side to their chart-topping cover of Neil Diamond's "I'm a Believer." Even the Raiders front Mark Lindsay believed "Steppin' Stone" belonged in the Shadows of Knight's Chicago garage, insisting to Sohns, "This song is you. You need to do this song."[32] The Shadows of Knight never did record "(I'm Not Your) Steppin' Stone."

Dunwich cut ties with the Shadows of Knight in 1968, dropping them from their roster. The aftermath was another well-known notorious narrative of artist-versus-label back-and-forths, rampant with allegations regarding royalties and rip-offs, and leaving those entangled wondering where the money went. "We unfortunately were signed to a bad record deal where we didn't get paid like most of the bands," summarized Sohns. "We kind of drifted 'cause everyone knew we were getting screwed out of money. So it was hard to keep them in it.... It was a bad situation we were in."[33]

Dunwich sold the Shadows of Knight master tapes to its parent company, Atlantic, for an obligatory sum of one dollar. One year later, without the band's consent or knowledge, Dunwich re-issued a "Gloria '69" single on the ATCO label. The updated recording featured overdubs by Peter Cetera, future member of the band Chicago, and Jim Donlinger of the local psych-rock group Aorta. The desperation and exploitation were glaring, and the single fittingly flopped.

Garage to Gumdrop: Blues, Bubblegum, Buddah, and Beyond

Sohns rocked on past the Dunwich prime and parting. He inherited the Shadows of Knight trademark—literally, loosely, and somewhat legally—and carried the band banner with him from Chicago to New York. There, he connected with Brooklynites Jerry Kasenetz and Jeffrey Katz and their Super K Productions, a tributary in a resourceful record label lineage. The former Cameo-Parkway producers were the principle proponents of "bubblegum pop." The thriving, teen-targeted subgenre was generally stamped with an upbeat, sugary sound, catchy, singalong-style choruses, childlike themes, and contrived innocence, with an occasional wink of sexual innuendo. Buddah Records became the chief distribution domain for the bubblegum brand that was mainly manufactured and managed by the entrepreneurial Kasenetz and Katz duo. The label was formed in 1967 by Art Kass, head of Kama Sutra Records, an MGM subsidiary whose flagship artist was the chart regulars the Lovin' Spoonful, out of Greenwich Village in New York. Of note, the group joined fellow 1960s act Gary Lewis & the Playboys as the only recording artists to place their first seven consecutive Hot 100 hits within the chart's Top 10.

Kass's appointment of 24-year-old Neil Bogart as Buddah's chief of operations quickly cascaded into his enlisting Kasenetz and Katz, who were colleagues of Bogart's from his time as head of A&R at Cameo-Parkway. The renowned Philadelphia record company, in operation since 1956, had been struggling since early 1964. The label's sharp decline was accelerated by *American Bandstand*'s westward move from hometown Philly to Los Angeles. The Dick Clark teen television dance show was considered Cameo-Parkway's primary source of publicity. In addition, the British Invasion's impact on the music tastes of the American record-buying public proved detrimental. Cameo couldn't keep pace, despite strategies that included licensing a handful of early British beat group singles, notably the first American releases by the Kinks—"Long Tall Sally" and "You Still Want Me"—though neither made the US charts. Bogart also signed Bob Seger to his first recording contract, with the label issuing his first five singles, which remained regional hits in Michigan with no national reach. In mid–1966, Bogart briefly shepherded a mild renaissance for the label, turning to garage and soul. The label's last hit single was the ? and the Mysterians garage classic "96 Tears," which topped the charts in the fall of 1966. Cameo-Parkway shut down in September 1967, and became ABKO the following year.

Buddah's bubblegum singles carved a notable niche on the charts between 1966 and 1969, with two bands as their primary pop purveyors. The Ohio Express placed "Yummy Yummy Yummy (I've Got Love in My Tummy)" (#4) and "Chewy Chewy" (#15) in the Top 20, with "Beg, Borrow and Steal" (as the Rare Breed on Attack Records) (#29); "Down at Lulu's" (#33); and "Mercy" (#30) reaching the Top 40. The 1910 Fruitgum Company's "Simon Says," "Indian Giver," and "One Two Three, Red Light" were gold records in the Top 5, with "Special Delivery" (#38) and "Goody Goody Gumdrop" (#37) also Top 40 tunes; "May I Take a Giant Step (Into Your Heart)" (#63), "The Train" (#57), and "When We Get Married" (#118) also charted. Even the Super K "supergroup," Kasenetz-Katz Singing Orchestral Circus, a fictitious Traveling Wilburys precursor, managed a #25 showing with the single "Quick Joey Small (Run Joey Run)." The Buddah label's lone #1 hit was "Green Tambourine" by the Lemon Pipers in February 1968. On a novelty note, double-sided hits were not a company priority, though many (but not all) Super K–produced singles were efficiently pressed with B-side tracks that were recorded backwards or as studio session instrumentals. This strategic flip side 45 method was also employed earlier by producers such as Phil Spector as a way of pointing a radio deejay to the "A" side of the singles for airplay.

Sohns recorded anonymously with a group of Super K studio musicians on many of Buddah's most popular singles. He also managed to consolidate a group to record as the "second generation" Shadows of Knight, in name only. There remained a waning glimmer of glory for the re-branded band to display. The single "Shake" was released in October 1968 on the short-lived Buddah subsidiary Team Records. The song effectually merged the Shadows of Knight's increasing hard rock preference with bubblegum's simplicity and a trace of Sam the Sham and the Pharaohs' catchiness. "Shake" rose to #46, becoming the Shadow of Knight's fifth and final entry on the charts. A subsequent single released the same year on Super K, "My Fire Department Needs a Fireman," was a 45 false alarm that went unnoticed beyond its title.

An album by the new edition of the band followed, one of the few to be released on Kasenetz and Katz's Super K label. The move seemed logical for the record company, considering Sohns's standing and the original Shadows of Knight reputation he carried, combined with the recent respectable chart run of "Shake." Though sort of sanctioned by Sohns, the unimaginatively self-titled LP, *Shadows of Knight* (1969), with the definite article "The" dropped from the name, felt incompatible with the phantom incarnation of the Arlington Heights/Mt. Prospect–based band. The substitution was not so much a slight of the original lineup as it was a glaring case of stolen identity. The album, the third and final LP in the band's discography, was a colliding amalgam of punk, proto-metal, and hard rock, with flimsy bubblegum footing and framework. Filled with fuzz and feedback, the prevailing sound lacked the characteristic Kasenetz-Katz production sheen. The album was more garaged up than it was goody goody gum dropped. Any traces of bubblegum were only in construction, not execution. The absurdly titled "Uncle Wiggley's Airship" featured feedback, lumbering surges, stutters, stammers, and starts. The song's comparably ludicrous lyrics, which describe the vessel as "a watermelon with wings," may have been Buddah brand worthy but was superseded by explicit echoes of Blue Cheer, Blues Magoos, the Troggs, Kinks, Captain Beefheart, and even Buffalo Springfield's "Bluebird" throughout. The record's odd fusion likely was not what the Super K production team expected or wanted, even from a diminished Dunwich Shadows of Knight assemblage. By the time *Shadows of Knight* was recorded and released in 1969, Sohns and Super K had also parted ways. In the separation aftermath, Kasenetz and Katz appeared indifferent to issuing a studio project consisting of what Sohns considered unfinished tracks and demos for other acts on the Buddah label.[34]

The critical reception, or rejection, of *Shadows of Knight* reinforced Sohns's (dis)contention. In an "Unsung: The Book of Seth" platform on the "Archdude" Julian Cope Presents Head Heritage UK website, the rock writer known as "The Seth Man" provides an improbably elongated and sharply colorful read of what he considers an "album in crisis," characterizing the recording's interesting, incorrigible, and improvisational nature as

> supernatural ... crudely produced and swept into a schizoid zone all its own where it barked and drooled while trying to behave. Which it did—badly. ... a catalog of first takes, mistakes, outtakes and every-other-kinda-takes as well as how NOT to produce a record; let alone one to rescue a diminishing career with some semblance of a return to form. ... with enough fuzz, junk, kicks and yucks for its half an hour duration, it scores a big time punk "fuck yeah."[35]

The Seth Man adds that the uneven production "tilts into a glorious train wreck" that was "sonically lopsided towards the vocals." The critique crescendos into a pronouncement of *Shadows of Knight* as "possibly one of the most inept rock records, ever. Not so much due to the performances as much the manner in which those performances were recorded and how the elements were juxtaposed."[36]

The steadfast Sohns returned home to Chicago, doggedly wearing the Shadows of Knight emblem. There, he reunited with Bill Traut to produce what in essence became a sendoff single for the Shadows of Knight, "I Am the Hunter." Released in 1970 on ATCO Records, the career-culminating cut was a days-gone-by growl with blatant ricochets of Joe Walsh and the James Gang. The song stiffed on the charts, signaling the end of the Shadows of Knight. Sohns's sex, drugs, and rock and roll legacy was eventually augmented by a punch-out of Sid Vicious and a jail term for drugs.

Garage's Greatest Year

The Shadows of Knight instigation of the Chicagoland national chart breakthrough in 1966 was a regional corollary that coincided with what is commonly considered "garage's greatest year." The Shadows of Knight were punk principals in the psychotic reaction that included the Count Five, ? and the Mysterians, the Leaves, Electric Prunes, Music Machine, Blues Magoos, Seeds, and Standells, among many other electrified, psychedelicized bands. However, the garage door was only open for a relatively short span. In the confining estimate of Colin Fleming, "pretty much just for a year." That year—1966—marked the midway and the peak of a prolific 1964–1968 pop rock parenthesis.[37]

The soundscape, scene, and music marketplace continued to evolve rapidly, the accelerated pace in tune with the constant motion and consciousness of The Times. The title of Jon Savage's insightful cultural chronicle, *1966: The Year the Decade Exploded* (2016), provides an apt "Big Bang" universe metaphor for the seismic cultural shifts that were taking place. Among the swings and turns, album interest and emphasis escalated among artist, industry, and audience alike, as 33⅓ LP sales began to challenge, and would soon eclipse, the exclusivity of the popular seven-inch 45 single.[38]

The year was pronounced with momentous works, many with mentions of masterpiece—the Rolling Stones' *Aftermath*; the Beach Boys' *Pet Sounds*; the Beatles' *Revolver*; Bob Dylan's *Blonde on Blonde*, the first double-album by a major artist; and Simon & Garfunkel's poetic pair, *Sounds of Silence* and *Parsley, Sage, Rosemary and Thyme*. All of the records were released just as the grungier garage offshoot of the rock genre was reaching its pinnacle. A new phase of rock was passing garage by, unseating its sonic supremacy and settling into place. "Psychedelia and hippie-dom killed off the toughs, you might say, and though garage-band careers could persist into 1967 and beyond, there was nothing like that kind of initial fervor of 1966," observes Fleming. The Shadows of Knight's concise, compelling trajectory was testament to that compact, impactful time frame. The swaggering Chicagoland punks crashed what Fleming labeled garage's "raucous national prom," bringing with them "Gloria" as their date and spiking the punch as they made the scene.

Chapter 4

It's Dunwich Man

> *A full decade before the Sex Pistols, Dunwich Records had unceremoniously ushered in punk in all but name.*
> —Dave Traut, curator, Classic Garage Rock Library[1]

The Shadows of Knight's rowdy rule at the vanguard of Chicagoland's emergence in the mid–1960s musical map transformed from possibility into an impactful presence, in part, through timing and the dynamic triangulation between WLS, the Cellar, and Dunwich Records. Though perhaps overshadowed by the volume and vivacity of the Windy City's AM radio reach and the region's teen club circuit, the Dunwich imprint was prominent in its hometown Chicagoland music scene's short-term, high-volume sound. Despite a conspicuously limited album output, Dunwich distinguished itself as a prolific record label during a succinct two-year stretch. Bracketed by the Shadows of Knight's "Gloria" in 1966 and "Someone Like Me" in 1967, Dunwich's abundant and vibrant singles catalog encapsulated the essence of the regional music scene.

A resourceful trio of jazz buffs—Bill Traut, Eddie Higgins, and George Badonsky—initiated and shaped the local independent label into a renowned production centerpiece that embraced an array of Chicagoland bands, both core and periphery, and enlisted key producers who helped generate a surplus of singles highlighted by some of the regions' most representative and enduring charting songs, while establishing broader record distribution ties with numerous national labels, among them Philips, Mercury, and Acta.

Mechanisms, Orchestrations, Triangulations

The production partnership between Traut, Higgins, and Badonsky evolved out of another music triumvirate, this one a corporate confluence involving Seeburg, Universal Studio, and Atlantic Records. Traut, Higgins, and Badonsky all had music backgrounds that spanned bands to business. Traut and Higgins were both jazz musicians: Traut a saxophonist and sessionist, Higgins a pianist, composer, and bandleader. Badonsky brought record industry experience to the mix, having worked, among other positions, as a regional sales director in Chicago for the New York City–based Atlantic Records label.

In the early 1960s, Traut and Higgins worked together programming and producing "background music" for the Seeburg Corporation, a pioneering manufacturer of automated musical vending equipment designed to accommodate 78 and 45 rpm record formats and sheet music. The J. P. Seeburg Piano Company was founded in 1907 by Justus Percival Sjöberg (the Swedish surname Americanized into "Seeburg"), who came to the United States at age 16 and settled in the Chicagoland area, initially in Rockford, 90 miles northwest, before drifting into the city. Seeburg worked in the piano industry as a mechanic and supervisor. While at the Marquette Piano Company, he and his associates constructed the first coin-operated pianos on location in Chicago.[2]

The Seeburg Company was at the forefront of the jukebox evolution. Early on, the firm distributed Marquette Piano's full output and became the premier producer of orchestrions in the United States. These automatic pianos contained several instruments inside that generated the sound of an entire band or orchestra. By the late 1920s, the company's concentration shifted to the production of coin-operated phonographs and player pianos. In 1928, Seeburg introduced the Audiophone, a jukebox antecedent that combined components of the nickelodeon and the phonograph. The bulky multi-select song machine featured eight separate turntables mounted on a rotating Ferris wheel–like device, which allowed the patron a choice of records for a nickel a song. The Selectophone model that followed featured 10 turntables/records, though its systematic complications such as warped spindles frustrated operators. The prototypes were not huge initial successes for Seeburg, and the competition was rapidly expanding. By the 1930s, other manufacturers such as Wurlitzer and Rock-Ola had entered the marketplace. Under the direction of J. P.'s son Noel, Seeburg remained competitive through the mid–1940s and World War II, producing reasonable and ritzy jukeboxes. The company's biggest impact came at the decade's end, marking the music machine timeline with their release of a mechanism that could play both sides of 50 records, a reliable 100-select jukebox. Seeburg emerged as the music marketplace leader through the 1950s, dominating jukebox production with advanced models that played 45 rpm records and provided a 200-song selection. Both features were firsts in the field.[3]

Seeburg leased a small space at Universal Recording in Chicago. The studio, co-founded in 1946 by Bill Putnam, Bernie Clapper, and Bob Weber, was among the city's preeminent in-house sound production facilities during the flourishing Chicago R&B and soul era of the 1950s and 1960s. The site was a rhythmic regional reflection of the Southern soul happening down the road in Memphis at Stax Records and its sister label, Volt, founded in 1957 as Satellite Records. Independent studios were plentiful in the Chicagoland vicinity during that period, a production proliferation spanning near North Side spaces that included the Universal complex located at 46 East Walton, to RCA on Lake Shore Drive, Sound Studios and Stereo-Sonic on North Michigan Avenue's Record Row, and Paragon on Huron, to P.S. Recording on the South Side.[4]

The opportunistic Traut took advantage of the Seeburg company's affiliation with Universal. In 1963, Clapper granted the aspiring producer limited after-hours access to Studio A, one of the largest in town, to work on recordings, with the agreement that if a record hit, there would be some recompense to Universal. The studio allowance gifted by Clapper was instrumental as a foundational stepping stone. In Traut's matter-of-fact view, "without Universal there never would have been a Dunwich at all."[5]

Traut and Higgins had their sights set on producing, arranging, and recording their own jazz records rather than making bland background music and jukebox tracks for Seeburg. Higgins had previously recorded an album of post-bop "hard" jazz, *The Ed Higgins Trio*, recorded at Bill Huck's Replica Studio 25 miles northwest of Chicago in Des Plaines, and released on the Replica label in 1958. Higgins, a native of Cambridge, Massachusetts, further established himself as a regular performer around some of Chicago's most prominent jazz clubs, among them Blue Note, the Brass Rail, Cloister Inn, Preview Lounge, Jazz Ltd., and London House, where he played opposite some of the era's jazz giants, including Cannonball Adderley, Bill Evans, Erroll Garner, Stan Getz, Dizzy Gillespie, Wes Montgomery, Oscar Peterson, Coleman Hawkins, and George Shearing, as well as notable sidemen bassist Richard Evans and drummer Marshall Thompson.

Traut and Higgins connected with Nesuhi Ertegun at Atlantic Records, a record label of legendary lineage formed by Nesuhi's younger brother, Ahmet, and Herb Abramson in 1947. Before being persuaded by his brother and Jerry Wexler, the "Father of R&B," to join them as partners in 1955 at Atlantic rather than defect to their competitor, Imperial Records, Nesuhi had established significant music cachet. A lifelong jazz aficionado with particular interest in the New Orleans style, Nesuhi married into Hollywood's sacred shrine, the Jazz Man Record Shop, wedding its owner, Marili Morden. Referred to as "the high priestess of Jazz," Morden was colorfully characterized throughout Cary Ginell's chronicle, *Hot Jazz for Sale: Hollywood's Jazz Man Record Shop* (2010), as "the seductive although restrained amorous cynosure of the traditional scene."[6]

Ertegun established the Crescent Records label, which eventually merged into Jazz Man Records, where he produced trombonist and bandleader Kid Ory revival recordings in the mid–1940s and other works by swing and Dixieland jazz musicians Pete Dailey and Turk Murphy. He also worked at Good Time Jazz Records with Lester Koenig, a screenwriter, film producer, and founder in 1951 of the jazz label Contemporary Records. Ertegun's expertise and proficiencies extended beyond the music studio into studious settings, where he exhibited the erudite Ertegun pedigree highlighted by the patriarch, Munir, who was appointed Turkish ambassador to the United States in 1935. Among other accomplishments, Nesuhi served as editor of *The Record Changer*, "the American Magazine of Jazz," and he was professed to be among the first to teach a history of jazz course for academic credit at UCLA.

As a vice president at Atlantic, Nesuhi Ertegun supervised the label's extensive jazz catalog and was noted for investing in the long play album market by improving recording sound quality and sleeve formats. As producer, he worked with jazz greats John Coltrane, Charles Mingus, and Ornette Coleman; was involved with the label's rhythm and blues and rock and roll rosters; and recruited the legendary songwriting partners Jerry Leiber and Mike Stoller. Both Nesuhi and Ahmet Ertegun were eventually honored as Rock & Roll Hall of Fame inductees.

The Lovecraft Label: "Getting Real About Rock 'N' Roll"

While working on jazz recordings at Atlantic, among them a Higgins album titled *Soulero* (1965), Traut and Higgins met Badonsky, a regional sales rep who had grown as restless with his role at Atlantic as Traut and Higgins were with Seeburg. Badonsky expressed interest in teaming with the pair on a music venture. In 1965, the trio's production partnership premiered as Amboy Records, a pre–Dunwich designation that paid homage to Badonsky's New Jersey origins in the Middlesex County municipalities "The Amboys," South and Perth. The Amboy record label launched with a promotional-only 45 single, "Bombay Bicycle Club"/"Silverthumb." Each side featured film score style instrumentals arranged by Higgins and Traut under the name the Univacs, with guitar purportedly provided by Steve Miller. The recordings, which received some airplay on WLS, were from studio sessions that Traut characterized as "not knowing what they were … but kind of our maiden attempts at rock 'n' roll."[7]

From that "Silverthumb" Amboy single forward, Traut, Higgins, and Badonsky "decided to get real about rock 'n' roll." Traut had "studied enough rock by that time" that he "knew a little bit about how it should be done." He also learned a lot about its sound and mixing from spending hours at Universal Studio with engineers Bob Kidder and Jerry DeClercq. Of the three producer partners, Badonsky was perhaps the most rock-oriented. "George was really into raw talent and I was into musicianship," said Traut. "Sometimes the two didn't always go together."[8] Such creative conflicts were commonplace, with varying end results. In retrospect, Traut suggested that the Shadows of Knight, despite some success, may have "suffered" and been caught between his and Badonsky's conflicting concepts of what the band should be.[9]

Seeking input from associates who might "show them the [rock and roll] ropes," Badonsky contacted Kent Beauchamp, who owned Royal Disc Distributing, Chicago supplier for ATCO Records, while Traut approached WLS program director Clark Weber.[10] They got a list of area bands to go out and see perform live as potential roster recruits. Those promptings led to—among other places, people, and performances—the suburbs, Paul Sampson, the Cellar, and the fledgling label's initial signing, the Shadows of Knight.

The timing was right, the atmosphere ripe, and the competition relatively sparse. Jim Golden with U.S.A. Records and the Destination label was the only one producing rock and roll in and around Chicagoland at the time. Those circumstances help contextualize how a surf tune cover of "California Sun" by the Rivieras, a South Bend, Indiana, band located 95 miles away, became recognized as Chicago's first rock and roll hit in 1964, reaching #5 on the *Billboard* Hot 100 and remaining on the charts for 10 weeks.

Amboy was a temporary title for the nascent record label. A New Jersey–inspired name for a Chicago-based record company proved provincially awkward, with an undercurrent of betrayal. And an echo of "not to be confused with" irony. There was no Amboyant connection between the record label title and the Amboy Dukes, a psychedelic/acid rock band that formed in Chicago in 1964, though they became based in Detroit. Their name derived from an Irving Shulman novel. The group featured Ted Nugent and is perhaps best known for cranking out a Top 20 garage classic in 1968, "Journey to the Center of the Mind." A permanent name replacement for "Amboy" emerged during a lunch meeting between the three partners, with Jersey boy Badonsky ironically the one to suggest that his hometown designation be supplanted by "Dunwich." The new name was a curious extraction from H.P. Lovecraft's short story "The Dunwich Horror," first published in fantasy pulp in 1929 in an issue of *Weird Tales*, and on its way to becoming one of the core works in the Lovecraft literary sphere known as Cthulhu Mythos. Both Traut and Higgins were avid Lovecraft readers. Traut, who carried a copy of the cosmic macabre horror classic with him, studied under Lovecraft's protégé, executor, and first publisher, August Derleth, while attending the University of Wisconsin. The music publishing credits on the sole Amboy release foreshadowed the label's Lovecraft loyalty, with the stamp "Dunwich Productions" appearing under Higgins's A-side, while Traut's "Silverthumb" B-side was marked by the more obscure "Yuggoth Music," a Lovecraft universe reference to a fictional planet on the edge of the solar system. The cryptic pattern persisted into 1967, when the label's Windy City Management group rebranded as "Arkham Artists," an allusion to the dark, fictional, isolated Massachusetts village that is an integral setting in stories by Lovecraft and other Cthulhu Mythos writers.[11]

The same year, in perhaps the most explicit deference, Dunwich produced the local psychedelic/acid rock band H.P. Lovecraft for the Mercury label subsidiary Philips. The group recorded songs on each of their first two albums that were ambitious musical interpretations of their namesake's literary works: "The White Ship," a mystical lighthouse keeper tale from 1919, and "At the Mountains of Madness," a 1930s novella about a geologist's disastrous Antarctic expedition.

The band's founder, George Edwards (born Charles Ethan Kenning), happened to be a solo figure at the musical forefront of Dunwich when the company commenced production in late 1965. A studio session with the local folkie was prelude within close proximity to Dunwich's discovery and signing of the Shadows of Knight, whose rebellious presence, white blues, and suburban sound embodied the commercial viability, hipness, and teen appeal that Traut, Higgins, and Badonsky were looking for to help establish their fledgling label. "Gloria" proved their initial instincts true, as the 1966 hit declared the dawn of Dunwich and transported Chicagoland into national music notoriety.

The emergent Dunwich's logo imprinted on a 45-single's inner label was plain with no graphics, in predominantly pink and yellow variations. The design and color were clever, contemporary, and calculated. "I had read an article in *Playboy* magazine about the sales power of colors, and that shocking pink, or fuchsia, was kind of a light version of that year's best-selling colors," explained Traut. "It was a hot color that year, used in all the movie posters, and the psychology was that if you made something that color, people would buy it."[12]

The Dunwich Records label and logo, and its music publishing and management group Yuggoth and Arkham Artists, were all inspired by the weird works of writer H.P. Lovecraft (Dunwich Ltd.).

Subsequent pressings of the label logo's left side featured a woman in a flowing dress with a lute on her lap, the image selected by Traut from a public domain graphic artwork book provided by art director Ron Fratell. Positioned above her head, a cartoon speech balloon contained the pronouncement accented with a sixties slang suffix, "It's Dunwich Man." The jazz tone hip phrase was added by Badonsky, which balanced his apparent aversion to the shocking pink color.

Cover Contrast, Convenience, and Miscalculation

Despite their inaugural display of instinct, savvy, and knack, the Dunwich team was still finding its way through the evolving intersection of music industry, audience, and marketplace, figuring out the fundamental balance between artist and label respect and selling records. The success of "Gloria" was neither fluke nor foreshadowing. Not every decision by Traut, Higgins, and Badonsky struck gold or platinum or made a mark that resonated beyond the Midwest region. That was clearly the case by Dunwich's second single release. In glaring commercial and cover contrast, when Dunwich swiftly followed the release of "Gloria" in 1966 with Edwards's version of the Beatles' "Norwegian Wood (This Bird Has Flown)," the 45 went largely unnoticed. Edwards's interpretation of the Lennon–McCartney song could not even break into the Top 100, stalling at #117. Cover song convenience and miscalculation may have contributed. Chicagoland music chronicler Jeff Jarema attributed the Edwards single's dismal reception to, among other factors, a "choice of cover material this time [that] was less inspired," and, interestingly, a false sense of security and expediency that "reflected Traut's daily grind at Seeburg cutting unnecessary covers of then-current hits."[13]

Though "Gloria" sounded with some familiarity along the scale from obvious to obscure, there was no higher profile in mid–1960s America and the UK than the Beatles. Borrowing from the Fab Four songbook was neither forbidden nor frowned upon. Covering songs from what was melodically materializing into one of history's most prominent songwriting duos in Lennon/McCartney was increasingly a sing-along standard, particularly in the wake of the delightful double feature of the Beatles' Richard Lester–directed jukebox films, *A Hard Day's Night* (1964) and *Help!* (1965) and their abundantly appealing set of accompanying soundtracks.

"Norwegian Wood" was the second track on side one of *Rubber Soul*, the Beatles' sixth studio album. Released in December 1965, the record was brimming, with "Drive My Car," "Nowhere Man," "Michelle," "Girl," "I'm Looking Through You," "In My Life," "If I Needed Someone," and "Run for Your Life" among its striking 14-song sequence. *Rubber Soul*'s initial impression and widespread influence endured to indisputable sanctified status among "all-time great albums." The record's creative and competitive impact on alpha Beach Boy Brian Wilson are particularly well documented. Wilson states unequivocally that he was "blown away," proclaiming *Rubber Soul* to be standard setting and life changing as "the first album [he] ever heard that every song went together like no album ever made before."[14] Professedly, the enraptured Wilson immediately proceeded to his piano, where he composed a set of songs, among them the renowned "God Only Knows," for the ambitious and sophisticated *Pet Sounds*, which was released less than six months later in May 1966.

Within *Rubber Soul*'s singular totality, "Norwegian Wood" carried its own significance. The instrumentation, featuring George Harrison's exotic sitar strands that were inspired by Ravi Shankar, foreshadowed, if not announced, Eastern, rāga, and psychedelic sounds that would soon be inserted into rock arrangements. The dulcet, extramarital account in "Norwegian Wood" attracted a crowd of covers. Edwards's version was among a striking sum of 14 that were recorded during 1966, with Brian Hyland, Waylon Jennings, Jan and Dean, and the Kingston Trio among the cadre of interpreters.

Song selection and Seeburg sabotage aside, there was some artist accountability as well attributed to Dunwich's second single falling flat. Edwards's lackluster rendition of "Norwegian Wood" was likewise less inspired. In Jarema's critical characterization, the recording was "an unexceptional single" that "neither touched on the wild abandon" of Edwards's earlier Dunwich-produced obscurity doing Bob Dylan's "Quit Your Low Down Ways" nor "hinted at the innovative music" that would soon follow when Edwards formed H.P. Lovecraft, Chicago's signature psychedelic group, in 1967.[15]

Macabre Music Undercurrents

H.P. Lovecraft emerged, or submerged, from the commercially neglected underground by way of folkster Edwards's in-house session presence at Dunwich. Faithful to the Dunwich Productions formula of adapting Brit hits, Edwards recorded a version of Chip Taylor's "Any Way That You Want Me," a Troggs' hit in the UK. Traut and Badonsky coupled the cover with an earlier Edwards outtake, "It's All Over for You." The single was released on Philips Records early in 1967 under the moniker H.P. Lovecraft rather than as a George Edwards solo record. With a name and a single in place, all that was needed was recruitment of band members. The initial H.P. Lovecraft lineup included Tony Cavallari on lead guitar, drummer Mike Tegza, and Tom Skidmore on bass briefly, before being replaced early on by former Shadows of Knight guitarist Jerry McGeorge. Classically trained multi-instrumentalist Dave Michaels was a complementary creative keystone to Edwards. The versatile Michaels's operatic range vocally, combined with his musical proficiencies on organ and piano, harpsichord, clarinet, and recorder, shaped the band's distinctive sonic palette, haunting ambience, and striking harmonies. H.P. Lovecraft's fusion of folk rock elements with a psychedelia sound was conceptually and stylistically more album oriented than it was singles suited. Their cover of the folk gospel "Wayfaring Stranger" that preceded their self-titled debut album release failed to chart in September 1967.

Driving the variations on H.P. Lovecraft was a nine-piece orchestra that produced a prevalent eerie musical undercurrent throughout the record true to the band's namesake's "macabre tales and poems of Earth populated by another race" (as was printed on the album's back cover). The sequence scattered a few originals in jazz ("That's How Much I Love You Baby [More or Less]") and vaudevillian veins ("The Time Machine") in between cover versions that included Chet Powers's hippie anthem to brotherhood, "Let's Get Together," which was popularized the same year (as "Get Together") by the Youngbloods, Randy Newman's "I've Been Wrong Before," and folk tunes from notables Travis Edmonson ("The Drifter") and Fred Neil ("That's the Bag I'm In," "Country Boy & Bleecker Street"). The album centerpiece was (the aforementioned) "The White Ship," a sprawling 6:30 atmospheric opus based on a Lovecraft short story. The muted soundscape featured baroque harpsichord passages, droning feedback, murmuring harmonies, and the chiming of an authentic 1811 ship's bell, which contributed to the production's "wavering, foggy beauty," as characterized by music historian/journalist Richie Unterberger.[16] "The White Ship" in its epic entirety was a favorite throughout the FM underground, while the edited single failed to chart on *Billboard*'s Hot 100.

Following a bi-coastal tour to promote their debut album, H.P. Lovecraft promptly and permanently departed its midwestern roots for the West Coast sphere with its conducive counterculture climate. Without calculation or cliché, the band's ephemeral weirdness and psychedelic sound had significant standing within the hippie population. In San Francisco's Bay Area, H.P. Lovecraft's inventive live performances were particularly well received and their album sales, though modest, spiked in the locality. Fabled concert promoter Bill Graham took notice, leading to H.P. Lovecraft bookings at the renowned Bay Area music venues the Fillmore and Winterland Ballroom. In a compact 1967–68 parenthesis, the group skillfully translated their elaborate music and production qualities on record into an imaginative presence and prowess performing live. The addition of Jeffrey Boyan from the group Saturday's Children on bass and vocals enhanced H.P. Lovecraft's live act. Boyan replaced McGeorge, who left a few months after the band's relocation west. H.P. Lovecraft accumulated an extensive résumé of California concerts and tours, playing on the same bills with Traffic, Buffalo Springfield, the Youngbloods, Pink Floyd, the Who, Jefferson Airplane, Moby Grape, and the mythical Haight-Ashbury's favorite freaks, the Grateful Dead, among other bands. In between their extensive touring dates, H.P. Lovecraft trended with bands benefiting from commercial tie-ins, cutting several radio and television spots for Ban roll-on deodorant.

In September 1968, H.P. Lovecraft released an unimaginatively titled follow-up album, *H.P. Lovecraft II*. Less focused than their debut, though expanding its musical approach, *II* featured another Lovecraft literary interpretation, "At the Mountain of Madness," along with a Brewer and a Shipley cover, "Keeper of the Keys," and several Edwards originals among its nine songs. Album sales fell short of charting. Signs of the band's unraveling that steadily surfaced late in '68, with Michaels leaving to return to school, culminated in collapse by early 1969.

There was the usual career continuity and crossover. Edwards returned to solo folk performance, while Tegza joined Bangor Flying Circus, a progressive/psych rock group that included Alan DeCarlo and former Shadows of Knight members David "Hawk" Wolinksi and Tom Schiffour (whom Tegza replaced on drums). The band's lone long play release, a self-titled album on Dunhill, peaked just inside the *Billboard* 200 in 1969. After the Circus left town and split up, Wolinski and DeCarlo formed Madura, which released two albums for Columbia in the early 1970s. Tegza was involved with a pair of H.P. Lovecraft variants, Lovecraft and Love Craft. Each group produced an album—the psych-free rock *Valley of the Moon* (1970, Reprise) and funk *We Love You Whoever You Are* (1975, Mercury)—with makeshift lineups that included Chicagoan recruits from Aorta (Jim Donlinger, Michael Been) and the Buckinghams (Marty Grebb).

Casting Shadows:
"Twenty Other Bands Around Chicago"

Each part of Chicago had their fave rave rock group.
—Bill Traut[17]

The Dunwich recording catalog was blatantly singles saturated, a reflection, in part, of the 45 revolutions per minute reverberating through the Top 40 times. And, despite popularity generated by local live performances and radio airplay, many bands simply did not have enough quality material to fill two sides of an album. The groups that did, such as H.P. Lovecraft, the Mauds, and American Breed, landed on labels outside Dunwich with national distribution, Mercury, Philips, and Acta among them. On the flip side of its substantial singles, Dunwich's long play inventory was a short list. The number of albums released exclusively on Dunwich totaled a mere three: the two Shadows of Knight LPs in 1966—*Gloria* and *Back Door Men*—and the rhythm-and-blues debut by funk and soul singer Amanda Ambrose, *Amanda* (1967). Still, the label's diminutive album discography did not imply a lack of production, as the company maintained a hyperactive roster of artists with its singles stock sustaining from recording to release as Dunwich Productions.[18]

Jimy Sohns's grousing grievance with Dunwich's "hot potato" recruiting reaction in the wake of the Shadows of Knight's breakthrough—suggesting that the record label "went out and signed up like 20 other bands around Chicago"—may have been a slightly inflated estimate, though not appreciably exaggerated.[19] Opportunity knocked, banged, if not kicked down the Dunwich door, shouting and sounding loudly from the stages of area teen clubs.

The Dunwich label's roster was packed, man. Local bands prevailed, with a few outlying midwestern intonations echoing and zig-zagging beyond Chicagoland's surroundings: 160 miles to south central Peoria, Illinois (the Warner Brothers); from there, 89 miles slightly southeast across to Champaign-Urbana, located 135 miles outside Chicago, and crossways into neighboring Indiana, 125 west to Indianapolis (Idle Few, Sounds Unlimited), which is 183 miles southeast of Chicago. Adoptions crossed over another state line into Michigan: 95 miles easterly to Niles, Michigan (the all-female group Luv'd Ones) and another 150 from there on to Ann Arbor (The Five Bucks, Byzantine Empire).

One single at a time, spinning and spanning the peripheries to the popular, the Dunwich label's lineup captured a representative profile of Chicagoland's mid-1960s happening teen scene and its sound, from garage to psych and some suburban and South Side soul. A punk presence was prevalent, along with routine riffs and recognizable ricochets from the Rolling Stones, Yardbirds, and Animals. Word jazz vocalist Ken Nordine's "Bachman"/"Crimson and Olive" (1966) was an anomaly on Dunwich. Nordine's novelty 45 featured a Johann Sebastian Bach homage with a color recitation on the flip side.[20] Among the Chicago-based Dunwich affiliates, the American Breed (on the ancillary Acta label) was the sole subsequent suburband to the Shadows of Knight that was able to navigate some national notoriety. The majority of the label's local groups—the Knaves, Saturday's Children, Del-Vetts, Banshees, Rovin' Kind, Little Boy Blues—remained relative obscurities and local heroes. Most were confined to circulation in the regional underground and clubscape as lively live acts and one-hit wonders or no-hitters who recorded a catchy debut or intermittent single and maybe a B-side that received airplay on WLS and WCFL. Despite the regional restraint and standard band transience marked by name changes and personnel turnover, many of these short-term groups and/or their signature song attained "garage classic" status over time, reemerging decades later as featured forgottens, deep tracks, and buried treasure on an array of regional, era, genre, and record label reissue collections and cool cult compilations.

Following the Edwards flop, Nordine's novelty, and a Luv'd Ones Rufus Thomas cover, "Walkin' the Dog," The Things to Come were next in the Dunwich '66–67 singles queue. The signing of the punk suburband from the conservative community of Wheaton, 30 minutes west of Chicago, signaled Dunwich's plans to echo, if not duplicate, their Top 10 approach that was employed with the Shadows of Knight and "Gloria." The fortuitous formula was simply to uncover a British Invasion tune, whether A- or B-side, that was not well-known or receiving radio airplay stateside and then have the band record and release an American version before anyone else did.

Traut was prone to tinkering with Dunwich roster recruits, altering band names and personnel as frequently as musical styles. He took his fine-tuning an idiosyncratic step farther with the Things to Come. Convinced that British branding would be beneficial, Traut decided to alter the band members' actual names, assigning them Anglo aliases. In the curious recasting of the Things to Come lineup, Ken Utterback became "Ken Ashley," Richard Cureton "George Heatherton," and Tom Mirabile "Keith St. Michael." Drummer Cliff Harrison's name was deemed "English enough" and he was spared the identity makeover. The "Things to Come" name itself was also Brit-fluenced, purportedly appropriated/inspired by the Yardbirds' song "Shape of Things." The name also foreshadowed the fictional Max Frost and the Troopers' psych-anthem "(Nothing can change) The Shape of Things to Come," featured in the counterculture classic film *Wild in the Streets* (1968).

As was a curious commonplace during the era and with many of the Chicagoland bands and their initial incarnations, there happened to be overlooked name duplication. In this case, with another Things to Come from Long Beach, California, a group that included Russ Kunkel as its drummer. Kunkel became a prominent session musician and member of the renowned Section, which backed a significant cross section of 1970s singer-songwriters in studio and on tours. The California Things to Come recorded and released a single, "Sweetgina," on Starfire Records in 1966.

The same year, in July 1966, Dunwich released the Wheaton, Illinois, Things to Come's excitable version of jazz and blues pianist Mose Allison's "I'm Not Talkin'." Their rousing rendition more closely echoed the Yardbirds' hyper interpretation with chord interplay between guitar gods Eric Clapton and Jeff Beck. Each version accented the emphatic "Well, that's all I got to say" couplet connecting "I'm Not Talkin'." Recorded at what was considered "garage group haven" at Sound Studios, the single also featured an impressive mid-tempo B-side ballad, "Till the End." The Things to Come were among the era's and region's long list of one-and-dones who delivered a striking single—an "undiluted masterpiece" of the garage rock genre that was enhanced by their energetic live performances—and then mysteriously vanished into 1960s oblivion.[21]

Pile Drivers and Protopunk Pioneers

The Knaves narrative not only perpetuated the prevalent punk pattern with similar blink-of-an-eye brevity but also was tinted with Chicago Mafia associations. With its roots across the Chicagoland northwest border suburbs—Morton Grove, Niles, Des Plaines, and Skokie, a predominantly Jewish suburb—the group was fronted by Howard Berkman, the music mentor who brought experience from previous membership in the Jesters, which included Steve Goodman, destined for fame as a folkie. Characterized by Knaves' drummer Gene Lubin as "a sort of blissed-out Buddah with a mischievous smile,"[22] Goodman may be best known for writing "City of New Orleans," the Illinois Central railway tune popularized by Arlo Guthrie in 1972 and a hit for Willie Nelson in 1984, among its many recorded renditions. Joining Berkman and Lubin in the initial Knaves lineup, "faking their way through 'Louie, Louie,'" were Johnno Hulbert (guitar, harmonica, vocals), Neal Pollack (bass), and Mark Feldman (guitar, vocals), alleged to have been recruited because of his resemblance to a member of the British hitmakers the Dave Clark Five. Stewart Einstein was enlisted as a replacement for Pollack after he was drafted in 1967.

The Knaves "came on like a group of Jerry Lee Lewis types playing hard-ass blues" and a rocking repertoire of British band covers, with four guitars and loud drums that attracted crowds at area high schools and the city's university grounds at Loyola and the University of Illinois Circle Campus. Thanks to an "ancient booking agent," the band paid further dues for a year circulating in what Berkman described as the "Go Go club road house wise-guy night club scene."[23] Before settling in as regulars playing the teen club circuit, the Knaves' early live performance path extended from Rush Street to Old Town to the South Side into Indiana, with Like Young, Pynk Phynk, Big Toe, The Way Out, The Limit, Mousetrap, Goldfinger, Bourbon a Go Go, Second Story, My Sister's Place, the Interlude Lounge, and Club Normandy among the many venues they were booked at. "At the end of the week sometimes we'd give our check to the cashier and they'd only give you two-thirds of the money," recalled Berkman. "If you mentioned it, they'd tell you: that's the way it works."[24]

Among the band's more conspicuous supporters were the Trilling brothers, local tile contractors with alleged organized crime affiliations. Bob and Geno Trilling adopted the Knaves because, according to Pollack, "they thought it would be cool to have a pet band" (though "house band" seemed suitable). The brothers employed the band members on construction jobs, where they had to tuck their long hair under their hard hats at job sites. The Trillings also let the Knaves practice in their floor tile storeroom. Neither the familiar Chicago "mob" suspicions, nor claims that their father was a bodyguard for notorious gangster Al Capone, nor their discovery that the brothers were armed when accompanying the Knaves on gigs deterred the band members from the alliance with the Trillings. "Back in the '60s, young people assumed that everything—especially the music business—was run either by mob, the government, or Wall Street," recollected Lubin. Echoing their bandmate, Berkman and Pollack expressed a similar shrugging indifference, demystifying the Trillings as "night club hangers on" and "junior wise-guy wannabes" who were not really connected to organized crime.[25]

Perhaps a consequence of exposure to the Trilling posturing, the Knaves fully embraced their name, a common Shakespearean signifier for "infidel," "scoundrel," "rascal," and "rogue." A more flattering usage references one of four face cards in a deck bearing the image of a young prince. Avant-gardians in attitude, look, and lyric, with leanings toward the British thugs the Pretty Things and the Troggs as much as the Kinks and Hollies, the long-haired garagers adopted phony English accents and outfitted themselves in ruffled shirts, morning coats with tails, and Beatles boots while claiming to be from Liverpool, which was not a Chicagoland suburb. Pollack described the band's dysfunctional, juvenile delinquent demeanor:

> We were driving, insistent, raw, confrontational, aggressive, and "in your face" ... we were all into music and had been listening to it all our lives so, consciously or subconsciously, we were influenced by everything we had ever heard. Bottom line is that it's all intervals. We were doing it balls to the wall, redlining on all eight cylinders. We weren't trying to fool anybody and were putting out the most honest expression possible of how we felt. No hype, no bullshit. Just pile-driving our anger, confusion and frustration down the throats of anyone who would listen. We wanted the world to know that if it wanted to fight with us, we might lose, but we were going to get enough licks in so that it knew it was in a fight.[26]

The Knaves elevated their songwriting emphasis beyond teenage relationships and romance to rage against The Establishment. Listen no further than the group's loud lone single, "Leave Me Alone," an edgy anti-authority anthem composed by Berkman and Hulbert. On the sound surface, the lashing song, laced with harmonica, is an edgier, more unrestrained reverberation of the Things to Come's "I'm Not Talkin'," with point-blank, piss-off posturing that pulls no punches punctuating couplets: "why don't you choke yourself and leave me alone."

"Leave Me Alone" and its contrasting folk rock flip, "The Girl I Threw Away," were recorded at Chess Studios in 1966 and initially issued as a single on the local

Glen label late in the year. During the same studio session, under production supervision of area promoter Paul Gallis, the Knaves recorded several songs that were unreleased, including a curiously incongruous cover of Cole Porter's American Songbook and *Casablanca* classic, "As Time Goes By." After Gallis managed to navigate the spikey single into the WCFL rotation, Dunwich swooped in, signing the Knaves and securing the "Leave Me Alone" master and its publishing rights. A follow-up record never happened, however. The Dunwich Productions recording, "Inside Out"/"Your Stuff," lingered on acetate. Though the songs featured a solid and simplified sound with notable Troggs tinges rather than revved up rave, the record remained unreleased. Speculation was that local radio resistance from WLS and WCFL was prompted by the veiled sexual suggestiveness on the record's A- and B-sides. Timing was also a sway, as months earlier, the local Mauds' cover of soul duo Sam & Dave's Stax smash, "Hold On, I'm Comin'," aroused content controversy with Chicago's radio rotation gatekeepers.

The Knaves broke up around mid–1967, with familiar fragmenting factors contributing to their fate: marriage, family, college, finances, drugs, drinking, and the draft. Oddly, their future was literally stolen, as larceny proved to be the notorious nail in the Knaves' coffin. According to Lubin, "the real killer was when some dastardly evil perpetrator drove off with our van full of instruments and equipment and no one had the money to even buy a guitar pick after that."[27]

Another band from the Skokie community, Little Boy Blues, is a frequent fine-print footnote in the Dunwich discography discussion. Though not initially on the label's roster, the group was loosely linked with George Badonsky and licensed with Yuggoth Music. During its arc between 1965 and 1969, the band released recordings on the local labels IRC and Ronco, and the Mercury subsidiary Fontana. The group's original members were University of Illinois at Chicago students Lowell Shyette (lead vocals), Paul Ostroff (lead guitar), Ray Levin (bass), and James Boyce (drums). Billy McColl also contributed vocals. Commonly considered protopunk pioneers, Little Boy Blues' sound proceeded from blues-based beginnings to borrowed British Invasion ("Look at the Sun"/"Love for a Day" [1965]) and back to blues (Willie Dixon's "I'm Ready" [1966]). Both were IRC releases that were Chicago favorites. The band's final recording for IRC, "I Can Only Give You Everything" (1966), marked a musical transition to a tougher, more aggressive sound. Little Boy Blues' noisy rendition of the Tommy Scott/Phil Coulter composition was packaged with a picture sleeve, perhaps making their recording a more conspicuous single situated in the middle of a cover crowd that included a familiar Van Morrison and Them version early in 1966, and interpretations by the Troggs and MC5 that followed in 1967.

With their series of songs popular on Chicago radio and a weekly club residence in the region, Little Boy Blues seemed positioned for a breakthrough beyond the Midwest. They landed gigs opening for international and national acts such as the Rolling Stones, Lovin' Spoonful, and the Association, and received further national exposure with an appearance on Dick Clark's weekday afternoon *American Bandstand* spinoff, *Where the Action Is*.

In September 1966, however, in a familiar sign of the tumultuous times, Uncle Sam intervened: Shyette was drafted into the army. With Frank Biner replacing their lead vocalist, the band left IRC for another local label, Ronco, a K-Tel counterpart. In late 1966, Little Boy Blues recorded their fourth single, "The Great Train Robbery." Produced by Badonsky associate Steve Heller, published with Yuggoth Music, and released in 1967, the record is commonly considered an acid/punk garage masterpiece. The recording features a harmonica opening simulating a train whistle, fastened to forceful fuzz driving, and a nursery rhyme transformation "Rain rain go away" into "Train train don't go away, I can't come another day."

Despite the arresting single, the band never quite solidified or regained momentum in the wake of Shyette's call to duty. The customary personnel changes and creative conflicts ensued, complicated by counterculture undercurrents. Disgruntled with the musical direction of the band, McColl and Ostroff left as the group moved further into psychedelia, playing at "be-ins" and headlining counterculture clubs the Cheetah and Kinetic Playground.[28]

Before the original members completely dispersed, Levin, Ostroff, and Boyce, along with Biner, recorded "You Dove Deep in My Soul" during a mid–1967 Dunwich session apparently supervised by Badonsky. Dunwich documentarian Jeff Jarema labeled the unreleased gem "the last great Little Boy Blues track," with the band slipping into a more soulful slant, accentuated by Biner's James Brown vocal aspirations. While the song features the familiar fuzz, there is also a flute (from Levin)— "never a good sign on a punk record," Jarema amusingly observes before concluding that "You Dove Deep in My Soul" serves as a "palatable middle ground" between their previous "The Great Train Robbery" and later "stoned jazz rock moves."[29]

Amidst the group's continual attrition that claimed Biner and Boyce, Little Boy Blues' reconfigured remainders and replacements—Bill Pollack (guitar), Marc Coplon (vocals), Bill Mooney (drums)—managed enough material to record a major label LP, *In the Woodland of Weir*, released on the Mercury imprint Fontana in 1968. "Patchwork" is perhaps the kindest and most convenient critical characterization of the last-gasp album. Little Boy Blues disbanded the following year in 1969.

Pride and Joy of the Lakeshore

The Del-Vetts flirted with being a '66 centerpiece for Dunwich, releasing multiple singles with some chart presence on the garage psychedelic sound cusp between September and November and through 1967. Formed circa 1963, the Del-Vetts activated as a quartet predominantly playing surf rock instrumentals inspired by the Ventures and Chuck Berry covers across the teen dance circuit in clubs such as the Rolling Stone and Cellar in the affluent suburbs of Chicago's north shore, Winnetka among them. Traut, acutely in tune with the territorial rule of suburban musical map, considered the Del-Vetts "the Northside's Shadows of Knight." "The Shadows of Knight definitely ruled Schaumburg and Arlington Heights, the northwest side of town," explained Traut. "The Lakeshore side of town—Lake Forest, Highland Park, and everything from Evanston north—belonged to the Del-Vetts."[30]

Traut, who lived on Chicago's North Side, followed the "noise" about the Del-Vetts written in the local newspapers and saw the group play live numerous times. Their high-volume energy and showmanship stood out. During one concert at their hometown Highland Park High School, they drove Corvettes into the gymnasium and jumped out and onto the stage to perform. The initial outfit consisted of Jim Lauer (lead vocals/lead guitar), Bob Good (bass), Lester Goldboss (guitar), and Paul Wade (drums). By mid-decade, following some personnel shuffling, the lineup solidified into the lively Lauer, Good (shifting to rhythm guitar/harmonica), Jack Burchall (bass), and Roger Deatherage (drums), and the group began to work with Bill Traut cutting tracks. A Seeburg jukebox single soon followed as prelude to signing with Dunwich. True to Traut form, the Seeburg song selection was a catchy cover, "Little Latin Lupe Lu," with a hot rod revved instrumental B-side, "Ram Charger." The original, composed by Righteous Brother Bill Medley, charted in the 40s on *Cashbox* and *Billboard* in 1963, and was subsequently re-recorded during the decade by Minneapolis surf rockers the Chancellors, the Kingsmen, and Mitch Ryder and the Detroit Wheels, whose version reached the Top 20 in 1966.

The Del-Vetts sound echoed the Yardbirds' fuzzy commotion and rave-up technique that resounded throughout the mid–1960s stateside garage genre. Perhaps the most ear-catching exemplar of the innovation was the Count Five's "Psychotic Reaction," which reached #5 nationally in the summer of 1966. Beyond its chart success, the song pointed toward a more psychedelic approach in musical method and attitude, one that invited improvisation and allowed for experimentation in tone and technique. Identifying this stylistic transition and the early psych-garage palette, Ann Johnson and Mike Stax detail the musicological incorporation by "Psychotic Reaction" of two rave-up sections as "the lead and rhythm both making some unconventional sounds, and the lead climbing up the scale with fuzztone effect ... accompanied by the rhythm scratching atonally in counterpoint to the drums" and a "subtle tape phasing effect adds to the overall mood of weirdness."[31]

The distinctive double-time rave-up method and moodiness was effectively and energetically adapted by the Del-Vetts on their first Dunwich single, "Last Time Around"/"Everytime." The influence of Jeff Beck's solo from "You're a Better Man Than I" is unmistakable. Traut was taken aback—or in this case, taken aBeck—at Lauer's note-for-note semblance, admitting, "I was so unknowledgeable about rock and roll at that point that I didn't realize that he'd copied the solo until long after the record was out."[32] Recorded in May 1966 at Universal Studio, the Del-Vetts' bold Dunwich debut was suitably sequenced and situated alongside and in between other punkish singles issued by the label—the Shadows of Knight's "Oh Yeah," days after the Things to Come's "I'm Not Talkin'," and two months before the Banshees' "Project Blue," an August release. Written by Lauer's friend, Dennis Dahlquist, whose contributions earned him the sobriquet "the fifth Del-Vett," "Last Time Around" was a top request locally at WLS, reaching #26 on the summer's charts and earning the Del-Vetts a reputation as one of Chicago's most promising young bands.

The Del-Vetts auspicious aura may have been modestly enhanced by a touch of vogue. The same month the band was recording their snarling single, Del-Vett front Lauer appeared on the May 13, 1966, cover of the popular weekly national publication *Life* magazine. The photo portrays Lauer along with three other lads in a groovy Carnaby Street, London look—dashing double-breasted jackets, bell-bottom flairs, boots, plaids, mop top coifs—posing on the landmark Michigan Avenue bridge over the Chicago River in the Marina Towers vicinity with a Wrigley Building background. The spotlight shined anonymously, with the cover caption simply identifying the foursome as "Chicago school students take to new mod gear," staging in advance of the "revolution in male clothes" fashion feature inside the *Life* issue. Cool, rather than school, apparently was the key modeling measure for the photo shoot and accompanying article. While Lauer may have fit the age group criteria, he was actually no longer a student, having dropped out of Stevenson High School in Lincolnshire following a principle versus principal clash over Lauer's nonconformist stance on school haircut standards, a familiar generational flashpoint and era chasm. Lauer and his cover boy companions were recommended to the magazine article's author by Cesar Rotondi, owner of the Man at Ease clothing shop located north of North Avenue on Wells Street in Chicago's historical hip(pie) Old Town neighborhood. Rotondi, who was at the fashionable forefront importing the latest London styles to Chicago, identified the four teenagers as typical young customers who frequented his trendy boutique. As a result, *Life* happened.

The Del-Vetts follow-up single, "I Call My Baby STP"/"That's the Way It Is," flopped. A late release in November 1966, the song's disappointing reception may have been evenly surprising and probable. The presumed momentum from the popular punk predecessor, "Last Time Around," did not sustain and instead mirrored the pattern of unfulfilled promise of ensuing singles that even a huge hit such as "Gloria" could not guarantee for the Shadows of Knight and their follow-up 45 "Oh Yeah" a year earlier. Bouncy and brief at 2:15, with Jan and Dean hot rod resonance, "I Call My Baby STP" underperformed despite product endorsement, appealing picture sleeve packaging, and an iconic STP decal included inside. The "STP" letters were abbreviated from "scientifically treated petroleum," a popular oil additive that was branded as "the racer's edge." The song's promotional petroleum product tie-in was blatant, the connection originating from a friend of Traut's who worked in advertising and had STP as a client. A chauvinistic undercurrent extends from the song's title to lyric innuendo that reaches a bit beyond Beach Boys basics—"hottest little wheels of the land," "hottest machine anywhere around," "take her out she's gonna score for me"—to the image on the 45's jacket, which portrays the Del-Vetts uniformly dressed in suit jackets and neckties sitting in a Corvette convertible (an STP sticker pasted prominently on the passenger side windshield) and gazing at a woman walking out of the frame.

The endorsement deal with "I Call My Baby STP" may have been a soul-selling sign for the Del-Vetts. Or, in the least, a turning point or a loss of innocence. In early 1967, with Dunwich restructuring, the Del-Vetts changed their name to the Pride and Joy. Though such improbable alterations were usually instigated by Traut, in this case the Del-Vetts acquiesced to their fan club's peculiar preference for the moniker makeover. In the conversion, the band, for the most part, abandoned their bite for a softer, more melodic sound. Pride and Joy's subsequent single for Dunwich, "Girl," another Dahlquist composition that had more Hollies harmony than Yardbirds riffage, reached #27 locally in May 1967. Its contrasting B-side, the denser "If You're Ready," appeared to be an attempt to revive the raunch and bring back the bite of "Last Time Around."

In follow-that-dream fashion from the Midwest to the West, Pride and Joy pursued a low-budget movie deal in California with Dick Clark Productions. The timing appeared to be a Monkees see–Monkees do move seeking *Where the Action Is*. The group shot scenes and recorded eight songs for the unreleased film, *Somebody Help Me*, the tentative title borrowed from a song by Steve Winwood and his brother Muff's band, the Spencer Davis Group, that Pride and Joy performed for the movie. Another soundtrack cut, "We've Got a Long Way to Go," written by the legendary hit songwriting partnership Cynthia Weil and Barry Mann, was eventually released as a Dunwich Production on the Acta label, a Dot Records subsidiary in Los Angeles. Despite its songwriting pedigree, the song surprisingly stiffed with no chart placement. Amidst a shifting music industry landscape, an unsettling outsider sense within the West Coast scene, and the band's internal creative differences and personnel departures, the once-Del-Vetts turned the Pride and Joy broke up the following year in 1968.

A Country Rock Quintet and Columbia Quartet

Various stylistic strands steadily surfaced amid Dunwich's prevalent punk presence. Among the more conspicuous was the Rovin' Kind, who inserted a rare trace of country into Chicagoland's garage soundscape. Before their formation in 1965, the group's members had accumulated considerable experience performing and recording with other teen bands dating to the late 1950s in south suburban Harvey. Co-founding front and accomplished guitarist Paul Cotton's extensive music résumé included local groups the Capitols, Carol Vega & Trio, and the instrumental outfit the Mus-Twangs, who released a surf-style single of Irving Berlin's "Marie"/"Roch Lamond" on the local Nero label. The record was picked up by the Chicago-based Mercury Records and distributed nationally on the company's Smash Records subsidiary.[33]

Mid-decade, the Alabama-born "King" Cotton, along with bassist Frank Bartell (née Bortoli) and drummer Fred Pappalardo (née Page), formed the Gentrys. The trio solidified into a popular quintet featuring a relatively rare double lead guitar configuration when joined by guitarist Kal David (Raskin) and keyboardist Mike Anthony. David had been the front for the Exceptions, a soul/pop/rock outfit formed in 1962 in Rockford, 90 miles northwest of Chicago. That band included notables Marty Grebb, a drummer/multi-instrumentalist who later became a Buckingham, and bassist Peter Cetera, who moved on to The Big Thing. Bigger things followed in 1967 when Grebb joined Terry Kath, Lee Loughnane, Robert Lamm, James Pankow, Danny Seraphine, and Walt Parazaider as the Chicago Transit Authority, a precursor that sooner than later became "Chicago" in 1969. The eventual horn rock supergroup's truncated title was in large part to avoid legal entanglement with the city's operator of mass transit. The Exceptions cut several singles in the early 1960s that were released on the local labels Ardore and Tollie, a Vee-Jay imprint followed by a cut on Capitol in 1966, "The Girl from New York"/"As Far as I Can See." The group also recorded a reverent five-song EP, *Rock 'N' Roll Mass*, in 1966 for the Flair label, a subsidiary of Modern Records that formed in the 1950s with a roster that included Elmore James, Richard Berry, and Ike Turner. The Catholic garage rock set, though lacking confessional songs in its repertoire, included adaptations of hymnal standards "Lord Have Mercy"; "Glory to God"; "Holy, Holy, Holy"; "Our Father"; and "Lamb of God." Despite the Exceptional sincerity with the prayerful playlist, the religious rotation invited and invoked secular sarcasm, amusing associations, and playfully non-pious parallels with the crosstown heathens Shadows of Knight song "Gloria."

A name change was imminent for the Midwest Gentrys, considering that "the other" Gentrys, a Memphis-based band, landed a single, "Keep on Dancing," at #4 on the *Billboard* Hot 100 in 1965. Their hit featured a false fade and drum fill to get the song to just over two minutes and was bouncier than the doo-wop rendition recorded by the Avantis two year earlier. The Top 10 tune led to national exposure for the Memphis group across the triad of television teen dance shows—*Shindig!*, *Hullabaloo*, and *Where the Action Is*—and on tours with the Beach Boys and Sonny and Cher. As a result, the Chicagoland Gentrys pragmatically retitled to "the Rovin' Kind" to avoid duplication. The name was presumably derived from a lyric in "Bound to Roam," a song written by band member Mike Anthony. However, the twin syndrome lingered, as the alteration to the Rovin' Kind was conspicuously comparable to another kind of band in the Chicagoland vicinity, the Wanderin' Kind. The folk group released a lone single, "Wynken, Blynken and Nod"/"Something I Can't Buy," on Dunwich in 1966.

The Rovin' Kind's new moniker was fairly fitting. The group drifted between multiple record labels with singles, beginning with "Everybody"/"Bound to Roam" in 1965 on another Chicago label, Contrapoint; followed by "Right on Time"/"Night People" on Roulette in 1966; before landing on Dunwich in December 1966, covering the Who's "My Generation" backed with a Beatles B-side, Lennon/McCartney's "Girl." The Rovin' Kind's Pete Townshend take, while more than a mere convenient American translation of a British classic, was not that distinctive either, agreeably resounding the thrust and stammering of the Who original. The single, though solid on both sides, stalled with little sway. In keeping with the Dunwich affinity for the familiar, the group's follow-up release in 1967 doubled down on commercial appeal with another admirable two-sided cover, the Tommy Boyce/Bobby Hart tune "She," which already had been recorded by the Monkees, paired with an exacting echo of John Sebastian's mellow-tronic Lovin' Spoonful tune "Didn't Want to Have to Do It."

The regional battle of the band winners maintained a persistent cover-concentrated live performance schedule, frequently alternating billings with Baby Huey & the Babysitters at clubs ranging from Busters to the Black Orchid in Stony Island. Among the better cash-compensated bands in the area, the Rovin' Kind's polished musicianship was in demand in studios and session work. At Dunwich, they also contributed to H.P. Lovecraft's first single, "Any Way That You Want Me," in 1966. Later the same year, the group backed WCFL disc jockey Barney Pip's novelty single on Smash Records, "You Really Turn Me On."

In 1968, the Rovin' Kind followed the Del-Vetts' flight pattern and name change precedent, and migrated west to Los Angeles. There, they connected with producer James William Guercio, a fellow Chicagoan with considerable cachet and imprint. Among other highlights, Guercio supervised the Chicago Transit Authority before they abbreviated into Chicago and produced the Buckinghams' string of highly successful singles in 1967. In what had become a trendy major label affiliation for Chicago-based bands—among the notable being the Buckinghams and Cryan' Shames—Guercio recruited the Rovin' Kind to Columbia Records, where they renamed again, this time as the Illinois Speed Press. Following "Right on Time"/"Night People," a single released on the Roulette label, their initial album in 1969 coincided with a trio of other Columbia inaugurations of fellow Chicagoland bands—the Chicago Transit Authority, the Flock, and Aorta. The four self-titled debuts were opportunely bundled in promotion as a professed "Chicago sound." The marketing strategy may have worked, or at least been a favorable factor, as all four records placed in the *Billboard* 200 album chart.

Chicago Transit Authority was a sprawling double album, highlighted by a sequence of standout singles that became standards in the band's brassy deep discography—"Does Anybody Know What Time It Is?," "Beginnings," and "Questions 67 and 68." Another track, "I'm a Man," was released as a single in the UK. Initial sales of the album were sluggish, perhaps hindered by the double record pricing. As *CTA*'s singles sustained on FM radio's album-oriented rock formats, the record climbed inside the Top 20. Sales subsequently certified gold, on the way to eventually attaining double platinum status. The staying power was striking, as the album lingered on the *Billboard* Hot 100 well into the 1970s, along with the band's subsequent

LP releases. *Chicago Transit Authority*'s 171-week stay set a record at the time for chart longevity. (The longest run, Pink Floyd's conceptual masterpiece *Dark Side of the Moon* [1973], eventually accumulated 1,000-plus weeks on the *Billboard* 200 album chart.) Chicago's debut album contributed to the band earning a Grammy nomination for Best New Artist of the Year, which was awarded to Crosby, Stills and Nash in 1970.

Illinois Speed Press, which settled modestly at #144, was the most eclectic and least brassy of the Chicagoland quartet of Columbia albums. The group's distinct dual lead guitar system spanned bluesy rock and bouncy acoustic with Southern rock and country strands. In one critic's view, the album "sounds at times like Chicago Transit Authority without the horns."[34] On a curiously humorous (liner) note, the comedy troupe Firesign Theatre contributed the newspaper-like inner sleeve transcript for the album. *Duet* followed in 1970, with Cotton's country-rock proficiencies and preferences at the forefront and co-founder David's blues-rock receding. The band folded shortly after the release. In the dispersal, the Illinois Speed Press's keystones continued. Kal David formed the Fabulous Rhinestones with ex-Electric Flag bassist Harvey Brooks in San Francisco in the early 1970s. Cotton was recruited to join the country-rock pioneers Poco, whose pronounced early lineup featured the briefly brilliant Buffalo Springfield refugees Richie Furay and Jim Messina (whom Cotton replaced), eventual Eagles Randy Meisner and Timothy B. Schmit, along with Rusty Young and George Grantham. Cotton remained with Poco until 2010, contributing significant songs along the way, among them "Heart of the Night," one of the band's biggest hits from one of their bestselling albums, *Legend*, in 1978.

The other pair of Columbia initiates, the Flock and Aorta, brought further variation to the Chicagoland music mix. The Flock's elongated eclecticism formed at the forefront of the "progressive rock" movement of the 1970s. As predecessors to their fellow local prog-rockers Styx, who emerged in 1972, the Flock's fusion unfolded into folk, blues, classical, and electric jazz, with plucking and wah-wah among its playful and complex arrangements. Songwriting was not a particular strength, with lyrics secondary to the instrumental emphasis. The group's stylistic stretching was highlighted by interplay between violin virtuoso Jerry Goodman and guitarist/vocalist Fred Glickstein. They were anchored by a rhythm section of Jerry Smith (bass) and Ron Karpman (drums), with Blood, Sweat & Tears–type horn section counterpoint provided by Rick Canoff (tenor sax), Frank Posa (trumpet), and Tom Webb (flute/sax/harmonica). The Flock's self-titled debut on Columbia contained only six songs, though the total running time reached 45 minutes. The shortest song was an expanded adaptation of the Kinks' "Tired of Waiting," which at 4:35 was two minutes longer than the Davies brothers' original. Two tracks in the six-song sequence—"Clown" and "Store Bought-Store Thought"—clocked in at 7:00 and 7:45, respectively, with the jazzy lines of "I Am the Tall Tree" at 5:37, and the concluding bluesy variation "Truth" winding down the album as a 15:25 fade. The group's stomping, swirling 1967 single on the Destination label, "Take Me Back," was a conspicuous absence from the debut LP. The song's handclaps and horns, an MG sound signature of the Monaco/Golden and Bobby Whiteside production trinity, provided a peppy, pleading, and unsung 2:35 prologue to the American Breed's "Bend Me, Shape Me."

The Flock's follow-up, *Dinosaur Swamps* (1971), was a less intriguing album than their debut. The record was dense and overproduced, with more fluctuation than flow musically. The album's cluttered repertoire ranged from psychedelia to country and folk tinges to spoken word and reverb. The band fell apart shortly after the album. The deflocking and fragmentation were largely spurred by Goodman's departure to join the Mahavishnu Orchestra, a jazz, psych, Indian music group who happened to be on the Columbia roster. The complex fusion ensemble was initially composed of John McLaughlin, Billy Cobham, Jan Hammer, and Rick Laird. Glickstein and the remaining Flock, primarily its rhythm section minus the horns, revived briefly to record a comeback album, *Inside Out* (1975).

Aorta was another Traut draftee for the Dunwich production roster. The group morphed out of the reconfigured Exceptions after its original members—Kal David, Marty Grebb, Peter Cetera, Denny Ebert—dispersed in different music directions and destinations. Their replacements—James Vincent Dondelinger (Donlinger), Jim Nyeholt, and Billy Herman—teamed with recruits Dan Hoagland (Hoogland) on tenor saxophone and bassist Bobby Jones and adopted the name Aorta in 1967.

In 1968, the group recorded a single, "The Shape of Things to Come," with Traut and Dunwich Productions for the Atlantic label. The same year, the formative version of that Barry Mann/Cynthia Weil composition was featured on the soundtrack of *Wild in the Streets*, produced by the independent American International Pictures, which specialized in low-budget teen film fare. Despite sharing a title, a similar daring spirit, and future gaze, the song was not derivative of or inspired by the H. G. Wells science fiction work from 1933, published two years after Aldous Huxley's *Brave New World*. Performed by Max Frost and the Troopers, which included comedian Richard Pryor portraying the band's drummer, the soundtrack version of "The Shape of Things to Come" emanates activist anthem qualities in its concise, resolute two-minute (1:57) advocacy and anticipation of new thoughts and dreams crowding out old realities with "revolution sweeping in like a fresh new breeze."[35] The fictional front Frost (Christopher Jones) is an archetypal activist antihero with a revolutionary rallying cry that includes voting rights for teenagers. The movie climaxes with Frost being elected president of the United States, then ordering everyone over age 30 into concentration camps, where they are forced to take LSD. Some of Frost and his Troopers' other protest songs, such as "14 or Fight," are as absurd as his political platform. "Shape of Things to Come" was recorded by the band the 13th Power but released under the film pseudonym "Max Frost and The Troopers" in order to capitalize on the movie's appeal to the youth audience. The inner label of Aorta's Atlantic 45 of "Shape of Things to Come" included a byline—"From A.I.P. Picture 'Wild in the Streets'"—above its production credits. The cross-media synergy proved an effective marketing strategy as the single eventually reached #22 on the charts.

Continuing from his supervision of the group's Atlantic single, Traut co-produced Aorta's self-titled debut album with Donlinger. The record's diverse and solid musicianship blended psychedelia, jazz, soul, folk, and rock, running a sound spectrum from fuzz guitar to strings and horns. Critical views were as varied as the album's arrangements, with characterizations misaligned from "startling" to "inventive" to "pretentious." Slight sales of their single "Strange" forecast a comparably low-level showing for *Aorta* on the *Billboard* album chart, placing at #167. In between recordings, the band toured regularly, opening for Led Zeppelin and Mothers of Invention, among other groups. *Aorta 2* followed early in 1970. Released on the Happy Tiger label in Los Angeles, the record had a radically different style that leaned toward country rock with Christian overtones. The band split shortly after, with personnel relocating briefly in editions of Rotary Connection and H.P. Lovecraft.

Girls with Guitars in the Garage

Dunwich's prevailing guys-in-the-garage gathering—a Midwest microcosm of the predominant male music mainstream—became genderfied with the signing of the full-female faction the Luv'd Ones. The most recognizable "girl groups," as they were branded in the era, were commonly characterized by soul, doo-wop harmonies and the (Phil) Spectorian wall of sound splendor. Among the majestics of the genre were a range that spanned Motowners such as the Supremes and Martha and the Vandellas to the Crystals, Dixie Cups, Chiffons, Ronettes, Shirelles, Blossoms, and Shangri-Las with a corpus of signature songs that included "Da Doo Ron Ron," "Chapel of Love," "Iko Iko," "He's So Fine," and "Leader of the Pack."

The Luv'd Ones personified a far less prevalent female profile at the time. They were girls with guitars. Electric, not acoustic. Rockers, rather than folk strummers and Joni Mitchell/Joan Baez aspirants. The proto-punk, proto-feminist group was also a Chicagoland outsider geographically, initially formed in the mid-1960s as the Tremolons in nearby Niles, Michigan. Following a single, "Please Let Me Know," backed with an instrumental, "Theme for a DJ," that was released on Wildwood Records in Benton Harbor, Michigan, the group changed labels—both record and band—signing with Dunwich as the Luv'd Ones.

Charlotte "Char" Vinnedge was the group's creative and musical centerpiece as songwriter, singer, lead guitarist, and artwork designer. She also handled equipment maintenance duties and drove the band van on tours. The rest of the Luv'd Ones was filled out by Char's sister Chris (bass), Mary Gallagher (rhythm guitar), and Faith Orem (drums). The band's swirling sound provided a fitting fuzzed-out framework for Char Vinnedge's icy vocals and edgy lyrics laced with somber shades and jealousy themes.

The Luv'd Ones were an early entry in the Dunwich label's singles swell of 1966, surfacing in the wake of the overshadowing "Gloria" and the underwhelming George Edwards single but before "Oh Yeah." The first of their three releases, "Walking the Dog," was a cover of Rufus Thomas's Stax single from 1963, which had in a short time reached standard status, accumulating a lengthy list of interpreters that included the Rolling Stones, Johnny Rivers, the Kingsmen, Sonics, Everly Brothers, and Mitch Ryder. The Luv'd Ones' debut's B-side, "I'm Leaving You," encored as a flip to the pulsating teen tune "Dance Kid Dance," with the single "Come Back"/ "Stand Tall" issued in between.

Though at the female forefront as Dunwich debutantes, the Luv'd Ones were not the only anomalies crossing the feminine folk divide to rock the Chicagoland garage. The Daughters of Eve, local teens from Chicago's Rogers Park/Edgewater neighborhoods—specifically Senn High School—emerged during the same time frame. Preceding the Luv'd Ones, the Daughters of Eve formed in late 1965 under the aegis of Carl Bonafede, a disc jockey known as "The Screaming Wildman" and a managerial mastermind who reconfigured the Centuries and Pulsations into the Chicagoland hitmakers the Buckinghams. Bonafede envisioned assembling a "sister group" to complement, and capitalize on, the Buckinghams, such a maneuver unique and unconventional in the mid–1960s male music mainstream. Even before putting together the group, Bonafede had to convince and/or charm parents into allowing their pre-teen/teenage daughters to join a band that was not the school marching musical unit. Bonafede managed to get parental consent, at least in the short term, though tensions persisted after the band was formed. He first proceeded to recruit singer/guitarists Judy Johnson and Marsha Tomal, before adding 13-year-old Andrea (Andee) Levin on bass and drummer Debi Pomeroy to complete the Daughters lineup. Marilou Davison and Lori Wax succeeded Levin on bass in the Eve-olution.

The "Daughters of Eve" name originated from Pomeroy's father, a pastor, recognized as "the Rock 'N' Roll Preacher" for his enthusiastic support of his children's musical pursuits. Pastor Pomeroy managed Deb's rebellious brother Justin's band, The Dirty Wurds, and he made the gymnasium inside his church an "upon this rock" space for his children's bands to practice in. Music routinely reached the family house, which was connected to the church. Enthralled with the vibrant folk music scene and inspired by the renowned Old Town School of Folk Music 20 minutes away, where Debi took guitar lessons, the Pomeroy siblings hosted hootenannies on a stage set up with lighting in the basement of the Pomeroy home.[36]

Bonafede was determined to enhance the inherent novelty nature of the all-female rock band with a (literally) uniform gimmick for gigs. Though matching outfits suited many mod male bands of the era, the Daughters wore their stylish scorn on their sleeves. Levin characterized the "first uniform when we actually got work" as "outfits that were so godawful, they were like green jeans and burgundy-colored, velour V-neck, and … we actually had pictures taken in them."[37]

Like their kindred spirited Luv'd Ones, the Daughters of Eve were a unique draw. Their music, energy, and progressive presence were well received by audiences, as they frequently opened shows for their local contemporaries. Still, the Daughters of Eve's run was brief and their recording output thin. Between their 1966 entrance and dissolution in 1968 when both Johnson and Tomal wed, the pioneering female band recorded a set of singles that were released on three different Chicago-based labels, beginning with producer Jim Golden's U.S.A. Records: "Hey Lover"/"Stand by Me" (1966), the Ben E. King cover from 1961, and "Symphony of My Soul"/"Help Me Boy" (1967), the B-side a captivating gender inversion of the Animals' "Help Me Girl." Of note, the genre brand—"All Girl Band"—is printed in parentheses beneath "Daughters of Eve" on the label of the group's debut 45. The band's two U.S.A. Records releases were followed by "Don't Waste My Time"/"He Cried" (1967, Spectra Sound) and "Social Tragedy"/"A Thousand Stars" (1968, Cadet).

Outliers and Obscurities

Though the Dunwich identity was undeniably hometown Chicagoland, the regional reach of Traut and company routinely drifted beyond the city limits, suburbs, and adjacent state lines with music in mind, seeking to uncover the sounds of promising bands and garage gems. In one direction, the Michigan-rooted Luv'd Ones were located 95 miles southeast of Chicago looping the lower tip of Lake Michigan on Interstates 90 and 94. Another 150 miles east in Ann Arbor were The Five Bucks, a mid–1960s formation of University of Michigan students. Among the group's midwestern makeup that spanned Detroit (drummer Jerry Daller) to Akron (keyboardist Bauchman Tom), Chris Rose and rhythm guitarist Steve Hearn had Chicago roots; Hearn was from Glencoe, 25 miles north of city. In 1966–67, the Five Bucks spent the summer in between semesters playing in Chicago. They recorded one-offs on three different labels: "No Use in Trying"/"Now You're Gone," which became a novelty misprint label as "Now You're Mine" (Afton); "I'll Walk Alone"/"So Wrong" (Omnibus); and "Breath of Time" (U.S.A. Records). According to bassist Bruce Kerr, Traut envisioned The Association echoing in The Five Bucks sunshine pop harmonies, a correlation that was further accentuated by the Asian-American representation in each group, with the Five Bucks' Bauchman Tom and Hawaiian-born Larry Ramos in the Association. A seemingly requisite group rename resulted in "the Byzantine Empire," a Middle Ages page borrowed from Kerr's history major in school. In 1968–69, the group recorded three 45s at Universal under the production supervision of Higgins and Bob Schiff. The singles, featuring four originals and two covers, including "Happiness Is" by the Association, were released on Amy-Mala-Bell Records. Despite the Five Bucks/Byzantine Empire's singles, some radio airplay on WLS, and routinely playing concerts at venues across the Midwest, from state fairs and college campuses to the Aragon

Ballroom in Chicago, and opening for the Hollies, Animals, Turtles, Doors, and Del Shannon, among other acts, the band's breakthrough never came before its breakup at decade's end.[38]

The Warner Brothers stretched "local" and the Dunwich domain 165 miles southwest to Peoria in central Illinois. The show biz name appropriating brothers Warner—Larry and Al—and "two mysterious cats" Kenny Elam and "Crazy" Tommy Stovall, made the midwestern record rounds. The group debuted on the Destination label in 1965 before delivering a single to Dunwich in 1966, followed by releases on the Balance, Everest, and Kandy Kane labels. Their inaugural single, "Please Mr. Sullivan," was an "Alley Oop"-ish novelty song featuring a playful plead to appear on *The Ed Sullivan Show*—"ready for Eddie / just tell us when." The Warner Brothers' lone Dunwich single combined a distinct folk-punk rendition of a frequently recorded Gerry Goffin–Carole King composition, "I Won't Be the Same Without Her," with a divergent, debauched, exuberant howl, "Lonely I." Jarema characterized the "ace pairing" as "a wild, double sided uptempo blast" that was "arguably Dunwich's most continually overlooked single."[39] A few outtakes from the Warner Brothers' 1966 Dunwich session, "Oleo Margarine," and the raunchy "Dirty Ernie," were uncovered in the vaults and later issued.

Peoria, set on the Illinois River, is also the birthplace and musical coming-of-age for popular 1970s–1980s singer-songwriter Dan Fogelberg. During the same mid-1960s time frame, Fogelberg was apprenticing with Peoria-area cover bands: the Beatles'-based Clan and the Coachmen. In 1967, the Coachmen recorded a single with two Fogelberg compositions, "Maybe Time Will Make Me Forget" and "Don't Want to Lose Her," precursors to many of his soft rock romantic ballads. The tracks were recorded at the Golden Voice Studio in nearby South Pekin, 10 miles away, and released on the Ledger Records label. As a student of the arts (theater, painting) at the University of Illinois, Fogelberg performed regularly in various venues across the coffeehouse, club, and café circuit in Champaign-Urbana. Aspiring music manager Irving Azoff, who had discovered and initiated promoting rockers REO Speedwagon in the same locality, noticed Fogelberg's folk-rock and solo acoustic sets and set his career in motion. Under the production direction of Norbert Putnam, a noted Nashville and Muscle Shoals session musician, Fogelberg recorded and released his debut, *Home Free*, in 1972, on his way to a highly productive and successful career until his death in 2007 in Maine at age 56.

Fogelberg's impressive gold- and platinum-plated discography includes 16 studio albums between 1972 and 2009, two LP collaborations with flutist Tim Weisberg, three live sets, and a steady stream of hit singles, 12 of which placed inside the Top 10, most comfortably on the adult contemporary chart. Four of the those songs reached #1—"Longer" (1979), the tribute to his father "Leader of the Band" (1981), "Make Love Stay" (1983), and "Believe in Me" (1984). Rounding out the top 10 tunes of familiar Fogelberg fare are "Heart Hotels" (#3, 1980), "Same Old Lang Syne" (#8, 1980), and "Run for the Roses" (#3, 1982). One of his most FM-friendly songs, and an essential in the abounding mid-decade singer-songwriter rotation along the James Taylor axis, "Part of the Plan," charted at #22 in 1975.

Though Fogelberg's career is commonly associated geographically with Jackson, Mississippi; Nashville; and Colorado, he paid homage to his midwestern roots with "Illinois" ("I'm your boy"), the second track on his second album, *Souvenirs* (1974, Epic), a country-tinged folk-rock set produced by guitarist Joe Walsh. The album went double platinum, reaching inside the Top 20 on the album chart at #17.

Sounds Unlimited extended the Dunwich reach a little farther, nearly 200 miles into Indiana. With an initial lineup consisting of guitarists Phil Brandt and Steven Foster, along with bassist Ken Mahlke and Wayne Wilson on drums, the group was part of a flourishing Indianapolis teen music scene that featured the Boys Next Door, Idle Few, and Sir Winston and the Commons among its most popular bands. Sounds Unlimited distinguished themselves in style and sound, disregarding dress standards and hair length, and preferring to perform more obscure album tracks rather than the most familiar songs of commonly covered British bands. The group was also known to replicate destructive Who-style finales during their live shows.

The band toured extensively, though their studio sessions in Chicago and in Philadelphia at the celebrated Cameo-Parkway Studios did not yield a single. The Philly session, arranged by Columbia Screen Gems and overseen by film and television music supervisor Lester Sill, was intended as an audition for *The Monkees* television series. Sounds Unlimited shredded selections from the Colgems Records catalog (Columbia Screen Gems in conjunction with RCA Victor), which strongly suggested the band was more comfortable and/or more interested in rackety renditions of the Blues Magoos' "Gotta Get Away" than they were mainstream music. The band's frenetic execution and punk'n'delic presence was not what Sill and the producers had in mind and did not earn the Chicagoans a callback. As pop rock lore has it, another notable, Steven Stills, despite his guitar proficiency, did not get a part either, purportedly due to thinning hair and bad teeth. Davy Jones, Michael Nesmith, Peter Tork, and Micky Dolenz got the gig to "Hey hey.... Monkee around."

Sounds Unlimited literally became a brother act following Mahlke's departure for college and a motorcycle accident involving Brandt, an unfortunate occurrence that ricocheted to Bob Dylan's mythical motorcycle crash in July 1966 in Woodstock, New York. Terry Talbot, and his younger sibling John, stepped in on lead and rhythm guitars, and Foster moved to bass. In 1967, the Sounds Unlimited new lineup delivered one of Dunwich's best pop efforts with their lone single, "A Girl as Sweet as You"/"Little Brother." The record had a significant Boys Next Door signature, with producer and writing credits from Boys bandmates Skeet Bushor, Steve Lester, and Jim Koss. Bushor also produced and arranged Idle Few's 1966 Dunwich single "Another World"/"Farmer John." The vocal harmonies and patterns on "A Girl as Sweet as You" pleasantly echoed the Five Americans' Top Five hits "Western Union," "Sound of Love," and "Zip Code." Unfortunately, and perhaps inexplicably, the record failed to chart. When Sounds Unlimited split in 1969, the Talbot brothers, upon Traut's urging, redirected their folk/country/rock partiality into Mason Proffit. The industrious Indianapolis group released five albums through 1973 and was at the forefront of an emerging sound that was a precursor to the Eagles' vein of country rock that was a touchstone of the prolific California canyons singer-songwriter circle of the 1970s.

Midwestern Mersey and Velvet

Saturday's Children may have been among the most anonymous of Chicagoland's garage obscurities. Led by versatile songwriter, lead singer, and bassist Geoff Bryan (Jeff Boyan), who had been a member of Dalek/Engam: The Blackstones with future Shadows of Knight Jerry McGeorge, the Hammond/Munster, Indiana, group also included guitarists Dave Carter and Ron Holder, organist Rick Goettler, and drummer George Paluch. The ambitious outfit featured a toned down sound that embraced the Zombies, Beau Brummels, and, of course, the Beatles. With a cool knack for melody more than thrashing, reverb, or fuzz strains, Saturday's Children was conveniently categorized as "Midwestern Mersey" and frequently clustered with other American Fab Four sound-alikes, Boston's Barry and the Remains and New Jersey's Knickerbockers, who were widely recognized for their precise Beatles imposture on "Lies" in 1965.

Saturday's Children's arc was as puzzling as it was momentarily promising. Factors for the band's advancement were favorable without reaching fruition. Dunwich was supportive, particularly Traut, who industriously searched for songs for the band to record. When he was in New York, Traut actively gathered songs from his friends in the music business. Among the finds, a friend in publishing shared a tape of Randy Newman, which "absolutely knocked out" Traut.[40] The studio production quality of Saturday's Children's recordings amplified the band's proficient musicianship that featured Farfisa organ flourishes. In addition, they were live favorites, often attracting larger crowds than the more established acts on the teen dance circuit and at club cornerstones such as the Cellar. The group's three Dunwich singles released in 1966–67 contained some curiosities—"You Don't Know Better"/"Born on Saturday"; a catchy two-sided seasonal 45, "Deck Five," which was at once a holiday inversion and a nod to the jazz standard by Paul Desmond and Take Five, with a flip, "Christmas Sounds"; and an early Randy Newman cover, "Leave That Baby Alone"/"Hardly Know Her."

Despite some appealing qualities, the singles merely dented the Chicago charts without generating sufficient sales to justify Saturday's Children recording an album. The group split in 1968. In the beyond, Bryan (as Jeff Boyan) joined a waning H.P. Lovecraft outfit as their third bass player in three years, while Carter ended up with the Cryan' Shames, who had recorded a Boyan/Holder song, "Dennis Dupree from Danville," that was the closing cut on their *A Scratch in the Sky* (Columbia, 1967).

The Banshees emblazoned the Dunwich playlist with one of the label's rawest recordings, "Project Blue." Released in the summer of 1966 with a calmly contrasting B-side ballad, "Free," the Banshees' sole single was a pounding proto-punk and blues-based song, driven by frenetic guitar distortion from lead guitar "whiz" Ron Rouse and a tormenting, "screw loose" howling vocal by Frank Bucaro.[41] The band also included Jack Smead (rhythm guitar), Rick Notolini (bass), and drummer Tom Leetzow. Formed in 1962 as the Fugitives before reconfiguring as the Prophets mid-decade, the young group was signed to a Dunwich contract by Traut after he happened upon their "Project Blue" demo recording session. In the ensuing Traut transformation, the band was "relieved of their non-musician bass player" Notolini, whose musicianship was characterized along a deviating scale from the polite "inexperienced" to the candid "incapable." "Rick couldn't play at all. 'Project Blue' was three notes and he couldn't even play that," Smead told *Kicks* magazine.[42] Notolini was replaced by English musician Peter Sheldon, who had relocated to Chicago. Perhaps more markedly than the personnel change, Traut assigned the band a more mystical moniker, converting the Prophets into the Banshees, the new name adapted from a legendary wailing female fairy spirit rooted in Irish mythology. Ironically, Bucaro carried the primal scream lead singer cross as fugitive, prophet, and banshee to eventually being ordained as a Catholic priest.

As an active live act across the tri-state Midwest circuit from the Chicagoland venues to Wisconsin and Indiana, the Banshees notched notable opening gigs for shows with the Yardbirds and Dave Clark Five. The Banshees were brief, disbanding in 1967, a familiar endpoint for many 1960s garage groups. Their single song identity with "Project Blue," though slight, sustained with unassuming significance within the era's playlist. Dave Traut, curator of the Classic Garage Rock Library website, credits the Banshees for avoiding "sounding like another suburban Stones knock-off," emphasizing that the band "almost telepathically mined the same territory as the Velvet Underground *White Light/White Heat*, only a full year earlier."[43]

Mister Rogers' Neighborhood: Suburban Soul Drippin'

> [Jimy] Rogers had it and he knew it. So did everyone who saw him and the Mauds perform.
> —Chicago musicologist/radio personality Bob Stroud[44]

Within the prevalent punk'n'delic profile of Dunwich Productions and the Chicagoland scene, the Mauds were misfits, contributing a standout strand of suburban soul and blues rock frequently and conveniently categorized as "white" or "blue eyed soul." The North Shore band starred another dynamic front named "Jimy," this one, Jimy Rogers of the Highland Park and Buffalo Grove suburbs. Following a fledgling formation with guitarist Bill Durling in 1965, Rogers regrouped in 1966 with a lineup that solidified with a versatile lead guitarist adept at urban jazz: Robert

"Fuzzy" Fuscaldo, who was recruited from Wauconda, 20 miles away; Tim Coniglio playing trumpet and rhythm guitar; Billy Winter on bass; and drummer Phil Weinberg. Though the Mauds' name derived from the hip Brit jargon "mod," the band was committed to a sound that was shaped by artists along the soul spectrum such as Curtis Mayfield, Otis Redding, and Sam & Dave, among others.

The Mauds' affiliation with the area's touchstone teen stomping ground, the Cellar, proved advantageous to the band's arrival and ascent. Club owner Paul Sampson and Shadows of Knight lead Jimy Sohns were dutiful Mauds mentors and managers. Among other opportunities and acts of support, Rogers substituted for kindred spirit Sohns as the Shadows of Knight lead on tour and locally when Sohns was resolving his military draft status. And, after Sohns and company moved on to follow their rock-and-roll dream beyond the regional realm, the energetic Mauds were the natural replacement for the Shadows of Knight as the house band at the Cellar.

The Mauds' rapidly rising popularity roused by Rogers's sweaty soul rock Jagger-like performance verve struck a responsive chord with the omniscient Traut. A deal with Dunwich ensued. The Mauds' debut single featured one of the group's live staples, a cover of the Isaac Hayes/David Porter R&B standard, "Hold On, I'm Comin'," which had been a huge hit for Sam & Dave on the Stax label the previous year. Recorded at Chess Studios, the pressing of the Mauds version was circulated throughout local record stores. While the savvy Traut maintained artistic control through Dunwich Productions, he wisely arranged a wider distribution deal for the Mauds with the major label Mercury Records, which willingly picked up the suburban soul song and released it in May 1967. "Hold On, I'm Comin'" swiftly climbed the charts (again), settling inside the summer's top 15 on Chicago's WCFL and WLS. However, the Mauds momentum decelerated into controversy over a suggestive lyric—"reach out to me for satisfaction / on my knees for quick reaction"—which registered objections from listeners. A cleaned-up radio edit of the song resulted.

In between its popularity and accompanying controversy, the Mauds' "Hold On, I'm Comin'," like any cover version, inherently invited comparison to the original. To his impartial credit, Jeff Jarema is among a slight counter critical camp who consider the Mauds' rendition musically inferior, not only to the Stax original, but overshadowed by its own B-side, "C'mon and Move," written by Fuscaldo and Rogers. The Chicago music chronicler's perspective pierced Eddie Higgins's "mock soul horn overdubs" as "the worst element of the Mauds studio sound," adding that Rogers found the production arrangements embarrassing.[45]

The Mauds' achy follow-up single, "When Something Is Wrong (with My Baby)," another Hayes/Porter composition, was a stark slowdown and letdown from "Hold On, I'm Comin'," with little commercial appeal. A Jerry Butler/Curtis Mayfield pairing "He Will Break Your Heart"/"You Must Believe Me" fared better. The Mauds' soul stance and comfort with R&B covers was further affirmed on the group's 11-song debut album, *Hold On*, a Mercury Records release in 1967. In addition to including their three singles, the long play's funk and soul sequence featured two originals, "C'mon and Move" and "You Made Me Feel So Bad," dotted among vigorous versions of "Harlem Shuffle"; "Ha Ha Ha"; "You Don't Know Like I Know"; "Look at Granny Run Run"; and another Stax single from '66, "Knock on Wood," by Eddie Floyd and Steve Cropper. All of the songs on *Hold On* clocked in under three minutes, with the exception of an extended 5:17 take on "Mercy, Mercy, Mercy." The cover version, which closes side one of the album, added lyrics (credited to Gail Fisher and Vincent Levy) to Cannonball Adderley's jazz instrumental composed by Joe Zawinul. The Mauds recorded the song around the same time as their local contemporaries, the Buckinghams, whose soulful rendition was a huge hit, reaching the top five on the national charts in 1967.

The Mauds' most meaningful mark musically and commercially came in 1968 with the single "Soul Drippin'." Written by Dick Monda, who later gained notoriety as "Daddy Dewdrop" with a (mostly) spoken word hit in 1971, "Chick-A-Boom (Don't Ya Jes' Love It?)," the production was supervised by post–Dunwich George Badonsky and Skeet Bushor. The single's arrangement foreshadowed the driving brassy "Chicago Sound," featuring players recruited from the Chicago Transit Authority's horn section—Walt Parazaider, Lee Loughnane, Jimmy Pankow, and Robert Lamm on keyboards—before CTA recorded their first album. A catchy, compact 2:25, "Soul Drippin'" touched the Top 10 in Chicago and broke into the national charts at #85. The song received further endorsement when recorded the same year by the Standells of "Dirty Water" garage classic notoriety.

The success of "Soul Drippin'" did not sustain as a stepping stone. The Mauds' ensuing single, "Only Love Can Save You," and its B-side folk hero tale with a counterculture undercurrent, "Sergeant Sunshine," fell flat. A full-page ad in *Billboard* featuring a "forthcoming album" plug did not notably heighten interest in the Mauds and their music or boost sales. Ad aside, in the longstanding tradition of antagonistic relations between artists and record labels, the Mauds were reportedly disappointed in Mercury's lack of promotion and support. Shifting radio formats at the time may have also been a contributing factor as AM Top 40 was forced to be more selective with songs in order to compete with emerging FM underground stations. The Mauds' sound was regarded as risky in reaching a wider audience. Airplay dwindled for their final Mercury single in 1969, "Satisfy My Hunger," backed with the instrumental, "Brother Chickie." A label relocation the following year to RCA, where they recorded a version of the Gerry Goffin/Carole King ballad "A Man Without a Dream," did not significantly redirect the band's diminishing arc. Fragmentation followed; the group members gradually dispersed, and the Mauds as a band were done in early 1971.[46]

As for the Mauds mythology, the group's soulful suburban North Shore strut with a South Side sound was significant on several levels. As the area's undisputable top white blues band, the Mauds were estimated to be pulling in a notable-in-the-day $3,000 per gig at their live performance peak, with their popularity close to eclipsing their fellow Cellar dwellers the Shadows of Knight. The archetypal dynamo Rogers rose to Local Legend supreme status as a front. And their single "Soul Drippin'" is generally considered one of the best recordings to come out of Chicagoland, and a favorite among the city's celebrated music figures such as Ides of March front Jim Peterik and radio's Dick Biondi.

Despite their popularity, presence, and some notable accomplishments live and on record, the Mauds' regional ripples were not as far-reaching or recognized as some of their suburband contemporaries. The band's place in the mid–1960s Chicagoland musical sphere is routinely revisited in discussion and debate, with midwestern insider and national outsider critical views remaining unsettled along a spectrum that includes points of appreciation, somewhat slighted, and occasionally discounted. Reasonable or not, the Mauds are rarely regarded among the Chicagoland band era elite—the Shadows of Knight, New Colony Six, Buckinghams, Cryan' Shames, and Ides of March. Even to those close to the mid-to-late-1960s scene, the Mauds commonly settle respectably in a blues note spot just outside the top five bandwidth, in the second tier as regional runners up or honorable musical mentions, alongside the American Breed, but ahead or above the multitude of the one hit-sters, the lesser knowns and obscurists, and the pervasive punks in Chicagoland's crowded garage and the Dunwich domain.

"Bend Me, Shape Me"

Akin to the Mauds, the American Breed were also situated outside the punk province, with a slightly more polished soul sound and a clean-cut demeanor. The band formed as Gary & the Knight Lites (also Nightlights, Nite Lites, Light Nites) in 1962 in Cicero, a suburb less than 10 miles west of the city, and adjacent to Berwyn, the Ides of March's home ground. Fronted by the Knight Lite namesake and lead vocalist, Gary Loizzo, the interracial quartet included bassist Charles Colbert Jr., Al Ciner on guitar, and drummer Lee Graziano. Colbert's presence as an African American band member brought diversity that was distinct in the day, part of the prelude of the period that included multicultural membership in groups such as Blood, Sweat & Tears and Sly and the Family Stone, a funky family of racially integrated male and female members in San Francisco.

Loizzo and Colbert were among band members who had accrued experience in local bands such as the Valiants, Trinidads, and Daylighters. Early on, the Knight Lites set out to replicate soul styles such as Stevie Wonder and the Temptations, with renditions of "Up Tight (Everything's Alright)" and "My Girl" (that were eventually recorded), and approached the music in what Traut characterized as a "bubble gum fashion." The group was particularly popular in the Italian sections of the city's South Side. Between 1963 and 1967, the Knight Lites released several singles and jukebox 45s under variants ranging from the inverted Light Nites to Nightlights, across local and national labels that included Nike, Las Vegas–based Prima,

Seeburg, U.S.A. Records, Amy-Mala-Bell, and Kedlen. An impressive output, though none of the singles were considered successful.

Enter Traut, who stepped in and fostered the group into the fold of Dunwich Productions. Their first recording with Dunwich—"Same Old Thing"/"One, Two Boogaloo"—reportedly struck such a negative cord with influential producer Jerry Wexler that it single-songedly became a catalyst for ending the Dunwich distribution deal with ATCO. Wexler was more interested in an authentic, rather than polished, R&B sound.[47] Traut responded with a requisite name improvement for the group, and the newly knighted "American Breed" signed with Acta, a short-lived division of Dot Records created as an outlet for psychedelic rock releases. Under Traut's production supervision that featured a more active studio role for Higgins, the American Breed's sound matured into a horn emphasis that was not characteristic of the Dunwich punk and rock and roll sound, blending soul strands with jazz, rock, and some elements of psychedelic. By most accounts, working with the group was generally agreeable for Traut, a contrast to some of his less compliant recording activities and associations. He found Loizzo and company to be "very malleable," adding that he "was able to get them to do the things [he] wanted them to do." Traut portrayed the band members as "even tempered, nice guys with no egos, no problems like the Shadows of Knight. I could actually mold them."[48]

A prolific parenthesis ensued for the American Breed in 1967–1968, marked by a stream of singles and a soundtrack song, multiple album releases, and commercial jingles and product endorsements that included Coca-Cola. There were also appearances on television's music variety shows, including several bookings on *American Bandstand*. The ample Gerry Goffin–Carole King Brill Building body of work proved to be a primary song supply initially for the Knight Lights and subsequently for the American Breed singles and album tracks. "I Don't Think You Know Me" was one of several songs borrowed from the legendary Brill Building songwriting duo. Though also spurned by Wexler, the group's slick rendition conspicuously reverberated in the Monkees' Michael Nesmith's "You Just May Be the One." Other adaptations from the Goffin-King songbook included "Don't Forget About Me," which settled outside *Billboard*'s Hot 100 at #107; two tracks on the American Breed's second album, "No Easy Way Down" and "Sometime in the Morning," which was also recorded by the Monkees and featured a lead vocal from drummer Micky Dolenz; and "The Right to Cry" on the band's third album.

The American Breed's bouncy, brain-bending version of Al Gorgoni and Chip Taylor's "Step Out of Your Mind," which enlisted "Same Old Thing" for a B-side encore, was a Top 10 tune locally. The single subsequently rose to #24 inside the national Top 40 in May 1967. The recording lived up to its title/lyric as a "step" that set in motion a succession of singles generated by the group. Six months later, in November, "Bend Me, Shape Me" was released and steadily ascended to an even higher chart place nationally at #5. The singles sequence cascaded into 1968 with "Green Light" (#39)—co-written by Annette Tucker, whose songwriting credits include the Electric Prunes garage classic "I Had Too Much to Dream Last Night"—"Ready, Willing and Able" (#84), "Anyway That You Want Me" (#88), and "Keep the Faith"/"Private Zoo." The same year, the American Breed also contributed "A Quiet Place" to the soundtrack of the film *No Way to Treat a Lady*, a dark serial killer comedy/thriller adapted from a William Goldman novel and starring Rod Steiger, Lee Remick, and George Segal.

The million-seller "Bend Me, Shape Me" naturally became the American Breed's signature song. Produced by Traut, the 2:25 single featured hooks, Higgins's horn arrangements and handclaps, and a galloping tom tom drum, along with a catchy sing-along chorus in its gliding two-and-a-half minutes. The song was co-written by Scott English and Larry Weiss, a duo who developed a notable knack for composing mid–1970s touchstone tunes. English's "Brandy" transformed (and rhymed) into the Barry Manilow hit "Mandy," and Weiss's country gold, "Rhinestone Cowboy," became a Glen Campbell emblem. Interestingly, the American Breed was not the first to record "Bend Me, Shape Me." The song initially appeared as a track on the Outsiders' album *In*, the Cleveland band's third LP, recorded in 1966 and released in January 1967. Fortuitously, the Outsiders' album previewed another Chicago hit, Jim Holvay's composition "Kind of a Drag," which followed "Bend Me, Shape Me" on *In*'s side one sequence. One month later, in February, "Kind of a Drag" topped the charts for the Buckinghams, while the American Breed's "Bend Me, Shape Me" arrived in the Top Five the next year. Adding to the lineage of "Bend Me, Shape Me" lineage within the same time frame, The Models, an aptly named group composed of Vogue fashion models, echoed a psychedelicized version on MGM Records in 1966, which some argue was the very first recording of the song. In 1968, the Welsh rockers Amen Corner's rendering reached #3 in the UK.

The American Breed's "Bend Me, Shape Me" is generally recognized as the benchmark version of the song, having routinely re-sounded for years in the solid gold/oldies radio rotations, respectably representing mid–1960s Chicagoland in companion queue with the area's other hit standards such as "Gloria," "Kind of a Drag," and "Vehicle." In addition, the American Breed's pleasant rendition continued to be conveniently and cleverly employed throughout the consumer realm over the years, adapted by advertisers in commercial soundtracks for a range of products that include the pharmaceutical Flexon, Sleep Number Mattresses, Gap, and Mercedes Benz with a slick rephrase "Benz me, shape me."

While the majority of Chicagoland bands were confined to 45s and generally lacking a sufficient amount of material to fill a 33⅓ long play, the American Breed managed to record a striking sum of four albums in a concentrated 12-month span between the falls of 1967 and 1968. The series started with a self-titled debut, followed by a trio of seasonally sequenced releases in 1968—*Bend Me, Shape Me* in February; *Pumpkin, Powder, Scarlet & Green* in May; and the soft rock *Lonely Side of the City* in the fall. All of the albums were produced by Traut and recorded at Universal Studios in Chicago, each with a relatively succinct running time under 30 minutes.

Under Dunwich Production supervision recording on Acta Records, the American Breed integrated a rock-jazz infusion into the Chicagoland sound. Their pop perfect rendition of the Outsiders' "Bend Me, Shape Me" placed in the top five on the *Billboard* Hot 100 in early 1968 and has remained a touchtone tune. Jumping (L-R): Gary Loizzo, Chuck Colbert Jr., Al Ciner, Lee Graziano (*Billboard* ad, October 28, 1967).

Covers, of course, were a common and convenient song source, prevailing over the sparse set of originals contributed by the group members. In addition to routinely gleaning from the Goffin-King inventory, Traut and the band drew from an impressive array of songwriters for album material, among them another renowned Tin Pan Alley pair, Barry Mann and Cynthia Weil ("We Gotta Get Out of This Place"); Steve Cropper and Eddie Floyd ("Knock on Wood"), Allen Toussaint (using the pseudonym Naomi Neville) ("Lipstick Traces"); Robert Higginbotham ("High Heel Sneakers"); Smokey Robinson and Ronald White ("My Girl"); Stevie Wonder/Henry Cosby/Sylvia Moy ("Up Tight [Everything's Alright]"); Van McCoy ("Before and After"); Curtis Mayfield ("I've Been Trying"); Chip Taylor ("Anyway That You Want Me"); and Carole Bayer Sager ("I'm Gonna Make You Mine").

Pumpkin, Powder, Scarlet & Green contained colorful conceptual accents outside and in. On the album cover photo, the band members are posed in suits that are color coordinated with the album title, the portrait outlined by the color-coded corresponding album title words. The back cover features four seasonal reflections inspired by the album's palette, written by the band members: Colbert (Autumn/Pumpkin), Loizzo (Winter/Powder), Graziano (Summer/Scarlet), and Ciner (Spring/Green). The poetic passages convey a greeting card ambience with image-laden phrases that conjure nature and mood, among them "rainbows, peace and tranquility of Indian Summer, soft snow, warm fireplace, early morning dew, soft fresh breezes, tender young leaves and pine needles and moss." The quartet of colors from the album title are further translated musically into four concise (1:12 and under) instrumentals arranged by Eddie Higgins and placed as parentheses as a nice production accent to open and close each side of the album.

Despite their arresting output and producing one of the biggest hits to come out of Chicagoland during the era, the American Breed could not maintain musical momentum beyond their 1967–68 surge. The non-album track, "Keep the Faith"/"Private Zoo," may have deserved better airplay and listenership but ended the group's singles chart streak in 1968 and foreshadowed the band's fade. "Walls"/"Room at the Top" from *Lonely Side of the City* was soft in style and sales, as was the fourth album itself, further indications of the group's descent. Personnel and musical shifts were in motion. Keyboardist Kevin Murphy joined the group and André Fischer replaced Graziano on drums. The addition of singer Paulette McWilliams further funked up the group's heavier R&B horn sound, evident in the transitional single "Hunky Funky" (shortened from "Everything Is Hunky Funky [I'll Be Anything If You Want Me]"), which placed outside the charts at #107 in 1969.

During the American Breed's '69 wane, Traut managed to land another soundtrack placement for the group, as they recorded the kitschy theme song for the French comedy *Le Cerveau* (*The Brain*), starring David Niven as a diabolically cool criminal mastermind. The title tune's lead couplet playfully evokes Niven's character: "Who's got a computer for a mind? Who's got an IQ like an Einstein?"

Despite Loizzo's efforts to advance the American Breed across the cusp into the new decade, their run was essentially over. The group's last official non-album single, "Can't Make It Without You," went unnoticed, affirming the band's finale. Loizzo swerved toward the production side of the music business as a recording engineer.

He established Pumpkin Studios, located in the southwest suburb Oak Lawn, where he produced commercials and bands, eventually receiving a Grammy nomination for his work with Chicago-based 1970s rock group Styx. His bandmates—Ciner, Colbert, Murphy, McWilliams, Fischer (who later married singer Natalie Cole)—regrouped in various configurations, metamorphosing from the American Breed to The Breed, into Smoke and then Ask Rufus, which abbreviated to Rufus in the early 1970s. With Chaka Kahn (Yvette Marie Stevens) eventually replacing McWilliams, Rufus rose to "funk royalty" as an influential Grammy-winning group during the decade. Among Rufus's achievements were four #1 R&B albums and an abundance of Top 40 singles that featured several #1s ("You Got the Love," "Sweet Thing," "Do You Love What You Feel", and "At Midnight (My Love Will Lift You Up)") and many others inside the Top 5, including "Tell Me Something Good" and "Once You Get Started."

The significance of the American Breed's jazz-rock fusion may be overlooked and understated within the group's one-hit legacy. Whether the group's presence should be regarded as predecessor or pioneer or some place in between, the integration of horns into the American Breed's oeuvre lies at the forefront of the brassy pop rock sound that was adopted and amplified by numerous bands that formed around the same time within and beyond the Midwest region. Fellow locals the Buckinghams, the Ides of March, Chicago, and the pre-progressive Flock—along with national acts Blood, Sweat & Tears; Chase; Lighthouse; and War—were among the horn-driven bands that established a jazz rock subgenre that carried from the mid-to-late 1960s into the 1970s with considerable success.

It's *Still* Dunwich, Man

By summer's end in 1967, less than two years and more than 20 bands into its operation, the Dunwich enterprise realigned. The record label itself stopped spinning, its cessation marked by the Shadows of Knight single finale and band farewell, "Someone Like Me," a non-album track that was backed by "Three for Love" from their LP *Back Door Men*.

Dunwich's abbreviated duration as a label was impeded, in part, by a swiftly progressing music culture, both commercially and creatively. Tighter, more selective playlists on hometown radio powers WLS and WCFL made it increasingly difficult for songs by lesser known local acts to get airplay, and their best shot at a breakout or breakthrough. The emergence of the Buckinghams and the Cryan' Shames, and their subsequent signings away from local labels to the major national Columbia Records, signaled a shift to an emphasis on a more accessible sound, one that was more pop than with punk underpinnings.

Despite the Dunwich discontinuance and the coinciding dispersal of its initiators, the late label's "lady with the lute" logo lingered as an imprint on record releases. When Traut and Badonsky bought out their partner Higgins's part of the company, Dunwich Records morphed into Dunwich Productions. Higgins, who was always more comfortable with jazz than he was with rock and roll, relocated to Florida. One year later, in the spring of 1968, Badonsky and Traut parted ways and the company amended again slightly, becoming Dunwich Productions Ltd. Badonsky became an celebrated restaurateur on the city's North Side.

Production continued, but was shipped out, with the masters sent to other record companies for pressing and distribution. National label linkages included Mercury/Philips and Acta, with Ronco and Glen among the liaisons on the local level. Despite the array of artists being re-located on other labels, the bubble above the lute player on the Dunwich logo could have been fittingly fine-tuned to pronounce, "It's *still* Dunwich man." The recordings remained registered Dunwich Productions and Dunwich Productions Ltd., keeping the Chicago identity and label legacy intact. The arrangement was the best of both music business worlds for Traut as it allowed him to maintain creative control while benefiting from broader exposure and distribution for the bands and their music.

Following the departures of his fellow founders and the Dunwich dissolution, the lone originator of the trio, Traut, did not miss a beat. He efficiently established a new partnership by bringing in proven Chicago area producers Bob Monaco and Jim Golden. The duo was well known, having made a mark as MG Productions, most notably on the record rosters and the ample singles catalogs of two other renowned local labels, U.S.A. and Destination, with bands such as the Cryan' Shames, Flock, and Rivieras among their extensive production credits.

The Dunwich/MG reconfiguration was relatively seamless. "By the time I got Golden and Monaco, we really knew what we were doing," said Traut. "We expanded the operation, we had better offices, more stuff going on, and we got along much better with each other than George [Badonsky], Paul Sampson [the Cellar], and I ever did."[49] The new Dunwich alliance continued to produce Chicago-based bands into the 1970s, among them, Aorta, the Hardy Boys, and Mason Proffit, for various record labels, from the major Columbia to the independent Happy Tiger. In 1971, Traut and Golden teamed with actor/producer/talent manager Jerry Weintraub to start the Wooden Nickel record label, with additional Chicago signings that included the Siegel–Schwall Band and Styx.

A *Punk*tuation Mark

Dunwich '66–'67 enfolded a pulsating and prolific punk parenthesis within the Chicagoland music chronicle. Dunwich's understated significance as a record label and production company is inextricable from its mastermind and manager Bill Traut, a music discoverer who went out and signed the Shadows of Knight and "20 other bands" around Chicago's neighborhoods, garages, and teen clubs. Traut's vision and impactful implementation as a Dunwich co-founder and producer merit placement alongside the region's renowned music scene shapers during the era. Traut was to Dunwich what Paul Sampson's unsung presence was to the Cellar; what the disc jockeys and radio programmers were to WLS and WCFL; and what the Jimys—Sohns and Rogers—were as charisma-coated fronts to the Shadows of Knight and the Mauds. As a compressed, energetic echo of the Chess label's celebrated soulful abundance of the 1950s into the 1960s in the same vicinity, Dunwich's brief and brilliant singles saturation accumulated into a collection that shaped a distinct identity through its roster of bands from the city's surroundings, assembled into a raucous representation that cataloged the sound and spirit of the time and place that was 1960s Chicagoland.

CHAPTER 5

Hey Baby, They're Playing Our Songs
The Buckinghams' Smashing '67

It's pretty easy to get a record deal when you have the #1 record in the country.
—Carl Giammarese, the Buckinghams[1]

The Dunwich record label predominance in Chicagoland 1966 was superseded almost *single*handedly—as in 45 rpms—by the Buckinghams the following year. The release of "Kind of a Drag" in late December 1966 on the local independent label, U.S.A. Records, foreshadowed the Buckinghams' banner '67. The single entered the Hot 100 at #90; seven weeks later it was sitting at #1. The two-minute song's opening six-second escalation of horns that bounces to a burst and titled lead lyric lament heralded the Buckinghams' unforeseen chart entrance.

The "kind of a" moment transcended the local music scene, ascending into a national arrival. "Kind of a Drag," written by Jim Holvay, topped the charts for two weeks in February 1967, notably ending a steadfast six-week supremacy of the Monkees' "I'm a Believer." The million-selling gold record was a Buckingham baptism that initiated an impressive string of five more singles that followed, with only one of those songs placing lower than #12. The band's subsequent soulful single released in May, "Lawdy Miss Clawdy," an oft-covered Lloyd Price tune, was the lowest ranked, settling between #36 and #41. After signing with the major label Columbia Records, the Buckinghams returned to the Top 10 twice, with "Don't You Care" (#6) in March and "Mercy, Mercy, Mercy" in June (#5). The Joe Zawinul song had been a hit for Cannonball Adderley the previous year. Later in the year, the singles "Hey Baby (They're Playing Our Song)" (#12) in September and "Susan" (#11) in December positioned just outside the Top 10.

The group's six-single sequence in '67 also displayed some staying power. With the exception of the respectable six-week run of "Lawdy Miss Clawdy," their other five songs remained on the charts between 10 and 14 weeks. The prolific playlist presence on the AM airwaves earned the Buckinghams *Billboard* magazine's distinction as the "Most Listened to Band in America" of 1967.

The Hit Parade: Singled Out in '67

The prominent chart placement of a two-minute tune from a clean-cut midwestern band recorded and released on an independent label seemed an unlikely equation, with an unanticipated effectual outcome. Yet, the accomplishment was not accidental. Unseating the telegenic teen idol Monkees from their prolonged stay at *Billboard*'s top spot in and of itself was notable. The Buckinghams' 45 feat within the singles-saturated '67 may be even more striking when considering the context of the climate and crowded competition, and the scope, scale, and significance of the surrounding songs and artists.

With many singles ricocheting from a progressively popular album format, the year's rich rotation overwhelmed the airwaves, transistors, and turntables with a vibrant range of recordings. From touchstone tunes destined for "classic" status (the Doors' "Light My Fire"; Aretha Franklin's "Respect," Procol Harum's "Whiter Shade of Pale," Van Morrison's "Brown Eyed Girl," Jimi Hendrix Experience's "Purple Haze") to first-timers and one-hit wonders (Bobbie Gentry's "Ode to Billie Joe," Keith's "98.6," Scott McKenzie's "San Francisco [Be Sure to Wear Flowers in Your Hair]," Every Mother's Son's "Come on Down to My Boat"). The variations in the expansive playlist included duos (Sonny and Cher's "The Beat Goes On"), dad/daughter duets (Frank and Nancy Sinatra's "Something Stupid"), family ensembles (Cowsills' "The Rain, the Park and Other Things"), and vocalists with middle-of-the-road appeal: Bobby Vinton, Vikki Carr, Petula Clark, Engelbert Humperdinck, Frankie Valli, Johnny Rivers, and Dionne Warwick ("I Say a Little Prayer"). Several hits became signature songs for their sources (the Turtles' "Happy Together," "Windy" by the Association, the Box Tops' "The Letter"), along with soundtrack themes (Lulu's "To Sir with Love," the chart-topping, year's best-selling title tune for the film starring Sidney Poitier as an immigrant interim teacher in an inner city school in London's tough East End brimming with rejects and troubled youth) and socio-political anthems (Janis Ian's "Society's Child," Buffalo Springfield's "For What It's Worth").

Among the cross section of genres and sound styles represented were folk (Peter, Paul and Mary; the Seekers' "Georgy Girl"), psychedelic and garage (Blues Magoos' "[We Ain't Got] Nothing Yet," Strawberry Alarm Clock's "Incense and Peppermints," Electric Prunes' "I Had Too Much to Dream," Music Explosion's "Little Bit o' Soul"), MOR pop (Spanky and Our Gang's "Sunday Will Never Be the Same"; the 5th Dimension's "Up, Up and Away") and rock (Jefferson Airplane's "Somebody to Love"). Naturally, the British Invasion was well represented, with groups commonly having multiple songs in rotation such as the Hollies, Dave Clark Five, Herman's Hermits, Kinks, the Rolling Stones ("Ruby Tuesday," "Let's Spend the Night Together"), the Who ("I Can See for Miles"), the Spencer Davis Group ("Gimme Some Lovin'"), Cream ("Sunshine of Your Love"); as was Motown, R&B, and soul with James Brown, Arthur Conley, Ray Charles, Jackie Wilson, Stevie Wonder, Wilson Pickett, Sam & Dave, the Supremes, Smokey Robinson & the Miracles, the Four

Tops, Temptations, Martha and the Vandellas, Gladys Knight & the Pips ("I Heard It Through the Grapevine"), and instrumentalists Booker T. & the M.G.'s. And of course the Beatles continued to magnify their mark from the mid–1960s. Beyond the release of *Sgt. Pepper's Lonely Hearts Club Band* in May, they generated a double A-side single, "Penny Lane"/"Strawberry Fields Forever," and non-album singles "All You Need Is Love" and "Hello Goodbye," later issued in November on the US LP *Magical Mystery Tour* soundtrack (a double EP in the UK). Paul Revere & the Raiders, the Grass Roots, Young Rascals, Mamas and Papas, Tommy James & the Shondells, and the Lovin' Spoonful were among American bands who placed multiple songs in the Top 40 before, during, and after 1967. As did the fruitful Monkees, whose "believer" songs bracketed the year—their version of Neil Diamond's "I'm a Believer" sustaining from 1966 into January and "Daydream Believer" in December 1967—with a rendition of the Carole King/Gerry Goffin composition "Pleasant Valley Sunday" and "A Little Bit Me, A Little Bit You" in between.

Within this voluminous and extraordinary 1967 singles setlist, the Buckinghams made their mark, and further affirmed and amplified the Chicagoland music profile that had been inaugurated by the New Colony Six, Shadows of Knight, and the Dunwich domain.

British Enough?

The Buckinghams formed in 1965, materializing out of a merger of members from two suburban bands who played drag strips and car shows, storefronts and Battle of the Band competitions. Carl Giammarese (guitar) and Nick Fortuna (bass) of the Centuries paired with the Pulsations' John Poulos (drums) and vocalists Dennis Tufano and George LeGros, who previously sang together in an acapella group, the DarSals. Dennis Miccolis (keyboards) also joined the band initially but departed in the early stages following a recording session at Chess Studios, while LeGros was drafted into service by the military. Miccolis was promptly replaced by Larry Nestor, who was subsequently supplanted by Marty Grebb, an addition that stabilized the group membership.

Becoming the Buckinghams was not quite the familiar same-school students band formation formula, as the members represented a cross section of the city's North Side neighborhoods, Albany Park and Roscoe Village, their avenue intersections—Belmont and Grand with Fullerton, Sacramento, and Lawrence—and high schools—Lane Tech, Gordon Tech, Roosevelt, and Niles West. Grebb was the lone outsider, a South Sider raised in Blue Island, 15 miles south of the Chicago Loop, and schooled at Mendel Catholic in Roseland.

Like many of their Chicagoland contemporaries, among them the colonial costumed New Colony Six, the Northwest Siders were in tune with the prevailing presence of the British Invasion, in sound and style. The import(ant) nature was further magnified when it was suggested by producers during the band's audition for the WGN-TV variety show *All Time Hits* that the group "wasn't British enough." The stage security guard, John Opager, overheard the producer's prompting. Opager dutifully proceeded to compile a list of potential Brit-based band names, which he politely presented to the group with hopes of solving their identity dilemma. The band's brief exile in nameless limbo ended when they adopted "the Buckinghams," preferred over "the Baker Street Irregulars." "The British bands were coming up with names for their groups that really didn't significantly relate to England, and here we were, a band trying to come off a little as British," said Giammarese. "And so it made sense to call us 'the Buckinghams.'"[2]

Bearing their new Brit band brand, the Buckinghams were subsequently booked for an extensive multiple-month run on *All Time Hits* as the show's weekly music performers. Ironically, when the Buckinghams later performed nationally on *The Smothers Brothers Comedy Hour*, the variety show's stage backdrop featured British Union Jack flags because the show's set designers thought the Chicagoans were a British band. The misperception was based on the band's name and their Carnaby Street style, from suits to mop-top haircuts. "They had already created the set so we did it," said Giammarese. "They didn't know that we were just a bunch of Italian kids from Chicago."[3]

The group's new designation signified dually with a British accent of Buckingham Palace and local color, conveniently connecting with Chicago's lakefront landmark, Buckingham Fountain, in Grant Park. "That way, we didn't feel like we were selling out Chicago to take a British sounding name," said Tufano.[4] The association was endorsed on the cover shot of the Buckinghams' debut album, *Kind of a Drag*, in 1967, with the group pictured in a Polaroid pose in the foreground of the city's famous fountain. The iconic water work was designed by Beaux-Arts architect Edward H. Bennett and its statues created by the French sculptor Marcel F. Loyau. The rococo wedding cake style design of the fountain was inspired by the *Bassin de Latone* and modeled after Latona Fountain at Versailles. As a Lake Michigan allegory, the representation features a set of seahorses symbolizing the four Midwest states that border the Great Lake: Illinois, Wisconsin, Michigan, and Indiana.

Around the Horn: *Jim*prints, Busy "B's," and MOB Ties

The Buckinghams' coalescence and swift development were beneficiaries of two indelible "Jimprints" who consistently contributed to the production credits that underscored the band's smashing '67. Namely, the Jims—Holvay and Guercio. The productive pair expanded the Chicagoland music scene's curiously common "Jim-names-ium" beyond the more familiar band leads—Sohns and Rogers, Pilster and Peterik—to include industrious behind-the-scenesters. Holvay and Guercio were essential figures who shaped a signature songwriting and sound style that became the best of the budding band. Holvay's compositions stood out, stamping the Buckinghams' biggest hits, beginning with "Kind of A Drag," followed by three more charting songs he co-wrote with Gary Beisbier: "Don't You Care," "Hey Baby (They're Playing Our Song)," and "Susan." Beisbier was among a trio of "busy Bs" also associated with the band, which included Buckinghams' "firsts": their first manager, Carl Bonafede, and first producer, Dan Belloc. The other "Jimpact" emanated from Guercio, who produced several of those Buckinghams' hit records, managed the group, and was instrumental beyond music in the Chicagolanders signing with the major label Columbia.

Holvay grew up in Brookfield, a village located 13 miles west of the city, renowned for its zoological magnificence. The Brookfield Zoo, founded in 1934, is an internationally acclaimed animal kingdom with nearly 500 species occupying its 216-acre west suburban sprawl. Holvay attended high school in nearby Lyons, playing in bands such as Jimmy and the Jesters along the way. His coming of age was marked musically by visits downtown to the city and Record Row along Michigan Avenue's legendary 10-block stretch between Roosevelt and Cermak roads, lined with studios and labels, Vee-Jay, Constellation, and Chess among them. The Mississippi Delta sounds from the South Side studios and record labels located there and meeting figures such as Leonard Chess, Willie Dixon, and Curtis Mayfield, made first and lasting heroic impressions on Holvay, prompting the adoption of the nickname "Jimmy Soul."

Holvay and his songwriting sidekick, saxophonist Beisbier, were founding members of The MOB. The musical group, *not* to be associated or confused with the notorious criminal confederation that was prevalent in and around Chicago. The MOB were pioneers—original gangsters—playing prominently as trumpeters of a template that was at the forefront of the renowned Chicago horn rock sound. The eight-piece R&B showband's polished horn style reverberated locally from the Buckinghams and Chicago to the American Breed and the Ides of March. The sound carried more broadly across country and continent to jazz rock outfits, notably Blood, Sweat & Tears, as well as Chase and the Toronto-based band Lighthouse, with each of the two producing huge hits in 1971—"Get It On," which spent 13 weeks on *Billboard*'s Hot 100, and "One Fine Morning," which topped the Canadian charts, respectively.

The MOB's metamorphosis into a full-blown, brassy showband with a Vegas vibe encompassed a compound, lengthy lineage of linkages, multifarious band formations, transformations, and tributaries, with continual musician membership movement, marked by routine additions and subtractions resulting from the military draft, National Guard duty, and college calling. Perhaps most notably, the groundwork for the celebrated band Chicago was part of a parallel progression that was rooted in The MOB's materialization and floating fragments of formulation.

The Chicagoland horn (r)evolution began to blossom in the early 1960s well west of the city, around Aurora, with the high school group The MayBees. The band's suburban soul was inspired by the R&B sound of records being produced in downtown Chicago. In the summer of 1963, three main MayBees—guitarist Holvay, Larry McCabe (trombone), and Gary Beisbier (tenor sax)—gravitated to the group the Chicagoans, a start-up show band that featured Jimmy Peterson and funky, heavy-footed drummer Bobby "The Cheeze" Ruffino. The group grew from playing Midwest record hops to becoming the house band on Jim Lounsbury's local television dance show, before touring across the country. During a demo session in New York, the midwestern outfit cut a horn and surf instrumental homage to the Fab Four, who had arrived stateside from England for their epic appearance on *The Ed Sullivan Show* in February, officially launching the British Invasion. The tape eventually made its way to WLS program director Clark Weber, who favored the sample's flip side, titling the promising, promotable untitled tune "Beatle Time." Weber wielded further wisdom and weight by fashionably suggesting the group rename from the "Chicagoans" to a more opportune Brit and Beatlesque sounding "Livers," short for the legendary local "Liverpool." Constellation Records released the Livers' 45, with the catchy, concise 1:35 single receiving ample airplay on WLS.[5]

Within the same time frame and vicinity, eventual MOB emcee and high register trumpeter Jimmy Ford was fronting the Kasuals, a four-piece jazz and R&B instrumental combo composed of Mike Sistak (guitar), Dwight Kalb (drums), and Ron Gately (bass). When Gately resisted the road, he was replaced by former MayBee Wayne Erwin. The group of accomplished musicians secured backup band and regular spots on the popular *Dick Clark's Caravan of Stars* tour during the mid-1960s. Following a swing through Nashville, the Kasuals encountered a first-come, first-served (as in legal documents) circumstance. The group was mandated to change its name after discovering that singer Brenda Lee's backing band had previously claimed "the Casuals" moniker, spelled with a capital "C." Thus, Chicago's Kasuals converted to a corporate recast as the Executives. Ford also assembled an offshoot tour band, the Executives #2, featuring an impressive lineup that included Holvay, Beisbier, Ruffino, Guercio, Rick Panzer (trumpet), and organist Kevin Murphy, in his band initiation preceding stints with the American Breed and Rufus. The group performed across North America through the fall of 1965 before dispersing to college, the National Guard, Chicago, and Los Angeles.[6]

In the fall of 1964, with the departures of Erwin and Kalb, the Executives' composition began to inconspicuously accumulate into the foundation of the group Chicago: Danny Seraphine on drums and Guercio, a pied piper of personnel, bringing in his friend from DePaul University, horn player Walt Parazaider, who subsequently enlisted Terry Kath on bass. When Ford and Sistak exited the Executives to join The MOB, the remainders (Seraphine, Parazaider, Kath) added vocalist Chuck Madden and formed The Missing Links. The group recorded a Holvay tune, "Makin' Up & Breakin' Up"/"You Hypnotize Me," released on Signett Records in 1966. The Buckinghams would later record the song and include it among the 12 tracks on their debut album, *Kind of a Drag*, released on U.S.A. Records in 1967.

The Missing Links expansion continued into early 1967, moving toward "that octave R&B sound"[7] with the additions of Parazaider's DePaul classmates trumpeter Lee Loughnane and trombonist James Pankow along with keyboardist Robert Lamm, who played as alter ego front in Bobby Charles and the Wanderers. Later that year, vocalist/bassist Peter Cetera from the Exceptions joined the six-member group. The Missing Links had outgrown their name, inflating into The Big Thing, another temporary designation in the fleeting succession of title alterations for the band. In 1968, under the direction of Guercio as manager/producer, The Big Thing migrated westward way to Los Angeles and converted yet again, this time into the Chicago Transit Authority. The group was signed by music mogul Clive Davis on Columbia Records, where Guercio had established considerable cachet beyond hometown group Chicago, having produced the similar sounding horn jazz/rock Blood, Sweat & Tears' self-titled second album for the major label, a #1 album that featured huge hits "Spinning Wheel" and "You've Made Me So Very Happy." Released late in 1968, the BS&T album won a Grammy for Album of the Year in 1970. Following the release of *Chicago Transit Authority* in April 1969, and the uncommon double-album debut's subsequent slow, sustained sales, striking signature singles, and chart stamina enhanced by a Grammy nomination for Best New Artist in 1970, the Chicago Transit Authority, commonly condensed to "CTA," was officially, permanently and (rock and roll) historically abbreviated to "Chicago" following a patent infringement notice from the group's namesake at the city's department of transportation.[8]

By early 1966, the MOB's membership was materializing toward completion, with its core of musicians in place—Holvay (Fender bass), Beisbier (sax, arranger), Sistak (trombone, guitar), Ruffino (drums), Ford (trumpet, congas, MC), and Tony Nedza (Hammond B3). Holvay's music savvy and sophistication, and his appreciation of the soul jazz sound, were evident in the selection of Nedza as a bandmate. Holvay recognized his unique ability as an organist to play solid bass lines on pedals. "There haven't been many players that can split their brain like that and not miss a beat while still playing the groove," said Holvay. "When we switched to a Fender keyboard bass, musicians couldn't believe their ears. They kept looking for the bass player on stage, but there wasn't one. Tony was 'the man.' If we were doing a Motown cover tune, Tony would break down that intricate, syncopated James Jamerson bass line and play it note for note while playing chords with his right hand and sometimes even singing a background part, all at the same time. Tony was an incredibly talented guy."[9]

The Herrera brothers, Artie and Al, proved to be the final pieces of the emergent group. The sibling singer and saxophonist were recruited from across the Wisconsin state line in the Milwaukee-based R&B combo, Little Artie and The Pharaohs. The Pharaohs were familiar. In 1965, as the duo Kane and Abel, the Righteous-sounding brothers recorded the Holvay-written "Break Down and Cry." The single, coproduced by Holvay, Beisbier, and manager Joe DeFrancesco, was released on another Chicago independent label, Destination Records. "We thought we could convince them to join the band, we were going to be the next Beatles," said a hopeful Holvay.[10]

In April 1966, following a gig, the group of eight gathered in the alley behind Dan Belloc's Holiday Ballroom on Chicago's North Side and agreed to formally form the super soul group known as The MOB. The band's notorious name—a natural fit considering Chicago's legendary gangster identity—originated from a late night TV movie and reflected the size of the group beyond the standard four- or five-member outfits. In Holvay's simple characterization, having a full-blown horn section, singers, and musicians meant "there'll be a *mob* of people on stage."[11] The MOB dressed the part, outfitted in uniform black pinstripe suits, dark shirts, white ties, and carnations, which contributed to their stylish showband aura.

The road-ready MOB was more stage savvy than studio suited. The band was at their best as a headliner in major showrooms on the club and hotel circuit from Nevada across North America. The MOB played and performed through the 1970s, notably backing Chad & Jeremy and opening for the Association, among other bookings and gigs. The Chicagoland outfit was particularly, if not peculiarly, popular in Hawaii and Puerto Rico, and was eventually inducted into South Dakota's Rock and Rollers Hall of Fame. Among other distinctions, The MOB was featured in the lineup performing at the initial Inaugural Youth Ball, held at the Eisenhower Theater of the John F. Kennedy Center for the Performing Arts in January 1973, commencing Richard Nixon's infamously abbreviated second term.

The MOB's pioneering horn sound, soulful style, and showband presence were more enduring musical marks than their own recordings. Their initial single, "Wait (Please Don't Walk Away)"/"Mystery Man," was released in May 1966 on Cameo-Parkway Records, one month after the group formed. Other recordings followed into and through the 1970s on the Daylight, Twinight, Mercury, Colossus, MGM, and Private Stock labels, and were confined to regional rotation rather than breaking nationally. The most notable may have been two Holvay/Beisbier songs recorded in 1970 on Colossus: "I Dig Everything About You"/"Love Has Got a Hold on Me" and "Give it to Me"/"I'd Like to See More of You" which reached inside the *Billboard* Hot 100 at # 83 and #71. On a note of archival interest, during that period, the Colossus catalog contained a cluster of hits by Dutch bands—Shocking Blue ("Venus"), the Tee Set ("My Belle Amie"), and the George Baker Selection ("Little Green Bag"). The MOB's two self-titled albums, released in 1971 and 1975, were fairly inconsequential recordings.

Made in the U.S.A.: Golden at 2131 South Michigan Avenue

The weekly exposure performing on WGN's *All Time Hits* was the Buckinghams' first break following their formation. Recording ensued. In 1965, the band released a 45 on the Spectra Sound label, "Sweets for My Sweet," a Drifters' tune. The group's cover comfort continued after signing with the hometown U.S.A Records the following year. They cut versions of James Brown's "I'll Go Crazy," which had appeared in the Hot 100, the Beatles' "I Call Your Name," and the Hollies' "I've Been Wrong Before." All of the singles were popular locally.

U.S.A. Records, though smaller scale than its fellow local label Dunwich, provided another rudimentary recording haven for the profusion of garage groups in the Chicagoland vicinity and surrounding cities and states. While the dominant Dunwich's roster generally leaned toward the tougher and grittier teen acts, U.S.A.'s production proclivity was for a bit more polished sound. The independent label, owned by Paul Glass, was an outgrowth of his Allstate Record Distributing Company in Chicago, which handled labels such as Chess and Motown. Accordingly, U.S.A.'s early output was generally aimed at the R&B market. The label's attractive logo was a seemingly star-spangled design, featuring a powder blue base bottom half with black song title and credits imprinted, with the upper half red and white striped with blue stars stacked and a United States silhouette in blue with "U.S.A Records" printed in white.

The fledgling music enterprise received its biggest impetus when Glass recruited Jim Golden from Lenny Garmisa's distributorship located across the street from U.S.A. to essentially run his tiny record company. Golden was destined to become another of the Chicagoland scene's unsung sound shapers and movers, a kindred spirit of Dunwich's managerial maestro Bill Traut. Golden worked in promotion and sales on his way to growing into a savvy record guy who loved the music business. Less practiced as a musician than Traut, Golden initially relied on intuition and pragmatism. He devoted his time to going around listening to groups, tuning his ear for a hit song (see/hear the Rivieras "California Sun"), and developing a feel for the youth market along the way. "I didn't know much about what the hell I was doing, quite honestly, in those days," said Golden. "But I knew what a hit sounded like, and unless you ruined it, it could still be a hit. That was basically my start."[12]

Golden embraced the promotional power, presence, and practicality of the 50,000-watt radio station in the regional room—WLS—and its disc jockeys among the key contributors to the conducive community setting of the music scene. "We cut records for practically nothing in those days," said Golden. "What I used to do is befriend all of the jocks at WLS…. It was a very friendly community. Not a lot of peacock walking, ego-crazed people. We loved the business. It was a great business…. There was none of this corporate crap: wait and get into a release schedule that is six months off. I could record something, go to Chess Records, cut a dub, and take that dub—not even a pressing—up to WLS that night to find if I had a hit."[13]

Sharing Traut's appreciation of homegrown talent, Golden, as a Chicagoland loyalist and ardent advocate of the abundant array of groups playing across the area, fostered a family atmosphere at U.S.A. Locals largely composed the label's lineup. The Buckinghams were among the city dwellers signed to the label, along with Daughters of Eve and Gary & the Knight Lites, whose U.S.A. release, "I Don't Need

Your Help," was a prelude to their progression into the American Breed. Signings were widespread, extending beyond the city limits and into the suburbs. The musical map includes: Lord of the Flies from north of the city in Winnetka; the Counts from 45 miles southeast in Joliet; Park Avenue Playground from Lansing (30 miles); Great Society from the western suburb of Villa Park (20 miles); the punkish The Lost Agency in Downers Grove (20 miles) and rooted a few miles away in nearby Westmont (22 miles); and The Shady Daze, who were regulars along with the Cryan' Shames at the happening Blue Village teen club in the vicinity and had the distinction of opening for both Buffalo Springfield and the Doors.

Golden opened "a tiny, tiny studio" located behind Batts Restaurant on 22nd and Michigan, across the street from Chess Recording Studio. There he started bringing in groups for demo sessions. The space had a garage and basement spirit, and, in the view of its proprietor/producer, "was a joke studio but we had some microphones and were able to get some kind of separation in terms of different instruments."[14] The setting was sufficient and certainly did not hinder Golden's standing or his music quest. "All these groups, they flocked to me because they knew I was a real, real strong supporter of local talent," said Golden. "They knew that I would stay up around the clock, let them have full access to my studio, let them into the studio, sit behind the board when I could and say, 'Hey go for it.' We would all listen, say it was great or let's do another one. It was really 'family' kind of stuff."[15]

And like Dunwich, U.S.A.'s midwestern identity was not exclusively Chicagoland band based, with its roster representation reaching across the region outside the Illinois borders. Golden set a precedent and a tone with his uncovering of the Rivieras and their ray of "California Sun" in South Bend, Indiana. Among other out-of-staters were Oscar and the Majestics from the unofficially annexed Chicago suburb of Gary, Indiana (30 miles southeast), and, representing Racine, Wisconsin (76 miles north toward Milwaukee), Trafalgar Square (initially the Revels), who recorded a Kinks' cover, "'Til the End of the Day." The most distant bands were each located about 300 miles from Chicago: the Bells of Rhymney/the Cherry Slush from Saginaw, Michigan (290 miles east), and the Messengers, with origins in Winona, Minnesota (305 miles northwest), before reconfiguring in Milwaukee (90 miles north of Chicago). The Messengers' version of the Wilson Pickett/Steve Cropper soul classic "Midnight Hour" released on U.S.A. made it to #5 in Chicago. The payola paid off in exposure as the Messengers signed a record deal with Motown and its Rare Earth imprint. At U.S.A., Golden and primo production partner Bob Monaco were left with a hit song but no band to promote it. A slight saga unfolded, as the producers devised a substitute group from well outside the Midwest in Massachusetts, assigning the moniker Michael & the Messengers, even though there was no band member named Michael. U.S.A. re-pressed "Midnight Hour," and the replacement Messengers followed with a charting version in 1967 of the Reflections' popular song from 1964 "(Just Like) Romeo and Juliet."

Golden's steadfast support of Chicagoland's music talent led him to set up additional record labels to accommodate the abundance of local bands aspiring to 45 feasibility. Destination Records was a comparable U.S.A. companion label and offshoot, featuring local favorites the Cryan' Shames and the Flock among the garage/psychedelic bands on its roster and issuing their popular songs "Sugar and Spice" and "Take Me Back." On the one-off Ginny Records, named after Golden's wife, Virginia, The Foggy Notions from the Near North Side held the distinction of being the sole teen group who cut a 45 on the label.

It Made Us Feel So Groovy

The Buckinghams' first recording sessions for U.S.A. took place at Chess Records, conveniently located in close proximity to U.S.A. Records on Chicago's mythical Michigan Avenue. U.S.A. resided at 2131 South Michigan, with the legendary Chess and Ter-Mar Studios located across the street at 2120 South Michigan Avenue, the landmark address immortalized by the Rolling Stones in an instrumental recording during their 1964 tour. Sound Studios also operated on the strip. Both renowned recording hubs were distinguished by their engineers extraordinaire, Stu Black and Ron Malo, who supervised sessions mixing, mastering, dubbing, and operating behind the studio soundboards. Pop-ish bands such as the Buckinghams were not commonly booked to record at Chess, which was the hallowed home to primarily blues artists. And the occasional bad Brit boys such as the Rolling Stones.

The Buckinghams' studio time at Chess was the run-up to their '67 breakthrough, propelled by the songwriting alliance with Jim Holvay that was initiated by Carl Bonafede, the group's manager. Bonafede was another unsung figure on the (behind the) scene, an active local music impresario, booking bands across the area record hop circuit in dance halls and ballrooms. When he and Holvay crossed paths at a gig, Bonafede asked if the songwriter had any tunes that might work for the new band he was supervising. Holvay strummed an acoustic rendition of "Kind of a Drag," a work in progress that he "had been dinking around on a spinet piano in a music practice room" at an area junior college.[16] Holvay thought the song might be better suited for the Beatles-oriented Buckinghams than his R&B-based band the MOB. Bonafede readily recorded the rendition in the dressing room with a Wollensak tape player and microphone and returned to the Buckinghams with the demo. Upon hearing the lo-fi sample, they "thought it was cool."[17]

Recording "Kind of a Drag" proved transformative for the Buckinghams. "It was pretty easy for us to play. The changes were pretty easy. I think we just played it the way that came naturally to us," said Giammarese. "We didn't think too hard about the arrangement. We knew what the chords were. But what changed it was our producer deciding to add horns."[18] The Buckinghams were not founded as a horn band, nor did they start out playing live with any brass backing. Incorporating horns was producer/bandleader Dan Belloc's idea. He brought in his big band trombonist, Frank Tesinsky, to handle the arrangement of "Kind of a Drag," with studio sound supervision provided by Chess's ace recording engineer, Ron Malo. "After we recorded the track and the vocals, we put these horns on and it really made the whole track come to life," said Giammarese. "It was a great song—the lyric, the melody, for that time—but the horns brought it up for us."[19]

Once adopted, recorded, and released, the catchy, two-minute "Kind of a Drag" catapulted the Buckinghams from regional recognition to the national spotlight and became the band's commercial and sonic foundation. The well-crafted, concise composition featured a tune tinted with a wistful tone steered by an insistent tempo to counter its teetering brink-of-breakup circumstance, with a lingering "I still love you." Tufano's buoyant vocal blends seamlessly smooth with the downtown, punchy horns, a keyboard bridge, and layered harmonies that convey holding out hope. The tone is downbeat but not desperate. "The guy sounds happy that his girl has left him," observes Giammarese.[20]

The context of "Kind of a Drag" contained a curious plot twist, with the Buckinghams finding themselves improbably located in record label limbo. According to Tufano, even though fans responded favorably to "Kind of a Drag" when the band played the song live, U.S.A. apparently never liked the cut and resisted its release after it was recorded. "Kind of a Drag" was among the Buckinghams' sides remaining from the dozen tracks the band had recorded. With the Buckinghams' U.S.A. contract expiring, the label's options were somewhat limited. U.S.A. released "Kind of a Drag," obviously without any expectation that the 45 was destined to be an overnight hit. On the single's B-side, the Buckinghams tapped into the British Invasion, delivering a garage rendition of the Zombies' "You Make Me Feel (So) Good," with Giammarese on lead vocal. The Buckinghams frequently performed the song during their live shows, as they were professed fans of the group and its lead, Colin Blunstone.

U.S.A. tried to re-sign the Buckinghams, but the two never came to renewal terms, leaving the label with a bouncy, brassy leftover recording, "Lawdy Miss Clawdy," which they released in late 1966. The independent record company's zenith coincided with the Buckinghams' #1 song "Kind of a Drag" in 1967. Predictably, the Chicagoland label took a hit when the Buckinghams took their hit elsewhere. U.S.A. ran its commercial course by 1968, a wane concurrent with Golden and his managing partner Bob Monaco (as MG Productions) joining Traut at Dunwich Productions Ltd. The trio eventually went on to form Wooden Nickel Records with Jerry Weintraub, launching the 1970s Chicago arena rockers Styx.

"U.S.A. was pretty disappointed," recalls Giammarese. "We were pretty young at the time and didn't know a lot about what was going on. If we were going to go beyond being one-hit wonders, we figured we better find a manager and record company that could take us to the next level."[21]

The Columbia Catalog

Departures dominoed in the Buckinghams' split from the Chicagoland record company. Dennis Miccolis, the band's keyboard player, moved on, as did their manager Bonafede, who felt he was limited as a "local guy" and couldn't take the band any further. The interval was a peculiar circumstance for the Buckinghams. They were missing a musician, minus a manager, and without a record label, while their single, "Kind of a Drag," ascended to the top of the national charts by February 1967. A search for missing pieces and replacements swiftly ensued. For starters, songwriter and multi-instrumentalist Marty Grebb (saxophone, guitar, keyboards) from the Exceptions joined the group, and the Buckinghams headed to California. There they connected with Chicago native James William Guercio, who had been working with Chad & Jeremy, among other artists. The youthful midwesterners why-not? innocence showed. "He [Guercio] seemed to know what he was doing, so we signed with him," said Tufano.[22] The Buckinghams' new manager approached prominent producer and record company executive Clive Davis on behalf of his home-towners carrying #1 record cachet. The Buckinghams were promptly back in business, signing with Columbia Records.

Along with the happening times, being on a major record label roster naturally elevated expectations for the Buckinghams. They were surrounded by an imposing label lineup of talent that included Bob Dylan, the Byrds, Simon & Garfunkel, Paul Revere & the Raiders, the Cyrkle, and their Chicagoland cohorts, the Cryan' Shames, who preceded them with a Columbia contract in 1966. The pace of production and performance accelerated into a "burn the candle at both ends with little sleep" mode for the Buckinghams. The group was in constant motion, hustling between recording and the road, which encompassed an estimated 280 to 300 gigs and numerous television appearances not confined to the local scene. Teen magazine features and national television exposure followed, with "big deal" performances scheduled across the popular variety show spectrum. Among the Buckinghams' bookings were *The Joey Bishop Show*, *The Jerry Lewis Show*, *The Smothers Brothers Comedy Hour*, and *The Ed Sullivan Show*, an appearance Giammarese singularized as a "when you knew you had made it moment."[23] The group also appeared on Dick Clark's *American Bandstand*. "From then on we were on the road all the time," said Tufano. "We'd record tracks occasionally. Then go back on the road. Then we might go back in a few months and add vocals. We did it all on the run. It was crazy."[24]

Billboard magazine's characterization of the Buckinghams as "the most listened to band in America" was not hyperbole, as a succession of Buckinghams' singles tracked a similar, albeit slightly less successful course than the chart topping "Kind of a Drag." In addition to the U.S.A. remnant release, "Lawdy Miss Clawdy," which settled midway on the charts, four subsequent Buckinghams songs—"Don't You Care," "Mercy, Mercy, Mercy," "Hey Baby (They're Playing Our Song)," and "Susan"—ordained the group's Columbia catalog. Each of the singles placed inside the Top 12 during 1967.

"Kind of a Drag" not only established the Buckinghams' horn sound as an instrumental underpinning (which Guercio continued to refine), but also presented the band's characteristic song style, primarily conveyed in the compositions contributed by the fellow Chicagoan co-write cornerstones, Holvay and Beisbier. "We were lucky that Jim and Gary wrote all of our stuff except for 'Mercy Mercy Mercy,'" said Tufano. "Because that gave us a continuum, like when you continue a conversation."[25] The compatibility and chemistry between the two songwriters and the band were strikingly smooth, as the lyrics were at ease with Tufano's flowing lead vocal deliveries and the band's musical arrangements. There was a consistent low-key quality and tone in the couplets that were more catchy than they were complex: "You said that you'd believe me/ then why'd you ever leave me" in "Don't You Care." Or, "It made us feel so groovy/We fell in love, just like in the movies," in the romantic reminisce of a pretty melody in, "Hey Baby, (They're Playing Our Song.)" And, in "Susan," "looks like I'm losin'…do you have to be confusin'."

Tufano considered the gift of the Holvay/Beisbier lyrics analogous with correspondence, saying that singing them was "like a personal love letter." He singled out "Kind of a Drag"— "great follow-up and nice, cool song"—and identified "Don't You Care" as his favorite. "It was comfortable to sing and a great opportunity to use my voice in the way the song presents itself," he said. "And the song is smooth, low, and so it seems personal." Instrumentally, Tufano also appreciated the drum lick that John Poulos added to the opening of the song: "Little things like that make those songs shine." "And there's no screaming," noted Tufano. "During that period of time a lot of songs were over-the-top yelling!"[26]

"Susan," another Holvay/Beisbier standout with an additional songwriting credit to producer Guercio, was routinely recognized for its odd psychedelic supplement or "freak out." Allegedly inspired by a crush on a go-go dancer at the Whisky a Go Go club on Sunset Strip in Los Angeles, "Susan" featured an incongruous insertion by Guercio of an excerpt of Charles Ives's composition "Central Park in the Dark" that echoed the trippy vibe in the Beatles' "A Day in the Life," the closing track of their 1967 album *Sgt. Pepper's Lonely Hearts Club Band*. Whether intended as homage or simply an impulsive burst of ingenuity, Guercio had "this crazy idea to add this backwards tape thing" in an abrupt 30-second break-like-bridge in the song.

The band was unaware of Guercio's spacey superfluities, and they did not hear the final mix of the recording until they were out on the road. The kaleidoscopic *Twilight Zone*–like orchestration did not play well with members of the Buckinghams. Giammarese said he "thought there was a defect in the acetate."[27] "Usually Guercio was a great producer and had a great ear, but putting that in there was a mistake," said Tufano.[28] Nor did radio stations find the song's unusual intermezzo appealing. Many programmers and disc jockeys edited the chaotic cacophony out of the song, concerned that listeners were tuning out and into other stations, prompted by the song's mysterious midway muddle. Despite Guercio's glaring production touch in the idiosyncratic interlude, the mid-tempo tune's tone and signature smoothness with strings, horns, and harmonies were enough for "Susan" to sustain for an extended 12-week stay on the *Billboard* Hot 100, peaking at #11.

The B-side to the "Susan" single, "Foreign Policy," was also noteworthy as an anti-war song. The Buckinghams were not an overtly political band. Their stance, or lack of one, was consistent with their regional colleagues as protest songs and political themes were not a priority. Radicalism and resistance were a rarity and not on record in the mid–1960s Chicagoland songbook. The sociopolitical silence was conspicuous, considering the tumultuous times. In late August 1968, less than nine months after "Susan" was released, the city of Chicago became a riotous epicenter during the Democratic National Convention, with "the whole world watching." Written by Guercio, "Foreign Policy" addresses ignorance, bigotry, and war—"children and the games to begin, thinking only we must win"—and features a spectral audio clip from assassinated President John F. Kennedy presenting peace as a matter of human rights.

The late showing of "Susan" in 1967 marked the summit of the Buckinghams' significant singles run and Top 40 chart presence that launched with "Kind of a Drag." The highest position attained by a Buckinghams' single subsequent to

The Buckinghams' "Susan," placing at #8 in the WCFL Sound 10 Survey in early 1968, marked the zenith of the impressive singles chart run by the "most listened to band in America" in 1967. (L-R): Dennis Tufano, Carl Giammarese, John Poulos, Nick Fortuna, Marty Grebb (WCFL-AM radio, Chicago; the Buckinghams).

"Susan" was "Back in Love Again," which peaked at #57 on *Billboard* and #53 on *Cashbox* during its short six-week stay on the charts in mid-1968. With the undercurrent of tensions triggered by the "Susan" freak-out interlude lingering between Guercio and the group, the Buckinghams settled on "Back in Love Again" as their next single after debating whether or not to release "What is Love" instead, a song that they performed together with "Susan" on their *Ed Sullivan Show* appearance.

Time and Changes

A confluence of factors sidetracked the Buckinghams' sustained single success, primarily the precipitous shifts in the maturing music industry and audience tastes. The music scene's evolution was reflected in radio's swift transition from singles-driven AM pop to FM formats with album-oriented emphasis and weightier rock sounding bands such as Cream. The changes presented significant commercial and creative challenges for Top 40 bands.

The LP was not an unfamiliar format for the Buckinghams; they had released two albums in 1967, *Kind of a Drag* and *Time & Changes*. *Kind of a Drag*, the hit single and the album, were foundational works that set standards of success and music style for the group. Critic Bruce Eder went as far as declaring *Kind of a Drag* "one of the most extraordinary albums of the 1960s." Conscious of its Chicago-based, garage band punk context, Eder suggests that the album's surprising qualities place the Buckinghams within some very prestigious company, as "one expected such great, diverse LPs out of the likes of the Beatles and the Rolling Stones, among others."[29]

The rock-oriented record was not sound specific or genre binding, particularly to the Buckinghams' categorizations that commonly drift dichotomously between garage punk and sunshine pop. Eder's critical view crisscrosses local with international correlations to frame the Buckinghams' debut album, stating that *Kind of a Drag* "isn't the kind of searing punk document that their Windy City rivals the Shadows of Knight presented with their two LPs—the latter group's work stood next to the Buckinghams roughly where the Who's albums did next to those of the Beatles."[30]

The Buckinghams' LP inauguration on the U.S.A. label was distinctly diverse without being a disorderly sequenced grab bag. On the album's 12 tracks, the band performs proficiently across a wide musical range, delivering soul, blues, garage punk, and British pop rock with comparable assurance. The compact set—with one track at 3:32 and the remaining running under 2:37—is anchored by cover songs and staples from the Buckinghams' apprenticeship, their early sessions, and the band's live local repertoire. Counter to the conventional course of leading the album with a smash single, "Kind of a Drag" was relegated to an unusual placement as the album's closing track. Instead, the Buckinghams start the set with soul in a punchy, brassy version of James Brown's "I'll Go Crazy." A robust mid-album cover sequence features lean garage guitar versions of "Sweets for My Sweet," a version that aligns more closely with the Searchers' interpretation rather than the Drifters' rendition of the Doc Pomus/Mort Shuman tune; the Hollies' "I've Been Wrong"; the Zombies' "You Make Me Feel Good"; an upbeat dance-to take on Lennon–McCartney's "I Call Your Name"; and the George Gershwin aria "Summertime," from *Porgy and Bess*. A subsequent remastered/reissued edition of *Kind of a Drag* (1997) adds the Buckinghams' interpretations of two oft-covered R&B standards by Lloyd Price and Bo Diddley, a lightweight "Lawdy Miss Clawdy" and a version of "I'm a Man" that echoes the Yardbirds' raw rendering.

On the Buckinghams' second '67 album and Columbia label debut, *Time & Changes*, the band appeared to take the title to heart, delving in a slightly different direction. Producer Guercio continued to shape the horn rock sound; modifying the group's sound toward a slightly heavier edge that could play alongside Cream, Jimi Hendrix, Janis Joplin, Santana, and many others infiltrating FM radio's rotations. Guercio's imprint was prominent as he arranged, conducted, and wrote or co-wrote six of the record's 10 songs. Rounding out the album's set were a Beatles cover, "I'll Be Back"; the Buckinghams' singles "Mercy, Mercy, Mercy" and "Don't You Care"; and another catchy, well-crafted Holvay/Beisbier co-write, "Why Don't You Love Me." Guercio's production presence bordered on being overstated, with heavy-handed horns and expansive, occasionally strange, orchestral arrangements, with some sounding suitable for film scores and jazz bands. The cumulative outcome was not quite quirky, but experimental enough to distinguish from the Buckinghams' approach on their hit singles. Interestingly, the requisite inclusion of the familiar "Don't You Care" and "Mercy Mercy Mercy" was conspicuous and oddly out of sync with the album's song sequence, despite being standout tracks.

In One Ear...

Duplicating their multiple album output of 1967, the Buckinghams released a pair of LPs in 1968, *Portraits* and *In One Ear and Gone Tomorrow*. Guercio's production supervision persisted through *Portraits*, though the tensions inflicted by his psychedelic "freak out" circumvention on "Susan" lingered. The band steered toward a more autonomous creative course, looking to find their own voice with original material rather than covering songs and moving beyond what had become their standard songwriting sources, the dynamic Holvay and Beisbier duo and Guercio. The Buckinghams became more involved writing (and publishing) their own songs, with Grebb emerging as the band's central songwriter.

On *Portraits*, the Buckinghams continued to stretch their material musically and lyrically with their own compositions. The band returned to Los Angeles and holed up in the Hollywood Hills writing and rehearsing. In the studio, they were given an unusual amount of leeway with their playing, creating and "doing certain things," which, according to Giammarese, amounted to "a pretty big leap for us."[31] Those "certain things" included employing different instrumentation, amps, effects, sounds, pedals, and a range of guitars: Epiphone, Gibson, Fender Stratocasters. The enhanced eclecticism featured psychedelic touches and polished production elements that included overarching string and horn arrangements courtesy of Guercio. Giammarese considered the experimental *Portraits* "a masterpiece of a concept album ... our *Sgt. Pepper*, so to speak."[32]

Despite their admirable, ambitious efforts to advance to something better and different with the album, the group strained to adapt to a heavier vibe and style comparable to the sounds circulating in the surfacing psychedelic rock scene in 1968. The experimentation resulted in disguise and diversion from their solid song compositions. The band was clearly more comfortable and better suited for the commercial confines of the AM friendly realm than they were with the FM album-oriented rock format. Similar to the presence of the Buckinghams' top-billing singles on *Time & Changes*—"Susan" and "Hey Baby (They're Playing Our Song)"—the songs did not ground *Portraits*, rather contributed to the album's uneven feel. The singles were well-intentioned interlopers and further reminders of how embedded the Buckinghams' AM brand was. The band was at its best delivering buoyant, breezy, brassy pop rock singles about elusive love, breaking up, and making up, all compressed into the couplets of a two- to three-minute time frame. Many of the running times of the tracks on *Portraits*, and later that year, *In One Ear and Gone Tomorrow*, were notably lengthier, often an outcome of expanded, though not necessarily overwrought, arrangements. Several songs doubled in running time and reached into the four-minute range, among them, "Have You Noticed You're Alive" (4:41), "C'mon Home" (4:08), and "Just Because I've Fallen Down" (4:13).

The soft reception to the Buckinghams' approach on *Portraits* was a disappointment to the band. "We thought that maybe the album would lift us from the lower pop, lighter music to something a little stronger and heavier," said Giammarese. "But our audience was not ready.... They still wanted to hear 'Kind of a Drag' and 'Don't You Care.' So it was a hard transition to take it to that level."[33]

The release of *In One Ear and Gone Tomorrow* later in 1968 did not appreciably alter, rescue, or reverse the band's trajectory. Guercio was gone. He and the Buckinghams parted ways, with the producer/manager moving on to work with Blood, Sweat & Tears, supervising their second album for Columbia late in 1968, and to further refine the horn sound with the Chicago Transit Authority (turned Chicago). In stark contrast to '67, and perhaps a corollary of Guercio's absence short of his lone contribution to the album producing "What Is Love," the Buckinghams were unable to generate a characteristic hit single from *In One Ear and Gone Tomorrow*'s 11 songs. The album's lead track and single, "Back in Love Again," featured the Buckinghams' recognizable and appealing horn arrangements, big hook, tempo, tone, and fade out, not to mention providing distinct foreshadowing of Chicago's jazz rock sound on the near horizon. Catchy and compact at 2:07, the song appeared to brim with Top

20 attributes. Yet, when released as a 45, "Back in Love Again" only managed to settle into midlevel placement, peaking at #57 on the Hot 100 and at #53 on *Cashbox* during its short stay on the charts.

Produced by Jimmy "the Wiz" Wisner, a classical pianist, *In One Ear and Gone Tomorrow* consisted of nine original songs—all written or co-written by Grebb—and a few Buckinghams' interpretations of compositions by renowned songwriting teams, Holland/Dozier/Holland ("Can I Get a Witness") and Burt Bacharach/Hal David ("Are You There with Another Girl)." The album's varied song sequencing, its tones and tempos, chill vocals and harmonies align along a varied sound spectrum. The range extends from rock riffs, jangles, and shuffles to bold brass and lush strings to old timey radio sounds and traces of the Moody Blues and other era echoes. Propeller and aeronautic gusts provide an atmospheric prelude for the lead lyric of "Song of the Breeze": "take a ride on a windy day." The depth and delicate delivery of "Simplicity" resounds in acquaintance with the melancholy moods of "Yesterday," "As Tears Go By," and perhaps the Lovin' Spoonful's "Darling Be Home Soon." One of the album's unsung tracks is the groovy gem that closes out side one, "Can't Find the Words." The track's four minutes are packed with sophisticated cool. The cymbal clattering, fuzzy growling guitars shredding, and a siren fade-out foster a kooky sixties film soundtrack vibe that evokes hip characters in turtlenecks and dancers shimmying on a shag carpet.

In One Ear and Gone Tomorrow was a quiet release, one that was largely overlooked in the mid–1968 shuffle, though the album (vint)aged well, frequently attracting "lost album of the sixties" citations and status over the years.[34] Ironically, the record's clever rephrase title proved to be a self-fulfilling prophecy. Not only did *In One Ear and Gone Tomorrow* close out the Buckinghams' trilogy of albums on Columbia, the long play record contemporaneously foreshadowed short play and their fatefully fast fade out as a Chicagoland band.

…And Gone Tomorrow

In the wake of their fourth and final album, the Buckinghams recorded and released a series of singles between September 1968 and late 1969, none of which placed on the charts. One of the recordings, "Where Did You Come From," appeared on the silver screen, as it was used (though uncredited) in the soundtrack of the film *The Guru* (1969). The composition, with a hint of the melody from Petula Clark's "Don't Sleep in the Subway," was a collaboration between renowned lyricist Don Black and composer Mark London, whose considerable credits include the hit title tune of the film *To Sir, with Love* (1967), sung by Lulu. *The Guru*, a comedy directed by James Ivory, features a premise seemingly inspired by Beatle George Harrison: British pop star Tom Pickle (Michael York) travels to Bombay, India, to learn to play the sitar from a renowned maestro.

The Buckinghams' set of late 1960s 45s were mostly originals and previously unreleased songs: "This is How Much I Love You," "It's a Beautiful Day (For Lovin')"/"Difference of Opinion," and "I Got a Feelin'"/"It Took Forever," with a few of the B-sides circulating tracks from *In One Ear and Gone Tomorrow* ("Song of the Breeze," "Can't Find the Words"). The series of singles completed the Buckinghams' Columbia catalog and their contract with the major record label.

The times were a-changin'. Evolution, revolution, or something was in the air. The music scene was a microcosm of the broader sociopolitical climate of conflict and youth in motion. Amidst the tumult of the times, the abiding acrimony and business-as-usual rift between artists and their record labels, and/or (mis)management, intervened in the Buckinghams' advancement as a band. Guercio's departure as producer, legal matters with song rights and licensing, financial mishandling and manipulation, contractual disagreements, and creative control conflicts—not to mention an incident involving drugs—combined to take a toll on the Buckinghams. Less than two years removed from being "the most listened to band in America," the Buckinghams disbanded by late 1969, another conspicuous case of evanescence and rock and roll realization. "You were starting to ask yourself what the hell are you going to do with the rest of your life," said Giammarese. "You find yourself at 22 and like a ship without a rudder."[35]

The Buckinghams' members dispersed across the music sphere. Poulos gravitated to management, while Fortuna was active as a session bassist and moved in and out of various bands. Grebb amassed extensive credits recording, touring, and working with Lovecraft, the Fabulous Rhinestones, Leon Russell, Elton John, and Roger McGuinn post–Byrds, among others. Grebb also had a particularly lengthy, short-of-permanent place playing with Bonnie Raitt.

Tufano and Giammarese paired up as a duo, recording three pleasant, though commercially flat, soft rock albums between 1973 and 1977: *Tufano and Giammarese*, *The Tufano & Giammarese Band*, and *The Other Side*. The single, "Music Everywhere," was a glimmer that placed in *Billboard*'s Hot 100 in 1973. The albums were released on Ode Records, the label of esteemed producer/music executive and Rock & Roll Hall of Fame inductee Lou Adler. Notable among Adler's producing acclaim are the touchstones *Tapestry* (1971), Carole King's Grammy-winning album, and the endlessly running cult classic film *Rocky Horror Picture Show* (1975).

Giammarese eventually repositioned as a high-volume commercial jingle vocalist and then embarked on a sustained solo career, while Tufano briefly pursued acting before circling back to the singing circuit in Bobby Vinton tribute guise. Tufano also has the trivia question distinction of teaming with actress Mindy Sterling to sing "Without Us," the theme song for the NBC network's prime-time situation comedy *Family Ties*. The Tufano/Sterling duet played during the series premiere season in 1982 and was replaced by Johnny Mathis and Deniece Williams's rendition beginning the following season. The popular television show, created by Gary Goldberg and starring Michael J. Fox, produced 176 episodes over its seven broadcast television seasons.

Over the decades, the Buckinghams routinely reunite, revisiting, restating, and presiding over their hit parade at various Chicago area events and as part of the line-ups of popular 1960s Solid Gold touring nostalgia shows. Among the most prominent and prevailing period roadshows is the Happy Together Tour, which has featured the Turtles, Grass Roots, Gary Lewis & the Playboys, Gary Puckett and the Union Gap, and Tommy James & the Shondells, among other Top 40 flashes from the era.

Six Singles Strong: A Sustaining Sound Scope

The Buckinghams' climb, crest, and culmination chronicled into a curiously compact course. From a basement band doing British Invasion and R&B, to bubbling under on *Billboard* before a big breakthrough, to bubble bursting into disbandment, all within four fleeting years. Music historian Rick Simmons dramatically characterizes the ephemeral Chicagoland group as "rock's greatest disappearing act," and their rapid recede as "one of the most perplexing falls in rock and roll history."[36] Though the Buckinghams' succinct span was fairly typical of the short-term duration of bands—whether of Midwest, national, or international origins—during the prolific period, their concentrated chart continuity and presence that transcended mere "one-hit wonder" repute undoubtedly heightened expectations of staying power, and conversely magnified the group's transience.

The Buckinghams' "in one ear and gone tomorrow" arc of achievement moved swiftly along a spectrum from surprising to significant. Or, perplexing. Aside from some of the extraordinary singles saturation of the era accumulating from bands such as the Dave Clark Five and indubitably, the Beatles, and their historical standard holding the top five spots on the *Billboard* charts in 1964, the Buckinghams' Top 40 chart persistence was an enduring and admirable accomplishment. Their succession of hit songs settled somewhere between smashing and sensational, with the Chicagoland band holding its own alongside the Hollies, Byrds, Paul Revere & the Raiders, Herman's Hermits, the Turtles, and other artists generating multiple hit singles within the mid-period's 45 revolutions-per-minute flourish.

The Buckinghams' enduring essence, on both regional and national levels, remains situated simply, soundly, and securely within a short term/long play that is six singles strong, more glaringly than a legacy resounding or residing in their albums or live performances. Beyond the notable chart positions and sales of the Buckinghams' records, the band's distinctive '67 single sequence, among other musical merits, embodied major record label validation and legendary studio settings, showcased a rising producer and pair of unsung songwriters, and advanced the horn rock sound as a brassy bridge between the bands The MOB and Chicago. Momentous, momentary, and mystifying, the Buckinghams' string of successful singles enriched and eclipsed the vibrant Midwest setting, further pronouncing the Chicagoland presence and indelibly imprinting its regional identity on the national musical map.

CHAPTER 6

It's a Cryan' Shame

As Chicagoland's major label breakthrough band, signing with Columbia Records in 1966, the Cryan' Shames brought an array of appealing musical qualities to the Midwest mid–1960s scene. The garage group demonstrated a unique knack for adeptly gleaning and intermingling familiar sounds and disparate elements and shaping them into their own song style signature that was textured with exquisite vocal harmonies and inventive instrumentation, attractive melodies, and sophisticated arrangements.

The Cryan' Shames' evolution as a Chicagoland suburband progressed as a fairly familiar "follow that dream" narrative that unfolded steadily, if not swiftly, from innocence to a relative regional state of stardom. Once the group established a following playing live locally, they connected with influential radio disc jockeys and then cut several singles that received heavy rotation airplay. The band networked appropriate music industry contacts, signed a record deal, and resourcefully managed the rock requisites such as the road, touring and gigs, rehearsals and recording sessions, and personnel swings along the way.

Recognized for their spirited live presence and some chart success with a sequence of 45s, the Cryan' Shames' profile, identity, and appeal tended a touch toward being more album-oriented than the majority of their fellow Chicagoland bands, notably the Buckinghams and New Colony Six, who established significant singles status. Following their debut 45 release on the local label Destination, "Sugar and Spice," which placed in the top 50 nationally, the Cryan' Shames signed with Columbia Records. The renowned major label was gravitating to folk, rock, and pop mid-decade during the record company's executive transition from Mitch Miller to Clive Davis. Between 1966 and 1969, the Cryan' Shames recorded and released three alliterative "s"-titled albums—*Sugar and Spice*, *A Scratch in the Sky*, and *Synthesis*—on Columbia, supplemented by eight accompanying singles during their succinct span. Several of those 45s featured both A- and B-sides that were non-album tracks. The majority of the singles were more solid than they were smashing successes, and predictably more popular in the Midwest than they were nationally. While many of the Cryan' Shames' 45s reached the Top 10 locally on the WLS and WCFL radio rotations, many of the group's singles spent significant stretches "bubbling under" outside the Hot 100 *Billboard* chart. The Cryan' Shames' singles' chart positioning patterned at peaks between 80 and 127.

Prowlers, Roosters, and "the Guy with the Hook"

The Cryan' Shames' origins reside 20 miles west of Chicago in the vicinity of the affluent suburb Hinsdale and the neighboring communities Lisle and Downers Grove. The group's configuration into one of the central suburbands during the mid-to-late 1960s was a synthesis similar to other local formative fusions, among them, the Buckinghams, who materialized by merging members of the Pulsations and the Centuries. The Cryan' Shames also took shape assembling personnel from a few local bands. The Prowlers, with individual sobriquets seemingly a coincidence, quirk, or peculiar condition for group membership, provided a foundational trio consisting of Gerry "Stonehenge" Stone (rhythm guitar), Lisle native Tom "Toad" Doody (lead vocals), and the versatile Dave "Grape" Purple (bass, keyboards, harpsichord). These elder 20-year-olds were joined by two younger, non-nicknamed musicians from the nearby Downers Grove band the Roosters: guitarist Jim Fairs and drummer Dennis Conroy, both age 18.

The emergent ensemble completed their youthful lineup by enlisting enthusiast Jim Pilster, a percussionist who was not affiliated with any active band, to join them on stage. Pilster, the band's tweener at 19, added another catchy pseudonym to the lineup: "J. C. Hooke." The moniker was in reference to Pilster's artificial extremity, the result of a congenital malformation that left him with an underdeveloped left arm. Pilster's performance prop may have been a novelty, but the appendage was fashioned out of necessity. His vigorous tambourine tapping on stage hurt his limb, so Pilster put together a makeshift hook that he screwed into a down rod and taped to his arm to cushion the continual impact. John Brown, who owned and operated a leatherworks shop in Piper's Alley located in Chicago's near north side neighborhood Old Town, the city's hip(pie) epicenter, commissioned a sculptor friend who was a professor in metallurgy at the Art Institute of Chicago to craft a thick sheath for Pilster. The cumbersome, costume-like casing, "a big harpoon-shaped thing" estimated by Pilster to weigh close to three pounds, was an incongruous, conspicuous accessory with the band's contemporary attire. "We were all wearing mod clothes—the waistcoats and ruffled shirts—and Brown thought a hook would add to my image," said Pilster.[1] Brown's leatherworks studio fashionably furthered the Cryan' Shames' common sound association with the Byrds as the Old Town artisan also designed the iconic moss-green cape worn by Byrd David Crosby.

Pilster/Hooke was first and foremost a performer. "Percussionist" was a convenient, requisite label listed on record liner note and sleeve credits. And, while Pilster provided another harmony vocal to the chorus, at his best he was a showman. As the group's fronting Mr. Tambourine Man, Pilster projected a swashbuckling, crowd-pleasing, prancing posture and presence, single-handedly delivering energetic acrobatic athleticism across the stage. "I started jumping around and we started doing some choreography," said Pilster. "It wasn't very sophisticated, but we were about the only energetic band around. Everybody else was like imitating the Rolling Stones, standing around and looking moody."[2] Bandmate Jim Fairs was among the many who appreciated Pilster's exuberant presence:

> It was kind of nice, because here was this guy who didn't have to figure out how to play his guitar. He could just get onstage and enjoy the music. I was trying to figure out how to put all this music together. Everyone was trying to figure out how to play their instruments or trying to look cool, and here was a guy who would get onstage and enjoy the music, to dance, to sing an occasional harmony, to play the tambourine and to have a good time.[3]

At Hinsdale Central High School, Pilster lettered for four years as a diver on the school's renowned swim team. He was a member of their very first state meet qualifying squad that inaugurated the school swim program's perennial championship level performance and placement. The singing swimmer's sardonic stage name was literally and figuratively a hook. Pilster's left-handed attraction was more a signature than a sideshow gimmick and became a pivotal part of Pilster's persona and the group's identity. Early on, the group was habitually and handily referred to as "the band with the guy with the hook."

According to Pilster, the initialed prefix "J.C.," derived from his bandmates' exclamations—"Jesus Christ Hooke!"—when they were accidentally poked or nicked by too close contact with Pilster's sharp prong, whether during performances or in passing. Pilster himself could not avoid inadvertent self-inflicted punctures during his hyperactive stage antics. "The hook was my trademark and a lot of fun," said Pilster. "But the hook also felt very uncomfortable and was very dangerous."[4]

Travelers' Destination

The Prowlers and Roosters coalition, plus Pilster, managed to avoid a formative fracas over band branding by calling themselves The Travelers. The budding band's developmental phase echoed many of the familiar sounds of the era. The suburban collective fervently rummaged around and through the corners and crevices of the musical garage, resourcefully retrieving and refining fragments that fit and were then assembled into an appealing synthesis of folk and rock with psychedelic sunshine pop.

Despite the multitude of similarities, strands, and samplings, the Travelers managed to forge their own sound with an instrumental repertoire that autonomously avoided the incorporation of what had become a Chicagoland music scene signature—horns and brass. Their evolving style was derivative, yet distinctive: an adept Byrdsian emphasis that also borrowed and blended some of the best of the British Invasion—requisite Beatles melodies, Hollies harmonies, Rolling Stones and Yardbirds riffs—while also assimilating accents of the Association, the Left Banke, and ripples of Beach Boys resonance stirred into suburban surf near the shores of Lake Michigan. In Pilster's simplified self-summation, "We were garage before there was garage. And we loved the Byrds. We weren't the average rock and roll band. We were music and show, and we could actually sing."[5] Vocally, the group's constitution was striking for its range, with multiple singers who could reach any octave, whether assuming the lead or contributing to multilayered harmonies. "We feel vocal development is more crucial to us at this point than trying to get a distinctive instrumental sound even though we have managed to do this too," said Doody of the group's emergent stage.[6]

The suburband made an impression performing live shows locally, covering their way through sets of rock and R&B renditions across the teeming local teen scene. Their appearances advanced from school sock hops and battle-of-the-bands contests to playing at community centers, auditoriums, and VFW halls to happenings hosted by the popular WLS and WCFL disc jockeys. The Travelers were also a big draw at the hotspots along the lively club circuit, frequently billed at Like Young on Old Town's active avenue, Wells Street, and at the Blue Village in Westmont, where they became the unofficial house band.

Prevailing innocence paralleled the band's increasing presence and popularity. "We didn't have a clue what we were doing, especially financially," said Pilster. "I mean, we were only 16 and 18 years old. We were just happy to be out there playing and meeting girls. And we heard our names on the radio."[7] In their rapid development, the group acquired burgeoning band essentials, among them their own transportation via an air-conditioned trailer, over $6,000 worth of music equipment, and a road manager. Fred Bohlander, a friend of the band, who was a regular hanging out at the Travelers' shows, inserted himself into a novice managerial role, which was initially being handled by Doody's brother, Jack. With no previous booking experience to draw from, Bohlander innocently and instinctively began scheduling some performance dates for the band at various venues. Most of the gigs initially were live within a convenient and confining 10-mile radius.

As the band's popularity and exposure amplified through their live performances, on radio airplay, and by word of mouth, the scope expanded to traveling to play road dates across the Midwest region. According to most accounts, from band members and from Midwest music chronicler Clark Besch, the group was consistently earning between $180 and $200 per performance. Despite being a six-way split, the sum was considered a decent fee at the time, particularly for a band who had yet to record. For Bohlander, the self-appointed agent apprenticeship for his friends' band turned out to be a backstage baptism. Bohlander continued to pursue his passion in artist management and representation from Chicago to Los Angeles, working in the music industry with talent and concert booking with the renowned agency IFA. He then formed the fabled boutique group Monterey Peninsula before becoming co-head of concerts for Paradigm Talent Agency, where he completed his distinguished 50-plus year career in 2019.[8]

Important alliances advanced the Travelers closer toward the brink of discovery and a record deal. WLS disc jockey Dex Card was a pivotal presence in the band's breakthrough. Impressed by what he heard and saw during the Travelers' live shows,

Card recommended the group to Bob Monaco, an associate who was the promotions manager for Jim Golden's fledgling local label, Destination Records. Destination was part of an industrious trinity of local record labels that also included U.S.A. Records and Dunwich. All were garage and psychedelia rock havens with a recording pipeline to and from Sound Studios on South Michigan Avenue and the supervision of audio ace recording engineers Stu Black and Ron Malo.

The Destination label had just broken through the WLS Top 40 with the single "Please Mr. Sullivan," a novelty tune by the Peoria, Illinois, group the Warner Brothers. Their partially spoken plead to be on Ed Sullivan's Sunday evening variety showcase features a "Louie, Louie" melody with name-dropping that cites popular comic and music figures from the era, among them Phyllis Diller, Jerry Lewis, and country singer Roger Miller (best known for his Nashville novelty tunes "King of the Road," "Dang Me," and "England Swings"). Destination's roster steadily accumulated area acts, among them Ronnie Ross & The Good Guys; the Boyz from southwest suburb Joliet; Chicago outliers across state lines, the Ricochettes, who were referred to as "Milwaukee's Beatles"; the Jokers from Valparaiso, Indiana, 55 miles east of the Windy City; and the Sheffields from Holland, Michigan, the farthest distance at 150 miles.

Golden signed the Travelers to Destination, and Monaco, as a finder's keeper reward, became the group's manager. From that point forward, the Monaco/Golden tandem, as MG Productions, imprinted the band's recording catalog over the next three years. As one of the group's main songwriters and musicians, Jim Fairs recognized the importance of the band's business association with Monaco and Golden and how it complemented their creative qualities as musicians. "There were any number of bands playing and active at the time, and some, like the Riddles, never got a fair chance," said Fairs. "The real difference for us was the business component. We learned ground-level promotion and sales from them [Monaco and Golden]."[9]

If I Needed Someone's Song

The Travelers' music industry initiation was accompanied by some interesting impediments. The band's proposed debut single in 1966 became a stumbling block instead of a starting block. After hearing their admirable live performance of the Beatles' "If I Needed Someone," Monaco recommended the Travelers follow up and cut a cover of the George Harrison tune as their first single. The song was highly compatible with the Travelers' sound and style. Monaco no doubt recognized that the Chicagolanders capably triangulated the mutuality that existed between the Beatles and the Byrds, specifically the three-part harmonies and the electric 12-string ringing Rickenbacker correspondence between Harrison and Jim (Roger) McGuinn. The distinct sound reverberated back and forth from the Beatles film *A Hard Day's Night* in 1964 and the tracks "What You're Doing" on *Beatles for*

Sale (1964) and "Nowhere Man" on *Rubber Soul* (1965) to the Byrds' "She Don't Care About Time" and "The Bells of Rhymney," among other record reciprocations from both bands' bursts of brilliance mid-decade.

The Travelers' recording of "If I Needed Someone" became part of the song's curious preliminary course and continuity. Written by Harrison for model Pattie Boyd, whom he married in 1966, the version of the song had not been formally released by the Beatles, though it was circulating in Chicago via radio airplay on WLS and WCFL. The original track was sequenced on the Beatles' album *Rubber Soul*, which was issued in the UK on December 3, 1965. In keeping with its peculiar recording withholding practices, Capitol Records' North American edition of *Rubber Soul* altered the original British EMI Parlophone edition and excluded "If I Needed Someone" from the album content. The track resurfaced six months later in June 1966 on the Beatles' next album, *Yesterday and Today*.

Even before its release, the resounding qualities of "If I Needed Someone" attracted another of the leading British bands, the Hollies, whose producer had received a demo of the song from the Beatles' producer, George Martin. The popular group, founded by Allan Clarke and Graham Nash, resourcefully recorded a version as a follow-up to their hit "Look Through Any Window," with a same-day single release that coincided with the Beatles' *Rubber Soul* album's December distribution. The Hollies' rendition of "If I Needed Someone," which featured notably snappy drumming by Bobby Elliott, reached the Top 20 in the UK, though the chart position was a lower placement than many previous Hollies' hit singles.

Despite the cover version marking Harrison's songwriting chart debut, the Beatle was critical of the Hollies' production, saying of their adaptation of his love song, "[It] is not my kind of music." "I think it's rubbish the way they've done it," said "the quiet Beatle." "They've spoilt it. They [the Hollies] are all right musically, but the way they do their records, they sound like session men who've just got together in a studio without ever seeing each other before. Technically they're good, but that's all!"[10] Predictably, the Liverpudlian derision was not well received by their Manchester rivals, particularly Nash, though the Harrison-Hollies dissonance did not escalate beyond a few brusque exchanges.

The version's vibe lingered in the crisscross between the Beatles' EMI and Capitol record releases in the UK and the US. In 1966, when the Travelers recorded their take of "If I Needed Someone," Jim Golden was unable to secure licensing permission from EMI to issue the song as the Travelers' Destination debut single. The publisher prohibition of the 45 release was purportedly due to the (un)availability of the Beatles' original cut stateside.

Beyond the record label and legal levels, Harrison's Hollies' disenchantment hovered, conveniently conjuring a curious and vindictive cover conspiracy. The Travelers' version of "If I Needed Someone" appeared to be singled out, literally and figuratively. Between October and November 1966, around the same time frame the Travelers recorded the Harrison song, two other interpretations of "If I Needed

Someone" emerged as singles and album tracks. The Kingsmen, of "Louie, Louie" renown, with a revamped lineup, delivered a faithful folk rock rendition as a single on the Wand label. The version was also included as a track among multiple covers on their LP, *Up and Away*. Harrison's song was also presented instrumentally on Hugh Masekela's *Next Album*, which featured the South African trumpeter's jazz adaptations of numerous popular songs from the era, with "Along Comes Mary," "The Sounds of Silence," "California Dreamin'," "Norwegian Wood," "Elusive Butterfly," and "It's Not Unusual," among the Masekela set.

Complications compounded into an accompanying blown cover case involving the Travelers. Not only was their debut single and premiere postponed, the band's identity became in doubt. In yet another instance of a Chicagoland musical group wearing a misappropriated moniker, the band learned that "The Travelers" was a duplicate designation. "Tommy and the Travelers," more specifically. As inadvertent imposters, the Hinsdale "Travelers" would have to change their name. By all accounts of local legend, lore, and compilation liner notes, in a frustrated response to the group's circumstance and sequence of setbacks, Jim Pilster pronounced, "It's really a cryin' shame!" The impulsive "Hooke" utterance struck a transformative chord that pierced the transitory title "the Travelers," while purportedly wordplay sniping at their front Tommy Krein's name (pronounced "cryan"). Krein apparently was approached by Pilster about joining the Hinsdale "Travelers," but he was not interested. The discarded "Travelers" tag was dismissed by Pilster as sounding like a "boat group," and the rebranded band was fortuitously baptized "the Cryan' Shames."

Single-Minded:
Searching for a Sweet Spot and Solving a Riddle

With their name tenable, the Cryan' Shames were single-minded, seeking another song to record for a debut 45 do-over. Their musical quest crisscrossed regional and international sound convergences between the local band the Riddles and the British group the Searchers. The Riddles' group membership represented a string of Chicagoland western suburbs along an 11-mile stretch of Route 83, from Elmhurst and Villa Park to two "brooks"—Oak Brook and Willowbrook. The band's lone single, released on Quill Records in 1967, was a cover of "Sweets for My Sweet," with a mod psych/rock B-side, "It's One Thing to Say." Co-written by the dynamic duo Doc Pomus and Mort Shuman, "Sweets for My Sweet" was originally recorded by the Drifters in 1961, then a few years later by the Searchers as their debut single in 1963. In 1965, the Buckinghams preceded fellow locals the Riddles' rendition with their recording of the Pomus/Shuman sweet tune, releasing it as a single on Spectra-Sound and later including it as a track on their U.S.A. Records debut album, *Kind of a Drag*, one of the band's three LPs released in 1967.

Quill Records was a local independent label founded by Peter Wright. The

Riddles were among a Quill roster that was packed with raw, edgy, moody Midwest garage rockers that included the Exterminators; Rooks; Chances R; the girl group High Schoolers; Commons Ltd.; Delights, who were billed as "Chicago's answer to the Zombies"; Skunks; Prophets; Night Flights; Proper Strangers; Ricochettes; Ronnie Rice & The Gents; and Jimmy Watson & The Original Royals. Many members from this array of relatively obscure outfits gravitated to more notable area bands such as the New Colony Six, Chicago Transit Authority/Chicago, Aorta, and Aliotta Haynes Jeremiah, among others.

The Riddles' run was fleeting. Beyond the flicker of their only 45 rpm, which was distributed nationally on Mercury Records, the band was active playing the resident live circuit. They also made several appearances on local television on the age 12-and-under dance show *Kiddie A-Go-Go* before the group simply, swiftly dissolved. According to drummer Ronald Fricano, "We just couldn't come up with another song and faded away into bars."[11] Of note, the Riddles' lead guitarist, Patrick "Rick" Harper, eventually relocated to Tennessee and became one of the session players in Kenny Rogers' band Bloodline from 1976 through 2001.

The Searchers represented a Riddles' "sweet spot" and a sound standard. In addition to the Riddles' rendition of "Sweets for My Sweet" as a single, their live repertoire also included "Sugar and Spice," written by Searchers' producer Tony Hatch under the pseudonym "Fred Nightingale." Hatch pitched the song to the band he was supervising as the work of an unknown songwriter rather than his own composition, hoping the Searchers would be more receptive to recording the composition. As the Searchers' follow-up single to "Sweets for My Sweet," "Sugar and Spice" reached #2 in the UK and #44 in the US in 1963.

Formed in 1960, the Searchers derived their name from film director John Ford's John Wayne Western epic in 1956. Musically, the band was at the Merseybeat vanguard of the 12-string hooks and Everly Brothers three-part harmonies that became a hallmark of the Byrds, among other bands, both British and American. With a sound that was pretty, polished, and pleasant, the Searchers aligned with mid-decade hit-generating, clean cut, uniformed outfits such as Herman's Hermits, Gerry and the Pacemakers, and Gary Lewis & the Playboys. Between 1963 and 1965, the Searchers populated the charts with 13 melodic singles that placed in the Top 20 in England and in the US. Three of those 45s reached #1. Their most familiar hits were charming covers. In addition to "Sweets for My Sweet," the Searchers' rotation of reinterpretations includes Jackie DeShannon's "When You Walk in the Room," along with her hit "Needles and Pins," co-written by Phil Spector sidekick Jack Nitzsche and pre–Cher Sonny Bono; Billy Jackson and Jimmy Wisner's "Don't Throw Your Love Away," which was an Orions' B-side; and the playful gypsy aphrodisiac tune from legendary lyricist/composer team Jerry Leiber and Mike Stoller, "Love Potion No. 9," originally recorded by the Clovers in 1959.

While it was naturally fitting to link the Byrds, Beatles, and Hollies trinity with the Cryan' Shames' explicit influences, the Searchers' style was an understated underpinning in their sound. Upon hearing the Riddles' perform the Searchers' "Sugar and Spice" during a live show in nearby Bensenville, a northwest suburb located near O'Hare International Airport, the group members were instantly enamored with the song. The discovery developed into the Cryan' Shames' deferred debut single for Destination.

The Cryan' Shames swooped on "Sugar and Spice," recording a racing 2:26 rendition in 45 minutes under the production supervision of Monaco and Golden in mid–June. As Doody tells it, following the instrumental take, "they put a microphone out in the middle of the floor, we all got around, balanced ourselves, and then we sang it ['Sugar and Spice']. Then we sang it again, they multi-ed it, and that was it! We learned it the day before."[12]

The night before their Sound Studios session, Doody urged Jim Fairs to come up with a B-side for the projected single. The rush order songwriting result from Fairs was a striking stylistic contrast titled "Ben Franklin's Almanac." The track is a hectic haiku of proto psych-punk and tenacious tambourine tapping in a racing running time just under two minutes. The frenetic flip side, a free-for-all in freefall, is, in Fairs's view, "a snapshot of the influences of the Kinks, Stones, Beach Boys, and 'Louie Louie.'"[13] Not to mention the song's Bo Diddley beat and explicit Yardbirds fuzz and distortion. Resourcefully recorded in 20 minutes, the garage rave-up is "a jumble and a blur" that threads three trippy stanzas of formless fragments in Beat poet spontaneity and without any reference (other than the song's intrinsic electricity) to Ben Franklin—whether the inventor or the five-and-dime arts and crafts chain store. The succinct surreal sensibility ricochets in colors and particle pairings such as "inside out/far and near/here or gone" before setting in a "frozen sun.[14] Fairs admitted that his lyrics may have "sounded deep … but [were] actually complete gibberish."[15] In his critical excavation and succinct summary of the mayhem of "Ben Franklin's Almanac" in 2001, the aficionado of the obscure and unsung, known as "The Seth Man," in the music platform *The Book of Seth*, aptly deems the B-side track "a tiny epic."[16]

According to Doody and common local lore of the era, while driving home after their session and "probably half a mile from the studio," the Cryan' Shames heard Clark Weber on WLS radio introduce the song they had just recorded. Backed by influential local radio programmers such as Weber, "Sugar and Spice" benefited from immediate airplay in a rotation that was increasingly occupied with Chicagoland bands, with the New Colony Six and Shadows of Knight among the locals stirring the scene. "The DJs were trying to discover Chicago groups because there was a wealth of talent," said Doody. "We were in the right place at the right time. 'Sugar and Spice' took off, it just went like a rocket ship."[17] By the end of July, the Cryan' Shames delayed debut—the Searchers' cover as a substitute single for George Harrison's "If I Needed Someone"—reached inside the Top 10 of both WLS (#4) and WCFL (#7), on its way to placing in the midway of the national charts, where it peaked at #49 on *Billboard* and at #52 on *Cashbox*.

... And All Things Nice: Columbia Records

The sprightly '66 smash single, with impressive sales of 400,000 copies in the Midwest region, caught the national attention of Columbia Records. Whether pure purloining or profitable professional persuasion, Columbia signed the Cryan' Shames to a contract. In the opt-out process from their Destination deal, the band became the Midwest region's pioneering major label representatives, with the Buckinghams soon to follow after graduating from U.S.A. Records and also signing with Columbia in 1967. The label had been in transition since mid-decade, as its Broadway soundtracks and conductor Mitch Miller's *Singalong Series* LP sales were waning. Miller, an influential industry figure, stepped aside as company president and was replaced by Clive Davis. Largely influenced by the Monterey International Pop Festival and the presence of dynamic acts such as Janis Joplin, who was among the performers live at the momentous June 1967 California event, Davis shifted Columbia's catalog emphasis to rock.

The Cryan' Shames joined a stellar record roster, enlisted alongside their kindred sound spirits, the Byrds, whose primary popular song source, Bob Dylan, was Columbia's headliner. Other noteworthy hitmakers on the label lineup at the time included Simon & Garfunkel, Paul Revere & the Raiders, and the Cyrkle, who charted songs "Turn Down Day" and "Red Rubber Ball," co-composed by Paul Simon and the Seekers' Bruce Woodley.

Looking to capitalize on the initial success of their new midwestern signees, Columbia insisted on a fast follow-up 45 from the Chicagoland band whom they initially and clumsily cross promoted as "the Mod Paul Revere & the Raiders." Fairs maintained his role as the Cryan' Shames' resident songwriting source of original material and delivered another pleasant, upbeat two-minute tune for their Columbia debut 45—"I Wanna Meet You," backed with the glistening B-side, "We Could Be Happy." A snare lick kick startles "I Wanna Meet You" into an admiring admission, a crush-at-first-sight with a magazine model the object of adolescent innocence and boyhood infatuation. While the song was suggested to be inspired by a Montgomery Ward catalog, its lyrical gaze contains a universality that could be cast in multiple directions beyond illustrated retail inventory volumes to *Seventeen* and *Teen Beat* onto an adult's copy of *Playboy* magazine (with a proverbial "just for the articles" rationalization).

A sound-alike synthesis is salient in the song. The Cryan' Shames' sparkling harmony blend accenting Doody's lead vocal markedly bounces into a breezy, buoyant Beach Boy blueprint, with a dexterous, jangling bridge that continues to confirm their Byrds and Beatles—McGuinn and Harrison—12-string influences. By December 1966, "I Wanna Meet You" reached the WLS Top 10 and peaked nationally at #65 on *Cashbox*. Despite the follow-up single's chart placement falling short of the reception for its predecessor, "Sugar and Spice," both 45s facilitated increased national exposure, validation, and an appealing presence of the midwestern band.

Songs accumulated swiftly. In addition to their pair of two-sided singles, the Cryan' Shames had assembled and recorded enough material to fill at least two sides of a Long Play record by late summer 1966, even before signing their major label deal. Among the early recordings were curiosities such as an adept cover of the Beatles' "You're Gonna Lose That Girl," which remained a vaulted rarity awaiting release for decades. "Columbia essentially bought our album as delivered when they signed us," said Pilster. "They didn't really know what to do with us."[18] Similar to the rapid writing, recording, and release of their initial 45s, the Cryan' Shames' debut album came together, in Doody's estimation, "insanely quickly." *Sugar and Spice* was recorded on a tight budget at Sound Studios in a mere but manic two days in August.

Both Doody's and Pilster's accounts of the band's adventures corroborated an exhaustive schedule that ricocheted back and forth between the band being on the road performing at live gigs to all-night recording sessions and catching a nap under the piano or wherever they could in between takes. "We were going on no sleep for two days," recalls Doody. "We just went in, did it, sang it, and moved on. Most of that stuff was one take…. Just like a live recording."[19]

In informal accordance with standard record company practice, "Sugar and Spice" was resourcefully replicated from its hit single status to being bannered as the album's recognizable title and simultaneously showcased as the obvious choice for the lead track. The song's "sweet" theme pervades the long play record outside and inside, from the red-tinted cover design photograph shot by Don Bronstein portraying the group gathered in the Sweet Tooth candy shop in Piper's Alley, Old Town, through the album's 11 tuneful tracks of musicconfectionary.

Sugar and Spice's sunny sequence of melodious psychedelic pop rock with garage attributes consists predominantly of cross-genre cover versions, from familiar to relatively obscure, interspersed with four Fairs compositions. Three of the Fairs tracks were the previously released single sides—"Ben Franklin's Almanac," "I Wanna Meet You," and "We Could Be Happy." The sole original not from one of their 45s, "July," is another petite pearl. The succinct and serene harmonic dreamscape floats, echoes, and melts for an ephemeral 1:34, in layers of light harmonies accented with adroit Byrdsian chime, a jig-like bridge, and crisp Dennis Conroy backbeat on drums. The four Fairs originals foreshadowed stylistic sound directions the band would pursue sooner than later.

The seven cover versions recorded as tracks on *Sugar and Spice* represent a cross section of era-contiguous popular songs, from Motown to British Invasion to the indispensable Byrds presence. The highlight of the set may be the inclusion of "If I Needed Someone," the Cryan' Shames' proposed but postponed debut single. Among other familiar selections in the sequence are adaptations from the prolific songwriting catalogs of the Holland-Dozier-Holland trio, with "Heat Wave," taken to Hitsville by Martha and the Vandellas in 1963 on Motown's Gordy subsidiary, and Barry Mann and Cynthia Weil's "We Gotta Get Out of This Place," a white-blues hit for the Animals in 1965. The Cryan' Shames' live version of the song closes the album and is the only track to run longer than three minutes. Doody delivers a peculiar spoken word preface to the performance, with affected British inflection while meandering, calling the song "kind of an old Scottish classic," citing Vietnamese revolutionary, Ho Chi Minh, and inverting the song's title to "Out of This Place, We've Gotten to Get." Doody's affectation may have been an echo of Cryan' Shames solidarity with the Brit in the Buckinghams' name and the New Colony Six's costumes, a fashion statement/faux paus that Portland, Oregon, natives Paul Revere & the Raiders colonized in the era.

Three of the seven *Sugar and Spice* covers were Byrds' derivatives. To producer Monaco's and the Cryan' Shames' credit, they did not rely on the most recognizable rendition route. Perhaps self-conscious Byrds' watchers, and keenly cognizant of the undeniable influence, the conspicuous connections and comparisons to their Columbia label mates, the Cryan' Shames' Byrds borrowing was admirably nuanced and carefully curated, favoring deep tracks, B-sides, and covers.

There were inevitable echoes of familiarity. With their version of "Hey Joe (Where You Gonna Go)," the Cryan' Shames joined a lengthy list of artists who performed and/or recorded the Billy Roberts composition into one of the era's garage punk standards. In the one-year span between the Leaves launch of the song as a single in November 1965 and the Cryan' Shames' album track 11 months later in the following October, "Hey Joe" saturated the 1966 cover calendar with near monthly recording regularity. The '66 sequence includes racing renditions by Arthur Lee & Love (March), the Tangents, Surfaris (April), Standells (May), Byrds (July), fellow Chicagolanders the Shadows of Knight (October), Music Machine (November), the Jimi Hendrix Experience (December).

The Cryan' Shames' interpretation leads with an oriental gong cymbal that vibrates into spacey reverb, aligning with the Byrds' psychedelic translation of "Hey Joe (Where You Gonna Go)" on *Fifth Dimension* (1966), the Byrds' third album for Columbia. Recorded following the departure of the group's primary songwriter Gene Clark, the LP features a striking slant toward an experimental sound style with rāga influences. The record was marked by another notable absence—Bob Dylan material, which had been central to the Byrds' repertoire. From the chart-topping "Mr. Tambourine Man" in April 1965 through 1970, the Byrds recorded 13 songs written by Dylan as singles or album tracks, among them "Chimes of Freedom," "My Back Pages," "You Ain't Going Nowhere," "The Times They Are a-Changin'," and "All I Really Want to Do." The popular appeal of the Byrds' Dylan variations in ringing electric folk rock arrangements was rumored to have prompted lead singer David Crosby to purportedly proclaim that the Byrds "play Dylan better than Dylan." Years later, in his *Chronicles: Volume One* (2004), Dylan writes in colorful appreciation of Crosby's talent and eccentricities, characterizing him as "an architect of harmony" and an "obstreperous companion" who "could freak out a whole city block by himself."[20]

The Cryan' Shames' curious, commendable choice to cover the 1939 British song "We'll Meet Again" is another Byrds' catalog cue. Sentimental and sophisticated, the lovely longing melody was composed by Hugh Charles and Ross Parker and popularized in 1953 by Dame Vera Lynn. In the mid–1960s, the song was featured as soundtrack accompaniment to images of nuclear holocaust in the closing scene of the Stanley Kubrick's 1964 film satire, *Dr. Strangelove or: How I Learned to Stop Worrying and Love the Bomb*, starring Peter Sellers and George C. Scott. The following year, the Byrds' recording of "We'll Meet Again" was sequenced as the closing track on their debut album, *Mr. Tambourine Man* (1965).

The lone Byrds' original that the Cryan' Shames recorded as a track on *Sugar and Spice* is another intriguing selection. The Gene Clark gem "She Don't Care About Time" is buried treasure in the Byrds' catalog. The song is the B-side to their chart-topping, "Turn, Turn, Turn" (1965), the Byrds' adaptation of the Book of Ecclesiastes passage that was popularized musically by Pete Seeger. The complex chording structure within "She Don't Care About Time" features a guitar solo in the bridge that is patterned after Bach-inspired riffs from "Jesu, Joy of Man's Desiring." George Harrison cited the drumming from "She Don't Care About Time," along with a riff from "The Bells of Rhymney," as impressionistic influences on his "If I Needed Someone," thus adding another layer and line to the Cryan' Shames/Byrds/Beatles triangulation. The gifted Clark's introspective composition was recorded during the Byrds' second album studio sessions between June and November 1965. Despite its release as a single side, "She Don't Care About Time" oddly was not included on the *Turn! Turn! Turn!* LP's final 11-song cycle. Over time, versions of the secluded, unsung song eventually appeared across Byrds' "best of" and "essential" editions, reissues, compilations, and box sets.

The 11 tracks that compose the Cryan' Shames' *Sugar and Spice* set were recorded over a tight two-day period in August. Columbia released the LP in both monaural and stereo formats in mid–October 1966. A banner across the top of the album's front cover jacket announces "Electronically Re-channeled for Stereo" though all the album tracks are true "stereo" except for the first two selections of side one. The Cryan' Shames' debut album rapidly reached the Top Five regionally, with a notably slower show nationally. The record eventually registered inside the *Billboard* 200, placing at #192 in May of '67, with a relatively short four-week stay. The Chicagolanders' Columbia Records trajectory ascended steadily from innocence and local color toward broader notoriety. The success of the Cryan' Shames' initial pair of singles, along with an appealing debut album circulating in the music marketplace, combined to propel the promising profiles of both the Cryan' Shames as a band and the nascent Chicagoland scene in which they were rooted. The Cryan' Shames were swept into major label motion as touring commenced to promote their debut album release across the Midwest and eventually across the country. During a whirlwind span of six to eight months that extended from their debut album release in the fall of 1966 into early 1967, the band was abound in multimedia mode. Coverage was widespread, ranging from airplay in radio rotations, both regionally and nationally, and performances on television dance shows, to print sources that included cover features in popular teen magazines and in ads promoting their records on the pages of the major music trade publications *Billboard* and *Cashbox*.

The band and MG Productions established a playful promotional presence even before their major label signing. An August 13, 1966, ad in *Cashbox* for "Sugar and Spice," is mildly incongruent. In the full-page layout, a headline of music industry appreciation graciously "thanks disc jockeys, promo men and sales personnel for making the [Destination] record single a hit"; this text is bannered above an image of the Cryan' Shames semi-circled in excitable boy posture around singer/actress Nancy Priddy.

The cameo was curious. And Priddy subsequently receives a fine-print appreciation in the album cover jacket notes of *A Scratch in the Sky*. Priddy accumulated an interesting array of 1960s–1970s music and performance credits. Starting out as Greenwich Village/Laurel Canyon bi-coastal folkstress, she was a member of the Bitter End Singers; contributed uncredited backing vocals to Leonard Cohen's debut album, *Songs of Leonard Cohen* (1967); and recorded a folk-rock psychedelia album, *You've Come This Way Before* (Dot, 1968). Perhaps better known for her acting, she appeared in the television series *Bewitched* and *The Waltons* and eventually passed along the expressive gene to her daughter, actress Christina Applegate. Priddy also dated Stephen Stills, and is rumored to be the subject of the Buffalo Springfield song "Pretty Girl Why."

Audiences for the Cryan' Shames' live shows spiked significantly, pushing teen club crowd capacities beyond their limits, with some estimates at 3,000-plus attending their shows. The flow of activity resulted in the formation of a national fan club. The band's proliferating following translated into a substantially inflated performance pay scale for the group. In a *Chicago Tribune Sunday Magazine* feature article in late January 1967, the band members stated that they reached the $1,000-a-night threshold "blowing people's minds" at their live shows.[21]

Reaching for the *Sky*: A Midwestern Masterpiece?

In the midst of the Cryan' Shames' hustling initiative, change within the group was inevitable. Flux was a common and unsettling sign of the turbulent times and the restless, revolutionary reverberations of the sociopolitical climate. With the mythic Summer of Love on the horizon and the presence of the burgeoning counterculture, the Vietnam War continued to escalate, with parallel protests proliferating across the country. Cryan' Shames' co-founding figure, Gerry Stone, and bassist Dave Purple were both drafted for military service at different times early in 1967. Following his tour of duty, Purple eventually returned to the music business, redirecting into a production position as a recording engineer. While working at the hometown Chess Studio and Stax in Memphis, Purple accumulated an impressive

Chapter 6. It's a Cryan' Shame

Thanks Disc Jockeys — Promo Men and Sales Personnel For Making This Record a Hit

SUGAR & SPICE

by

The Cryan' Shames

DESTINATION 2624

A product of MG Production Co

The headline of a *Billboard* ad of appreciation from MG Productions acknowledges multiple music industry contributors to hit single success of the Cryan' Shames' "Sugar and Spice," on Jim Golden's Destination Records label. The full-page layout features an image of the band congregated around singer/actress Nancy Priddy (*Billboard*, August 13, 1966).

set of credits, highlighted by a Grammy Award for his engineering contributions to the groundbreaking soul score and soundtrack of the 1971 "blaxploitation" film *Shaft*, featuring the Isaac Hayes R&B funk hit "Theme from Shaft."

The Cryan' Shames managed to maintain continuity without missing a beat in the wake of the dutiful departures from the selective service syphoning off their bandmates. Experienced musicians and songwriters Lenny Kerley and Isaac Guillory were enlisted from local bands the Squires and Revelles as replacements for Purple and Stone. Kerley, who brought a high vocal to the Cryan' chorus, proved to be an attuned songwriting partner for Fairs. The pair quickly began crafting a composition that would become the Cryan' Shames' third single, "Mr. Unreliable." The song, which features an inimitable Beatles' "Day Tripper" guitar intro, is conspicuously edgier, with less emphasis on the shared group harmonies. The stylistic swing is even more evident on the single's B-side, "Georgia," which features a country arrangement and a traditional, old-timey tone but resists Southern vocal affectation.

In a typical charting pattern for the band's 45 releases, "Mr. Unreliable" made the Top 10 of the local radio airwaves (#7 on WLS; #12 WCFL). The single never gained much traction nationally, however, peaking at #127, despite its accompanying ad in *Billboard* declaring "how the Midwest was won." Columbia was relatively content more than the record company was clamoring or concerned with the Cryan' Shames' regional confinement. The single's 80,000 copies sold was a proportionally profitable performance and an indicator of sustaining success in a major market such as Chicago from a band Columbia considered to be a cost efficient member of its major label lineup. Musically, both sides of the single signaled a perceptible shift away from the sweetness and familiarities of *Sugar and Spice*. The layered vocals and swirling harmonies remained at the forefront, but with a divergent, expanded accompanying sound that settled "somewhere between the Beach Boys and psychedelic jazz," as characterized by the group members and cited in a June 27, 1967, *Billboard* feature.[22]

The release of the Cryan' Shames' fourth single, "It Could Be We're in Love," pronounced the band's sound-shaping transition. The recording premiered as a 45 with the mesmerizing B-side "I Was Lonely When" in late June 1967. The upbeat possibility-of-love song is highlighted by a charming lead vocal, accented by flourishing harmonies and tempo changes that crescendo and echo and a peculiar middle break interjected with toy bells and laughter, the placement reminiscent of the curious colliding psychedelic break in the Buckinghams' "Susan." There is Beach Boys similitude and vibrations. Brian Wilson–like production touches thread the song's bounce and churning arrangement, locating lyric phrases such as "walk along the sand last night" along the Pacific coast as much as along Chicago's Oak Street beach and the Lake Michigan shoreline. While the Cryan' Shames had previously recorded much of their material for the album as precipitously as possible with minimal takes, "It Could Be We're in Love" took an uncommon four days of studio time.

The extended span of the studio session was time well spent. "It Could Be We're in Love" surged onto the local charts, entering the Top 40 midway at #20. By August, the heavily requested song became a certified Chicagoland smash, reaching #1 on both WLS and WCFL. The song's popularity persisted. "It Could Be We're in Love" exhibited solid staying power, holding down the top spot on WLS for a month amidst a formidable and varied rotation of ballads, rock, and psychedelic singles. Among the songs circulating in the radio airplay at the same time were Frankie Valli's "Can't Take My Eyes Off You"; Bobbie Gentry's rural Mississippi bridge jump narrative, "Ode to Billie Joe"; Grace Slick's enigmatic *Wonderland* hallucination "White Rabbit," with Jefferson Airplane; and Jim Morrison and the Doors' epic "Light My Fire."

Nationally, the Cryan' Shames' single steadied into a mid–80s peak position on the *Billboard* chart, while rising to #70 on *Cashbox* later in the year. Sales of the record across the Midwest markets were particularly and predictably impressive, totaling 100,000 copies. In addition to the Cryan' Shames' personnel changes, variables such as the band's sustained live appeal, their debut album's solid showing, and the accompanying successful singles combined to provide momentum that impelled the band along a course of creative curiosity steering toward the studio to record a follow-up album.

"It Could Be We're in Love" resonated as a concise (2:28) and pretty prelude that simultaneously announced and confirmed the Cryan' Shames' musical exploration and stylistic sound expansion that advanced into an ambitious new album, *A Scratch in the Sky*. The title originates from Jim Pilster's roadside observation of a jet stream vapor trail in the sky above an Iowa cornfield while traveling with the band during a Midwest tour. The follow-up album was another Bob Monaco/Jim Golden MG Production, with the recording taking place at Columbia's state-of-the-art eight-track studio in New York. Engineers Fred Catero and Glen Kolotkin supervised the session during a four-week span from late summer into early fall of 1967, with the album's release in December in time for Christmas. A banner across the top of the album's cover once again pronounced that the record was "electronically rechanneled for *STEREO*, '360 Sound,'" which meant a slightly higher price than a Mono edition. Fairs also asserted production presence in the studio, overseeing the recordings that the band had meticulously rehearsed and rearranged, practiced and performed live, from Fairs's basement to the teen club Blue Village. "Fairs was a perfectionist," said Pilster. "He loved the studio setting and rehearsing more than he liked playing live."[23]

The tracks that compose *A Scratch in the Sky* display a notable level of musical maturity from the band. Rather than staying along the safe route in the immediate aftermath of their well-received cover-concentrated debut from less than one year earlier, the Cryan' Shames took a bold artistic step. The addition of multi-instrumentalists Kerley and Guillory fortified, expanded, and enriched the band's creative approach. Musically, the group progressed well beyond their core of guitars, drums, keyboards, and bass to a more eclectic and sophisticated soundscape. An impressive assortment of exotic instrumentation was incorporated into *A Scratch in the Sky*, generating a wide sound spectrum that includes bagpipes, harpsichord, French horn, cello, church bells, "backward" cowbell, flute, autoharp, accordion, mandolin, and tamboura. "We played every instrument," declared Pilster. "I played French horn on 'Up on the Roof,' and I didn't even play French horn. We must have done 92 takes of the song, in an expensive studio."[24] Vocally, the group's signature layering also swelled from two- and three-part blendings to ethereal, choir-like five-part harmonies. The collective ingenuity produced a more detailed, polished, and amplified folk-garage amalgam and a specialized sunshine psych-pop strand.

The Cryan' Shames' songwriting scheme also shifted in conjunction with their coinciding personnel and sound style reinventions. The group began to employ a fresh emphasis that transcended their cover band character, which was an initial identity that extended from staples of their live sets to the tracks on *Sugar and Spice*. The conversion from cover comfort toward a focus on original material was stirred in part from a cautionary compliment they received from a Byrd during the whirlwind period touring and performing in support of their debut album. As the opening act for a show at Chicago's McCormick Place in 1966, on a bill that featured the We Five, known for their hit cover of Ian & Sylvia's "You Were on My Mind," and their headlining heroes, the Byrds, Jim (pre–Roger) McGuinn told the Chicagoland opening act afterwards that as a band they were "really, really good, but you will never get anywhere unless you do your own songs."[25] The irony, of course, is that this advice was proposed by the front of a band that became well known, in part, by recording traditional tunes such as Pete Seeger's Ecclesiastical "Turn! Turn! Turn! (To Everything There Is a Season)" and multiple songs from the Bob Dylan catalog into popular hits. Nonetheless, McGuinn's suggestion struck a responsive chord and was a steering mechanism in the Cryan' Shames' redirected musical course.

All but two of the tracks that compose *A Scratch in the Sky*'s 11-song set are Fairs/Kerley collaborations. The compositions consistently circumvent conventional song structures, mingling sophisticated melodies and arrangements with often impressionistic lyrics. The productive pair's nine contributions to the album are rounded out by two borrowed tunes from other songwriting duos—the renowned Brill pop composers Carole King and Gerry Goffin, and fellow locals Jeffrey Boyan and Ron Holder of the group Saturday's Children. The richer songwriting extended *A Scratch in the Sky*'s running time, with the fullness of the new compositions and the two covers averaging one minute longer per track than the succinct standard 2:30 range of those on *Sugar and Spice*.

The band's overarching production aim with *A Scratch in the Sky* was to make each track a distinct creative component that shaped the whole of the album's varied and detailed arrangements into an intricate sonic atmosphere. Even their three 45 sides received minor makeovers, with the single versions of "It Could Be We're in Love," "I Was Lonely When," and "Mr. Unreliable" fine-tuned and presented differently as album cuts. The resourcefulness in the resulting Long Play recording avoids overt experimentation and pretentiousness and streams seamlessly in the song-to-song, side-to-side sequencing without being cute or cluttered.

The album's opening three-song succession establishes the breadth of the arrangements that thread throughout the record's tracks. From church bells, choir-like harmonies, and tempo shifts between gentle and bouncy in "A Carol for Lorelei" into the full-blown, evocative psychedelia and trippy droning ambiance of "The Sailing Ship" (appropriated by the Brian Jonestown Massacre in 2001 as "Sailor") to the baroque and jazz styles informing the captivating French feel of "In the Café." Beatles' *Revolver* rhythms resound in the garage edge of the single "Mr. Unreliable," with riffs that echo "Day Tripper" as well as the B-side of "Paperback Writer," "Rain." Side one of *A Scratch in the Sky* eases out with the nostalgic, painterly dreamscape "The Town I'd Like to Go Back To," its hallucinatory sense of yearning dissolving into an atmospheric instrumental that stretches into delicate delirium in a two-minute wane with a hint of Grateful Dead.

The Cryan' Shames' interpretation of King/Goffin's starry-eyed "Up on the Roof" that leads off side two became *A Scratch in the Sky*'s subsequent third single, following the album's prefix 45s, "Mr. Unreliable" and "It Could Be We're in Love." The sunshine fine MOR delivery, with sufficient appeal to reach #85 on the national charts, distinguishes the floating Chicago skyline view among the Brill Building standard's many rooftop renderings, from the Drifters' initial R&B 1962 classic through the Carole King and James Taylor mellow 1970s companion versions to contemporary takes that range from Edie Falco's guilt-ridden mother-to-daughter karaoke scene in the Showtime cable series *Nurse Jackie* in 2009 to Beach Day's 2013 hipster rendition also used in a LensCrafters ad. The Cryan' Shames gracefully weave teenage magic, youthful rebellion, and romantic angst into panoramic splendor with a lullaby tone in a fluctuating tempo arrangement accented with mandolin flurries.

Next in the side's sequence, the lush, harmony-rich pre-album single "It Could Be We're in Love" inserts a Midwest Malibu medley of Beach Boy beauty in shades of "Wouldn't It Be Nice"/"In My Room"/"God Only Knows" followed by the tougher tempo of "Sunshine Palm," which contrasts into the hypnotic "I Was Lonely When." In a style foreshadowed by the "Mr. Unreliable" B-side, "Georgia," "Cobblestone Road (She's Been Walkin')" contributes a catchy country-tinged tune accentuated with handclaps in an acoustic pick-and-strum Beatlesque manner that anticipates the rural charm of early solo Paul McCartney. Boyan and Holder's loosely biographical character sketch of one of their friends in "Dennis Dupree from Danville" closes the album with a funky edge-blending happening hippie rock and a bluesy progression, with a "whooo!" as a punctuation mark.

The sum of song craft, textures, and varied sequence of the tracks assembled on *A Scratch in the Sky* reveal the Cryan' Shames' remarkably rapid musical maturation between records. The band implements and embraces their many artistic influences inventively and naturally into a set of fresh and accessible tracks. *A Scratch in the Sky* reflects the era's musical spirit more discernibly than the album personifies the sociopolitical tenor of the times. While the Cryan' Shames were guided by their foundational Byrds, Beatles, and British Invasion affinities, their advanced arrangements, melodic instrumentation, and swirling multi-layered California chorus harmonies take supplementary cues from the enterprising sonic shifts, textures, and experimentation that were taking place and accentuating prominent recordings of the period such as the Beach Boys' *Pet Sounds* (1966) and the Beatles' *Sgt. Pepper's Lonely Hearts Club Band* (1967). Also evident in *Sky*'s intricate expanse are traces of the lush flourishes associated with the Association; the exquisite baroque and roll of the Left Banke, defined by a gorgeous rotation that includes "Walk Away Renee," "Pretty Ballerina," "Desiree," and "She May Call You Up Tonight"; and lesser hints of Procol Harum and Arthur Lee & Love, among other groups, sounds, and recordings.

The Cryan' Shames adroitly draw from some of the best qualities of these many musical makers and markers, inventively shaping them into a salient soundscape with a sense of singularity. There is a distinctiveness in the derivative disguise that undercurrents through *A Scratch in the Sky*'s 11 tracks. The band realizes an uncommon artistic achievement through their proficient and adventurous adopting and disassembling, recasting and reconfiguring such an array of familiar snippets and segments of sounds, styles, and melodies into a cohesive collage of a song cycle. While "Midwestern masterpiece" may be a mild overstatement for *A Scratch in the Sky*'s undeniable distinguishing musical accomplishment, the rich and resonant record, deep in tracks, is an unsung treasure and touchstone sequence of songs within the vibrant and vibrating Chicagoland 1960s music mecca.

Sky's the Limit

Two albums in, the Cryan' Shames maintained their popular profile in the Midwest, though they were unable to establish much parallel status across in the rest of the country. On the surface, and as a major label release, *A Scratch in the Sky* seemed to have multiple factors in its favor. With follow-up momentum from *Sugar and Spice*'s decent debut, the record displayed fine production and musicianship, charming qualities, and admirable artistic advances beyond the inaugural album. Columbia provided "blow your mind sky high" promotional pronouncements, highlighted by catchy advertisements placed in the major music trade magazines.

In April, less than one month after the memorable "How the West Was Won" declaration appeared in the mid–March edition of *Billboard*, another historical-based page plugging the "Mr. Unreliable" single subsequently surfaced in *Cashbox*. The layout headlines in plural—"The Chicago Fires"—a history repeats reference to the "flame-outs" 1871 cow kick combustion in the O'Leary barn. Below the banner are bovine and band images juxtaposed, with minimal text that maximizes the fire motif throughout. "She was first," utters the accusatory cow caption. The arson associations continue in the copy beneath the band's picture: "Put the blame on the Cryan' Shames for the second Chicago Fire." "Their new single is as big as all blazes in the Windy City … and it's spreading like wildfire. Your town is next!" In flaming footnote fashion, pyro puns in promotion underscore a small *Sugar and Spice* album cover image positioned in the bottom right corner of the page: "And a red hot album to match: Where the Cryan' Shames spark the action. On COLUMBIA RECORDS."

In addition to the carefully crafted marketing campaigns for *A Scratch in the Sky*'s lead single, Columbia solicited a full back cover essay from Gloria Stavers, the celebrated editor in chief of the popular teen publication, *16 Magazine*. Curiously, Stavers's prestigious publishing presence was lost on the band. "Columbia had a lot of weight," said Pilster. "Though we never even heard of her [Stavers]."[26] Stavers's noteworthy handwritten composition, in fairy tale tones that cast "five very groovy cats—and a Toad," is accompanied by a black-and-white illustration that references songs/lyrics in picture puzzle–like fashion: a waterside town, café, cobblestone, sunshine, roof tops, Danville and Chicago arrow signs, and a lone person walking—perhaps Dennis Dupree? Despite the prominent sponsorship, Stavers's high-profile endorsement printed on the *A Scratch in the Sky*'s back cover may have been countered somewhat by the album's front cover design. There was some speculation that the collage of Cryan' Shames concert and performance images may have been a marketing misstep that visually suggested the album was a live recording.

Among other factors and forces, *A Scratch in the Sky*'s circulation was situated in the chaotic crevice of the Midway between the youth culture movement's 1967 Summer of Love and "the whole world watching" during the disorderly Democratic National Convention in Chicago the following August 1968. Predictably popular

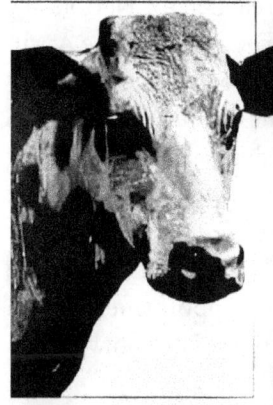
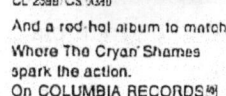

In another of the Cryan' Shames' patented playful promotions, the pyro-themed full-page ad for their single, "Mr. Unreliable," references the Great Chicago Fire, highlighted by an O'Leary cow cameo (top left). Standing (L-R): Dennis Conroy, Jim Fairs, Dave "Grape" Purple, Tom "Toad" Doody. Kneeling: (L-R): Jim Pilster (J. C. Hooke), Gerry "Stonehenge" Stone. Not pictured are Isaac Guillory and Lenny Kerley, who replaced Purple and Stone in the band (*Cashbox* magazine, April 1967).

locally and in the Midwest, *A Scratch in the Sky* entered the charts with more immediate surge than its popular predecessor *Sugar and Spice* and remained in Chicago's Top 10 through the early months of 1968. On a national scale, *A Scratch in the Sky* sold slightly better than the Cryan' Shames' debut LP, reaching #156 on *Billboard*. With little single support to steer and sustain a run, however, the album's staying power was limited. Again, the regional/national dichotomy was plain. Despite its delayed designation as a single from *A Scratch in the Sky*, "Up on the Roof" was a Top 10 record in Chicago on both WLS and WCFL, where it reached #7. Nationally, the 45 peaked at #85 on *Billboard* and slightly higher on *Cashbox* at #70 in late April.

A Scratch in the Sky was not the breakthrough, triumph, or significant stepping stone for the Cryan' Shames that the band members, their producers Monaco and Golden, and the Columbia record label had together hoped for. While the album surpassed the sales of their appealing cover comfortable debut, *Sugar and Spice*, and charted respectably in the crowded music market, *A Scratch in the Sky* did not approach the commercial measures that matched the record's musical merit or the Cryan' Shames camp's expectations. "There was definitely disappointment," said Pilster. "We considered the album transcendent and in that 'magic' category. It was our *Pet Sounds*."[27]

Synthesized....

The period at large continued to be prolific with music's fabulous field increasingly crowded and competitive. Radio's hit parade was expanding, if not exploding, with pop and rock genres and subgenres emerging and trending, with a stylistic range from psychedelic to bubble gum, and sounds beyond and in between. Station playlists simultaneously tightened, particularly for many local groups who became less prioritized or passed over by programmers with preferences for bands with big label backing.

In the midst of the shifts within the evolving music industry and marketplace, the Cryan' Shames faced the recurring internal challenge of personnel transitions. As the group planned new material to follow *A Scratch in the Sky*, both guitarist Jim Fairs and drummer Dennis Conroy decided to move on in 1968. The key musician departures may have affected the band's continuity more decidedly than previous membership makeovers. Fairs's exodus was particularly significant beyond his lead guitarist role. He was a formative figure, unofficially wearing the leader of the band badge as its core composer and arranger. Their replacements were locals: guitarist Dave Carter repositioned from the disbanded Saturday's Children, along with Squires/Boston Tea Party drummer Alan Dawson, whose stay was brief. In the conversion, standbys Kerley and Guillory stepped up to fill the songwriting void left by Fairs's departure, composing more songs individually than they did collaboratively as a duo.

Chapter 6. It's a Cryan' Shame

Non-original compositions also continued to provide viable variations for the regrouped group to interpret and record. In May, the Cryan' Shames hastily followed their "Up on the Roof" single with the release of a less obvious borrowed tune, "Young Birds Fly," written by William Oliver Swofford. Professionally known as "Oliver," Swofford became best known for two musical and film soundtrack songs in 1969: "Good Morning Starshine," from the popular, counterculture musical *Hair*, and "Jean," which received an Academy Award nomination for Best Original Song as the theme to the British film adaptation of the novel/stage play *The Prime of Miss Jean Brodie*. The chart course of "Young Birds Fly" was fleeting. After peaking locally outside the WLS Top 10 at #15 in late June and nationally settling at #86 in *Cashbox* and #99 in *Billboard*, the Cryan' Shames' melodious soft pop rock single faded fast.

In an opportune booking amid the Cryan' Shames' looming personnel transitions and meek chart placement, the Chicagoland band landed their first national television appearance in July on *Showcase '68*. The summer series, hosted by pop TV personality Lloyd Thaxton, aired on the NBC broadcast network Tuesday evenings in a 10-week run from mid–June to early September. Music variety dance shows targeting teen audiences were happenings across mid–1960s television lineups, with Dick Cark's midday and afternoon programs, *American Bandstand* and *Where the Action Is* among the most notable productions. Similar series such as *Hullabaloo* (1965–66, NBC) and *Shindig!* (1964–66, ABC) provided appealing prime-time fare.

As a distant precursor to the contemporary reality series sing-offs *American Idol* and *The Voice*, *Showcase '68* was a talent competition that traveled to different locations across the country. Premiering in San Francisco, the 30-minute episodes featured a lineup blending established and emerging musical acts performing before a panel of judges. Neil Diamond, Bobby Goldsboro, Bobby Vinton, the Box Tops, Tammy Wynette, the Chambers Brothers, and Archie Bell & the Drells were among familiar artists who appeared on the show. The Chicagoland scene was well represented, with the New Colony Six (June 25) and the American Breed (July 2, September 3) joining the Cryan' Shames (July 23) as Midwest regional recruits to the *Showcase* roster. The 10 weekly winners from the series' succinct seasonal span, with the American Breed among the qualifiers, then faced off during a one-hour finale. Sly and the Family Stone, whose funky psychedelic soul single "Dance to the Music" hit the Top 10 in late 1967, was chosen as *Showcase '68*'s overall winner and awarded the $10,000 grand prize.

The Cryan' Shames' July appearance on the sixth installment of *Showcase '68* was set on the University of Illinois campus in Champaign-Urbana, 135 miles south of Chicago. Also billed on the episode's lineup were Archie Bell & the Drells, carrying with them their #1 R&B hit "Tighten Up"; actress Carmen McRae; and contestants Joe Lee Wilson, a jazz singer, and supper club vocalist Janet Evans. Wilson was selected as the episode's winner by a panel of judges that included a pair of WLS radio disc jockeys, Clark Weber and Floyd Brown. Appearing to take full advantage of the television exposure, the Cryan' Shames premiered two unreleased songs,

"First Train to California" and "The Warm," both written by Jim Fairs. The broadcast debuts had a swan song undercurrent that was a prelude to Fairs's farewell appearance as a member of the Cryan' Shames one week later on July 29 at their gig at the New Place in Algonquin, Illinois.

Curiously, the Cryan' Shames' television introduction of the pair of new songs was not a timely preview of their subsequent singles release as an album lead-up. With the hopes of finding a formula that might invigorate their chart presence, the band veered in a different direction and recorded a Fairs/Guillory collaboration, "Greenburg, Glickstein, Charles David Smith & Jones." The novel, law firm–length title frames the lyrics' greedy, big business tone: "countin' all his money in the sky" and a clear company policy that the "customer's always wrong." The compact rocker at 2:14 sharpens the lyrical edge with notably heavier, phased production qualities anchored by driving guitar work accompanied by the group's initiation into brass. The new sound style single, with a contrasting lovely atmospheric B-side ballad, "The Warm," was released in mid–September. With negligible promotional support from Columbia due to the group's flattening 45 sales, the new single peaked just outside the Top 10 on WLS. Beyond the Midwest region, the 45 bubbled under at #115 on *Billboard* and gradually rose to #73 in *Cashbox* by early December.

The modest momentum did not deter the Cryan' Shames' new lineup from proceeding with recording the group's third album in as many years. The working title, *Games*, evolved into a more fitting alchemic designation, *Synthesis*. The album was released in late December 1968. Carryover strands of stability and similarity from *A Scratch in the Sky* were minimal as the reconstituted Cryan' Shames pursued an even more eclectic, exploratory style on their third LP's 11 adventurous new set of songs. Fairs's absence and presence simultaneously continued to resonate, as the lead tracks of each side of *Synthesis* are the lingering contributions from the freshly former member of the group. Filling out the set are three Kerley compositions, four intricate Guillory originals—two of which conclude each of the album's sides—and three complementary cover songs sequenced in between.

The single, "Greenburg, Glickstein, Charles, David Smith & Jones," opens side one with its heavy horn and guitar phased production. Back to back cover versions follow. The first, "Baltimore Oriole," is a tasteful, captivating selection, written by Tin Pan Alley composer Hoagy Carmichael with lyrics by Paul Francis Webster. The Cryan' Shames' evocatively arranged jazz/folk/rock rendition of the avian love song features an elongated running time of 4:31, surpassing the dreamy "The Town I'd Like to Go Back To" (4:27) on their previous album as the group's lengthiest recording. With the ensuing track, "It's All Right," the band returns to the hometown songbook of Saturday's Children, from which they had earlier sourced "Dennis Dupree from Danville" for *A Scratch in the Sky*. Co-written by crossover member Carter and his former bandmates Holder and Boyan, the Cryan' Shames' adaptation of "It's All Right" adds a comfortable country inflection to the *Synthesis* set. The style suited the band, as demonstrated in their prior recordings such as "Georgia" and "Cobblestone Road." Chicagoland music chronicler Clark Besch astutely identifies the similarities between the Cryan' Shames' take on "It's All Right" and Monkees material during the era, specifically the country-rock accents introduced by their wool hat wearing guitarist, Michael Nesmith, as a sound style that balanced the telegenic band's Brill Building borrowings.[28] Nesmith, a Texas native, along with Flying Burrito Brother and Byrd Gram Parsons, are commonly recognized for their pioneering efforts at the forefront of "cosmic American music," coining, defining, and expanding the country/folk/rock fusion. In mid-1968, as a Monkees member, Nesmith was breaking ground recording country-flavored solo songs during a session with the Nashville Cats in the RCA studios in Music City. The local lineage of "It's All Right" also includes an earlier Chicagoland edition on a 45 cut by the Centuries in 1965 before they fragmented into forming the Buckinghams. *Synthesis*'s side one sequence rounds out with "Your Love," a gentle ballad that makes a quiet case for being the Cryan' Shames' most affectionate meditation, followed by Guillory's elaborately arranged "A Master's Fool."

The progressive production touches from the initial side's closing track carry over to side two, which is marked by inserts, flourishes, and segues that thread the entire six-song sequence. Similar extended time and transition techniques were voguishly presented in suites/medleys by the Beatles on *Abbey Road* (1969) and in the seven-member Chicago's mini-opera "Ballet for a Girl in Buchannon" (also known as "The Ballet" and "Make Me Smile Medley"), which sprawled across seven tracks—three of which are instrumentals—that occupy 12:55 of side two of *Chicago II* in 1970.

Six months after its television unveiling on *Showcase '68*, "First Train to California" went from visual to vinyl as the lead track of the *Synthesis* album's second side. The song's westward ho separation scenario fittingly emanates with California canyon echoes, its brisk and bright manner evocative of the Mamas & the Papas. "First Train to California" establishes a pleasant, engaging tone that pervades the entire progression of side two and its subsequent five disparate tracks. Guillory's "Painter Man" provides a psych-pop palette with a far-out, kaleidoscopic late-sixties sensibility. In the portrait, colors flow from the "funny painter's hand" into heart and soul insights of his subjects illustrated with vivid imagery—"earthen jar, morning star, bluebird wings, golden strings, lullabies." The stylistic divergence proceeds in a delightful direction via a pair of Kerley compositions: the acoustic Beatlesque good time handclapping harmonease of "Sweet Girl of Mine" (despite a peculiar, if not pointlessly [mis]placed phone/bell ringing in the intro) followed by the percussive exotic rhythms of "20th Song."

The album's third cover song, "Let's Get Together," is suitably socially conscious, with Alan Dawson a singing substitution for Tom Doody on lead vocal. The original song was written by Chet Powers, a curious character whose multiple pseudonyms include the stage name Dino Valenti/Valente and a songwriting signature, Jesse Oris Farrow. The singer-songwriter's other notable career marks include being one of the founders of the San Francisco psychedelic rock band Quicksilver

Messenger Service in 1965 and a contested copyright crisscross with Tony Roberts over the garage classic "Hey Joe."

From the initial recording of "Let's Get Together" in 1964 by the Kingston Trio, the quintessential clarion call to harmony and brotherhood attracted an array of interpreters during the conflict and chaos of the times. The cross section of artists who recorded the song (frequently as "Get Together") included The (Chad) Mitchell Trio, featuring John Denver; the We Five; Jefferson Airplane; Linda Ronstadt and the Stone Poneys; the Staple Singers; Smith; Andy Williams; the Carpenters; Della Reese; Ed Ames; Anne Murray; and the Dave Clark Five (as "Everybody Get Together" in 1970). On a local level, H.P. Lovecraft's psychedelic spin on "Let's Get Together" in '67 preceded their fellow Chicagolanders' contrasting chorale crescendo cover on *Synthesis*. Probably the most familiar version of Valenti's peace petition is by the Youngbloods, featuring Jesse Colin Young. Initially a track on the band's self-titled debut album on RCA in 1967 (later retitled *Get Together* in 1971), their "Get Together" reached the Top Five when released as a single two years later in 1969. The folk anthem that garnered gold status for the group was the Youngbloods' only hit. Side two of *Synthesis*'s pleasantry concludes with another Guillory pop epic, "Symphony of the Wind." The album finale, with its grandiose approach in shades of Moody Blues, is an orchestral companion that is symphonically symmetrical to side one's closing, "A Master's Fool."

... Right Out the Door

The *Synthesis* album's chart presence was slightly paradoxical if not puzzling. The album's two singles never provided much push for the LP, nor did Columbia as its parental record label. The substandard showing of the 45s may have been a circumstantial sign of the times and the music marketplace, a fate perhaps foreshadowed by the group's non-album track, "Young Birds Fly," that bridged *A Scratch in the Sky* and *Synthesis*. The selection of "Greenburg, Glickstein, Charles, David Smith & Jones" rather than "First Train to California" as a prelude 45 for their new album initially invited second-guessing whispers of a minor miscalculation. In addition to the exposure from its television introduction on *Showcase '68*, "First Train to California" radiated a sunny demeanor with considerable charm. The song's appeal was perceived by music critic Richie Unterberger to be the band's "almost self-conscious straining for an MOR AM radio hit."[29] The runner-up tune received record redemption and was subsequently released as the *Synthesis* LP's belated second single in early February 1969. The weak chart performance pattern persisted, however. While the Fairs 45 fared well in smaller markets, frequenting the Top 20, "First Train to California" was unable to place or even "bubble under" nationally on the *Billboard* charts. The record's failure to register on the hometown WLS listings was a particularly conspicuous absence.

Interestingly, if not ironically, *Synthesis*'s longevity surpassed both *Sugar and Spice*'s and *A Scratch in the Sky*'s, almost doubling the chart shelf life of its pair of long play predecessors. Yet, the Cryan' Shames' third LP only managed a meager position on the *Billboard* chart, peaking at #184 in mid–April 1969, four months following its release. The chart performance was a portent. "We got *Synthesiz*ed right out the door," word played Pilster.[30]

The band began to splinter, with members dabbling in other productions, from commercial jingles and public service announcements to crossover cameos, contributions, and collaborations with local groups. Many of the recording projects were associated with the Monaco and Golden MG Productions merger with Bill Traut's Dunwich Ltd. Among the bands were the psychedelic Aorta and the underground rock Coven's debut, *Witchcraft Destroys Minds & Reaps Souls* (1969, Mercury). The album's tracks featured occult themes, Latin phrases, chanting, and a 13-minute "black Mass," the first to be recorded. The band subsequently had a Top 40 hit in 1971, "One Tin Soldier," the theme song to the film *Billy Jack*.

In October 1969, the Cryan' Shames released what would be their final single, exiting as they had entered, with a cover song. The group recorded Harry Nilsson's "Rainmaker," excerpted from the B-side of Nilsson's single version of folk figure Fred Neil's "Everybody's Talkin'" from 1966. The song was included as a track on the Brooklyn-born, Los Angeles–based Nilsson's 1968 album, *Aerial Ballet*, and released as single in July. "Everybody's Talkin'" was featured in the 1969 Academy Award–winning film *Midnight Cowboy* starring Jon Voight and Dustin Hoffman. When re-released as the movie's theme song, the soundtrack single became a Top 10 hit on *Billboard*'s Hot 100 and Easy Listening charts.

The Nilsson 45's flip side, "Rainmaker," was another curious cover choice by the Cryan' Shames. The dusty, hitch-your-wagon narrative set in Kansas contains a nursery rhyme couplet as a fadeout chant—"Rain rain go away / Come again another day." The Cryan' Shames' recording also has the distinction of a rare A-side vocal by someone other than Tom Doody, with Guillory front and center singing the song. The single's B-side, "Bits and Pieces," underscores Kerley's continued gravitation toward country-rock influences. The song settles comfortably along the sound spectrum between Buffalo Springfield and Poco, who formed in 1968 with Richie Furay and Jim Messina migrating from the herd of Stephen Stills, Neil Young, Bruce Palmer, and Dewey Martin in the wake of the supergroup collective's split following a brief but brilliant two-year stint. "Rainmaker"/"Bits and Pieces" went unnoticed with the fastest fade-out of any Cryan' Shames 45.

The group disbanded in the immediate aftermath. Three albums in three years and the run was over, in a fairly common "done too soon" trajectory. The end of the year marked the end for the Cryan' Shames, with their farewell live performance in December 1969 at the eminent northwest suburban teen club the Cellar in Arlington Heights, a somewhat surprising sendoff spot considering their house band base at the Blue Village in Westmont. The characteristic post-breakup pattern persisted.

In the dispersal, some of the group members repositioned and continued careers in music, with Fairs, Guillory, and Kerley the most active as musicians, performers, and producers. Cryan' Shames' reformations, reconfigurations, reunions, and commemorative cornerstone concerts ensued in intermittent recurrences through the decades, mainly on the local level. None of the gatherings at any juncture following the band's breakup resulted in new recordings.

Despite the absence of new material, the Cryan' Shames' sunshine garage sound and spirit were represented in numerous 1960s era compilation cameos, and in welcome record reissues of their catalog—its singles, B-sides, albums—that were released along the way as valued vestiges lending credence to the group's legacy. As early as the 1970s, the Cryan' Shames' 1966 Destination hit, "Sugar and Spice," was enshrined as a musical emblem alongside an admirable array of other mid-to-late 1960s psychedelic and garage rock singles in *Nuggets: Original Artyfacts from the First Psychedelic Era (1965–1968)*. Released in 1972 on Elektra Records, the seminal double album compilation was curated by Lenny Kaye, Patti Smith Group guitarist and writer and record store clerk at New York's Village Oldies. Kaye's *Nuggets* liner notes are recognized for featuring one of the earliest uses of the term "punk rock."

The "Sugar and Spice" B-side, "Ben Franklin's Almanac," and a demo of the Cryan' Shames' take on the Beatles' "You're Gonna Lose That Girl" (a favorite Lennon–McCartney rendition of producer Monaco's), are part of an abundant and arcane 40-track set culled from the U.S.A. and Destination record label rosters and assembled into the compilation *2131 South Michigan Avenue* (Sundazed, 2009). On the individual long play set, Columbia Legacy and the independent archival and rarities label Sundazed Music reissued the Cryan' Shames' trio of albums early in the new millennium in 2002. The vault visitation featured the standard "previously unreleased" materials such as demos, mono recordings, unissued 45 versions, rarities, and cover versions, among them Bread's soft rock "It Don't Matter to Me." Twelve years following that appealing bundle with bonus tracks, *A Scratch in the Sky* was singled out with an exclusive "Deluxe Expanded Mono Edition," reconfigured with the original monaural mix. The 2014 reissue, released on the UK indie Cherry Red/Now Sounds label, further reasserts *A Scratch in the Sky*'s enduring and understated importance as buried treasure from the Chicagoland mid-to-late-1960s music scene five decades earlier.

Bubbling Under

The image of a jet's vanishing vapor trail that inspired the Cryan' Shames' *A Scratch in the Sky* album title in 1967 contains a streak of simile for the Chicagoland group's ephemeral trajectory, a transience that was a catching, chronic condition and prevailing production pattern for many bands during the prolific period. Contextualizing the Cryan' Shames' evanescence summons the exuberant spirit of Jim

Pilster/J. C. Hooke's expression of disappointment when discovering that he and his emergent group of bandmates could not be known as "the Travelers." The tone and susceptibility conveyed in Hooke's "it's a cryan' shame" groan comes full circle.

The notion is conveniently comparable when redirected toward the Cryan' Shames' confined, condensed chronicle. The reasoning and rumination shared by frustrated fans and followers, critics, and musicians—past, present, and in retrospect—situate between curious and confounded. The mystification reluctantly, inevitably, arrives at the recognition tinged with some regret that the Cryan' Shames "never made it big." A common consensus of consolation among loyal locals and midwestern regionalists who came of age in the mid-1960s, and more broadly, the informed sectors of the national critical base, suggests that the Cryan' Shames probably deserved a better destiny as a band, rather than being bound to "bubbling under" like many of their singles.

The Cryan' Shames' musical merit was arguably worthy of fuller recognition and appreciation. The group exhibited some of the most attractive layers of sparkling vocal harmonies and versatile musicianship that emanated from the flourishing mid-decade midwestern musical sphere. The rich song craft and resourceful, stylistic sound appropriations and arrangements on display in the Cryan' Shames' singles, their three-album catalog of recordings, and in their live repertoire presumably should have/could have sufficiently enabled the group to sustain successfully for longer than they did. Nonetheless, within their abbreviated arc, the Cryan' Shames still managed to make a meaningful mark as Chicagoland's major record label breakthrough suburband, skillfully scratching the scenic 1960s soundscape with an enduring unsung inscription.

Chapter 7

Ba Da Ba Ba Dah

Brass and the Bungalows of Berwyn

We were always the kids from Berwyn going, "Gee, are we lucky to be here."
—Jim Peterik, Ides of March[1]

The Ides of March completed the Chicagoland music scene's prolific progression that arose in the mid-1960s, extending the remarkable regional run toward its zenith in the early 1970s. As the title of their 2015 anthology proclaims, the Ides of March were the "last band standing." The original group's arc unfolded for nearly a decade, spanning 1964 through 1973, defined in large part by its prominent hard-driving horn hit, "Vehicle," and featuring the foremost rock star persona to emerge and endure from the region during the era in Jim Peterik.

In quiet contrast to some of their fellow local music groups at the time who sustained bursts of sudden hits, the Ides of March's origins and evolution as a band followed a somewhat similar, albeit a more measured trajectory, toward a breakthrough and chart status, with a comparable recording output. The Ides chronicle includes a band name change; style, sound, and personnel fine-tuning; and recording for multiple labels—independent, subsidiary, and major.

Roller Coaster Ride: From the Shondels to Parrot

The band's basement beginnings, humble and innocent, were situated 12 miles and 20 minutes west of Chicago in blue-collar Berwyn, a predominantly Czechoslovakian conservative community, surrounded by the suburbs Cicero, Oak Park, Riverside, and North Riverside. Having grown up together as Cub Scout packmates and elementary school pals, the brotherly bond between Berwyn boys Jim Peterik, Larry Millas, Bob Bergland, and Mike Borch was well established by the time they reached Morton West High School. The bonus was that they all happened to play instruments. Peterik, the youngest of the group, possessed leader-of-the-band qualities. His youthful inauguration performing in front of a live audience came during a *Teen Search* contest in Berwyn as he delivered a rendition of Wilbert Harrison's "Kansas

City." After the applause, Peterik was hooked; rock and roll was confirmed as his music mission.

In October 1964, the four friends formed The Shondels (variously spelled Shon Dels, Shon-Dels, or Shon Dels Unlimited, and occasionally hyphenated). The name originated from singer Troy Shondell, Fort Wayne, Indiana–born Gary Wayne Schelton, who had an early 1960s hit single, "This Time." The attentive Peterik thought the name was cool, so he borrowed it for his band in formation.[2] Peterik fronted the group as its primary songwriter, lead guitarist, and vocalist, accompanied by Millas on guitar, Bergland on bass, and drummer Borch, all who also contributed backing vocals and harmonies.

During their early rehearsals, the teen musicians claimed to have never taken themselves too seriously as a music group. Typical of beginner bands of the times, the Berwyners wanted to be (like) the Beatles. The first song they played together was from the Lennon/McCartney Beatles catalog: "Tell Me Why." "We had no idea what we were doing," confessed Peterik. "We never thought we would make records or make a career out of playing music. We were just having fun making music."[3] They persisted and played on, eventually becoming the high school house band at Morton West. The Shondels recorded a garage sounding single featuring two Peterik/Millas compositions: "Like It or Lump It" with its tamer doo-wop flip side, "No Two Ways About It." The resourceful group pressed the 45 on their own local imprint, Epitome Records, and made copies available for cheap (usually a dollar) for distribution at their live local gigs.

The Shondels were signed to Parrot Records, with its playfully distinct logo in yellow and green, featuring a stylish, strutting bird in spats, bow tie, and cane, tipping a top hat. A subsidiary of London Records, Parrot's roster was perhaps best known for hosting the Zombies' hit singles, "She's Not There" and "Time of the Season." The label routinely released 45s licensed by Decca Records, with artists that included Tom Jones, Them, Lulu, Engelbert Humperdinck, and the one-hit wonders Hedgehoppers Anonymous with their sunnily suspicious and ironically timeless 2:16 social commentary/protest song "It's Good News Week."

Peterik wasn't the only midwestern musician captivated by Troy Shondell at the time. One hundred miles east of Chicago in Niles, Michigan, Tommy Jackson, who adopted the stage name Tommy James, retitled his band (originally the Echoes) from the Tornadoes to the Shondells. In 1966, Tommy James & the Shondells' chart-topping "Hanky Panky" initiated an impressive string of hit singles with the group through 1969, with many of the songs reaching the Top 10. Among their hits on the Roulette Records label were "I Think We're Alone Now"; "Mirage"; "I Like the Way"; "Out of the Blue"; "Mony, Mony"; "Crimson and Clover"; "Sweet Cherry Wine"; and "Crystal Blue Persuasion."

Peterik and his merry band of Chicagoland Shondels "had no clue" about the designation duplication and/or the twin-titled Tommy James and his Shondells (with two *l*'s) in a neighboring state across Lake Michigan until "Hanky Panky" announced their arrival and subsequent Top 40 presence. Suddenly in need of a new name to accompany their forthcoming first recording, the Berwyn band resorted to required reading (or compressed CliffsNotes) from their high school lit list. Shakespeare struck a chord. Bergland cited the soothsayer's caution to Julius Caesar, "Beware the Ides of March," suggesting that the mid–March death day reference be adopted as the band's new name, replacing their one-*l* Shondels.

During the next two years, the Ides of March recorded and released five singles on the Parrot label. Their set of songs adroitly integrated familiar elements of the popular British Invasion sound, from Kinks chords to chiming Hollies harmonies. The two-chord riff that leads and threads their debut, "You Wouldn't Listen" (B-side "I'll Keep Searching")," is a precariously precise echo with a note or two variance of the Davies brothers Kinks' classic "Tired of Waiting for You" from early 1965. Peterik calls it "the Kinks meets Curtis Mayfield" because of its R&B chord progression.[4] The Ides' adaptation into a smooth jangling arrangement and its cautionary relationship ricochet refrain display a precocious level of music and melody, vocal harmonies, and songwriting savvy for a composition that was conceived at Peterik's 15th birthday party sleepover.

The debut single, and the band's accompanying aspirations, were bolstered by hometown WLS disc jockey Ron Riley's call-in to host Dick Clark on the popular teen show *American Bandstand* on ABC television. Their concise conversation on the *Bandstand* hotline was purely promotional, a lead-in to the show's highlight "Spotlight Dance" segment. Riley plugged a tune "by a group of fellows from Chicago that's big and new … really happening and potentially pretty doggone good." Their song proved Riley pretty prophetic. "You Wouldn't Listen" became a regional hit, reaching #7 in Chicago in the spring and into the summer of '66 and settling midway on the national charts for seven weeks, peaking at #42 on the *Billboard* Hot 100.

In contrast to their melodious debut single, the Ides' tougher, up-tempo follow-up, "Roller Coaster" (B-side "Things Aren't Always What They Seem"), exuded an edgier garage disposition with some punkish posturing. In the "Song of the Day" curation, *Ten Records* music blogger Stu Shea characterizes "Roller Coaster" as "a perfect American riposte to the new mod British pop."[5] Like its popular 45 predecessor, "Roller Coaster" was relationship related and its guitars jangled, though with rougher edges and more exuberance. In addition to being a metaphor for emotional unevenness, there was also an element of literal ode along for the up-and-down ride. The idea for the song came to Peterik during a day at Chicago's iconic amusement park, Riverview. Located in the Roscoe Village neighborhood, the popular park's 74-acre sprawl was bound on the south by Belmont Avenue, on the east by Western Avenue, Lane Tech High School on the north, and on the west by the North Branch of the Chicago River. Among Riverview's main attractions was a fleet of thrill-ride roller coasters—The Bobs, Comet, Silver Flash, Fireball, Jetstream, and single-car sharp-turning Wild Mouse. Several of the structures were wooden, making the rides rickety and the twists and turns along the tracks even more unsettling. After operating for 63 years after its opening in 1904, the landmark amusement park closed in 1967. The Ides of March recorded "Roller Coaster" at Chicago's celebrated Sound Studios under the production supervision of ace engineer Stu Black. The band's producer/manager Mike Considine had lofty visions of Phil Spector–like compression for the track, wanting the production to explode like the Lovin' Spoonfuls' chart-topping "Summer in the City." According to Peterik, "to get that bass sound.... Stu Black put the whole mix through a giant compressor so it captured that sound, like Tom Petty before his time."[6]

"Roller Coaster" was a crowd pleaser at the Ides of March live shows, but its reception in the AM rotation and record buying audience ranged from decent to disappointing. The single reached the local Top 20 at #14 and nationally slipped in just inside the Hot 100, stalling at #92. There were some notable pockets of support for the song across the country. On New York City's WABC, the nation's top Top 40 station, "Roller Coaster" received "Pick Hit" status and remained in the rotation for several weeks. The critical consensus, past and present, is that the Ides' "Roller Coaster" was a cluttered two-and-a-half minute raw ride with reverb, a record that perhaps deserved better. In retrospective unsung focus, Stu Shea for one, wondered if the lukewarm reception may have been attributed to the song being too muscular and messy, too far out, and the production perhaps a shade tinny.[7] Peterik later admitted that one key vocal phrase in the song's chorus didn't even use actual words.

All contrasts and critiques considered, the Ides of March's initial singles on Parrot stand the test of time and are commonly regarded among some of the band's best works. "You Wouldn't Listen" and "Roller Coaster" have received a measure of respectful redemption and recognition as gems and overlooked obscurities among garage aficionados and Chicagoland music chroniclers, and have been included as tracks in *Nuggets* volumes.

The Ides of March's third release on Parrot in '66, "You Need Love," which featured a discerning Small Faces homage, "Sha-La-La-La-Lee," as its B-Side, was a no-show on the charts. Two more singles followed in 1967—"My Foolish Pride," a composition by Decca producer Jeff Milne that contained a "Purple Haze" hook (B-side "Give Your Mind Wings,"), and "Hole in My Soul"/"Girls Don't Grow on Trees," the Ides' only tracks recorded in stereo.

Despite the Ides of March's productivity, their emphasis on original material, and some small-scale signals of success with their initial 45 releases, Parrot never committed to the band recording an album for the label. The record company wanted a bigger breakthrough beyond the regional hit realm and were looking, listening, and hoping for songs with national reach. The Ides of March's promise and potential without generating sufficient profit or countrywide recognition resulted in their parting from Parrot.

Horning In: Blood, Sweat, and Ides

Say aren't you the fella that used to sing with B, S & T?
—Jim Peterik (Ides of March), "Friends of Feeling" (1971)

The Ides of March's set of '66 singles on Parrot foreshadowed, or more literally, trumpeted the band's future. In a continued effort by the Ides musicians to advance the scope of their sound, the group recruited trumpeter Steve Daniels from nearby Lyons, and Ray Herr, a folk singer and rhythm guitarist from the northwest suburb Arlington Heights in 1967. Horn accompaniment in arrangements had become widespread across the soundscape by that time, though most bands relied on studio musicians rather than having their own internal horn section personnel. The lively "Hole in My Soul" showcased the band newcomers, with Daniels's feisty trumpet front and center and Herr's Ides lead vocal debut on the flip side, "Girls Don't Grow on Trees."

Post Parrot parting, the Ides of March lulled, though the group managed to avoid lingering in label-less limbo. The gap was somewhat counter to the characteristic concentrated recording clusters of other Chicagoland bands such as the Buckinghams and New Colony Six. The Ides of March signed with Kapp Records, an independent label founded by David Kapp. His brother, Jack, helped set up Decca Records in the US in 1934. The Kapp label consolidated with MCA in New York City, with record licensing associations with the Decca and London labels. The Ides of March's first and only release on Kapp in 1968—the moody "Nobody Loves Me" backed with the semi-psychedelic "Strawberry Sunday"—became an obscurity in the band's discography. The single was highlighted by Herr's lead vocal, a whispering smooth contrast to Peterik's measured growl. In their shared singing spotlight for the Ides, Herr was well suited for the ballads while Peterik's delivery fit the up-tempo tunes. Both performers were naturals and showy fronts, which led to an undercurrent of tension between the two that persisted without sidetracking the band's progress. Herr's tenure would be brief, lasting only into 1970.

The Ides of March left Kapp Records hoping to find another record company that would be receptive to their new style. During the label lull, the Berwyn band remained very active and were a big draw throughout the youth center and sock hop circuit and thriving local teen scene and its accustomed clubs, from Like Young on Wells Street in Old Town to the Blue Village in Westmont and Valley View Young Adults Club in Frankfort, 35 miles south of the city. The band continued to refine their sound along the way, building upon their repertoire of borrowed tunes and melodies from the catalogs of Brit bands from the Beatles to the Hollies, occasional surf strands of the Ventures and California dreaming with the Mamas & the Papas. Other show highlights included vigorous versions of the garage essential "Tobacco Road" and the Frankie Valli/Walker Brothers' "The Sun Ain't Gonna Shine Anymore." While the Ides were adept at a variety of garage and pop rock stylings, their live sets also steadily integrated the sounds of soul, covering James Brown, Curtis Mayfield's "People Get Ready," and Arthur Conley's "Sweet Soul Music," among other rhythmic renderings.

The search for musical identity is a natural part of the developmental process and coming of age for any band. The Ides of March were no exception. "We were all 18, 19 years old," said Peterik. "We were still looking for a sound."[8] The period between 1968 and into 1969 marked a significant turning point in the Ides of March's development. In late 1969, despite Daniels's departure, the band doubled down on horns, expanding their lineup by adding local trumpeters John Larson and Chuck Soumar, who was classically trained. With the additions, the group reconfigured its garage foundation into a more emboldened brassy presence, with a stronger emphasis on Peterik's sturdy, smoker suspicious vocals. Bassist Bergland also horned in, providing tenor saxophone from his multi-instrumental repertoire to select songs in the Ides' sets and songbook. The musical shift may not have been as sudden as it seemed on the sound surface, particularly when considering the group's gravitation toward integrating British Invasion sound with R&B moments in their live repertoire.

The Ides of March's stylistic exploration and inclinations received significant impetus when they attended a live performance by the jazz rock outfit Blood, Sweat & Tears at the Kinetic Playground on Clark Street in uptown Chicago. The set kicked off with "More and More" from their recently released. "We got religion ... they blew us away," testifies Peterik. "Got real hip to their first album, with Al Kooper, and by the time we saw them they had David Clayton-Thomas."[9]

BS&T's horn rock style was a Chicagoland imprint shaped by renowned manager/producer James William Guercio in between his production supervision of local contemporaries the Buckinghams and Chicago, and by the American Breed, whose arrangements were accented by producer Bill Traut. Blending brass was a boost that proved a smooth and suitable sound direction for the Ides of March moving forward. The degrees of derivative may have been undeniable, though as echoes of influence, they were short of precise parroting. Comparisons were convenient and inescapable. Not only did the Ides of March instrumentation markedly resonate Blood, Sweat & Tears—albeit with slightly less brass bombast—Peterik's vocals were a resounding echo of BS&T lead singer Clayton-Thomas's throaty projection. The channeling was so striking "people in the studio said it was scary," said Peterik, who maintained that the spot-on similarity was not calculated.[10] Manager/producer Frank Rand wondered if Peterik was intentionally imitating the BS&T lead and insisted that the Ides lead vocalist "just be Peterik." The admonishment motivated the Ides lead singer to knock out "a real pissed-off take" that was, ironically, "the money take" for "Vehicle."[11]

Peterik placed the sound-alikeness in vocal hierarchical terms that delicately reciprocate somewhere between idolatry, influence, and imitation, and suggested that his BS&T hero David Clayton-Thomas "wanted to sing like Ray Charles and I wanted to sing like him [Clayton-Thomas]. On down the food chain."[12] Several years later, Peterik, perhaps self-consciously and presumably good-naturedly, referenced the BS&T/Clayton-Thomas semblances in the lyrics to "Friends of Feeling," a track on the Ides of March's second album, *Common Bond* (1971).

In mid–1969, Blood, Sweat & Tears was in the midst of a gold record rush. From March through August, their series of singles—"You've Made Me So Very Happy," "Spinning Wheel," and "And When I Die"—all reached #2 on the Hot 100, with each 45 certifying sales of 500,000 copies. The Ides of March's own AM chart ascent awaited.

Saga of a Smash Single: Subtracting 13 Seconds to Success

Along with their materializing music mode, the Ides of March began an affiliation with a management team. Local promoters Bob Destocki and Frank Rand approached the group after they opened a show for Neil Diamond and initiated a business association. Destocki, who worked as a regional promo rep for Warner Bros. Records, used his position to navigate and negotiate a major label deal for the Ides of March.

The band's initial late '60s send-up single, "One Woman Man"/"High on a Hillside," was released in 1969 on Warner Bros.-Seven Arts Records. The pleasant pledge of allegiance featured a string arrangement and a light sound described by Peterik as "more like the Association with brass. We were a harmony band with horns at that point."[13] While "One Woman Man" was a charming, lovely listen, the song did not resonate comparably with the analogous Association slow-dance ballads such as "Cherish" and "Never My Love," both of which were national chart toppers in 1966 and 1967. "One Woman Man" gently came and went, destined for a deep track slot on the Ides' subsequent debut album in 1970.

Warner Bros. remained interested in adopting and developing the Ides of March on their roster. The band put together a demo to further their audition for a major label deal. The four-song set submitted by the Ides included "Lead Me Home, Gently," a tender tune with a crescendoing chorus; the chugging "Something Comin' On"; and the Blood, Sweat & Tears–sounding "The Sky Is Falling." Last in line on the tape was "Vehicle," which was intentionally sequenced behind the three songs that the band members considered stronger possibilities for recording.

The band valued "Vehicle" on a different level than their record label did. Warner heard a potential smash to cash in on, while the Ides naively underestimated the song, primarily regarding the propelling tune as a vigorous, crowd-pleasing staple of their live shows. "It was not a song I would have chosen to be released on record," said Peterik. "We had certain distinctions for songs. Some were good to play live, while others were good to record. 'Vehicle' was one of the songs we felt was better accepted in a live situation. The first time we played the song the audience went wild so we kept playing it at our shows. Every time the ba-da-ba-ba-dah horn riff hit, the dance floor would fill up and people would be hooting and hollering. But we never had any plans to record 'Vehicle.'"[14]

The head of Warner's A&R department was fine with the first three songs on the demo tape but considered the last track the clear standout, hearing a surefire hit in "Vehicle." So did WLS disc jockey Art Roberts. The influential local music advocate liked what he heard when the Ides of March's manager shared a copy of the song with him at the radio station. Roberts was so impressed, he further suggested that the band add a shout-and-response chorus to the song to heighten Peterik's lead vocal. The Ides dutifully complied, adding a "Love ya (love ya), Need ya (need ya), I want ya / Got to have you child" preceding "great God in heaven you know I love you"—Peterik's spontaneous vocal invocation that he "suspected must have been a throwback to his Catholic upbringing."[15]

The Ides of March returned to the studio to record "Vehicle" with Roberts's suggested chorus conversion among other fine-tunings before sending the song Warner Bros.' way. The recording session took place at a CBS studio in Chicago that was primarily reserved for radio and television voice-over work. "They didn't know rock and roll from a hole in the wall," observed Peterik, acknowledging that there was a learning curve involved and a "feeling of experimentation" for both the band and the recording engineers.[16]

The studio circumstance, coupled with the audio-tape technology of the times, almost resulted in the undoing of "Vehicle" before the single's recording was completed. During the dubbing process, an engineer hit the wrong button and inadvertently erased part of the best take of "Vehicle" on the multitrack master tape. A 13-second sequence spanning the song's second "great God in heaven" up to the first note of the guitar solo disappeared. Peterik recalled the panic that immediately set in: "We spent two hours thinking 'Our career is over' because at this time we knew we had something."[17]

Fortunately, an engineer managed to rescue the recording by inserting a replacement segment extracted from a previous take into the void in the best take. Despite the seamless splice, the notorious vanishing audio act left a mark. Though relieved that his guitar solo was spared from the accidental eradication and that he did not have to replicate his self-proclaimed "magical" performance that he still doesn't know how he played, Peterik remained cognizant of what could have been a career-catastrophic 13 seconds. The Ides' front insisted that, from that studio moment forward, he heard the abrupt note within the audio edit every time he listened to "Vehicle."

Lyrically, "Vehicle" drew from several sources—from a lurking drug dealer or leering abductor, to a cool car, driving demands and tongue-in-cheek sexual innuendo among the song's bases. At the suggestion of Peterik's college roommate Bill Griner, the song's opening line—"The friendly stranger in the black sedan" with pictures and candy—was copped directly from a caption of an illustration in a

"Vehicle" drove fast and furious, sounding its horn on the way toward the top of the charts, arriving at #2 in *Billboard*'s Hot 100 in 1970. The casual band portrait on the 45 picture sleeve edition of the smash single was likely a photo image the band expected to be used on their *Vehicle* album cover design, rather than the disconcerting baby doll depiction Warner Bros. selected. (L-R): Ray Herr, Chuck Soumar (seated in chair), John Larson, Jim Peterik, Larry Millas, Mike Borch, Bob Bergland (seated on floor) (Ides of March; Warner Bros. Records, 1970).

government-issued anti-drug pamphlet distributed to high schoolers. The image depicted an undesirable cruising the curb seeking a susceptible student. Such stranger danger conjures the archetypal parental precautionary tale of potential peril that summons every mother's warning to their children about returning home safely from school, in an era before "missing" milk carton postings and AMBER Alerts. The ominous lurking line replaced Peterik's pre-pamphlet lyric lead, "I got a set of pretty wheels baby...." Couplets that follow, such as the main declaration, "I'm your Vehicle, baby / I'll take you anywhere you want to go," were more literal than nuanced. The stanzas spring from Peterik's relationship with his intermittent high school girlfriend and eventual wife, Karen, frequently calling him and asking for a ride somewhere in his souped-up 1964 Plymouth Valiant.

The hit song instincts of the music industrialists, combined with the Ides' skillful implementation of bold and brassy soulful strands, proved prophetic and profitable. Though a trendy, streamlined, AM-friendly echo of a number of the Ides' horn contemporaries, locally and nationally—from the Buckinghams and Chicago to Blood, Sweat & Tears, Lighthouse, and Chase—the opening horn pronouncement of "Vehicle" managed to maintain a distinctiveness. The signature sound sequence instantly imprinted the Ides of March and resonated into an indelible music mark on the scene, the region, and the era.

Released in March 1970 with "Lead Me Home, Gently" as its B-side, "Vehicle" endured its missing 13 seconds and became the fastest breaking single in Warner Bros. history at the time. By May, the single soared to #2 on the *Billboard* Hot 100, though the song was unable to overtake the Guess Who's "American Woman" for the top spot. "Vehicle" was also a Top 10 in the less prestigious *Cashbox* chart, reaching #6.

Vehicle, the Album

The Long-Play namesake of "Vehicle" debuted mid-year, launching a succession of albums in each of the next three years on two different labels. The Ides of March's inaugural studio album on Warner Bros. assembled a music meld of jazz, pop, and rock with psychedelic flourishes and occasional funk.

Eclectic echoes of influence are prevalent in the 41-minute, 10-song set. Blood, Sweat & Tears' progressive jazz rock fusion is a primary thread throughout, channeled in punchy tracks such as "The Sky Is Falling," "Time for Thinking," and "Bald Medusa," a sassy, sneaky adolescent hormone-driven double entendre. Crosby, Stills & Nash affectations accent Peterik's lead vocals accompanied with layers of harmonies. Other discernible inspirations include Creedence Clearwater Revival in the working-class "Factory Band." And the pledge "Home" conjures Neil Diamond in tone and tempo, with a delicate melody that settles in a song spectrum between Reg Presley's Troggs' "Love Is All Around" and Chip Taylor's "Angel of the Morning," a Top 10 hit that snagged Merrilee Rush a Grammy nomination in 1968.

The lovely arrangement of "Home" is composed by Hoyt Jones, a familiar recording studio figure in the Chicagoland vicinity who had orchestrated several lush New Colony songs, notably "I Could Never Lie to You," "Things I'd Like to Say," and "I Will Always Think About You." Jones's sound engineering elegance is also evident in the Ides of March's overlooked pre-album single "One Woman Man," which brings a ray of sunshine pop to *Vehicle*, and the B-side of "Vehicle," "Lead Me Home, Gently," which was not included as an album track.

"Lead Me Home, Gently" and "Home" share a common composition condition with lyrics that sporadically undermine splendid string weaves and crescendos and Peterik's cross-my-heart delivery. Sad and lonely lines such as "I sit staring at my dictionary/trying to find the meaning of life," the woeful "I'm just a grain on a cold deserted beach / waiting to be carried out to sea," and the cringe-worthy couplet "your sink needs a plumber / and you need a man" foreshadow intermittent maudlin verses in fellow Illinoisan (from Peoria) Dan Fogelberg's copious soft rock songbook that would soon emerge on FM airwaves and in his albums in the 1970s.

The infectious, gallivanting "Aire of Good Feeling" is geographically grounded with local color via a western suburb reference to meeting at "Miller Meadow, glistening with dew." The Forest Preserve Park, a popular picnic ground and teen make-out hangout, is located on 1st Avenue south of Roosevelt Road along the Des Plaines River. The Forest Park locale is adjacent to the Ides' home neighborhood of Berwyn and connects with the corners of suburbs Oak Park, Maywood, Broadview, and North Riverside.

Each side of *Vehicle* the LP is punctuated by elaborately arranged, tempo-shifting cover versions. Side one features an extended seven-minute medley that curiously converges Crosby, Stills & Nash's "Wooden Ships" with "Dharma for One," an Ian Anderson instrumental track (eventually lyricized) and a live staple on Jethro Tull's debut album, *This Was* (UK Island 1968/US Reprise 1969). *Vehicle*'s side two closes with further grandeur in an expansive nine-minute-plus re-version of the Beatles' *Revolver* (1966) single "Eleanor Rigby" titled "Symphony for Eleanor (Eleanor Rigby)." The elaborate, elongated arrangement contains echoes of Santana-sounding guitar solos and the Association's "Along Comes Mary" riff as detectable deft citations within the prolonged piece. Peterik acknowledged that selecting a Jethro Tull album track that features a flute and an extended Clive Bunker drum solo for reinterpretation by the Ides may have been mildly mystifying, but borrowing from the Beatles' Lennon–McCartney compositions was commonplace. "It was very au courant at the time, I think every band had their 'Eleanor Rigby,'" said Peterik. "It was kind of, like, required."[18]

Peterik was clearly tuned into the times and his musical surroundings. The array of artists covering the original song from *Revolver* (1966) before the Ides recorded their 1970 interpretation of "Eleanor Rigby" was an unusually lengthy list that included The Standells, Johnny Mathis, Joan Baez, Richie Havens, Vanilla Fudge, Frankie Valli, Jackie Wilson, Gene Chandler, Tony Bennett, Paul Anka, Bobbie Gentry, Ray Charles, the Four Tops, Aretha Franklin, and Rare Earth.

The composite of *Vehicle*'s vigorous 10 tracks solicited convenient critical characterizations such as "potpourri," "inchoate hodge podge," and "BS&T knockoffs," with the pair of extended side-ending suites diverging between "ambitious" and "pretentious" and "portentous and overblown … like Vanilla Fudge with horns."[19]

With hit single momentum and an album release support, the Ides of March toured extensively during 1970. They were minus Herr, who left the band abruptly that summer. Accounts of his departure varied, between Herr's having to resolve issues with selective service draft status to him being kicked out of the band after leaving unannounced. Herr changed his name to Ray Scott and aliased into a solo music career. Along the route of the Ides' promotional parade, the Chicagolanders opened for many top tier acts, among the more notable Led Zeppelin and both Jimi Hendrix and Janis Joplin before they tragically joined the mythical mortal 27 Club less than one month apart in September and October that year. During their West Coast swing, the Ides of March were booked at the renowned Los Angeles club Whiskey a Go Go, where they opened for major national acts Stephen Stills and Tony Joe White, who was riding his 1969 swamp sound signature "Polk Salad Annie" into his composition "Rainy Night in Georgia," made popular by Brook Benton in 1970. The Ides also logged numerous television performances, among them a June 1970 appearance on the ABC variety show *Get It Together*, a Dick Clark production hosted by Cass Elliot of the Mamas & the Papas.

Vehicle made it to the midway of the national album charts, peaking at #55. The position was a decent debut destination for the brassy band of Berwyners, considering the rich fullness of the music marketplace during 1970. The prolific period was highlighted by a steady stream of genuinely remarkable record releases. Standouts from the thriving singer-songwriter scene included albums by James Taylor (*Sweet Baby James*), Joni Mitchell (*Ladies of the Canyon*), Van Morrison (*Moondance*), Randy Newman (*12 Songs*), and Neil Young (*After the Gold Rush*). Among notable band entries were Young with his compadres Crosby, Stills & Nash (*Déjà Vu*), Creedence Clearwater Revival (*Cosmo's Factory*), and The Grateful Dead with a pair of impressive works, *Workingman's Dead* and *American Beauty*. Miles Davis (*Bitches Brew*) and James Brown (*Sex Machine*) represented jazz and soul. There were also prominent split ups that generated fine farewell albums, among them the Beatles' parting (*Let It Be*), Simon & Garfunkel's swan song (*Bridge Over Troubled Water*), and Lou Reed's departure from the Velvet Underground (*Loaded*). Beatle George Harrison's abundance of material in the long songwriting shadow of fellow Fabs Lennon and McCartney accumulated into a striking spiritual Spectorian solo triple album, *All Things Must Pass*.

Design, Dissent, Discount Department Store

Vehicle's presence in the music marketplace during the forefront of a new decade may have been somewhat self-sabotaged by its awkward album cover design that was delivered by Warner Bros. The composition depicted a bare baby doll lying in a roadside field with an ominous black sedan lurking in the background. The Ides members were more confounded than complicit in the questionable cover conceptualization. The band initially thought the jacket was a joke, as they were expecting their debut release to feature a group portrait from a photo shoot they had with a prominent Chicago photographer. According to Peterik, the band was "shell-shocked and scorched" at the label's "careless choice of marketing material." "We were apoplectic," recalls Peterik. "All that work to be marginalized by the most literal and perverted translations." In retrospect, Peterik leaned on parody for perspective, labeling the episode "a Spinal Tap moment," in reference to the critically acclaimed cult classic rock mockumentary *This Is Spinal Tap* (1984).[20]

The baby doll discord crept into controversy. The Ides of March were not alone in being affronted by the *Vehicle* jacket design. One of the nation's largest record retailers, the discount department store E.J. Korvette, refused to stock *Vehicle* in its vast vinyl inventory, fearing repercussions from the album cover imagery being on display with the record available for sale. The prohibition hit close to home, as the North Riverside Korvette store, located in Cermak Plaza Shopping Center at the southeast corner of the Harlem Avenue (IL Route 43) and Cermak Road (22nd Street) intersection, was adjacent to the Ides' hometown of Berwyn and a mere quarter-mile walk from Morton West High School, the band members' alma mater.

The Cermak Plaza locale on the Berwyn–North Riverside boundary opened in 1956 with a wide variety of retail shops and stores—five and dime (F. W. Woolworth, G. C. Murphy), shoes (Kinney, Thom McAn), grocery (Jewel, Hillman's), candy (Fannie Mae), bakery (Burny Bros.), card, gift, jewelry, clothing, and tire and auto, among others.[21] Two decades later, the setting had a cameo in the Mike Myers/Dana Carvey film comedy *Wayne's World* (1992), which highlighted the shopping center's parking lot landmark, a 50-foot steel spike skewered with eight cars. The stacked sculpture, titled *Spindle*, was assembled by artist Dustin Shuler in 1989 and stood tall in the space until 2008.

What began as a loss of innocence for the Ides of March advanced more tangibly into a loss of revenue. "That tasteless cover cost us thousands in sales," stated Peterik.[22] The bandleader's lament was not an overreaction. Though not a full-blown boycott, the retail record restriction was significant due to E.J. Korvette's proximity and the store's prominent, profitable presence in the era's music marketplace. E.J. Korvette was a pioneering suburban shopping centerpiece, founded in 1948 by Brooklyn buddies and World War II veterans Eugene Ferkauf and Joseph Zwillenberg. Counter to the urban folk legend that the "E.J. Korvette" designation was an acronym for "Eight Jewish Korean War Veterans," the store name derives from the two co-founders' forename initials, combined with the cool car "K" spelling instead of "C" that was adapted from the naval term for a Canadian sub-destroyer. "I thought the name had a euphonious ring," explained Ferkauf. "When it came time to register the name, we found it was illegal to use a naval class identity, so we had to change the spelling to 'K.'"[23] "Korvette's," minus its "E.J." initials, became the common consumer shorthand, an efficient abridgement similar to fellow franchises (S. S.) Kresge, (F. W.) Woolworth, and Sears separated from Roebuck.

Along the retail shopping spectrum's evolution/revolution, E.J. Korvette was an innovative enterprise that defined discount department stores, though its company preference was to be branded as "promotional" rather than "discount." The Korvette company emphasis was on low prices, with a variety of goods available within a spacious, one-stop-shopping setting with tasteful surroundings. The chain overshadowed, if not supplanted, the five and dimes of the times such as Kresge, McCrory, and Woolworth and was a precursor to the low-price Class of '62 advents, Wal-Mart and Kmart, and the eventual warehouse clubs, Sam's and Costco, which initiated two decades later in 1983.

Following its debut in Manhattan, Korvette's steady growth from New York through the Northeast corridor accumulated into six stores by 1956, then doubled to a dozen by 1958. By the early 1960s, the visionary company was building expansive 200,000-square-foot "Korvette cities" with adjoining supermarkets, furniture/carpet centers, and tire stores.[24] At its peak, the flourishing franchise consisted of 58 stores nationally. Korvette's entrepreneurial founder Eugene Ferkauf, who challenged fair trade laws, was featured on the cover of the July 6, 1962, issue of *Time* magazine with the banner "Consumer Spending: Discounting Gets Respectable."

Around the same time, Korvette's began its expansion into the Midwest region, with Chicago, Detroit, and St. Louis among the desirable discount destinations. The inaugural push into the Chicagoland suburbs launched in 1963: west in Elmhurst at Illinois Highway 83 and St. Charles Road, and southwest in Oak Lawn at 87th and Cicero Avenue. Two more openings in opposite outlying directions followed later that year, south in Matteson and north in Morton Grove. By mid-decade, the aforementioned North Riverside store became the fifth E.J. Korvette to open in the Chicagoland vicinity.[25]

The Midwest movement followed the franchise prototype. Korvette stores were predominantly and strategically sited in suburban strip malls along arterial roads leading out of urban areas and away from central business districts, often arriving before department store competitors such as Macy's and Gimbels. The largest, most modernized Korvettes were voluminous, with a capacity that contained apparel, home furnishings, sporting goods, pet supplies, electronics (with high-end home entertainment units, stereos, and tape decks), an automotive and tire center, a supermarket, and a pharmacy.

And music. Korvette's record department became renowned as a store signature and as a central music supplier, eclipsing independent and specialty shops, as well as its direct retail competition such as Polk Brothers and Sears, which also stocked vinyl records. Korvette's distinctive record department inserted itself naturally into the Chicagoland scene as an unlikely yet essential infrastructure ingredient of the suburban setting. The discount chain positioned prominently alongside and in conjunction with the area's other core components, renowned sound sources, and activity centers, such as the area teen clubs, record labels, recording studios, and radio stations.

As the store core, the revenue-rich record department uniformly occupied a quadrant of Korvette's, usually a second floor space. An escalator provided an escort to and from an abundant inventory of 33⅓s and 45s. The vast wall of vinyl stock had dual demographic appeal that attracted Long Play preference adult buyers and youth culture consumers drawn to rock and roll. At the time, the typical cost of an LP recorded in monaural ranged from $2.79 to $2.99, with the stereo format costing approximately one dollar more for its superior sound quality. Singles were priced under one dollar, commonly between 69 and 79 cents, with a worst-case cap at 99 cents. And the well-stocked cut-out bins were enticing, with the only drawback to the low-priced vinyl product being the obligatory hole punched in the corner or the sleeve.

Korvette's regularly revolving sales were unique in that the price markdowns were record label based rather than artist-centric. While the all-star rosters of major labels such as Columbia, RCA, Capitol, Warner Bros., and Motown were among the most desirable of the designated discounts deals, the record buyers' bonanza was Korvette's banner "Spectacular All Label Sale," a happening vinyl event that foreshadowed the contemporary annual springtime occurrence Record Store Day.

E. J. Korvette's fabulous "All Label Sale" signaled the spectacular low-price pinnacle of reductions regularly rotating in the vast vinyl inventory of the "World's Largest Record Department" located within the pioneering discount department store chain (*Chicago Sun Times* newspaper ad, circa 1968).

E.J. Korvette sustained through the 1970s before being mismanaged into declaring bankruptcy. The franchise's noteworthy, resourceful retail run ended in 1980, with its marketplace legacy not discounted, particularly as a vinyl record source. Rarely is there a discussion or documentation of E.J. Korvette, past or present, that does not highlight the department store's renowned and revered record space. References ricochet as requisite and reverent recollections. Nostalgic Baby Boomer reminiscences that chronicle coming-of-age, vinyl-virginity record-buying rituals (that include tales of youthful indiscretion and attempted single smuggling) at the fabled Korvette abound in threads, posts, and commentaries across the blogosphere and a variety of internet sites, with samplings and submissions that range from *The Steve Hoffman Music Forum* to *Pleasant Family Shopping*.

(Un)*Common Bond*?

The *Vehicle* cover art quandary marked a rite of passage for the Ides of March. In Peterik's view, the album dilemma was the band's "first, but not last, encounter with the scourges of the music business."[26] Another disagreement loomed, this one single rather than album-oriented. Delivering a (tough act to) follow-up single to the Ides' million-selling "Vehicle" devolved into a proverbial band-versus-record-label wrangle.

With its predictable profit prioritization and corporate commitment to capitalizing on continuity, Warner Bros. wanted a "Vehicle" clone, from hook and horns to melody and arrangement. The Ides favored the vibrant strumming folk, horn, and harmony of "Aire of Good Feeling," a "killer" song in Peterik's partial, though apt, estimation. In addition, the atypical spelling of "Aire" added a trace of sophistication and charm. Not surprisingly, the record label's preference prevailed, and the Ides of March dutifully recorded and released the similar sounding "Superman" as a mandatory "Vehicle" encore/rewrite.

With Peterik's vocal delivery in full David Clayton-Thomas (of BS&T) mode, the lyrically light damsel-in-distress superhero song leans on caped comic book hero conventions, from the phone booth to X-ray eyes. The first stanza phrasing is explicit: "faster than a speeding bullet," "able to leap tall buildings in a single bound," "more powerful than a locomotive." And the derivative remains more distinguishable than disguised throughout, musically with a horn lick from Cat Stevens's "Matthew and Son" and an citation of a Hendrix riff of Dylan's "All Along the Watchtower." The "Vehicle" lyric "great God in heaven" deciphers into a patent paraphrase of "Great Caesar's ghost" on "Superman."

The subsequent single "Superman," which charted at a not-so-super #64, was not included on *Vehicle*'s album track sequence. The single served dual promotional purposes, however, bridging "Vehicle," the single and the LP, with the Ides of March's second Warner Bros. album, *Common Bond*, released the following year in 1971. "Superman" was sequenced as the lead track on side two of the album.

There is suitable sound continuity between *Vehicle* and *Common Bond*, a kindred recording companionship short of double-album symbiosis. Like its predecessor, *Common Bond* is 10 tracks deep, a five-song split on each side of the LP. The 41-minute set is varied and ambitious, polished and progressive in places, yet achieves continuity and cohesiveness. The harmony and horn influences remain recognizable, initialized in CS&N and BS&T, whom Peterik playfully self-references in the lyrics of the album's opening track, "Friends of Feeling."

The Ides' maturing musicianship is manifest in proficient arrangements that range from tight to expanded, acoustic, and brassy, with the horns showing some signs of sounding slightly more restrained. The band's blend of folk/rock/pop/jazz/soul advances naturally into some progressive rock strands and stylings marked by tempo changes. Borch's drumming emerges from backbeat to the forefront with fills and flair in the percussion patterns that guide some of *Common Bond*'s longer tracks. Throughout, Peterik's versatile and vigorous vocals vacillate between gruff and delicate deliveries of elongated syllables and note bending. The raunch to reflective is routine, smoothly transitioning from the deeper soulful tones of the album's initial two tracks, "Friends of Feeling" and "Ogre," then softening into the wistful "L.A. Goodbye" before escalating to the majestic MOR ballad "Hymn for Her." Side one closes with the "L.A. Goodbye" single's B-side, "Mrs. Grayson's Farm," a five-minute-plus narrative inspired by an Ides tour stop.

The varied stylistic pattern continues through the long play recording. Side two's sequence leads with the vigorous "Vehicle" sequel "Superman," followed by three part Crosby, Stills & Nash affectations cascading in "We Are Pillows." A 28-second instrumental bridge "Prelude to Freedom" announces the gentle acoustic strum and flutter of "Freedom Sweet," which contains a melodic echo of the "lie la-lie, lie la lie-la lie la-lie" refrain in Simon & Garfunkel's "The Boxer." The singer-songwriter sensibility of "Freedom Sweet" made the song suitable for B-side status on a non-album track, "Giddy-Up Ride Me," a "Vehicle"-sounding sibling single released in September 1971.

The band's epic endeavors that marked the *Vehicle* LP persist, though this time only on one side of the album. *Common Bond*'s closing track, "Tie-Dye Princess," which winds down in a gradual 11:31, occupies one-fourth of the record's total running time. The protracted progressive rock track is a hippie fairy tale that projects an incense and tapestry vibe, conceivably a midwestern mapping of Chicago's Northside neighborhood, Old Town, a locality analogous with the counterculture haven Haight-Ashbury district in San Francisco.

The continued consensus is that "L.A. Goodbye" is clearly *Common Bond*'s standout track, the delegated "Superman" single aside. Wrapped in a flowing mid-tempo melody rich in triple-tracked textured harmonies, the song's wistful wavelength exudes regional reciprocity. The Sunset Strip field trip from Chicago to Los Angeles and back is at once a melancholy midwestern ode and a fond farewell to the West Coast. Peterik wrote the lyrics on an air sickness bag on the plane during a return flight from California, where the band been promoting "Vehicle"/*Vehicle*. "We were out there for over a week and we were just gobsmacked ... and got to meet Dick Clark," said Peterik. "On the way back it was a bittersweet feeling because we just had such an amazing time but we also kind of missed the bungalows of Berwyn, Illinois."[27]

Following its release as a single in February 1971, "L.A. Goodbye" ascended toward an impressive five-week stay at the top of the regional charts, placing in the top five on both WLS and WCFL. The soothing single's popularity did not project as soundly beyond the Midwest, however, as it only managed to reach #73 nationally. The modest peak position on *Billboard* was surprising, if not disappointing, considering the well-crafted song's regional success as a 45. "Chicago used to be the test market," said Peterik, in reference to the disappointing national fate of "L.A. Goodbye." "If it [a single] made it in Chicago, it was a pretty good chance it would make it everywhere. Well, it didn't happen." Peterik further suggested that the transition of the Ides of March's record label, Warner Bros., from major to independent distribution was a significant shift that may have impacted the Ides' single. "The story we got [was] that 'L.A. Goodbye' really got lost in the shuffle between distributors," said Peterik.[28]

The lack of a broader reception and appreciation did not inhibit the beloved hometown status of "L.A. Goodbye," or its enduring, calming presence that contrasts the brassy blare of "Vehicle" in the Ides of March songbook. The wavelength and "sentimental breakdown" of "L.A. Goodbye" gracefully glide as a cross-country canticle, accentuated by the Peterik proclamation, "And now I feel light years away / from the West side of Chicago." That particular lyric carved a chorus line of local legacy, a sing-along citation dually punctuating and perpetuating the prolific period and the place. Although three late-entry New Colony Six 45s issued on the Sunlight label reached the charts in 1971–72, the Ides of March's "L.A. Goodbye" wore the crown as the suburband seemly sendoff, the concluding, consequential single produced by the eras' Chicagoland collective.

In a song semblance situated within a few months of "L.A. Goodbye" in 1971, John Denver's "Take Me Home, Country Roads" curiously conveyed a similar ache of displacement. The single, co-written with Denver by Bill Danoff and Taffy Nivert, became a homesick hit following its mid–April release, reaching #2 on *Billboard* Hot 100 in August. In addition to its natural adoption as an "almost heaven" West Virginia anthem, the "radio reminder of a home far away" with memories gathering around, teardrops, and feelings of belonging transcended its stateliness and evolved into a national nostalgic refrain. The contemporary "Somewhere Over the Rainbow" looking back with longing lyricism by the "Take Me Home" trio of songwriters and by Peterik with "L.A. Goodbye" were reminiscent of a reflective rotation of songs within the time frame. Locally, there was the Cryan' Shames' trippy rumination in the *A Scratch in the Sky* deep track, "The Town I'd Like to Go Back To," with other prevalent melancholy musings and melodies that included

Ray and Dave Davies Kinks classics "Waterloo Sunset" and "Days" in 1967–68; Lennon–McCartney Beatles' compositions "Yesterday," "In My Life," and "There's a Place"; and Ron Wood and Ronnie Lane's "Ooh La La" with the Faces that followed in 1973.

Changing Majors:
Brass Passé and "Bakersfield Country"

Common Bond signaled a transition for the Ides of March on multiple levels—corporate, creative, and band personnel. The record culminated the Ides' two-album affiliation with the prestigious Warner Bros. label. The band subsequently signed with another major, RCA, and released two albums over the next two years, *World Woven* (1972) and *Midnight Oil* (1973).

The pair of new label recordings featured a notable sound swing across the cumulative 19 tracks sequenced on the pair of albums. To their creative credit, the band didn't settle comfortably or stand still stylistically; rather the Ides of March demonstrated a willingness to explore and expand their musical identity, adding to a progression that included British Invasion, jangle and harmony, and Blood, Sweat & Tears brass. The music modification at this stage was underscored by the addition of Dave Arellano, a blind keyboardist whom the Ides happened to discover playing at a hotel bar while they were touring in Canada. "This guy just had it," recalls Peterik, who characterized Arellano's dexterous, funky skill set as a "cross between Billy Preston and Stevie Wonder."[29] Arellano brought multiple instrumentation and sound enhancements, adding swirling B3 organ, gospel stylings, and Moog synthesizer and Mellotron, both relatively rare at the time.

In addition to Arellano's presence, there were rumblings from management and formidable industry figures such as Clive James suggesting that "brass was passé," which prompted the Ides' musical makeover. The fluctuation induced the departure of the group's piercing trumpeter John Larson. Fellow horn comrade Chuck Soumar remained with the core due to his versatility, which included percussion and vocals. In the transition, the Ides' signature brassy emphasis receded from the forefront of arrangements to a well-placed, select solo, a bridge, or a triumphant crescendo. Soumar's majestic trumpet solo on the global jukebox "Flip Side" provides an insular, resplendent reminder.

The Ides of March's RCA albums feature an adept array of music styles that range from blue-eyed soul and balladry to mid-tempo Southern rock and country accents. The band's trendy prog/art rock inclinations also persist, notably in the shifts and shimmers of the extended seven-minute "Children." The lead and closing tracks that bracket *World Woven*'s 40-minute, nine-song sequence feature jubilant sing-along choruses that span the Pacific to the pulpit. The opening, "Mother America," was inspired by Peterik's honeymoon balcony ocean view, while the album finale, "All Join Hands," rises to revival reverberations—"form a ring around the world, spread the word"—with a heavenly hopeful, celebratory churchy chant "lalalalalala-sha-na, hey-hey, hey-hey."

The Ides continue to exhibit a notable knack for laid back, accentuated with melodious touches in *la la la*'s, *na na na*'s, and textured harmonies. The enchanting "Landlady" glides across the meadow, mellow and meditative, with mandolin flutters and light layered vocals that thread the lovely earthy reverie. The spellbinding vision of nature—grasshoppers, a pussy willow standing ovation, sunset, grass—in a charming atmospheric, if not psychedelic, soundscape, conjures the singing, swaying animated short, *Flowers and Trees*, the pioneering production in the early 1930s that is part of Walt Disney's *Silly Symphony* animated series in three-strip Technicolor. Similarly smooth but slightly more sprightly, "Colorado Morrow" is a territorial tune. The melodic mid-tempo Rocky Mountain echo is a "hitchhike away from sorrow" traveling companion/geo-song sequel to "L.A. Goodbye," all aboard Crosby, Stills & Nash's "Marrakesh Express," destined for "an Illinois today." The album deep track is analogous to *Vehicle*'s unsung "Aire of Good Feeling" and its 45 fate, with both songs seemingly well suited but passed over for single selection.

The band's genre journey continues into the following year on *Midnight Oil* (1973). The Ides' infatuation with country rock emerges into a variant that Peterik labeled "Bakersfield country." The album's 10 tracks draw sounds, styles, accents, and cadence from the Byrds, whom they had toured with, and from Mason Proffit, formed in Indianapolis and relocated down staters based in Champaign, among other influences. Perhaps the most discernible mark came from a slightly more serendipitous source, Poco, forerunners of the Southern California country rock sound.

The Ides of March crossed production paths with the pioneering outfit, which happened to be recording at the RCA studio on Sunset Boulevard at the same time. Multi-instrumentalist Rusty Young sat in on the Ides' session, contributing dobro and his virtuoso pedal steel to "Roadie Ode" and the laid back "Lay Back," which, coupled with Soumar's harmonica, emanate a campfire lullaby atmosphere. The Ides wear Western well, as if it was not their first sound rodeo. The galloping "Quicksilver" saddles up with cinematic soundtrack qualities that evoke corrals, sagebrush, spurs, and swinging saloon doors. The album's rocking, rowdy "Hot Water," "Heavy on the Country," and "Ride the Music" are nicely balanced by smooth, harmonious tracks such as the prayerful "Holy Love," "Chicago's Got the Blues," and a cover of a William Lehman soul composition, "Do What You've a Mind To," which was also recorded and released the same year on RCA by the girl group greats the Shirelles.

Despite the Ides of March's versatile, proficient musicianship; their well-crafted, arranged, tightly produced sets of songs; and major record label support from Warner Bros. and RCA, neither *World Woven* nor *Midnight Oil* managed to attract much critical or commercial attention in the increasingly crowded, competitive album-oriented music marketplace of the early 1970s.

Solo Survivor

Jim Peterik was seduced by the solo siren song. The Ides' primary composer had become enamored with the flourishing singer-songwriter surroundings of artists such as Cat Stevens, Paul Simon, and Elton John. He was convinced he could fit that music mold. In the summer of 1973, Peterik informed his fellow Ides that he was intent on pursuing his own path and "seeing what was out there in the world of music."[30] The declaration of departure from the leader of the band caught the group members by surprise. Despite their best efforts, the Ides were unable to convince their founder, front, and face to change his mind and remain with the band.

In November 1973, the original configuration of the Ides of March culminated their near 10-year run in a final live performance at Morton West High School in Berwyn where the band began playing mid–1960s sock hops. The disbanded/*abandoned* Ides members dispersed in directions within and outside of music, from joining new musical groups and working behind the scenes recording, to accounting and the family upholstery business.

In the immediate aftermath of his Ides exodus, Peterik shifted into full follow-that-dream mode. He carried on and embraced the rock stardom quest, which included his fashioning a persona and presence that featured mod glasses, a colorful coif, and costume-like clothing. With a hint of a Liverpudlian Lennon light look, Peterik's panache regularly attracted attention and turned heads of curious passersby in public.

After releasing a solo album, *Don't Fight the Feeling* (1976), on Epic Records and short-term touring with the Jim Peterik Band, Peterik formed Survivor with Frankie Sullivan in 1978. Peterik recruited some previous collaborators for the group, including a commercial jingle cohort Dave Bickler of the Downers Grove suburb band Jamestown Massacre, teen clubbers who recorded at Chess, released songs on Destination and Warner Bros. The band is probably best known for their breezy beach convertible hit single, "Summer Sun," which slipped inside the *Billboard* Hot 100 at #90 in 1972. Also enlisted were Gary Smith and Dennis Keith Johnson, former rhythm sectionists of another BS&T/Chicago horn style, jazz-rock fusion outfit, Chase, whose "Get It On" stayed on the national charts for 13 weeks in 1971, peaking at #24. Peterik's vocal compositions "Run Back to Mama" and "Love Is on the Way" were among the six tracks on Chase's third and final album, *Pure Music*, released on Epic in February 1974. The group's founder, Bill Chase, died later the same year in August, at age 39, in a twin engine charter plane crash in Minnesota en route to a scheduled performance at a county fair.

Peterik's breakthrough came in 1982, and it was huge. He and Survivor sidekick Sullivan collaborated on "Eye of the Tiger," a theme song commissioned by actor, writer, and director Sylvester Stallone after Queen spurned his initial interest in "Another One Bites the Dust" to score another cinematic round of Rocky in the ring. Survivor's rousing rival-ready soundtrack centerpiece of the boxing threequel,

Rocky III, reached #1, occupying the chart's top spot for six weeks. The song, which received heavy airplay on MTV, remained in the Top 10 for 15 consecutive weeks. The protracted chart stay aligned "Eye of the Tiger" alongside other long-running 1980s hits—John Mellencamp's "Hurt So Good," Olivia Newton-John's "Physical," and the aforementioned "Another One Bites the Dust."

Accolades followed. "Eye of Tiger" received an Academy Award nomination for Best Original Song and for Song of the Year for songwriting. "Up Where We Belong," the Joe Cocker/Jennifer Warnes duet from the film *An Officer and a Gentleman*, and "Always on My Mind," co-written by Wayne Carson, Johnny Christopher, and Mark James, and a #1 hit for Willie Nelson in 1982, were the respective category winners. Not bound to runner up, a third nomination was a charm as Survivor was awarded a Grammy for Best Rock Performance by a Duo or Group with Vocal.

The achievement propelled Peterik into a personal platinum songwriting trajectory that accumulated into an impressive body of collaborative credits through much of the 1980s. Taking a cue from the triumphant sports arena anthem, Peterik continued writing big rather than ballad. His compositions were tailored to the hard rock and Southern rock veins, with sound suitability for stadium settings. In addition to Survivor's smash "Eye of the Tiger," Peterik composed the band's best-sellers—"The Search Is Over," "High on You," "I Can't Hold Back," and "Burning Heart." He also collaborated with other artists and groups, notably Sammy Hagar on "Heavy Metal," which was used in the same-titled animated science fiction film and its soundtrack, and with .38 Special, contributing "Fantasy Girl," "Rockin' into the Night," "Wild-Eyed Southern Boys," "Hold on Loosely," and "Caught Up in You."

Peterik's solo and Survivor pursuits, and the requisite references to his rock résumé, did not appear to carry considerable cachet or kindle much curiosity or coverage of his Ides of March origins. Whether Peterik or a publisher preference for bandleader branding purposes, the Ides of March and/or "Vehicle" did not receive top billing for Peterik's 2014 memoir, *Through the Eye of a Tiger: The Rock 'n' Roll Life of Survivor's Founding Member*. The Survivor symbiosis extended further, as "Eye of the Tiger" was eventually adopted as a standard part of Ides of March set lists of their later live performances.

The Ides of March Way

The Ides of March attained an enduring and endearing Chicagoland eminence established during their initial 1964–1973 course. Their run was highlighted in bold by one huge horn hit, and accented, if not fortified, by a few subsequent charting singles, four albums, and a dynamic live performance presence. Beyond the regional confines of the Midwest, the band's national profile tends to be commonly, and perhaps conveniently, classified in the One (huge) Hit Wonder category.

The lofty single status of "Vehicle," with its distinct horn pronouncement and sturdy swirl, is undeniably at the core of the Ides of March identity. The indubitable "ba da ba ba dah" opening horn hook became a signature sound sequence of Chicagoland and the era, trumpeting and transcending the notable chart capacity of their local colleagues—multiple New Colony Six, Buckinghams and Cryan' Shames singles, the Shadows of Knight's "Gloria," and the American Breed's "Bend Me, Shape Me."

The *motor*-ious musical legacy of "Vehicle" continues to dot the cultural landscape, its automatic transmission navigating naturally from car commercials to cover versions and soundtracks. The classic has been cast in campy, consumer, creepy, corporate, and comic contexts. General Motors is among the numerous car companies, from national auto manufacturers and distributors to local dealerships, to conveniently capitalize on the brash branding and "take you anywhere you want to go" allure of "Vehicle" as a theme song for an extensive national advertising campaign in 2001.

Performances of the song have also persisted toward plentiful. Among the most recognizable, *American Idol* contestant Bo Bice, who finished as runner-up to Carrie Underwood during the popular sing-off show's fourth season in 2005, delivered renditions of "Vehicle" in his live repertoire during the competition. He subsequently included the song as the B-side to his RCA same-year single, "Inside Your Heaven." Ironically, Bice also performed Blood, Sweat & Tears' "Spinning Wheel" on *Idol*, enlisting in the longstanding Peterik/David Clayton-Thomas vocal chorus.

"Vehicle" also reached the animated realm, providing a fitting music video–style soundtrack sequence for a scene in Seth MacFarlane's long-running offbeat sitcom series *Family Guy* (Season 16, episode 5, "Three Directors"), in which family father figure Peter Griffin gets fired from his job at the brewery.

Nearly 20 years after their 1973 split, the Ides of March reassembled in 1990 and have continued playing to the present, their modified membership merged with originals Bergland, Borch, Millas, and Peterik. The latter-day Ides of March have been primarily performance-oriented, routinely booked for shows nationally and regionally across the 1960s pop nostalgia tour and seasonal festival circuit. The geezer gigs include the longstanding Turtle-titled "Happy Together" lineup, milestone cultural and seasonal events and Cornerstone concerts with fellow Chicagoland music cohorts in various configurations.

In addition to recurring home team sporting event appearances, from national anthem renditions to seventh inning stretch singalongs at Wrigley Field, the band was also cast as choirboys from Berwyn. In 2005, at the request of Monsignor Daniel Mayall, pastor of downtown Chicago's hallowed Holy Name Cathedral, the Ides of March performed their carol, "Sharing Christmas," at the landmark church's eminent Christmas Eve mass. Since that occasion, the Ides of March have continued to be the heaven-sent "house band" for the annual holiday gathering.

New recordings by the band have been minimal, with record releases largely limited to live sets, reissues, and compilations, among them volumes cleverly and fittingly titled *Ideology* (2006), *Friendly Strangers: The Warner Bros. Recordings* (2007), *Still 19* (2010), a *Last Band Standing* box set (2015), the band's guest-laden 55th-anniversary *Play On* (2019), and a *Best of Christmas* collection.

In 2010, local veneration of the Ides of March approached a crowning apex. Hometown hero homage reverberated from song, sound, and stage to symbolism. Namely, in street signage of a Berwyn boulevard in the vicinity of the band's home room and hallways at Morton West High School. In recognition of the group of "gee, lucky to be here" teens who belted out a once upon a timeless tune with a bold and brassy signature sequence of notes and made their mark among the countless clusters of music-minded youth during their era, the community officially designated a stretch of Home Avenue between Riverside Drive and Cermak Road "The Ides of March Way."

The spirit of the avenue appellation of vehicular Ides idolization and appreciation is not confined to the Berwyn band and bungalows. The signpost, though specific in its sanctification, also signifies as a summation. The Way is passage and portal, a block party in chorus as an acknowledgment of the Ides of March's achievement, and as a tribute to the totality of the time and place, the spirit and soul that was Chicagoland's mid–1960s suburban scene.

In a Berwyn Boulevard commemoration fitting for a "Vehicle," a section of Home Avenue located near Morton West High School was dedicated to local music heroes the Ides of March in 2010 (Personal photo archive).

CHAPTER 8

Cornerstone Coda
In One Ear and Gone Tomorrow

And now I feel light years away / from the west side of Chicago.
—Jim Peterik, Ides of March, "L.A. Goodbye"
(c) Jim Peterik Music (1971)

In a compressed course consistent with the relatively short-term togetherness of pop rock garage and sunshine bands of any origin and locale during the flourishing mid–1960s time frame, most of the Chicagoland groups, including the productive, higher profile "Suburbs Seven," began to splinter by late 1968. The evaporating vibe and fleeting fateful fade may have been curiously coded in allegory and anticipatory analogy one year earlier, in December 1967, with the Cryan' Shames' bellwether album title, *A Scratch in the Sky*. Months later, in July 1968, the collective wane was casually corroborated with a shrug of album acquiescence in the Buckinghams' *In One Ear and Gone Tomorrow*. In another six-month span, by 1969, the emblematic coincidences of the local Long Play titles became prophecies fulfilled as five of the seven core Chicagoland groups had disbanded. Only the New Colony Six and Ides of March remained intact and continued to record into the early 1970s.

In 1971, the Ides of March settled the accumulation of charting Chicagoland singles during the era into a 50s totality, as "L.A. Goodbye" reached the Top 5 on WLS and WCFL and #72 nationally. In the two years to follow, neither of the Ides of March's subsequent albums—*World Woven* (1972) and *Midnight Oil* (1973)—yielded any singles for the local last band standing. The impressive Chicagoland chart run that commenced six years earlier—late in 1965, with the New Colony Six's Centaur single "I Confess," followed closely by the Shadows of Knight's Them cover, "Gloria"—culminated into crescendo with the mid-tempo harmonease of the Ides of March's "L.A. Goodbye." The soothing west side suburban ode was a fitting finale and fond farewell in 45 rpm, with Jim Peterik presiding, in verse and vocal, as valedictorian of the Chicagoland music Class of Mid–1960s. The proverbial Peterik principle of proximity provides a practically perfect parting note, its wavelength a little longer, in a "light years away" breezy feeling that adroitly synthesizes steadfast and sentimental into a commemorative conclusion of the vibrant vicinity's prospering pop rock garage period.

Bubble Burst: Leaving Oz

The thriving Chicagoland scene stalled into a state of transition and looming cessation, the diminishing almost as abrupt as its mid-decade dawning. The once-upon-a-timeness, the aire and era of good feeling, the communal magic and motion, the means and mood that Cryan' Shames' front Jim Pilster/J. C. Hooke gleefully gloried as "our own little bubble" had basically burst. The disappearing apex of the Midwest music mecca's magic act.

The triumphant trajectory that extended from the spangled sphere of sudden success to a post-peak place of uncertainty receded rapidly into a realm of relative anonymity. The shift was unsettling on multiple levels for its youthful participants. For the majority of the band members, most of whom were in their twenties, the loss of innocence and identity were palpable. "It was emotional hard times more than anything," said the Cryan' Shames' Tom Doody. "It was very difficult."[1] "That was a strange time ... and it happened so fast," added Buckingham Giammarese. "My world had come to a standstill by 1970. It was incredible to be 22 and to feel like your life is over, like you're old."[2]

There were numerous contributing factors simultaneously surrounding, shaping, and subtracting from the setting. Stability during the decade was elusive, a sign of the turbulent times across the sociocultural landscape and its political climate. The kaleidoscopic milieu spanned Woodstock and Watergate, the counterculture and Vietnam, Charles Manson and Neil Armstrong's "one small step" moon landing. Flux was a constant—in contrast, conflict, and chaos—and incongruous with continuity. WLS disc jockey Ron Riley offers an AM radio rainbow refrain on the era's drift:

> Well, the Sixties in general, up and about after the Beatles and the Stones were a nice transition and the music was good. And then it became sociologically unclean. There were rifts, there was Vietnam, there were the Nehru jackets, the flower girls and all that kind of stuff. We kept along with that change, the psychedelic music and all that. But I think after a while it got a little out of hand and I think a lot of that was like leaving Oz.[3]

Situated within the volatile societal circumstance, the common band burdens and proverbial rock myth narratives were present internally and externally among the Chicagolanders. Late decade, positioning became increasingly precarious within the highly competitive, congested music environment regionally and nationally. The music business continued its development and prompt progress toward pop profitability. Radio station programmers responded with playlists and rotations that reflected the shifts in music genres and evolving listener taste preferences. While singles sustained as hooks, album-oriented rock gained traction, along with free-form and underground FM formats.

Commercial and creative conflicts, management issues and demands, and record label meddling were requisite components of the emergent dynamic of navigation and negotiation, newness and naiveté, between the young artists and music industry personnel. Carl Giammarese summarizes the Buckinghams' experiences and epiphanies along the way before the band's breakup at the beginning of 1970:

> We were all a bunch of arrogant little kids. We thought we knew it all and we weren't taking crap from anyone. We had that kind of attitude. We started to realize that rock music was a big business and there was money to be made, and our managers were making it all and we weren't.
>
> We thought it was just easier to fire our manager and get a new manager and fire our producer and get a new producer. We found out that it was a lot easier said than done because at that time our record company didn't care much about what the Buckinghams did. They were too concerned with Janis Joplin and whoever else. We were given one bad producer after another. If we could've been given a real producer that could've been the key to our survival. It turned into a disaster, basically. It seemed rather hopeless at that time.[4]

Nick Fortuna echoes his Buckinghams bandmate: "We didn't think at all about any of our business. The only thing we thought about was what we were going to wear that day and how hard we were going to party afterwards. Back then, mostly, we were existing. That merry-go-round was never going to end, but it does. Everything comes to an end."[5]

The Chicagoland bands were not exempt from artistic differences and infighting. Conflict was fairly universal bandmate behavior and a chronic condition that steered to disintegrating harmony. The discord and restlessness were commonly complicated by jealousy, insecurities, the trappings of notoriety, and the price and pressures of popularity. "You couldn't go somewhere without somebody knowing you," said Pilster.[6]

Personnel and lineup comings and goings certainly took a toll, altering and/or undermining a band's sound consistency and creative chemistry. In addition, college, drugs, the draft, and military service were among the multiple contributing factors and forces that cultivated fragmentation and foundational fractures that led to abbreviated band runs and sooner-than-later dissolution.

In the immediate aftermath of the Chicagoland band breakups, members dispersed in particles of participation that scattered in many directions. In an attempt to reroute and reinvent their musical identities, many musicians relocated to different groups seeking and salvaging some measure of career continuity, with Rufus, Bangor Flying Circus, and Survivor among the numerous relocations and refuges (as documented in previous chapters). Other occupational reconfigurations for exiting band members included solo, duo, session players, producers, and studio sound engineers, with placement across a range of music genres and record label affiliations, major and indie, local and national.

Locale Legacy:
Currents of Curation and Continuity

While the multifaceted, fostering framework of flourishing teen clubs, recording studios, record labels, and powerful radio stations were pivotal, the essence of the mid–1960s Chicagoland scene and its legacy demonstrably reside in the music—the sound and the songs, in singles and in albums, recordings and live performances.

Chapter 8. Cornerstone Coda

The reverberating resonance from the rich, radio-driven regional rotation, particularly the music from the "Suburbs Seven," remains an irrefutably significant undercurrent in the swell of the prolific playlist of the 1960s hit singles soundscape. The most popular songs from the area and era surface across the music terrain beyond the Midwest home front in varying destinations and degrees of notoriety, including streaming sources, variety show karaoke-style cover competitions and sing-off spectacles, film soundtracks, advertising and radio retro rotations of Classic Rock and Oldies. The Buckinghams' popular singles, notably the #1 "Kind of a Drag"; the American Breed's Outsiders adaptation "Bend Me, Shape Me"; the Shadows of Knight's garage glorified Them take, "Gloria"; and the Ides of March's smash "Vehicle," with its signature horn hook, endure as a tetrad of touchstone tunes.

The individual catalogs of recordings of many of the era's suburbands have been compiled and reissued in remastered packages by archival record labels Rhino, Bob Irwin's Sundazed Music, Columbia Legacy, Cherry Red, Varèse Sarabande, BMG, and Collector's Choice. Beyond these impressive editions of individual band recordings, Sundazed dispensed other comprehensive compilations that featured selections from Chicago record label rosters. Deep in tracks and buried treasure, the singular sets showcase an extensive cross section of the city, suburban, and regional music from the era in multi-record, various artist volumes.

Among the noteworthy record roster anthologies are a *Best of Dunwich Records* pair, *Oh Yeah!* (Volume 1) (1991) and *If You're Ready!* (Volume 2) (1994), and the dynamic duo twin set, *2131 South Michigan Avenue: 60's Garage and Psychedelia from U.S.A. and Destination Records* (2009). Inconspicuously positioned at the forefront of these record label compilations is *Early Chicago Volume 1* (1971), issued on the short-lived indie Happy Tiger Records (1969–1971). The edition's early era emphasis features an eclectic range of area artists and some cool cover versions among its 12 tracks. Fast forward to 2015 and a *Sound Stage Cornerstone of Rock* collection.

These carefully curated compilations receive complementary contextualization in the accompanying informative liner note essays crafted by quintessential Midwest music chroniclers Clark Besch and Jeff Jarema. Adding to the critical curatorial co-op, their fellow archivist extraordinaire and music maven Kent Kotal founded the *Forgotten Hits* website in 1999 as an oldies newsletter, with "damn-near daily postings" of riffs and residue that continue to be a central source of sustainable citation of the Chicagoland mid–1960s music milieu and mythology.

Others who have contributed splendidly and significantly as documentarians arranging a stock of interviews and images, profiles, and period perspectives include Dean Milano's scenic view in the photo journal for the Arcadia series *Images of America* (2003); WLS radiohead historian Stew Salowitz; Mike Dugo in *The Lance Monthly*; multi-faceted avant-gardian Steve Krakow as "Plastic Crimewave" with the illustrated bi-weekly info-strip "The Secret History of Chicago Music" in *The*

Chicago Reader; the late Jeff Lind's similar series, "History of Chicago Rock," which appeared (circa 1980s) in the same alternative weekly newspaper; Dave Traut and *Classic Garage Library*; Mike Baker and *The Forgotten 45s*; and Ken Voss, founder, publisher, and steward of the monthly music magazine and blog *Illinois Entertainer* (since 1974) and the depth-defying Illinois Rock 'N Roll Music Archives.

Live music performances remain a priority for the Chicagoland bands and fan base alike, providing period pulse and perpetuation, and persisting as a central and sentimental strand of legacy sponsorship. The foremost 1960s suburbands have routinely reassembled, often collectively as a conglomerate and/or with variable measures of original representation of membership. The reformations and their regional reunion shows have been branded as the Cornerstones of Rock. The Arcada Theatre, a 1960s sound sanctuary in suburban St. Charles, located 45 miles west of the city, has become a home stage residency for the Cornerstone Concert series.

The scope of the bookings also includes the casino and cruise line circuits, holiday occasions, Chicago and regional commemorations, festivals, and retro events with high appeal among the Midwest baby boomer demographic. Many of the recognizable local groups have frequently allied with the popular national nostalgia road shows, on land and sea. Among the notable engagements are the "Solid Gold Sixties Tour," "Flower Power Cruise," and "The Happy Together Tour," which organized in the mid–1980s, enlisting an eclectic lineup of popular 1960s bands. The live reunion performances have taken precedence over recordings for the Chicagolanders with the studio setting subordinate to the stage.

With the exception of an intermittent commemorative cut, new recordings by the suburbands have been a rarity, with reissues and retrospectives a more common course and path of preservation. Sustaining solo has also yielded sporadic recordings. The Buckinghams' Carl Giammarese's individual album releases span *Trying Not to Fade* (2002) and *Living in the Moment* (2016). In between, *My Journey* (2011) was conceptualized as a companion soundtrack to his autobiography, *Reinventing the Buckinghams*, a writing collaboration with Dawn Lee Wakefield. The 19-song set features stripped down, unplugged arrangements of Buckinghams' essentials, tunes from the Tufano and Giammarese catalog, a cover of the Beatles' "I'm A Loser," and two new songs. In 2021, Giammarese contributed the track "I Don't Mind" to the Badfinger tribute album *No Matter What: Revisiting the Hits* (2021). The cast recording renditions for the power pop collection included Rick Wakeman, Ian Anderson, Sonny Landreth, Matthew Sweet, Albert Lee, and Todd Rundgren. Giammarese has also recorded several songs with singer, songwriter, producer, and Cher impersonator, Lisa McClowry.

Scattered sources in print and in visual media productions provide additional retrospective on the productive period. Memoirs are minimal. In addition to Giammarese's journey, Ides of March front Jim Peterik dispensed the lone Chicagoland band member's autobiography from the era, though his Berwyn beginning band did not get top billing in his rise-to-rock-stardom story's title, *Through the Eye of a Tiger:*

The Rock 'n' Roll Life of Survivor's Founding Member (2014). Carl Bonafede, whose impactful presence included launching and guiding the careers of the Buckinghams and Daughters of Eve, provides mid-1960s impresario insights in *The Screaming Wildman: Vibrations from the Dawn of Chicago Rock* (2016). Bonafede's unique behind-the-scenes viewpoint features interviews with musicians, artists, promoters, disc jockeys, and others central to the scene.

From page to screen, *The Voice That Rocked America: The Dick Biondi Story* (2018), an independent film documentary directed by Pamela Pulice, chronicles the life and career of the legendary disc jockey and the impactful presence of local radio and its dynamic personalities on the region during the era. More broadly based beyond individual bios, *When Chicago Rocked the '60s* (2001) highlights the area's "Golden Age of Top 40" in one of the 30-minute episodes of the docu-series *Chicago Stories*, produced by public television station WTTW. The presence of the mid-1960s music scene in the PBS series slate is a notable acknowledgment as the inclusion situates the garage suburbands adjacent to prominent figures, landmarks, and events from the area's rich ethnic and cultural heritage. Among the subjects documented in the series' diverse lineup include the Great Chicago Fire, the Union stockyards, improvisation comedy, the birth of gospel music, the Staple Singers, Koko Taylor, Major League Baseball owner and promoter Bill Veeck, mayors Richard J. Daley and Jane Byrne, the city's Pablo Picasso sculpture, Midway airport, serial killer John Wayne Gacy, and Riverview Amusement Park.[7]

The inevitability of loss also rests (in peace) within the Chicagoland legacy as a number of notable figures from the period have passed away over the years. In memoriam, among the departed include New Colony Sixer Les Kummel (1978); Cryan' Shames musicians Isaac Guillory (2000) and Dave Purple (2001); producers/record executives Bob Monaco (2008), Jim Golden (2014), Bill Traut (2014), and his Dunwich associates Eddie Higgins (2009) and George Badonsky (2016); disc jockeys Art Roberts (2002), Dex Card (2018), Clark Weber (2020), and Dick Biondi (2023); *Kiddie A-Go-Go* children's television personality and pioneering producer tandem, Elaine and Jack Mulqueen (2012, 2016); Ides of March members Ray Herr and John Larson (2011); Knaves drummer Gene Lubin (2015); Buckingham Marty Grebb (2020); and a trio of Suburbs Seven band fronts, the Mauds' Jimy Rogers (2010), Gary Loizzo of the American Breed (2016), and the Shadows of Knight's Jimy Sohns (2022).

Geomusic Markers and Measures

Measuring the scale and standards of any music scene and its soundtrack's significance during any period is certainly a subjective stance, with impact ratios relative and proportionate. Chicagoland's spirited mid-1960s suburban shindig certainly invites, if not insists upon, curiosity, consideration, and critical comparison with notable parallel pop rock parentheses and pockets across eras and settings.

Among that wide range of analogous geomusic markers include New York City's 1970s Greenwich Village folk scene, with punk, new wave, salsa, funk, soul, and disco dispersed across surrounding boroughs, a diverse sound span vividly chronicled in Will Hermes's *Love Goes to Buildings on Fire: Five Year in New York That Changed Music Forever* (2011).

In the opposite direction cross country reside the legendary, luxuriant West Coast songwriting sanctuaries in the echoes of twin California canyon communities, Topanga and Laurel, skirting Los Angeles, and reaching into West Hollywood, Santa Monica Boulevard, and Beverly Hills in the late 1960s and early 1970s. Up the Pacific Coast to San Francisco's Haight-Ashbury district's psychedelia and on to the Pacific Northwest passage stretching from Seattle grunge to Portland's "rude-jazz" and the "Sea-Port Beat," the region's rich roots documented in detail by Peter Blecha in *Stomp and Shout: R&B and the Origins of Northwest Rock and Roll* (2023).

Across the Deep South, pockets include the Swampers and the Muscle Shoals Sound at Rick Hall's Fame Studios in Alabama to Gainesville, Florida, and Athens, Georgia, alternative of the 1980s and 1990s. And major music metropolitans across the country—Music City Nashville and Memphis, Minneapolis, and Detroit, Philadelphia, Boston, and Austin, Texas.

The distinctive presence and pulse of productivity generated by the Chicagoland suburbands during the span between late 1965 and into the early 1970s should not be undervalued or overstated. The dynamic period embodies a pop rock garage cluster that is perhaps a prolific pocket more than a panorama; a strong undercurrent more than an overtone; a meaningful moment more than a full-scale music movement. The magnitude and gravity of mid–1960s Chicagoland may not necessarily register, ring, or ripple with rock revolution resonance or trigger transcendence beyond Midwest memory and declaration. Even within Chi-Town's Windy City vicinity, the accomplishments and identity of the Suburbs Seven and the gamut of garage groups were routinely overshadowed by their long playing resident contemporaries, Chicago, playfully proclaimed as "the band so great they named a city after it."

By broader benchmarks, cross-country comparisons, and contextualization, the Chicagoland bands of the era, particularly the Suburbs Seven, were proportionally larger-than-local regionally, though smaller than singular sensations on a larger coast-to-coast scale. The respectability was relatively restrained, despite generating a number of hits comparable to the output of many of the national and international artists and groups that were their music chart companions. Their shared achievement and presence were notable considering that there was no groundbreaking genre, no singular sound or uniform stylistic identity that emerged in the catalog of music produced in the vicinity. The convincing case, compelling context, and persisting proof for Chicagoland, in large part, lies solidified in the popular playlist and its locality, the collective concentration and catalog of songs imprinted with an indelible 1960s suburb stamp.

Mapping the Mid–1960s Midwest: Come on Feel the Illinoise[8]:

> *I think we were all trying to put Chicago on the map.... There was a lot of talent here and everybody had been passing it over. We were trying to compete all at once to make Chicago and the Midwest noticed.*
> —Jimy Sohns, Shadows of Knight[9]

The multitude and magnitude of the sounds and spirit of the Chicagoland sphere across the Midwest during the era were certainly visible and valued. The legion of local suburban garage groups grooved their own momentous mark, collectively carving a cornerstone across the pop rock panorama and into the region's rich music map and its legacy. The striking abundance of the period furthered and more firmly fixed Chicagoland's prominent place in the center third of the country, congruent with Mick Jagger's "make it in the Midwest" manifesto that he imparted to Shadows of Knight front Jimy Sohns.

The tableau totality of the happening mid-decade music(o)ccurrence enriched the larger locality's eclectic "Sweet Home Chicago" heritage of blues, jazz, soul, R&B, gospel, house, rap, folk, funk, rap, and rock. The notable Illinoise g-g-g-generated within the prolific pop rock garage parenthesis between late 1965 and the early 1970s settled with suburban significance as a prelude and bridge, verse and chorus, authenticating a noteworthy niche along the celebrated music timeline of "that toddlin' town."

That local lineage of origins, whether birthplace, based in or bordering, alphabetizes eminently from A to Z, from Laurie Anderson to Warren Zevon. In between lies a *soul*stice of notables that includes Paul Butterfield, Ramsey Lewis, Curtis Mayfield and the Staple Singers; significant strands of country/folk rock singer-songwriters, from Byrds front (Jim) Roger McGuinn to humorists Steve Goodman and John Prine; along with Dan Fogelberg and bluegrass fiddler Alison Krauss, whose roots extend southbound to the Peoria-Decatur-Champaign triangle.

The bountiful city soundscape stretches from prominent points such as the Fred Fisher "Chicago" composition in 1922—popularized by Frank Sinatra's finger-snapping, shoulder-sling rendition in 1957—and a nightclub circuit that showcased giants such as Bing Crosby and Benny Goodman to the Chess Records and Vee-Jay soul-filled studios and early record label legacies in a 10-block stretch down South Michigan Avenue into a broad embrace of contemporary sounds, styles, and settings, emanating from genres and subgenres, in currents and tones that penetrated the Chicagoland atmosphere.

A genre-spanning divergence spins from Earth, Wind & Fire's funky Afro pop to the progressive rock of Styx on to REO Speedwagon and Cheap Trick (from Rockford, 90 miles east) and the Gold Coast convertible cruise anthem "Lake Shore Drive/L.S.D." by Aliotta Haynes Jeremiah in the 1970s; the infiltrating musicomic characters later in the disco decade with *Saturday Night Live* accomplices Dan Aykroyd and Second City alum John Belushi as the Blues Brothers, "Joliet"

Jake and Elwood; into 1980s alt rockers Smashing Pumpkins, to a steady stream of 1990s indie rock stock that featured lo-fi, whip smart Liz Phair exiting Guyville, multi-instrumentalist Andrew Bird, and the prolific alt country folk rockers Wilco; and onto a roster sampling that includes Plain White T's (formed late 1990s), *American Idol/Dreamgirls* Jennifer Hudson, Fall Out Boy, Beach Bunny, Whitney, Horsegirl, and Dehd.

Landmarks and locales route across park publics and communities, winding from Wilco's Northwest warehouse loft and recording hideout on Kedzie Avenue near Irving Park and their musical presence that threads "Via Chicago" through trailer, opening theme, scenes, and soundtrack of *The Bear* (2022–present), the superb Italian beef restaurant FX/Hulu streaming series to the fabled Old Town School of Folk Music in Lincoln Park to the long-running Lollapalooza Music Festival, which settled in as a permanent late summer resident of Grant Park along the lakefront. And renowned recording studios and radio stations, music venues and record labels, scatter on and across, in between and beyond the blocks of city and suburb neighborhoods, along the streets, roads, and avenues of the north, south, and west sides, echoing and connecting points past and present.

A Prevailing P*rocks*imity

The mid–1960s Chicagoland music scene's status may be slightly susceptible to a tempered tone. Critical observations, particularly those originating outside the Midwest region, may be prone to overlooking or minimizing the merit of the area's era-imprinting accomplishment and its relevance. Some views may credibly and conveniently enunciate and emphasize the scene as an evanescent event, while borrowing the Buckinghams' album title, "in one ear and gone tomorrow."

To those, such as myself, predisposed to personal coming-of-age partialities and proclivities—and with the benefit of hindsight and blind spots—the epoch endures evocatively, romantically tintend above and beyond the "own little bubble," the "aire of good feeling," and "glorious time" that situated with consequence in the suburban sprawl of the city's surrounding peripheries from the mid–60s to early 70s. The vibrant, voluminous vista sustains as a significant vestige. Its rhythmic remnants resonate emblematically; a distant constellation shimmering as a metaphorical and meaningful scratch in the soundscape sky, and a cornerstone, settling and standing steadfastly. A center of gravity.

The Chicagoland mid–1960s music scene's "once upon a time" presence and profuse playlist persevere in sound and spirit, a prevailing *procks*imity and period within the region's rich chronicle. The timeless timbre and essence resound, abiding as confirmation of the Shadow Knight Sohns-ian sense and sensation of "being a part of something bigger and more important." A "make it in the Midwest" measure. Memorable and magnificent. A mecca and mythic marker on the Music Map.

Selected and Annotated Discography
The Sounds of Mid–1960s Chicagoland

The following selected and annotated discography of recordings compiles and arranges the Chicagoland mid–1960s music catalog in its various forms and (re)configurations, samplings and sound sources, ranging from singles and albums to reissues and compilations. The categories in litany lean toward emphasis on the productive core Chicagoland suburbands and their music spanning the mid–1960s into the early 1970s, along with more recent reissue releases.

Among notable points and patterns along the way: (1) the striking concentration of 40 (give or take) charting singles between 1966 and 1968; (2) the solid chart staying power for many of the singles; (3) the productivity of the Buckinghams in 1967 resulting in the group being named *Billboard*'s "most listened to band of the year"; (4) the bands' various record label transitions—local, regional, and major; (5) the album-oriented Cryan' Shames' moderate chart placement; and (6) a conspicuous four-year gap between singles and record labels for the Ides of March, from 1966 to 1970. And a discographic disclaimer, determination, or excused absence that lives up to its billing as "selected": There is simply not enough room in this space for the 38 album-plus recording catalog of the eminently successful Chicago band Chicago.

Charting Chicagoland Singles

THE SUBURBS SEVEN, SPANKY, AND "SUMMER SUN"

1966–1972

The neighboring South Bend, Indiana, garage group, the Rivieras' "California Sun," a surf cover that reached #5 in The Hot 100 and remained on the charts for 10 weeks in 1964, was a prelude to Chicagoland's prolific suburban singles run from the mid–1960s into the early 1970s. The year 1966 marked an arrival for Chicagoland suburbands, as the core began to chart a concentrated collective course through the increasingly crowded mid-decade songscape, with the New Colony Six's "I Confess" and the Shadows of Knight's "Gloria," at the forefront of the inauguration that launched in late 1965. This chart overview highlights the notable productivity of the core Suburbs Seven, while also embracing Spanky and Our Gang's 1960s sunshine singles sequence, a few MOB cuts in the 1970 wane and the Jamestown Massacre's "Summer Sun" setting on the singles scene in 1972.

Year
(number of singles)

Band. "Song" (Record Label) # Peak National Chart Position / Weeks on Charts (if available) * Includes singles that placed outside the *Billboard* Hot 100

1966
(11 singles)

Buckinghams. "Kind of A Drag" (U.S.A.)	#1 / 13
Cryan' Shames. "Sugar and Spice" (Destination)	#49 / 9
____. "I Wanna Meet You" / "We Could Be Happy" (Columbia)	#85 / 4
Ides of March. "You Wouldn't Listen" (Parrot)	#42 / 7
____. "Roller Coaster" (Parrot)	#92 / 1
New Colony Six. "I Confess" / "Dawn Is Breaking" (Centaur)	#80 / 4
____. "I Lie Awake" (Sentar)	#111 / 2
Shadows of Knight. "Gloria" (Dunwich)	#10 / 12
____. "Oh Yeah" (Dunwich)	#39 / 6
____. "Bad Little Woman" (Dunwich)	#91 / 2
____. "I'm Gonna Make You Mine" (Dunwich)	#90 / 1

1967
(15 singles)

American Breed. "Step Out of Your Mind" (Acta)	#24 / 9
____. "Bend Me, Shape Me" (Acta)	#5 / 14
Buckinghams. "Lawdy Miss Clawdy" (U.S.A.)	#41 / 6
____. "Don't You Care" (Columbia)	#6 / 14
____. "Mercy, Mercy, Mercy" (Columbia)	#5 / 12
____. "Hey Baby (They're Playing Our Song)" (Columbia)	#12 / 10
____. "Susan" (Columbia)	#11 / 12
Cryan' Shames. "Mr. Unreliable" (Columbia)	#127 / 3
____. "It Could Be We're in Love (Columbia)	#85 / 8
New Colony Six. "Love You So Much" / "Let Me Love You" (Sentar)	#61 / 6
____. "You're Gonna Be Mine" (Sentar)	#108 / 4
____. "I'm Just Waitin' (Anticipatin' for Her to Show Up)" (Sentar)	#128 / 4
Spanky and Our Gang. "Sunday Will Never Be the Same" (Mercury)	#9 / 8
____. "Making Every Minute Count" (Mercury)	#31 / 7
____. "Lazy Day" (Mercury)	#14 / 4

1968
(16 singles)

American Breed. "Green Light" (Acta)	#39 / 7
____. "Ready, Willing and Able" (Acta)	#84 / 3
____. "Anyway That You Want Me" (Acta)	#88 / 4
Buckinghams. "Back in Love Again" (Columbia)	#57 / 6
Cryan' Shames. "Up on the Roof" (Columbia)	#85 / 3
____. "Young Birds Fly" (Columbia)	#99 / 2
____. "Greenburg, Glickstein, Charles, David Smith & Jones"	#115 / 2
Mauds. "Soul Drippin'" (Mercury)	#85 / 4
New Colony Six. "I Will Always Think About You" (Mercury)	#22 / 13
____. "Can't You See Me Cry" (Mercury)	#52 / 8
____. "Things I'd Like to Say" (Mercury)	#16 / 16
Shadows of Knight. "Shake" (Team)	#46 / 8
Spanky and Our Gang. "Sunday Mornin'" (Mercury)	#30 / 8
____. "Like to Get to Know You" (Mercury)	#17 / 11
____. "Give a Damn" (Mercury)	#43 / 8
____. "Yesterday's Rain" (Mercury)	#94 / 3

1969
(6 singles)

New Colony Six. "I Could Never Lie to You" (Mercury)	#50 / 8
____. "I Want You to Know" (Mercury)	#65 / 6
____. "Barbara I Love You" (Mercury)	#78 / 5
Spanky and Our Gang. "Anything You Choose" (Mercury)	#86 / 3
____. "And She's Mine" (Mercury)	#97 / 1
____. "Echoes (Everybody's Talkin')" (Mercury)	#126 / –

1970
(4 singles)

Ides of March. "Vehicle" (Warner Bros.)	#2 / 12
____. "Superman" (Warner Bros.)	#64 / 5
MOB "I Dig Everything About You" (Colossus)	#83 / –
____. "Give It to Me" (Colossus)	#71 / –

1971
(3 singles)

Ides of March. "L.A. Goodbye" (Warner Bros.)	#73 / 9
New Colony Six. "Roll On" (Sunlight)	#56 / 9
____. "Long Time to Be Alone" (Sunlight)	#93 / 4

1972
(2 singles)

New Colony Six. "Someone, Sometime" (Sunlight)   #109 / 2
Jamestown Massacre, "Summer Sun" (LUV/Warner Bros.)   #90 / 5

Chicagoland @ 33⅓

The core "Suburbs Seven" bands, along with the area inner outlier, Spanky and Our Gang, not only produced the majority of charting singles but contributed the preponderance of album-length recordings within the Midwest's single-centric mid–1960s scene.

American Breed. *American Breed*. (Acta/Dot, 1967)
_____. *Lonely Side of the City*. (Atlantic, 1968)
_____. *Bend Me, Shape Me*. (Acta, 1968)
_____. *Pumpkin, Powder, Scarlet and Green*. (Atlantic, 1968)

Aorta. *Aorta* (Columbia, 1969)
_____. *Aorta 2*. (Happy Tiger Records, 1970)

Buckinghams. *Kind of a Drag*. (U.S.A., 1966)
_____. *Time and Changes*. (Columbia, 1967)
_____. *Portraits*. (Columbia, 1968)
_____. *In One Ear and Gone Tomorrow*. (Columbia, 1968)
_____. *Greatest Hits*. (Columbia, 1969)

Coven. *Witchcraft Destroys Minds & Reaps Souls*. (Mercury, 1969)
_____. *Coven*. (MGM Records, 1971)
_____. *Blood on the Snow*. (Buddah Records, 1974)

Cryan' Shames. *Sugar and Spice*. (Destination/Columbia, 1966)
_____. *A Scratch in the Sky*. (Columbia, 1967)
_____. *Synthesis*. (Columbia, 1969)

Five Emprees. *Little Miss Sad*. (Freeport Records, 1965)

Flock. *The Flock*. (Columbia, 1969)
_____. *Dinosaur Swamps*. (Columbia, 1970)

H.P. Lovecraft. *H.P. Lovecraft*. (Philips, 967)
_____. *H.P. Lovecraft II*. (Philips, 1968)
_____. (as Lovecraft) *Valley of the Moon*. (Reprise, 1970)

Ides of March. *Vehicle*. (Warner Bros., 1970)
_____. *Common Bond*. (Warner Bros., 1971)
_____. *World Woven*. (RCA, 1972)
_____. *Midnight Oil*. (RCA, 1973)

Illinois Speed Press. *Illinois Speed Press*. (Columbia, 1969)
_____. *Duet*. (Columbia, 1970)

Little Boy Blues. *In the Woodland of Weir*. (Fontana, 1968)

Mauds. *Hold On*. (Mercury, 1967)

Mason Proffit. *Wanted*. (Happy Tiger, 1969)
_____. *Movin' Toward Happiness*. (Happy Tiger, 1971)

The final album recorded and released on the independent label. The Indianapolis group, formed by the Talbot brothers after Sounds Unlimited disbanded, was at the forefront of emerging country folk rock sound. The group recorded several other albums between 1971 and 1973: *Last Night I Had the Strangest Dream* (Ampex, 1971), *Rock Fish Crossing* (Warner 1972), and *Bare Back Rider* (Warner Bros., 1973).

New Colony Six. *Breakthrough*. (Sentar, 1966)
_____. *Colonization*. (Sentar, 1967)
_____. *Revelations*. (Mercury/Sentar, 1968)
_____. *Attacking a Straw Man*. (Mercury/Sentar, 1969)

Rivieras. *Let's Have a Party*. (U.S.A. Records, 1964)

Jim Golden garage discovery for U.S.A. label. Chicagoland's unofficial first 45 hit single via the "California Sun" in South Bend, Indiana.

Robbs. *The Robbs*. (Mercury, 1967)

Debut from the Oconomowoc, Wisconsin, brother band, leading with the single "Race with the Wind."

Shadows of Knight. *Gloria*. (Dunwich, 1966)
_____. *Back Door Men*. (Dunwich, 1967)
_____. *Shadows of Knight*. (Super K, 1969)

Spanky and Our Gang. *Spanky and Our Gang*. (Mercury, 1967)
_____. *Like to Get to Know You*. (Mercury, 1968)
_____. *Anything You Choose b/w Without Rhyme or Reason* (Mercury, 1969)
_____. *Spanky's Greatest Hits*. (Mercury, 1969)
_____. *Live*. (Mercury, 1970)

Band Anthologies, Compilations, Best-Ofs, Reissues

Since the Chicagoland music scene's dissolution in the early 1970s, assorted volumes in band, various artists, and record label configurations have been released on prominent recording archival labels such as Sundazed, Rhino, Columbia Legacy, Real Gone Music, and Now Sounds/Cherry Red. The configurations include career-spanning compilations, commemorative collections, single album reissues, anthologies, deluxe expanded remastered editions, EPs, essentials, and best-ofs. The packages contain the standard curatorial music content: B-sides, early works, previously unreleased, unissued, non–LP, and bonus tracks, rarities, demos and outtakes, single versions, alternative takes, and remixes. The plentiful music content is enhanced by liner note booklets that include photos, interviews, and insightful commentary by the usual suspects in the lineup of Chicagoland music chroniclers and archivists, with Clark Besch, Jeff Jarema, and Jerry Schollenberger among the contributors.

American Breed. *The Uttermost Incredible Complete Recordings.* 5 LPs/3 CDs. Happy Tiger Records TH 1017. 1993.

All songs from studio albums, rare and early 45 releases, film soundtrack songs, and radio spots.

Buckinghams. *Mercy, Mercy, Mercy: (A Collection).* Columbia Legacy CK 47718. 1991.

The requisite rotation from the charting collective leading the Chicagoland hit parade, with a lone "previously unreleased" among the 18 tracks.

Cryan' Shames. *A Scratch in the Sky.* (Deluxe Expanded Mono Edition). Cherry Red/Now Sounds. 2014.

The band's second album presented in its original mono, with seven bonus tracks.

_____. *Sugar & Spice* (Reissue). Sundazed Music SC 6186. 2002.

Highlights include previously unissued versions of the Beatles' "You're Gonna Lose That Girl," Bread's "It Don't Matter to Me," and compositions from Jim Fairs and Lenny Kerley.

_____. *Sugar and Spice: A Collection.* Columbia Legacy CK 47905, 1992.

A solid sampling from the band's three albums, with several unissued 45 versions of songs. Features the band's final 45, a cover of "Rainmaker," the B-side of Harry Nilsson's Top 10 single "Everybody's Talkin'," from October 1969.

Del-Vetts. *The Del-Vetts* (Compilation). Sundazed Music SEP 10–170. 2008.

_____. *Last Time Around.* Sundazed Music SEP 124. 1997.

A four-track EP: "Last Time Around," "Everytime," "I Call My Baby STP," and "That's the Way It Is."

Five Emprees. *A Whole Lotta Five Emprees: Singing Little Miss Sad. The Complete Studio Recordings 1965–1968.* Arf! Arf! Records AA 095. 2004.

Hello Benton Harbor, Michigan! With sensational centerpiece "Little Miss Sad."

Ides of March. *Last Band Standing: The Definitive 50 Year Anniversary Collection.* Ides of March (I.O.M.) Records. 2015.

The 4 CD & Live DVD set is as billed in the title, definitely definitive.

_____. *Vehicle (Expanded Edition).* Real Gone Music RGM 0430. 2014.

Selected and Annotated Discography

Modestly expanded, in slip case packaging, with four additional tracks—early "High on a Hillside"; the B-side of "Vehicle," "Lead Me Home, Gently"; "Melody"; and the single version of "Vehicle"—and liner notes by long-time music writer Richie Unterberger.

_____. and Dick Biondi. *Sharing Christmas.* Jim Peterik Music. 2006.

Mini-album/EP with four original holiday songs and radio icon Biondi narration: the title tune, "The Five Snowflakes," "A Distant Trumpet," and "All Join Hands." A pleasant seasonal soundtrack carol to accompany the Ides of March's annual Christmas Eve performances, a Chicagoland holiday tradition.

_____. *Beware! The Ides of March Live.* I.O.M. Records. 2002.

A rich two-record set that includes Ides essentials; Peterik solo and Survivor classics "The Search Is Over," "High on You," and "Eye of the Tiger"; and an homage to garage roots, "Tobacco Road," the Kinks' "Tired of Waiting," and Curtis Mayfield's Impressions' "I've Been Trying."

_____. *Friendly Strangers: The Warner Brothers Recordings.* Rhino Handmade. 2003.

_____. *Vehicle* and *Common Bond.*

Compiles complete tracks from albums *Vehicle* (1970) and *Common Bond* (1971); non-LP B-sides "High on a Hillside" and "Lead Me Home, Gently"; the non-LP single "Melody"; and the single version of "Vehicle."

_____. *Ideology. 1965–1968.* I.O.M. Records 2000.

Early Epitome and Parrot label material and Shondels songs.

_____. *Ideology Version 11.0 (1966 to present).* I.O.M. Records 10882 1970 2. 2000.

Features a curious closing chorus of tracks: "Spirit of Chicago," featuring Frankie Sullivan and American Breed's Gary Loizzo, among others; "Star Spangled Banner"; and "Wild-Eyed South Side Boys."

Illinois Speed Press. *The Illinois Speed Press.* Columbia CS 9792. 1969.
Reissued on Columbia Legacy (2021).

Knaves. *Leave Me Alone.* Sundazed Music LP-SEP 10166. 2007.
Eight-track, 33-minute EP includes an instrumental version of the antiestablishment anthem "Leave Me Alone." Issued in 2014 in limited edition translucent gold vinyl.

Luv'd Ones. *Truth Gotta Stand.* (Compilation) Sundazed Music SC11050. 1999.

Mason Proffit. *Come and Gone.* Warner Bros. 2S-2746. 1973.
Double album reissue of Indianapolis country folk rock group's Happy Tiger releases, *Wanted* (1969) and *Movin' Toward Happiness* (1971).

New Colony Six. *Colonized! Best of The New Colony Six.* Rhino Records R2 71188. 1993.
_____. *At the River's Edge* (Reissue). Sundazed Music Inc. SC10–166: 1993.
_____. and the Raymond John Michael Band. *Sides.* Rev-Ola, 2007.

Rivieras. *Let's Have a Party!* (Reissue) Oldays Records 6488. 2017.

Reissue of South Bend, Indiana, garage group's U.S.A. Records LP in 1964, recorded at Columbia Studios in Chicago, and featuring Chicagoland's unofficial first hit single, "California Sun." Plentiful bonus tracks.

The Robbs. *Before, Then & After*. Wet World Records. WWIX 2011.

A Dick Clark discovery from Oconomowoc, Wisconsin, the pre-psych and sunshine band of Robb brothers with Wilbury-like aliases, recorded on Mercury, Atlantic, and ABC/Dunhill. Their catalog includes a self-titled debut; a double LP radio sampler, *Sounds Like the Navy*; and an LP as Cherokee, the name of their mid–1970s Hollywood recording studio. Some interesting cover versions included. Buyer beware: consumer reviews have consistently expressed few stars and disappointment in the collection.

Shadows of Knight. *Dark Sides: The Best of the Shadows of Knight*. Rhino Records R2 71723. 1994.

_____. *Raw 'n' Alive at the Cellar, Chicago '66!* Sundazed Music SC 11013, 1992.

Spanky and Our Gang. *Spanky and Our Gang* (Reissue). Mercury SR 11624 (original 1967).

Multiple reissues and formats of the Bloomington/Peoria folk group's debut between 1982 and 2016 in various countries. Features notables "Lazy Day," "Sunday Will Never Be the Same," "Making Every Minute Count," and a cover of the John Denver composition, "Leaving on a Jet Plane," popularized by Peter, Paul and Mary.

_____. *The Best of Spanky and Our Gang: Millennium Collection: 20th Century Master*s. Universal Music Group. 2005.

One of several Spanky greatest/Best-of collections (Rhino/WEA 1990; Mercury 1999). Basics without filler or bonus tracks, concise 10 essential tracks include version of Fred Neil's "Everybody's Talkin'."

_____. *The Complete Mercury Recordings*. 4 CD set. Hip-O Select B0003620-02 (2005).

_____. *The Complete Mercury Singles*. 21 tracks. Real Gone Music RGM 0270 (2014).

Local Record Label Roster and Various Artist Volumes

The mid–1960s Chicagoland music scene is certainly worthy of a multi-record box set treatment. Thus far, such a vast and varied volume has not fully materialized. The *Early Chicago Volume 1* on the independent Happy Tiger Records provided a sound sampling as early as 1971. Since then, the handful of various artist compilations have been exclusively assembled according to local legendary record label rosters—U.S.A., Destination, Dunwich, and Vee-Jay. The sets provide an admirable and representative regional rotation of recordings from the era. There is an enticing glimpse of a Suburbs Seven set in a *Sound Stage* Cornerstone Concert series compilation, issued in multiple formats—live/original recordings (CD, 2015; CD/DVD; 2018).

Various Artists. *2131 South Michigan Avenue: 60's Garage & Psychedelia from U.S.A. and Destination Records.* 2 CDs. Sundazed Music SC 11201. 2009.

As striking impressive a sound assemblage and summation of the Chicagoland mid–1960s scene as any vantage point or listening station. Double-disc document packed with 40 tracks from the garage rosters of prolific local record labels U.S.A. and Destination, including hitmakers the Buckinghams, Cryan' Shames, Flock, and a representative selection of local hero lesser-knowns: the Boyz, Cherry Slush, Counts, Daughters of Eve, Foggy Notions, Great Society, Jokers, Lord and the Flies, Lost Agency, Messengers, Oscar Hamod and the Majestics, Park Avenue Playground, Ronnie Ross and the Good Guys, Ricochettes, Shady Daze, The Sheffields, Trafalgar Square. Package features photos, band bio capsules, and an interview with producer/label owner Jim Golden.

_____. *Early Chicago, Volume 1.* Happy Tiger Records HT-1017. 1971.

At the forefront of Chicagoland compilations, this various artist set is not as record label specific as it is producer tinged (the Traut, Monaco, Golden trinity) with early era emphasis. The suburband sampler features predominantly cover versions by a representative range, from George Edwards to the Shadows of Knight, Mauds, American Breed, and the Cryan' Shames (their coveted take on the Beatles' "You're Gonna Lose That Girl") to Saturday's Children, the Trolls, Little Boy Blues, the Rovin' Kind, Del-Vetts, the Flock, and H.P. Lovecraft.

_____. *Oh Yeah! The Best of Dunwich.* Sundazed Music/Tutman Records SC 11010. 1991.

Roster representation includes Del-Vetts, Rovin' Kind, Saturday's Children, Warner Brothers, Little Boy Blues, 30-song sampling of the Dunwich roster with previously unreleased material and alternative versions by Sounds Unlimited, the Knaves, the Mauds, and the original recording of Shadows of Knight's "Uncle Wiggley's Airship," with fun filler radio spots featuring the American Breed and a Ban roll-on ad with H.P. Lovecraft.

_____. *If You're Ready! The Best of Dunwich Records…. Vol 2.* Sundazed Music/Here 'Tis Records SC11019. 1994.

Further testament to the Dunwich presence with another 28 tracks: The Pride and Joy, Shadows of Knight, Things to Come, Luv'd Ones, Saturday's Children, the Knaves, Wanderin' Kind, Rovin' Kind, Light Nites, American Breed, the Warner Brothers, Sounds Unlimited, H.P. Lovecraft, the Troys, an unissued track by Beau Gentry, and two cover cuts (George Edwards & Friends, Shadows of Knight) culled from the Happy Tiger Records *Early Chicago* compilation (1971).

It's a Foot Note, man!: The comprehensive Dunwich discographies compiled by Mike Callahan, Dave Edwards, Patrice Eyries at Both Sides Now Publications (2005):

singles (https://www.bsnpubs.com/chicago/dunwich45.html) and album: (https://www.bsnpubs.com/chicago/dunwich.html) are excellent supplementary sources to these Dunwich *Best Of* volumes.

_____. *Sound Stage Presents*: *Cornerstones of Rock: American Garage* (Sound Stage Classics Series). CD/DVD. BMG 5383915202018. 2018.

Documentation of an October 2015 Chicagoland Cornerstone concert, produced by WTTW/Chicago as part the public television station's splendid *Sound Stage Classics Series*. Jim Peterik and the Ides of March host as house band with their local garage group standbys delivering a set of their popular mid–1960s to early 1970s songs live on stage. The lineup features members of the New Colony Six, Cryan' Shames, American Breed, Shadows of Knight, and Buckinghams. Also performing: local Ted Aliotta of Aliotta Haynes Jeremiah, with the scenic Chicago anthem, "Lake Shore Drive"; out-of-town guests the Music Explosion ("Little Bit o' Soul"), Rick Derringer of the McCoys ("Hang on Sloopy"), and the Standells ("Dirty Water"); and a tribute to the late jazz rock band Chase ("Get It On"). Among the multiple formats, a 19-track CD edition in 2015 with the original (rather than live) versions of the suburband hit songs serves as a suitable sampler of the "best of" mid–1960s Chicagoland with dual appeal for long-time fans or as an introductory starter kit for the less familiar. The three non–Chicagoland band classics ("Little Bit o' Soul," "Dirty Water," and "Hang on Sloopy") from the performance are also included in the sequence (though not as "bonus tracks"), also in their original recording rather than live formats. "Lake Shore Drive" is the notorious omission from the set.

_____. *The Quill Records Story: The Best of Chicago Garage Bands*. Collectables COL-0662, 1997.

Additional archival affirmation of the scope of the soundscape the era and area, in the local record label shadows Dunwich, Destination, U.S.A. and Chess. Another enterprise of record promoter and New Colony supervisor Peter Wright, the 25-track compilation includes Ronnie Rice and the Gents, the Ricochetts, Riddles, Exceptions, and girl group the High-Schoolers, among others.

_____. *Vee-Jay: The Definitive Collection*. 4-CD box set. Shout! Factory. 826662-10485, 2007.

83 tracks culled from a soul-deep 13-year run (1953–1966) as an early African American–owned record label, making a mark alongside renowned Motown and cross town Chess and recognized for being the first American record label to release the Beatles' debut album and singles. The abundant collection spans blues, doo-wop, rhythm and blues, soul, jazz, and gospel from a roster that includes Jimmy Reed, Jerry Butler, John Lee Hooker, the Staple Singers, Elmore James, the Dells, and Billy Preston.

Chapter Notes

Prelude

1. Jock Hedblade and Lou Hinkhouse, dirs., *Chicago Stories*, "How Chicago Rocked the '60s," WTTW-Chicago/PBS, Don't Blink, Inc./Chicago Historical Society, 2001.
2. Miles Raymer, "Garage-Rock Pioneer Jimy Sohns Has Seen Enough for Ten Lifetimes," *Vice*, September 17, 2015, https://www.vice.com/en/article/exq5gk/garage-rock-pioneer-jimy-sohns-has-seen-enough-for-ten-lifetimes-916.
3. Mike Dugo, "The Knaves," *The Lance Monthly*, http://www.beyondthebeatgeneration.com/knaves.html.
4. Jim Pilster, personal phone interview with the author, February 25, 2017.
5. On November 6, 1967, one month before the release of the Cryan' Shames' *A Scratch in the Sky*, Gloria Stavers's colorful Doors profile, "Meet Jim Morrison," was published in *16 Magazine*. And I celebrated my 12th birthday.
6. The Beach Boys' song title is adopted by the late rock journalist/biographer Timothy White in the band bio/social history, *The Nearest Faraway Place: Brian Wilson, the Beach Boys and Southern California Experience* (New York: Henry Holt & Co., 1994).
7. Jim Peterik, "L.A. Goodbye," Bald Medusa Music, ASCAP, 1971.
8. John Ford, Henry Hathaway, and George Marshall, dirs., *How the West Was Won*, Prod. Bernard Smith, Screenplay by James R. Webb (Hollywood, CA: MGM Studios, 1962).
9. Conversely, the bigger, more important, inclusive "Chicago" is simply more convenient to comprehend, particularly for those outside the region. Case in point: In the mid–1970s, a friend invited me home for the weekend in rural Mississippi, 50 miles south of Jackson. While at a fishing hole, I was explaining to my friend's father that my hometown in Illinois was North Riverside, a suburb 20 minutes or so west of Chicago. Before I could complete my Midwest geography orientation, he declared flatly, as if correcting me, while casting his line, "You're from Chicago."
10. Homage to latter-day local legends Wilco via *Summerteeth* (Reprise Records, 1999). "Via Chicago" Words Ampersand Music/(BMI) You Want a Piece of This Music/(ASCAP).
11. For a more detailed, confessional account of my vinyl coming-of-age experiences at the E.J. Korvette record department, high/low-lighted by a moment of misguided youth for under one dollar in 1967, please see "My Back Pages," my personal preface (pp. i–ix) to *B-Sides, Undercurrents and Overtones: Peripheries to Popular in Music, 1960 to Present* (Farnham, UK: Ashgate, 2009). After coming across my reminisce of the single smuggling, Bobby (Barbara) Ferkauf Kurzweil, daughter of the discount department chain founder, Eugene Ferkauf, graciously contacted me via an email dispatch in February 2011.

Introduction

1. Adam Langer, "Glory Days," *Chicago Reader*, January 12, 1989, https://chicagoreader.com/news-politics/glory-days/.
2. Jim Golden, "Recollections," liner notes, *2131 South Michigan Avenue: 60's Garage & Psychedelia from U.S.A. and Destination Records*, Compilation by Bob Irwin, Jeff Jarema, and Mike Markesich, Sundazed Music, 2009.
3. Hedblade and Hinkhouse, "How Chicago Rocked the '60s."
4. Mike Dugo, "The Knaves," *The Lance Monthly*, RV Stewart Productions/Lance Records/Cool Links Publishing, http://www.beyondthebeatgeneration.com/knaves.html.
5. *Ibid.*
6. Langer, "Glory Days."
7. *Ibid.*
8. Originally Cook and the Chefs in high school (named after singer Don Cook), the band changed their name to the Impressions and then the Five Empressions before signing a recording contract with the small Chicago indie label Freeport Records. Although their single "Little Miss Sad" was originally released under the name the Five Empressions, the name was quickly changed after the famous soul group the Impressions issued an injunction against them. See Gary Burns's insightful liner note essay, "Shakin' With the Five Emprees," in *A Whole Lotta Five Emprees: Singing Little Miss Sad. The Complete Studio Recordings 1965–1968*, Arf! Arf! Records AA 095, 2004.

9. Langer, "Glory Days."
10. Hedblade and Hinkhouse, "How Chicago Rocked the '60s."
11. Carl Giammarese, Personal phone interview with the author, December 19, 2016.
12. *Ibid.*
13. Langer, "Glory Days."
14. WLS radio requested that the song's chorus be edited from "Hold on, I'm comin' / Hold on, I'm comin'" to "Hold on, don't you worry / Hold on, please." See Mike Callahan, Dave Edwards, and Patrice Eyries, "Dunwich Singles Discography," Both Sides Now Publications, https://www.bsnpubs.com/chicago/dunwich45.html.
15. The remastered edition of the Cryan' Shames' *Sugar and Spice* album (Sundazed Music, 2014) includes their cover versions of the Beatles' "You're Gonna Lose That Girl" and Bread's "It Don't Matter to Me," recordings that were buried in the vault for decades.
16. Langer, "Glory Days."
17. *Ibid.*
18. Carl Giammarese, personal phone interview with the author, December 19, 2016.
19. Langer, "Glory Days."
20. *Ibid.*
21. Graham Nash's song "Chicago/We Can Change the World," a track on his solo debut album, *Songs for Beginners* (Atlantic, 1971) and released as a single, was a protest song in response to the 1968 Democratic Convention and the subsequent Chicago Eight conspiracy. The line "Won't you please come to Chicago just to sing" is believed to be Nash's plea to bandmates Stephen Stills and Neil Young to come to Chicago to play a benefit concert for the Chicago Eight defense fund.
22. See Gary Burns, "No Guns at Geezer Rock," *Popular Music and Society* 41, no. 3 (2018): 349–50.
23. Langer, "Glory Days."
24. Jim Pilster, Personal phone interview with the author, February 25, 2017.
25. Hedblade and Hinkhouse, "How Chicago Rocked the '60s."
26. Jim Peterik, with Lisa Torem, *Through the Eye of the Tiger: The Rock 'n' Roll Life of Survivor's Founding Member* (Dallas, TX: BenBella Books, Inc., 2014), 83–4.
27. Raymer, "Garage-Rock Pioneer."
28. Langer, "Glory Days."
29. *Ibid.*
30. See Kent Kotal, "Clubbin' in Chicago…in the Late '60's and early 70's," *Forgotten Hits* (blog), May 7, 2019, http://forgottenhits60s.blogspot.com/2019/05/clubbin-in-chicago-in-late-60s-and.html.
31. Carl Giammarese, Personal phone interview with the author, December 19, 2016.
32. Langer, "Glory Days."
33. *Ibid.*
34. *Ibid.*
35. Mike Dugo, "Up Close with Ray Graffia Jr. of New Colony Six," *The Lance Monthly: 60s Garage Bands*, April 2004 in *MusicDish e-Journal*.
36. Carl Giammarese, Personal phone interview with the author, December 19, 2016.
37. Langer, "Glory Days."

Chapter 1

1. Jeff Jarema, liner notes, *2131 South Michigan Avenue: 60's Garage & Psychedelia from U.S.A. and Destination Records*, Sundazed Records (SC 11201), 2009.
2. Jim Peterik, "Vehicle," Bald Medusa Music/ASCAP, 1970.
3. Chicago and Then Some (Judith), "Chicago's Historic Music Legacy: Interview with Carl Giammarese of the Buckinghams," *ChicagoAndThenSome* (blog), December 13, 2012, http://chicagoandthensome.blogspot.com/2012/12/chicagos-historical-music-legacy.html.
4. Stew Salowitz, *Chicago's Personality Radio: The WLS Disc Jockeys of the Early 1960s* (Bloomington, IL: Chicago Radio Book/Bloomington Offset Process, 1993), 30.
5. Jeff Davis, "Introduction," in *Images of America: Chicago's WLS Radio*, by Scott Childers (Chicago: Arcadia Publishing, 2008), 11–13.
6. *Ibid.*, 8.
7. Salowitz, *Chicago's Personality Radio*, 35.
8. *Ibid.*, 7.
9. See "The History of WLS Radio," http://www.wlshistory.com/WLS60/.
10. Salowitz, *Chicago's Personality Radio*, 8.
11. *Ibid.*, 44.
12. *Ibid.*, 8.
13. Rick Kaempfer, "Ron Riley," *Chicago Radio Spotlight* (blog), January 22, 2011, http://chicagoradiospotlight.blogspot.com/2011/01/ron-riley.html.
14. Salowitz, *Chicago's Personality Radio*, 58.
15. The WLS "official radio record surveys" are displayed at various online archives, among them http://www.vidiot.com/WLS_Surveys/1964.html. Perhaps the most comprehensive archive of WLS material is compiled and curated by radio historian Jeff Roteman; see http://user.pa.net/~ejjeff/jeffwls1.html.
16. Salowitz, *Chicago's Personality Radio*, 4.
17. *Ibid.*, 90–91.
18. *Ibid.*, 88.
19. Ted Okuda and Jack Mulqueen, *The Golden Age of Chicago Children's Television* (Carbondale, IL: Southern Illinois University Press, 2016), 129.
20. *Ibid.*, 126.
21. Salowitz, *Chicago's Personality Radio*, 88.
22. *Ibid.*, 89.
23. Okuda and Mulqueen, *The Golden Age*, 131.
24. *Ibid.*, 131.
25. *Ibid.*
26. Kent Kotal, "Who Played The Very First Beatles Record In America?" *Forgotten Hits* (blog), http://forgottenhits.com/who_played_the_very_first_beatles_record_in_america.

27. See Mike Callahan, David Edwards, and Patrice Eyries, "The Vee-Jay Story," Both Sides Now Publications, http://www.bsnpubs.com/veejay/veejaystory1.html.
28. *Ibid.*
29. Michael Ribas, liner notes, *Vee-Jay: The Definitive Collection*, Shout! Factory, 2007.
30. Callahan, Edwards, and Eyries, "The Vee-Jay Story."
31. Salowitz, *Chicago's Personality Radio*, 89.
32. *Ibid.*, 8, 10.
33. *Ibid.*, 60.
34. "WLS Magazine Sales Over 100,000," *Billboard*, May 13, 1967.
35. Salowitz, *Chicago's Personality Radio*, xi.
36. *Ibid.*, xii.
37. *Ibid.*, 84.
38. *Ibid.*, 27.
39. *Ibid.*
40. *Ibid.*, 41.

Chapter 2

1. Ray Graffia, email correspondence received by the author in 2017: June 12 and 28, August 4, September 22, and October 24.
2. Mike Dugo, "Up Close with Ray Graffia, Jr., of New Colony Six," *Lance Monthly/60's Garage Bands*, April 4, 2004 in Music Dish e-Journal (February 17, 2017) and/or http://www.beyondthebeatgeneration.com/newcol.html.
3. Jerry Schollenberger, liner notes, *Colonized! Best of The New Colony Six*, Rhino Records R2 71188, 1993.
4. Ray Graffia, email correspondence with the author, September 22, 2017.
5. Schollenberger, *Colonized!*
6. George Plasketes, "Paul Revere's (Last)ing Ride (1938–2014)," *Popular Music & Society* 38, no. 4: 522–525.
7. Ray Graffia, email correspondence with the author, September 22, 2017.
8. Richie Unterberger, "New Colony Six," in *Music USA: Rough Guide* (London: Rough Guides, 1999), 268.
9. George Plasketes, "In Memoriam: Terry Melcher (1942–2004)—Lost in the Mid-60s Sun?" *Popular Music & Society* 30, no. 2 (May 2007): 267–273.
10. Plasketes, "Paul Revere's (Last)ing Ride."
11. Dugo, "Up Close."
12. *Ibid.*
13. *Ibid.*
14. Schollenberger, *Colonized!*
15. Dugo, "Up Close."
16. Ray Graffia, email correspondence with the author, September 22, 2017.
17. *Ibid.*
18. Langer, "Glory Days."
19. Dugo, "Up Close."
20. Unterberger, "New Colony Six," 268.
21. Jeff Jarema, liner notes for The New Colony Six, *At the River's Edge*, Sundazed Music Inc. SC11016, 1993.
22. Dugo, "Up Close."

Chapter 3

1. Raymer, "Garage-Rock Pioneer."
2. Jeff Jarema, liner notes, *Dark Sides: The Best of the Shadows of Knight*, Rhino Records R2 71723, 1994, 6.
3. Raymer, "Garage-Rock Pioneer."
4. Mark Paytress, "What Goes On? Nuggets Unearthed: The Shadows of Knight: 'Oh Yeah,'" *Mojo*, January 2017, 22.
5. Kent Kotal, "Your All-Time Favorite Garage Band!!! #1. The Shadows of Knight," *Forgotten Hits* (blog), December 8, 2012, http://forgottenhits60s.blogspot.com/2012/12/your-all-time-favorite-garage-band-1.html.
6. Gary James, "Interview with Jimy Sohns of the Shadows of Knight," http://www.classicbands.com/JimySohnsInterview.html.
7. *Ibid.*
8. Mark Deming, "Biography: Shadows of Knight," *AllMusic*, https://www.allmusic.com/artist/shadows-of-knight-mn0000791247.
9. Laura E. Hill, "When DuPage Rocked," *Chicago Tribune*, December 31, 1995, https://www.chicagotribune.com/news/ct-xpm-1995-12-31-9512310188-story.html.
10. *Ibid.*
11. Deanna Isaacs, "Group Efforts: Flashback to a Legendary Teen Hangout," *Chicago Reader*, July 29, 1999, https://chicagoreader.com/arts-culture/group-efforts-flashback-to-a-legendary-teen-hangout/.
12. *Ibid.*
13. Steve Marovich, "Last Time Around Part II: The Majestic Hills Bandstand Was a One-Time Hot Spot," Kenosha.com, December 11, 2021, https://www.kenosha.com/2021/12/11/last-time-around-part-ii-the-majestic-hills-bandstand-was-a-one-time-hot-spot/.
14. Bill Traut, liner notes, *If You're Ready! The Best of Dunwich Records... Vol. 2*, Sundazed Music SC11019, 1994.
15. Hugh Hart, "Recalling Their Star," *Chicago Tribune*, July 4, 1991, https://www.chicagotribune.com/news/ct-xpm-1991-07-04-9103160773-story.html.
16. Raymer, "Garage Rock Pioneer."
17. Kotal, "Your All-Time Favorite."
18. *Ibid.*
19. Raymer, "Garage Rock Pioneer."
20. Clark Weber and Neal Samors, *Clark Weber's Rock and Roll Radio: The Fun Years, 1955–1975* (Chicago: Chicago's Books Press, 2008), 87–88.
21. Langer, "Glory Days."
22. *Ibid.*
23. *Ibid.*
24. Jarema, *Dark Sides*, 6.
25. Paytress, "What Goes On?"

26. Ibid.
27. Jarema, *Dark Sides*, 8.
28. James, "Interview with Jimy Sohns."
29. Colin Fleming, "10 Wild LPs from Garage Rock's Greatest Year," *Rolling Stone*, June 3, 2016, https://www.rollingstone.com/music/music-news/10-wild-lps-from-garage-rocks-greatest-year-99345/.
30. Jarema, *Dark Sides*, 9–10.
31. James, "Interview with Jimy Sohns."
32. Ibid.
33. Ibid.
34. Jarema, *Dark Sides*, 12.
35. The Seth Man, "Shadows of Knight," *The Book of Seth*, October 2008, https://www.headheritage.co.uk/unsung/thebookofseth/shadows-of-knight.
36. Ibid.
37. Fleming, "10 Wild LPs."
38. Jon Savage, *1966: The Year the Decade Exploded* (London: Faber & Faber, 2016).

Chapter 4

1. Dave Traut, "The Banshees," Classic Garage Rock Library, http://www.classicgaragerock.comindex.php/bands/bio/3.
2. See "Jukebox Companies: Seeburg Corporation," http://www.jitterbuzz.com/jukeboxes_companies.html#sjuk and Kerry Seagrave, *Jukeboxes: An American Social History* (Jefferson, NC: McFarland, 2015).
3. Antique Clock Guy, "J.P. Seeburg Company: An Extensive History," https://www.clockguy.com/SiteRelated/SiteReferencePages/SeeburgHistory.html.
4. The essential book of record and region is Robert Pruter's *Chicago Soul* (Champaign, IL: University of Illinois Press, 1992).
5. Traut, *If You're Ready!*
6. Cary Ginell, *Hot Jazz for Sale: Hollywood's Jazz Man Record Shop* (self-published, lulu.com, 2010), 40, 118–120.
7. Traut, *If You're Ready!*
8. Ibid.
9. Ibid.
10. Ibid.
11. The liner notes in both volumes of *The Best of Dunwich Records* (Sundazed 1991, 1994) present accounts by Bill Traut and Jeff Jarema of the adoption of "Dunwich" as the record label name.
12. Traut, *If You're Ready!*
13. Jeff Jarema, liner notes, *Oh Yeah! The Best of Dunwich Records*, Sundazed Music/Tutman SC 11010, 1991.
14. Caspar Llewellyn Smith, "Beach Boy Brian Wilson Listens to *Rubber Soul*," *The Guardian*, June 10, 2011, https://www.theguardian.com/music/2011/jun/11/beach-boys-brian-wilson.
15. Jarema, *Oh Yeah!*
16. Richie Unterberger, liner notes for H.P. Lovecraft, *H.P.Lovecraft//H.P. Lovecraft II*, http://www.richieunterberger.com/hplove.html.
17. Traut, *If You're Ready!*
18. Mike Callahan, David Edwards, and Patrice Eyries have compiled Dunwich Record label discographies for Both Sides Now Publications: "Dunwich Singles Discography" (https://www.bsnpubs.com/chicago/dunwich45.html) and "Dunwich Album Discography" (https://www.bsnpubs.com/chicago/dunwich.html).
19. James, "Interview with Jimy Sohns."
20. Nordine's credits included (uncredited) vocal coach for Linda Blair in her possessed role in *The Exorcist* (1973).
21. "The Things to Come," Classic Garage Rock Library, https://classicgaragerock.com/index.php/bands/bio/26.
22. Mike Dugo, "The Knaves," *The Lance Monthly* (RV Stewart Productions/Lance Records), http://www.beyondthebeatgeneration.com/knaves.html.
23. Ibid.
24. Ibid.
25. Ibid.
26. Ibid.
27. Ibid.
28. Jason Ankeny, "Little Boy Blues Biography," *AllMusic*, https://www.allmusic.com/artist/little-boy-blues-mn0000258279/biography.
29. Jarema, *Oh Yeah!*
30. Traut, *If You're Ready!*
31. Ann Johnson and Mike Stax, "From Psychotic to Psychedelic: The Garage Contribution to Psychedelia, *Popular Music & Society* 29, no 4. (October 2006): 415.
32. Traut, *If You're Ready!*
33. Bruce Eder, "Illinois Speed Press Biography," *AllMusic*, https://www.allmusic.com/artist/illinois-speed-press-mn0002138693.
34. Jim Newsom, Review of *Illinois Speed Press*, *AllMusic*, https://www.allmusic.com/album/illinois-speed-press-mw0000852106.
35. Brian Craddock and Michael Pelonis, "Shape of Things to Come," Sony/ATV Music Publishing LLC, Universal Music Publishing Group, Warner Chappell Music, Inc., 1968.
36. Bess Korey, "Chicago's First All-Girl Band: Daughters of Eve. (Debi Pomeroy and Andrea Parness share their recollections of being member of Chicago's first all-girl band)," *Girlsinthegarage's Blog* (blog), April 27, 2010, https://girlsinthegarage.wordpress.com/2010/04/27/chicagos-first-all-girl-band-daughters-of-eve/.
37. Ibid.
38. Chris Bishop, "The Five Bucks 'No Use in Trying' and The Byzantine Empire," *Garage Hangover.com*, December 13, 2009, https://garagehangover.com/five-bucks/.
39. Jarema, *Oh Yeah!*
40. Traut, *If You're Ready!*
41. Jarema, *Oh Yeah!*
42. Traut, "The Banshees."
43. Ibid.
44. Bob Stroud, "Jimy Rogers and the Mauds: Biography," http://www.themauds.com/bio.htm.
45. Jarema, *Oh Yeah!*

46. Kotal, "Forgotten Hits Remembers Jimy Rogers and the Mauds," *Forgotten Hits* (blog), August 25, 2014, http://forgottenhits60s.blogspot.com/2014/08/forgotten-hits-remembers-jimy-rogers.html.
47. Jarema, *Oh Yeah!*
48. Traut, *If You're Ready!*
49. *Ibid.*

Chapter 5

1. Carl Giammarese, Phone interview with the author, December 19, 2016.
2. *Ibid.*
3. Casey Chambers, "Interview—Carl Giammarese (The Buckinghams)," *The College Crowd Digs Me*, December 14, 2015, https://www.thecollegecrowddigsme.com/2015/12/interview-carl-giammarese-buckinghams.html.
4. Rick Simmons, "Dennis Tufano, The Buckinghams, and Rock's Greatest Disappearing Act-Part 1," *ReBeat Magazine*, November 20, 2014, http://www.rebeatmag.com/dennis-tufano-the-buckinghams-and-rocks-greatest-disappearing-act-part-1/.
5. Mike Baker, "The Mob—Chicago Band. The Mob Story," https://mikebaker45s.weebly.com/the-mob-story.html. See also "The Mob," *Mike Baker and the Forgotten 45s@MikeBaker45s* (blog), https://mikebaker45s.wordpress.com/the-mob/.
6. *Ibid.*
7. "On This Day in 1967: The Start of the Big Thing That Turned into Chicago," February 15, 2017, https://www.rhino.com/article/on-this-day-in-1967-the-start-of-the-big-thing-that-turned-into-chicago.
8. William Ruhlmann, liner notes, *Chicago Group Portrait* (Box Set), Columbia Records C4K 47416, 1991.
9. Baker, "The Mob—Chicago Band. The Mob Story."
10. *Ibid.*
11. *Ibid.*
12. Golden, *2131 South Michigan Avenue.*
13. *Ibid.*
14. *Ibid.*
15. *Ibid.*
16. Carl Bonafede, *The Screaming Wildman: Vibrations from the Dawn of Chicago Rock*, ed. Joel Bierig (Chicago: CreateSpace Independent Publishing Platform, 2016), 217.
17. Chambers, "Interview—Carl Giammarese."
18. Carl Giammarese, "Carl Giammarese of The Buckinghams on 'Kind of a Drag,'" Antenna TV, December 1, 2019, YouTube video, 18:23, https://www.youtube.com/watch?v=zFcBEhzpwzs.
19. Andrew S. Hughes, "Music Still Not a Drag for Buckinghams," *South Bend (Indiana) Tribune*, June 23, 2011, SouthBendTribune.com, http://articles.southbendtribune.com/2011-06-23/entertainment/29697492_1_buckinghams-carl-gaimmarese-horns.
20. *Ibid.*
21. Carl Giammarese, Personal phone interview with the author, December 19, 2016.
22. Simmons, "Dennis Tufano."
23. ChicagoAndThenSome (Judith), "Chicago's Historic Music Legacy."
24. Simmons, "Dennis Tufano."
25. *Ibid.*
26. *Ibid.*
27. Carl Giammarese, Phone interview with the author, December 19, 2016.
28. Simmons, "Dennis Tufano."
29. Bruce Eder, review of The Buckinghams' *Kind of a Drag*, *AllMusic*, https://www.allmusic.com/album/kind-of-a-drag-mw0000044664.
30. *Ibid.*
31. Chambers, "Interview—Carl Giammarese."
32. *Ibid.*
33. *Ibid.*
34. Giggens, "Album Review 118. The Buckinghams—In One Ear and Gone Tomorrow," June 20, 2018, YouTube video, 18:23, https://www.youtube.com/watch?v=6GQhCeElgq8.
35. Hughes, "Music Still Not a Drag."
36. Simmons, "Dennis Tufano."

Chapter 6

1. Jim Mueller, "Back With the Cryan' Shames," *Chicago Tribune*, September 3, 1995, http://articles.chicagotribune.com/1995-09-03/features/9509030081.
2. Langer, "Glory Days."
3. *Ibid.*
4. Jim Pilster, Personal phone interview with the author, February 25, 2017.
5. *Ibid.*
6. Charles A. Barrett, "Shames in Harmony on a Vocal Identity," *Billboard*, June 27, 1967, 24.
7. *Ibid.*
8. Paradigm Talent Agency, "Executive Profile: Paradigm's Fred Bohlander Looks Back on 50-Year Career, But Don't Say He's 'Retiring,'" *Paradigm Land* (blog), January 25, 2019, https://the.land/paradigm/blog/Executive-Profile-Paradigms-Fred-Bohlander-Looks-Back-On-50-Year-Career-But-Dont-Say-Hes-Retiring.
9. Jarema, *2131 South Michigan Avenue.*
10. Dave Rybaczewski, "'If I Needed Someone' History," Beatles Music History: The In-Depth Story Behind the Songs of the Beatles! http://www.beatlesebooks.com/if-i-needed-someone.
11. Steve Krakow, "The Riddles' Lone 1967 Single Made Its CD Debut in 2008," The Secret History of Chicago Music, *Chicago Reader*, July 15, 2015, https://chicagoreader.caom/music/the-riddles-lone-1967-single-made-its-cd-debut-in-2008/.
12. Tom Doody, "Toad Tales," liner notes for The Cryan' Shames, *Sugar and Spice* (Reissue), Sundazed Music SC 6186, 2002.
13. Jarema, *2131 South Michigan Avenue.*

14. Jim Fairs, "Ben Franklin's Almanac," Destination Music BMI, 1966.
15. Clark Besch, "Sugar and Spice and All Things Nice," liner notes for The Cryan' Shames, *Sugar and Spice* (Reissue), Sundazed Music 6186, 2002.
16. The Seth Man, "The Cryan' Shames—'Sugar and Spice/Ben Franklin's Almanac,'" The Book of Seth, headheritage.co.uk, October 2001, https://www.headheritage.co.uk/unsung/thebookofseth/the-cryan-shames-sugar-and-spice-ben-franklins-almanac.
17. Doody, "Toad Tales."
18. Jim Pilster, Personal phone interview with the author, February 25, 2017.
19. Doody, "Toad Tales."
20. Bob Dylan, *Chronicles: Volume One* (New York: Simon & Schuster, 2004).
21. Clark Besch, liner notes for The Cryan' Shames, *Sugar and Spice (A Collection)*, Columbia Legacy CK 47905, 1992.
22. Barrett, "Shames in Harmony," 24.
23. Jim Pilster, Personal phone interview with the author, February 25, 2017.
24. *Ibid.*
25. Scott Schinder, liner notes for The Cryan' Shames, *A Scratch in the Sky* (Deluxe Expanded Mono Edition), Now Sounds/Cherry Red Records, CRNOW 48, 2014.
26. Jim Pilster, Personal phone interview with the author, February 25, 2017.
27. *Ibid.*
28. Besch, liner notes for The Cryan' Shames, *Sugar and Spice (A Collection)*.
29. Richie Unterberger, review of The Cryan' Shames' *Synthesis*, AllMusic, https://www.allmusic.com/album/synthesis-mw0000217604.
30. Jim Pilster, Personal phone interview with the author, February 25, 2017.

Chapter 7

1. Bill DeYoung, liner notes for The Ides of March, *Friendly Strangers: The Warner Bros. Recordings*, Warner Bros. Records, Rhino Records RHM2 734/ Rhino Handmade RHM2 7834, 2003, http://www.billdeyoung.com/music-archives/friendly-strangers-the-ides-of-march/.
2. Beverly Paterson, "Up Close with Jim Peterik," *MusicDish eJournal*, January 7, 2006, http://www.musicdish.com/mag/index.php3?id=10739.
3. *Ibid.*
4. Warren Kurtz, "Fabulous Flip Sides interviews Jim Peterik of the Ides of March," *Goldmine*, July 6, 2020, https://www.goldminemag.com/columns/fabulous-flip-sides-interviews-jim-peterik-of-the-ides-of-march.
5. Stu Shea, "Song of the Day: The Ides of March 'Roller Coaster,'" *Ten Records* (blog), May 6, 2017, http://tenrecords.blogspot.com/2017/05/may-6-2017-normal-0-false-false-false.html.
6. Kurtz, "Fabulous Flip Sides."
7. *Ibid.*
8. DeYoung, liner notes, *Friendly Strangers*.
9. *Ibid.*
10. Richie Unterberger, liner notes for The Ides of March, *Vehicle*, Expanded Edition, 1969, 1970, 2014 Warner Bros. Records/Real Gone Music RGM-0289 (2014).
11. *Ibid.*
12. DeYoung, liner notes, *Friendly Strangers*.
13. *Ibid.*
14. Paterson, "Up Close with Jim Peterik."
15. Rockaeology: Unearthing the Secrets Behind Rock's Greatest Hits "The Ides of March: 'Vehicle,'" Rockaeology.com, March 18, 2011, http://rockaeology.com/2011/03/18/the-ides-of-march-vehicle.aspx.
16. DeYoung, liner notes, *Friendly Strangers*.
17. *Ibid.*
18. *Ibid.*
19. Rob Horning, "The Ides of March: Vehicle," *Pop Matters*, August 15, 2006, https://www.popmatters.com/the-ides-of-march-vehicle-2495686020.html.
20. Jim Peterik, with Lisa Torem, *Through the Eye of the Tiger: The Rock 'n' Life of Survivor's Founding Member* (Dallas, TX: BenBella Books, 2014), 119.
21. See https://cermakplaza.com/history/.
22. Peterik, *Through the Eye of the Tiger*, 119.
23. Neil Gale, "The History of E.J. Korvette Department Stores and the Truth About Their Name," *Digital Research Library of Illinois History Journal*, October 16, 2021, https://drloihjournal.blogspot.com/2021/10/history-of-ej-korvette-department-stores.html.
24. Dave Aldrich, "E.J. Korvette: The Dawn of Discounting," *Pleasant Family Shopping* (blog), http://pleasantfamilyshopping.blogspot.com/2007/11/ej-korvette-and-dawn-of-discounting.html.
25. Fred Farrar, "E.J. Korvette Chain Opening in Suburbs," *Chicago Tribune*, April 17, 1963, 57.
26. Peterik, *Through the Eye of the Tiger*, 119.
27. Kurtz, "Fabulous Flip Sides."
28. Richie Unterberger, liner notes for The Ides of March, *Common Bond*, http://www.richieunterberger.com/commonbond.html.
29. Peterik, *Through the Eye of the Tiger*, 139.
30. *Ibid.*, 141.

Chapter 8

1. Langer, "Glory Days."
2. *Ibid.*
3. Salowitz, *Chicago's Personality Radio*, 84.
4. Langer, "Glory Days."
5. *Ibid.*
6. Jim Pilster, Phone interview with the author, February 25, 2017.
7. See the complete list of subjects featured on WTTW *Chicago Stories* archive at https://interactive.wttw.com/chicago-stories/archive.

8. The nifty phrase "Come on feel the Illinoise" originates as an "invitation" from indie artist Sufjan Stevens, presented on the cover of his LP *Illinois* (Asthmatic Kitty, 2005). The Detroit native considered the coastal neighboring state across Lake Michigan the "center of gravity of the American Midwest." Recorded in Brooklyn, the album's tracks reference places, events, and persons associated with the Land of Lincoln. *Illinois* followed *Michigan* (2003); both were supposedly conceptualized to be at the forefront of a 50 state–themed album series that would present history, culture, literature, art, and geography specific to each setting. Stevens's ambitious project has yet to make it out of the Midwest; the lower 48 states remain, awaiting songwriting and recording.

9. Langer, "Glory Days."

Bibliography

Aldrich, Dave. "E.J. Korvette: The Dawn of Discounting." *Pleasant Family Shopping* (blog). http://pleasantfamilyshopping.blogspot.com/2007/11/ej-korvette-and-dawn-of-discounting.html.

Ankeny, Jason. "Little Boy Blues Biography." *AllMusic.* https://www.allmusic.com/artist/little-boy-blues-mn0000258279/biography.

Antique Clock Guy. "J.P. Seeburg Company: An Extensive History." https://www.clockguy.com/SiteRelated/SiteReferencePages/SeeburgHistory.html.

Baker, Mike. "The Mob." *Mike Baker and the Forgotten 45s @MikeBaker45s* (blog). https://mikebaker45s.wordpress.com/the-mob/.

———. "The Mob—Chicago Band. The Mob Story." https://mikebaker45s.weebly.com/the-mob-story.html.

Barrett, Charles A. "Shames in Harmony on a Vocal Identity." *Billboard*, June 27, 1967.

Besch, Clark. Liner Notes for The Cryan' Shames. *Sugar and Spice (A Collection).* Columbia Legacy CK 47905, 1992.

Bishop, Chris. "The Five Bucks 'No Use in Trying' and The Byzantine Empire." *Garage Hangover.com*, December 13, 2009. https://garagehangover.com/five-bucks/.

Bonafede, Carl. *The Screaming Wildman: Vibrations from the Dawn of Chicago Rock.* Edited by Joel Bierig. Chicago: CreateSpace Independent Publishing Platform, 2016.

Burns, Gary. "No Guns at Geezer Rock." *Popular Music and Society* 41, no. 3 (2018): 349–50.

———. "Shakin With the Five Empress." Liner Notes. A Whole Lotta Five Empress: Singing Little Miss Sad. The Complete Studio Recordings 1965–1968. Arf! Arf! Records AA 095, 2004.

Callahan, Mike, Dave Edwards, and Patrice Eyries. "Dunwich Album Discography." Both Sides Now Publications. https://www.bsnpubs.com/chicago/dunwich.html.

———. "Dunwich Singles Discography." Both Sides Now Publications. https://www.bsnpubs.com/chicago/dunwich45.html.

———. "The Vee-Jay Story." Both Sides Now Publications. http://www.bsnpubs.com/veejay/veejaystory1.html.

"Cermak Plaza." https://www.cermakplaza.com/history/.

Chambers, Casey. "Interview—Carl Giammarese (The Buckinghams)." *The College Crowd Digs Me*, December 14, 2015. https://www.thecollegecrowddigsme.com/2015/12/interview-carl-giammarese-buckinghams.html.

Chicago and Then Some (Judith). "Chicago's Historic Music Legacy: Interview with Carl Giammarese of the Buckinghams." *ChicagoAndThenSome* (blog), December 13, 2012. http://chicagoandthensome.blogspot.com/2012/12/chicagos-historical-music-legacy.html.

Craddock, Brian, and Michael Pelonis. "Shape of Things to Come." Sony/ATV Music Publishing LLC, Universal Music Publishing Group, Warner Chappell Music, Inc., 1968.

Davis, Jeff. "Introduction." In *Images of America: Chicago's WLS Radio*, by Scott Childers, 11–13. Chicago: Arcadia Publishing, 2008.

Deming, Mark. "Biography: Shadows of Knight." *AllMusic.* https://www.allmusic.com/artist/shadows-of-knight-mn0000791247.

DeYoung, Bill. Liner Notes for The Ides of March. *Friendly Strangers: The Warner Bros. Recordings.* Warner Bros. Records; Rhino Records RHM2 734/ Rhino Handmade RHM2 7834. 2003.

Doody, Tom. "Toad Tales." Liner Notes for The Cryan' Shames. *Sugar and Spice.* (Reissue). Sundazed Music SC 6186, 2002.

Dugo, Mike. "The Knaves." The Lance Monthly. RV Stewart Productions/Lance Records/Cool Links Publishing. http://www.beyondthebeatgeneration.com/knaves.html.

———. "Up Close with Ray Graffia, Jr., of New Colony Six." *The Lance Monthly: 60s Garage Bands.* April 4, 2004 in *MusicDish e-Journal* (February 17, 2017) and/or http://www.beyondthebeatgeneration.com/newcol.html.

Dylan, Bob. *Chronicles: Volume One.* New York: Simon & Schuster, 2004.

Eder, Bruce. "Illinois Speed Press Biography." *AllMusic.* https://www.allmusic.com/artist/illinois-speed-press-mn0002138693.

Eder, Bruce. Review of The Buckinghams' *Kind of a Drag. AllMusic.* https://www.allmusic.com/album/kind-of-a-drag-mw0000044664.

Fairs, Jim. "Ben Franklin's Almanac." Destination Music BMI, 1966.

Farrar, Fred. "E.J. Korvette Chain Opening in Suburbs." *Chicago Tribune*, April 17, 1963. https://

www.newspapers.com/clip/18650249/ej-korvette-to-open-store-elmhurst-1963/.

Fleming, Colin. "10 Wild LPs from Garage Rock's Greatest Year." *Rolling Stone*, June 3, 2016. https://www.rollingstone.com/music/music-news/10-wild-lps-from-garage-rocks-greatest-year-99345/.

Ford, John, Henry Hathaway, and George Marshall, dirs. How the West Was Won. Prod. Bernard Smith. Screenplay by James R. Webb. Hollywood, CA: MGM Studios, 1962.

Gale, Neil. "The History of E.J. Korvette Department Stores and the Truth about their Name." *Digital Research Library of Illinois History Journal*, October 16, 2021. https://drloihjournal.blogspot.com/2021/10/history-of-ej-korvette-department-stores.html.

Giammarese, Carl. Phone interview with author. December 19, 2016.

———. "Carl Giammarese of The Buckinghams on 'Kind of a Drag.'" Antenna TV. December 1, 2019. YouTube video, 1:30. https://www.youtube.com/watch?v=zFcBEhzpwzs.

Giggens. "Album Review 118: The Buckinghams—In One Ear and Gone Tomorrow." June 20, 2018. YouTube video, 18:23. https://www.youtube.com/watch?v=6GQhCeElgq8.

Ginell, Cary. *Hot Jazz for Sale: Hollywood's Jazz Man Record Shop*. Self-published, lulu.com, 2010.

Golden, Jim. "Recollections." Liner Notes. *2131 South Michigan Avenue: 60's Garage & Psychedelia from U.S.A. and Destination Records*. Compilation by Bob Irwin, Jeff Jarema, and Mike Markesich. Sundazed Music, 2009.

Graffia, Ray. Email correspondence with author in 2017: January 2, June 12 and 28, August 4, September 22, and October 24.

Hart, Hugh. "Recalling Their Star." *Chicago Tribune*, July 4, 1991. https://www.chicagotribune.com/news/ct-xpm-1991-07-04-9103160773-story.html.

Hedblade, Jock, and Lou Hinkhouse, dirs. Chicago Stories. "How Chicago Rocked the '60s." WTTW-Chicago/PBS, Don't Blink, Inc./Chicago Historical Society, 2001.

Hermes, Will. *Love Goes to Buildings on Fire: Five Years in New York That Changed Music Forever*. New York: Farrar, Straus & Giroux, 2012.

Hill, Laura E. "When DuPage Rocked." *Chicago Tribune*, December 31, 1995. https://www.chicagotribune.com/news/ct-xpm-1995-12-31-9512310188-story.html.

"The History of WLS Radio." http://www.wlshistory.com/WLS60/.

Horning, Rob. "The Ides of March: Vehicle." Pop Matters, August 15, 2006. https://www.popmatters.com/the-ides-of-march-vehicle-2495686020.html.

Hughes, Andrew S. "Music Still Not a Drag for Buckinghams." *South Bend* (Indiana) *Tribune*, June 23, 2011. http://articles.southbendtribune.com/2011-06-23/entertainment/29697492_1_buckinghams-carl-gaimmarese-horns.

"The Ides of March: 'Vehicle.'" Rockaeology.com, March 18, 2011. http://rockaeology.com/2011/03/18/the-ides-of-march-vehicle.aspx.

Isaacs, Deanna. "Group Efforts: Flashback to a Legendary Teen Hangout." *Chicago Reader*, July 29, 1999. https://chicagoreader.com/arts-culture/group-efforts-flashback-to-a-legendary-teen-hangout/.

James, Gary. "Interview with Jimy Sohns of the Shadows of Knight." http://www.classicbands.com/JimySohnsInterview.html.

Jarema, Jeff. Liner Notes. Dark Sides: The Best of the Shadows of Knight. Rhino Records R2 71723, 1994: 6.

———. Liner Notes. *If You're Ready! The Best of Dunwich Records... Vol 2*. Sundazed Music SC11019, 1994.

———. Liner Notes. *Oh Yeah! The Best of Dunwich*. Sundazed Music/Tutman SC 11010, 1991.

———. Liner Notes for The New Colony Six. *At the River's Edge*. Sundazed Music Inc. SC11016, 1993.

———. 2131 South Michigan Avenue: 60's Garage & Psychedelia from U.S.A and Destination Records. Sundazed Records (SC 11201). 2009.

Johnson, Ann, and Mike Stax. "From Psychotic to Psychedelic: The Garage Contribution to Psychedelia." Popular Music & Society 29, no. 4 (October 2006): 415.

"Jukebox Companies: Seeburg Corporation." http://www.jitterbuzz.com/jukeboxes_companies.html#sjuk.

Kaempfer, Rick. "Ron Riley." *Chicago Radio Spotlight* (blog). January 22, 2011. http://chicagoradiospotlight.blogspot.com/2011/01/ron-riley.html.

Korey, Bess. "Chicago's First All-Girl Band: Daughters of Eve. (Debi Pomeroy and Andrea Levin Parnes share their recollections of being members of Chicago's first all-girl band.)" *Girlsinthegarage's Blog* (blog). April 27, 2010. https://girlsinthegarage.wordpress.com/2010/04/27/chicagos-first-all-girl-band-daughters-of-eve/.

Kotal, Kent. "Clubbin' in Chicago…in the Late '60's and early '70's." *Forgotten Hits* (blog). May 7, 2019. http://forgottenhits60s.blogspot.com/2019/05/clubbin-in-chicago-in-late-60s-and.html.

———. "Forgotten Hits Remembers Jimy Rogers and the Mauds." *Forgotten Hits* (blog). August 25, 2014. http://forgottenhits60s.blogspot.com/2014/08/forgotten-hits-remembers-jimy-rogers.html.

———. "Who Played the Very First Beatles Record in America." *Forgotten Hits* (blog). 2002. http://forgottenhits.com/who_played_the_very_first_beatles_record_in_america.

———. "Your All-Time Favorite Garage Band!!! #1. The Shadows of Knight." *Forgotten Hits* (blog). December 8, 2012. http://forgottenhits60s.blogspot.com/2012/12/your-all-time-favorite-garage-band-1.html.

Krakow, Steve. "The Riddles' Lone 1967 Single Made

Its CD Debut in 2008." The Secret History of Chicago Music, *Chicago Reader*, July 15, 2015. https://chicagoreader.com/music/the-riddles-lone-1967-single-made-its-cd-debut-in-2008/.

Kurtz, Warren. "Fabulous Flip Sides interviews Jim Peterik of The Ides of March." *Goldmine*, July 6, 2020. https://www.goldminemag.com/columns/fabulous-flip-sides-interviews-jim-peterik-of-the-ides-of-march.

Langer, Adam. "Glory Days." *Chicago Reader*, January 12, 1989. https://chicagoreader.com/news-politics/glory-days/.

Lyons, John T. *Joy and Fear: The Beatles, Chicago and the 1960s*. Brentwood, TN: Permuted Press, 2021.

Marovich, Steve. "Last Time Around Part II: The Majestic Hills Bandstand Was a One-Time Hot Spot." Kenosha.com, December 11, 2021. https://www.kenosha.com/2021/12/11/last-time-around-part-ii-the-majestic-hills-bandstand-was-a-one-time-hot-spot/.

Milano, Dean. *Images of America: The Chicago Music Scene: 1960s and 1970s*. Charleston, SC: Arcadia Publishing, 2009.

Mueller, Jim. "Back with the Cryan' Shames." *Chicago Tribune*, September 3, 1995. http://articles.chicagotribune.com/1995-09-03/features/9509030081.

Newsom, Jim. Review of *Illinois Speed Press*. All Music. https://www.allmusic.com/album/illinois-speed-press-mw0000852106.

Okuda, Ted, and Jack Mulqueen. *The Golden Age of Chicago Children's Television*. Carbondale, IL: Southern Illinois University Press, 2016.

"On This Day in 1967: The Start of the Big Thing That Turned into Chicago." February 15, 2017. https://www.rhino.com/article/on-this-day-in-1967-the-start-of-the-big-thing-that-turned-into-chicago.

Paradigm Talent Agency. "Executive Profile: Paradigm's Fred Bohlander Looks Back on 50-Year Career, But Don't Say He's 'Retiring.'" Paradigm Land (blog). January 25, 2019. https://the.land/paradigm/blog/Executive-Profile-Paradigms-Fred-Bohlander-Looks-Back-On-50-Year-Career-But-Dont-Say-Hes-Retiring.

Paterson, Beverly. "Up Close with Jim Peterik." *MusicDish eJournal*, January 7, 2006. http://www.musicdish.com/mag/index.php3?id=10739.

Paytress, Mark. "What Goes On? Nuggets Unearthed: The Shadows of Knight: 'Oh Yeah.'" Mojo, January 2017.

Peterik, Jim, with Lisa Torem. "L.A. Goodbye." Bald Medusa Music, ASCAP, 1971.

———. *Through the Eye of the Tiger: The Rock 'n' Roll Life of Survivor's Founding Member*. Dallas, TX: BenBella Books, 2014.

Pilster, Jim. (J.C. Hooke). Phone interview with author. February 25, 2017.

Plasketes, George. "In Memoriam: Terry Melcher (1942–2004)—Lost in the Mid–60s Sun?" *Popular Music & Society* 30, no. 2 (May 2007): 267–273.

———. "Paul Revere's (Last)ing Ride (1938–2014)." *Popular Music & Society* 38, no. 4 (October 2015): 522–525.

Pruter, Robert. *Chicago Soul*. Champaign: University of Illinois Press, 1992.

Raymer, Miles. "Garage-Rock Pioneer Jimy Sohns Has Seen Enough for Ten Lifetimes." *Vice*, September 17, 2015. https://www.vice.com/en/article/exq5gk/garage-rock-pioneer-jimy-sohns-has-seen-enough-for-ten-lifetimes-916.

Ribas, Michael. Liner Notes. *Vee-Jay: The Definitive Collection*. 4-CD box set. Shout! Factory. 826662–10485, 2007.

Roteman, Jeff. *Jeff Roteman's WLS Radio Website*. http://user.pa.net/~ejjeff/jeffwls1.html.

Ruhlmann, William. Liner Notes. *Chicago Group Portrait* (Box Set). Columbia Records C4K 47416, 1991.

Rybaczewski, Dave. "'If I Needed Someone' History." Beatles Music History: The In-Depth Story Behind the Songs of the Beatles! http://www.beatlesebooks.com/if-i-needed-someone.

Salowitz, Stew. *Chicago's Personality Radio: The WLS Disc Jockeys of the Early 1960s*. Bloomington, IL: Bloomington Offset Process, Inc., 1993.

Savage, Jon. *1966: The Year the Decade Exploded*. London: Faber & Faber, 2016.

Schinder, Scott. Liner Notes for The Cryan' Shames. *A Scratch in the Sky* (Deluxe Expanded Mono Edition), Now Sounds/Cherry Red Records. CRNOW 48, 2014.

Schollenberger, Jerry. Liner Notes. *Colonized! Best of The New Colony Six*. Rhino Records R2 71188, 1993.

Seagrave, Kerry. *Jukeboxes: An American Social History*. Jefferson, NC: McFarland, 2015.

The Seth Man. "The Cryan' Shames—'Sugar and Spice/Ben Franklin's Almanac.'" The Book of Seth, headheritage.co.uk, October 2001. https://www.headheritage.co.uk/unsung/thebookofseth/the-cryan-shames-sugar-and-spice-ben-franklins-almanac.

———. "Shadows of Knight." The Book of Seth, headheritage.co.uk, October 2008. https://www.headheritage.co.uk/unsung/thebookofseth/shadows-of-knight.

Shea, Stu. "Song of the Day: The Ides of March 'Roller Coaster.'" *Ten Records* (blog). May 6, 2017. http://tenrecords.blogspot.com/2017/05/may-6-2017-normal-0-false-false-false.html.

Simmons, Rick. "Dennis Tufano, The Buckinghams, and Rock's Greatest Disappearing Act-Part 1." *ReBeat Magazine*, November 20, 2014. http://www.rebeatmag.com/dennis-tufano-the-buckinghams-and-rocks-greatest-disappearing-act-part-1/.

Smith, Caspar Llewellyn. "Beach Boy Brian Wilson Listens to *Rubber Soul*." *The Guardian*, June 10, 2011. https://www.theguardian.com/music/2011/jun/11/beach-boys-brian-wilson.

Stroud, Bob. "Jimy Rogers and the Mauds: Biography." http://www.themauds.com/bio.htm.

Traut, Bill. Liner Notes. *If You're Ready! The Best*

of Dunwich Records... Vol 2. Sundazed Music SC11019, 1994.

Traut, Dave. "The Banshees." Classic Garage Rock Library. https://www.classicgaragerock.com/index.php/bands/bio/3.

———. "The Things to Come." Classic Garage Rock Library. https://classicgaragerock.com/index.php/bands/bio/26.

Unterberger, Richie. Liner Notes for H.P. Lovecraft. Compilation/Reissue. *H.P. Lovecraft / H.P. Lovecraft II*. Collectors' Choice 139–2, 2000. http://www.richieunterberger.com/hplove.html.

———. Liner Notes for The Ides of March. Compilation/Reissue. *Common Bond*. Collectors' Choice. CCM 646–2, 2006. http://www.richieunterberger.com/commonbond.html.

———. "New Colony Six." In *Music USA: Rough Guide*. London: Rough Guides, 1999.

———. Review of The Cryan' Shames' *Synthesis*. *AllMusic*. https://www.allmusic.com/album/synthesis-mw0000217604.

———. *Vehicle*. Expanded Edition. 1969, 1970, 2014. Warner Bros. Records/Real Gone Music RGM-0289, 2014.

Weber, Clark, and Neal Samors. *Clark Weber's Rock and Roll Radio: The Fun Years, 1955–1975*. Chicago: Chicago's Books Press, 2008.

White, Timothy. *The Nearest Faraway Place: Brian Wilson, the Beach Boys, and the Southern California Experience*. New York: Henry Holt & Co., 1994.

"WLS Magazine Sales Over 100,000." *Billboard*, May 13, 1967.

"WLS Official Radio Record Surveys." http://www.vidiot.com/WLS_Surveys/1964.html.

Index

Numbers in ***bold italics*** indicate pages with illustrations

Abbey Road 177
ABKO Records 90
Abner, Ewart 46–8
Abner Records 46
Abramson, Herb 95
Acta Records 28, 93, 102–103, 110, 125, ***127***, 130
Adderly, Cannonball 95, 132
Addrisi Brothers 16
Adler, Lou 151
The Adventures of Peter Fugitive (radio serial) 41
Aerial Ballet 179
"Aire of Good Feeling" 5, 192, 197, 201
Aliotta Haynes Jeremiah 160, 213
"All Along the Watchtower" 197
"All Join Hands" 200
"All Right Now" 81
All Time Hits (TV show) 135, 139
Allen, Bernie 25, 36, 41, ***53***
"Alley Oop" 31, ***32***, 118
Allison, Mose 104
"Along Comes Mary" 159, 192
"Always on My Mind" 202
Amanda 102
Amboy Dukes 97
Amboy Records 96–97
Ambrose, Amanda 102
American Bandstand 25, 41–42, 56, 58, 60, 89, 107, 125, 144, 175, 184; *see also* Clark, Dick
American Breed 13, 16, 18–19, 21, 23, 28, 88; 102–103, 114, 124–***127***, 128–130; 136–137, 141; 175; 187, 204, 209, 211
American Idol 175, 204, 214
"American Woman" 18, 191
Amy-Mala-Bell Records 117, 125
"And When I Die" 188
Anderson, Laurie 213
"Angel of the Morning" 191

Animals 14, 20–21, 61, 66, 76, 102, 117–118, 163
Anita Kerr Singers 31
"Another One Bites the Dust" 202–203
Aorta 16, 70, 89, 102, 112–115, 130
"Apache" 75
Aragon Ballroom 117
Arcada Theatre 210
"Are You There with Another Girl" 150
Arellano, Dave 200
Arie Crown Theater 27
Art Institute of Chicago 154
Ask Rufus 88, 129; *see also* Rufus
Association 18, 20, 60, 62, 69, 78, 106, 117, 133, 139, 155, 171, 188, 192
At the River's Edge (album) 72, 73
"At the River's Edge" (song) 66, 70
Atco Records (*also* ATCO) 89, 91, 96, 125
Atlantic Records 27, 80, 93, 95
Attacking a Straw Man 69
Autry, Gene 34, 40
Axton, Hoyt 34, 46

Baby Huey & the Babysitters 16, 112
"Baby It's You" 46
Bacharach, Burt 150
Back Door Men 85, 87, 102, 129
"Back in Love Again" 147, 149–150
"Bad Little Woman" 56, 74, 87–88
Badfinger 210
Badonsky, George 82, 93, 96–100, 106–107, 123, 130, 211
Baez, Joan 10, 115, 192
Baker, Mike 210
"(The Ballad of the) Wingback Mamaduke" 67

"Ballet for a Girl in Buchannon" 177; *also* "The Ballet"; "Make Me Smile Medley"
"Baltimore Oriole" 21, 176
Bangor Flying Circus 88, 101, 208
Banshees 16, 193, 109, 121
Batman (TV series) 41, 50, 60
Beach Boys 3, 20, 32, 65, 69–70, 78, 82, 84, 92, 109, 111, 155, 161, 168, 171, 225n6
Beach Bunny 214
The Bear (TV series) 114
Beatlemania 15, 22, 38, 41, 45, 84
Beatles 2, 6, 9, 11, 14, 17, 19–22, 38, 41, 44, 50, 54, 57, 60, 66, 69, 75, 79, 92 99, 105, 112, 118, 120, 134, 137, 139–140, 142, 145, 147–148, 152, 155, 157–158, 160, 162–163, 165, 167, 170–171, 177, 180, 183, 186, 192–193, 200, 207, 210; first U.S. radio airplay 45; and Vee-Jay Records 45, 47–48
Beau Brummels 18, 76, 120
Beauchamp, Kent 96
Beaudin, Ralph 34–37, 51
Beck, Jeff 84, 104, 108
Bedino, Howard 63
Bee Gees 9, 11
"Beginnings" 112
Beisbier, Gary 136–139, 145, 148; *see also* Buckinghams; The MOB
Bell, Archie & the Drells 175
Belloc, Dan 136, 139, 143
"Ben Franklin's Almanac" 161–163, 180
Bend Me, Shape Me (album) 126
"Bend Me, Shape Me" (song) 13, 18, 20, 72, 114, 125–***127***, ***146***, 204, 209
Bennett, Edward H. 135; *see also* Buckingham Fountain
Bergland, Bob 182–184, 187, ***190***, 204

Index

Berkman, Howard 105–105
Berry, Chuck 20–21, 85, 107
Berry, Richard 60, 81, 111
Besch, Clark 156, 177, 209
Bice, Bo 204
Bickler, Dave 202
"Big Boy" 44
"Big Girls Don't Cry" 47
Big Thing 17, 111, 138; see also Chicago (band); Chicago Transit Authority (band)
Billboard Magazine 166; ads 123, **127**, 166–**167**, 168, 172, 178; album charts 101, 112–113, 115, 165, 174; Hot 100 82, 97, 108, 125, **127**, 112–113, 115, 133, 136, 146–147, 151–153, 161, 168, 174–176, 178–179, 184, **190**, 191, 199, 202; "Most Listened to Band in America (1967)" (Buckinghams) 18, 132, 144, 215;
Billy Jack 179
Biondi, Dick 17, 25, 36–37; 41, 45, 47–49, 53, 124; bio film documentary 211; Beatles' US radio airplay debut 45; "The Pizza Song" **40**
"Bits and Pieces" 179
Black, Don 150
Black, Stu 142, 157, 185
Blecha, Peter 212
Blood, Sweat & Tears 19, 76, 113, 124, 129, 136, 138, 149, 187–188, 191, 200, 204
Blues Brothers (Dan Aykroyd & John Belushi) 213
Blue Cheer 91
Blue Village (teen club) 27, 77, 141, 156, 169, 179, 186; see also teen clubs
blues 3, 17, 19–20, 46, 64, 72, 75–76, 79, 81, 84–85, 89, 96–97, 102, 104, 106, 113, 121, 123–124, 142, 147, 163, 213
Blues Magoos 92, 119, 133
Blunstone, Colin 143
Bogart, Neil 89
Bohlander, Fred 156
Bonafede, Carl 116, 136, 142, 144, 211
Bonzo Dog Doo Dah Band 32
The Book of Seth (music platform) 91, 161
Booker T. & the M.G.'s 79, 134
Boone, Pat 23
Borch, Mike 182–183, **190**, 204
Box Tops 11, 18, 55, 133, 175
Boyan, Jeff 101, 120, 170–171, 176; see also Bryan, Geoff
Boyce & Hart (Tommy & Bobby) 44, 61, 87–88, 112
Boyd, Pattie 158

Boys Next Door 119
Bracken, James 45–46; see also Carter, Vivian; Vee-Jay Records
Bread 180
Breakfast Club (radio show) 35
Breakthrough 55, 64–66, 72
Brewer & Shipley 101
Brill Building (songwriters) 20–21, 61, 64, 125, 170, 177
Britain, Ron 25, 49–50
British Invasion 11, 14–15, 17, 45, 48, 54, 57, 59, 66, 72, 74–75, 89, 103, 106, 133–134, 137, 143, 150, 155, 163, 171, 184, 187, 200
Bronstein, Don 163
Brookfield Zoo 6, 136
Brown, Floyd 175
Brown, James 20–21, 107, 133, 140, 147, 187, 193
Brown, John 154
"Brown Eyed Girl" 44, 133
Browne, Jackson 10–11
Bryan, Geoff 120; see also Boyan, Jeff
bubblegum pop 19, 68, 72, 89–91, 124
Buckingham Fountain 135
Buckinghams 13, 15–20, 22–24, 26–27, 29, 31, **38**, 44, 56–57, 62, 67–68, 70, 88, 102, 112, 116, 123–124, 126, 129, 132–137, 139–140, 142–**146**, 147–154, 159, 162, 164, 168, 177, 186–187, 191, 204, 206, 208–211, 214
Buddah Records 90–91
Buffalo Springfield 76, 78, 91, 101, 113, 133, 141, 166, 179
"Bus Stop" 9
Bushor, Skeet 119, 123
Butler, Burridge D. 33–34
Butler, Jerry 44, 46, 122
Butterfield, Paul 213
Buttram, Pat 34
Byrds 11, 20–21, 44, 61–62, 76, 78, 83, 87, 144, 151–152, 154–155, 157–158, 160, 162–165, 169, 171, 201, 213
Byzantine Empire (also The Five Bucks) 102, 117

Cadet Records 46, 117
"California Sun" 14, 66, 97, 140
Cameo-Parkway Records 64, 84, 89–90, 119, 139
Campbell, Glen 43, 126
"Can I Get a Witness" 150
"Can't Find the Words" 150
Capitol Records 38, 47–48, 68, 111, 158, 196
Caravan of Stars 25, 84, 137; see also Clark, Dick

Card, Dex 25, **26**, 36, 38, 51, **53–54**, 77, 156, 211; see also Wild Goose
Carmichael, Hoagy 21, 176
Carnaby Street (London) 11, 22, 109, 135
"A Carol for Lorelei" 170
Carter, Calvin 47–48
Carter, Dave 120, 174
Carter, Vivian 45–46; see also Bracken, James; Vee-Jay Records
Cashbox (magazine) 13, 69, 74, **86**, 108, 147, 150, 161–162, 166, 168, 172, **173**, 174, 176–74, 191
Cavern Club (Liverpool) 79
The Cellar (teen club) 27, 77–78, 79–80, 82–83, 93, 96, 107, 120, 122–123, 130; see also Sampson, Paul; teen clubs
Centaur Records (also Centaur/Sentar) 27, 71–73, 62, **63**, 64, 67, 69–70, 71–73
"Central Park in the Dark" 145
Centuries 15, 22, 116, 134, 154, 177
Cermak Plaza 8, 194
Cermak Road 6, 24, 144, 205
Cetera, Peter 89, 111, 114, 138
Le Cervau (The Brain) 128
Chad and Jeremy 50, 139, 144
Champaign, IL (also Champaign-Urbana) 102, 118, 175, 201, 213
Chance Records 46
Chancellors 108
Chandler, Gene 46, 192
Charles, Hugh 165
Chase 19, 129, 202
Chase, Bill 202
Cheap Trick 213
Chelsea Girl 10
Cherry Red/Now Sounds (record label) 180, 209
Cherry Slush 16, 141
Chess, Leonard 27, 45–46, 136
Chess, Phil 27, 45–46
Chess Records/Studio 20, 27, 45–46, 64, 84, 105, 122, 131, 134, 136, 140–142, 166, 202, 213
Chicago (band) 17, 19, 88–89, 111–112, 129, 136–138, 149, 177, 187, 191, 212; see also Big Thing; Chicago Transist Authority
Chicago Board of Trade Building 25, 42
Chicago Reader 210
Chicago Seven 17
Chicago Stories (WTTW-PBS series) 211
Chicago suburbs/neighborhoods/villages:

Index

Albany Park 134; Algonquin 77, 176; Arlington Heights 77, 79, 90, 108, 179, 186; Bensenville 61; Berwyn 3, 6, 8, 11, 18, 24, 182, 184, 186, 192, 194, 199, 202, 204, **205**, 210; Blue Island 134; Broadview 6, 192; Brookfield 6, 136; Buffalo Grove 121; Cicero 24, 124, 182; Crete 33; DeKalb 4; Des Plaines 79, 95, 104; Downers Grove 141, 154, 202; Edgewater 116; Elgin 77; Elmhurst 51, 159, 195; Evanston 68, 108; Forest Park 192; Glencoe 117; Glenview 79; Harvey 110; Highland Park 108, 121; Hinsdale 11, 3, 11, 154, 155, 159; Joliet 4, 51, 141, 157, 213; Lake Forest 108; Lansing 141; Lincoln Park 214; Lincolnshire 109; Lisle 154; Lyons 136, 186; Maywood 192; Morton Grove 104, 195; Mt. Prospect 11, 75, 79–80, 90; Niles 104, 134; North Riverside 6–8, 11, 182, 194–195, 225n9; Oak Brook 8, 159; Oak Lawn 129, 195; Oak Park 7, 8, 11, 182, 192; Park Ridge 79; Riverside 6, 8, 11, 182; Rockford 80, 94, 111, 213; Rogers Park 134; Roscoe Village 134; Roseland 134; St. Charles 77, 210; Schaumburg 108; Schererville 51; Skokie 104, 106; Stony Island 112; Villa Park 141, 159; Westmont 78, 141, 156, 179, 186; Wauconda 122; Waukegan 51, 77–78; Wheaton 103; Willowbrook 159; Winnetka 79, 107, 141
"Chicago Sound" 65, 112, 123
Chicago Sun Times **196**
Chicago Transit Authority (band) (*also* Chicago) 17, 19, 88, 111–113, 123, 138, 149, 160
Chicago Transit Authority (album) 112–113, 138
Chicago Tribune 4, 22, 166
Chicago's Personality Radio: The WLS Disc Jockeys of the Early 1960s (Salowitz) 52
Chickenman (radio series) 50
"Children" 200
Christie, Lou 63, 81
Ciner, Al 124, **127**–129
Clapper, Bernie 94–95
Clapton, Eric 84, 104
Clark, Dick 25, 41–42, 56, 58–59, 84, 89, 107, 110, 137, 144, 184, 193, 199; *see also American Bandstand; Caravan of Stars; Happening '68*
Clark, Gene 21, 164–165; *see also* Byrds
Clark, Petula 133, 150
Clarke, Allan 158
Classic Garage Rock Library 93, 121, 210; *see also* Traut, Dave
Coachmen 118
"Cobblestone Road (She's Been Walkin')" 171, 177
Cocker, Joe 202
Cohen, Leonard 166
Colbert, Chuck, Jr. 23, 124, **127**–129
Colgems Records 119
Colonization 21, 61, 118, 123, 125, 127, 134, 170
"Colorado Morrow" 201
Colossus Records 139
Columbia Records 1, **2**, 19, 21, 23, 27, 59–60, 64, 68, 101, 110, 112, 114, 119–120, 129–130, 132, 136, 138, 144, 148–151, 153, 162–165, 167–169, 172, 174, 176, 178, 180, 196, 209
Comiskey Park 37, 45 *see also* Dahl, Steve; Disco Demolition Night
Common Bond 188, 197–198, 200
Conley, Arthur 21, 133, 187
Conroy, Dennis 154, 163, **173**–174
Constellation Records 137
Contemporary Records 95
Contrapoint Records 111
Coonley, Avery 6
Cornelius, Don 42
Cornerstones of Rock (concert series) 209–210
Cotton, Paul 110–111, 113
Count Five 92, 108
Counts 141
Coven 179
Cowsills 43, 68, 133
Cream 76, 133, 147–148
Creedence Clearwater Revival 191, 193
Crescent Records 95
Cropper, Steve 123, 141
Crosby, Bing 40, 45, 213
Crosby, David 154, 164 *see also* Byrds
Crosby, Stills & Nash 21, 113, 191–193, 198, 201
Crowley, Mort 35–36, 54
Cryan' Shames 1–6, 13, 15–17, 20, 24, 27–28, **38**, 56, 75, 78, 87, 112, 120, 124, 129–130, 141–142, 144, 153–154, 159–**167**, 168–172, **173**, 174–177, 179–181, 199, 204, 206–207, 211
Cyrkle 70, 144, 162

Dahl, Steve 37
Dahlquist, Dennis 109–110
Daley, Mayor Richard J. 22, 211
Dante & the Evergreens 32
The Dark Side of the Moon 113
Daughters of Eve 16, 116–117, 140, 211
Dave Clark Five 10, 11, 14, 17, 41, 60, 62, 66, 104, 121, 133, 178
David, Hal 150
David, Kal (*also* Raskin) 111–114
Davis, Clive 61, 64, 138, 144, 153, 162
Dawson, Alan 174, 177
Day, Doris 60
"A Day in the Life" 145
"Day Tripper" 16, 167, 170
"Daydream Believer" 134
Decatur (IL) 213; *see also* Champaign (IL); Peoria (IL)
Decca Records 68, 183, 185–186
De Clercq, Jerry 96
Dehd 214
Del-Vetts 16, 103, 107–110, 112
Democratic National Convention (1968) 17, 146, 172, 226n21
"Dennis Dupree from Danville" 120, 170–172, 176
Denver, John 178, 199
Derleth, August 97
DeShannon, Jackie 160
Destination Records 14, 16, 21, 27, 31, 96, 113, 118, 130, 138, 142, 153, 155, 157–158, 161–162, 166, **167**, 180, 202, 209; *see also* Golden, Jim
Destinations 44
Destocki, Bob 188
Diamond, Neil 17, 88, 134, 175, 188, 191
Diddley, Bo 21, 64, 74, 84–85, 148, 161
Dino, Desi, Billy 65
Dinosaur Swamps 114
disc jockeys (WLS, WCFL) 5, 7, 25, 36–37, 49–**53**, 54, 70, 131, 140, 145, 153, 156, 166, **167**, 175, 211; Swinging Seven 17, 36, 54
Disco Demolition Night 37; *see also* Dahl, Steve
Dixon, Willie 21, 85, 87, 106, 136
"Does Anybody Know What Time It Is?" 112
Dolenz, Mickey 119, 125; *see also* Monkees

Index

Donlinger, Jim 89, 102, 114, 115
Don't Fight the Feeling 202
Don't Look Back (rockumentary) 80
"Don't Sleep in the Subway" 150
"Don't You Care" 17, 132, 145, 148
doo-wop 46, 111, 115, 183
Doody, Tom 28, 154, 156, 161–164, *173*, 177, 179, 207
Doors 2, 14, 55, 62, 66, 83, 118, 133, 141, 168 *see also* Morrison, Jim
Dot Records 27–28, 110, 125, 166
Draper, Ken 49
Drifters 139, 148, 159, 170
Duet 113
Dugo, Mike 209
"Duke of Earl" 46
Dunbar, Jim 32, 26
Dunwich Records 16, 27–28, 79–80, 85–**86**, 88–89, 91, 93, 95, 97, 99–100, 130–132, 134, 140–141, 157, 209, 211; American Breed production supervision 125–**127**; Arkham Artists 97–**98**; *Best of* compilations 209, 224; dissolution and realignment of 129–130; "Gloria" 82–83; label logo **98**–100; local and regional roster recruits on 100–120; Lovecraft literary links 97; Mauds and 121–124; Productions and Ltd. 97–98, 100, 102, 106, 114, 121–122, 125, 130 143, 179; "Silverthumb" single 96; Yuggoth Music 97–**98**, 106–107; *see also* Badonsky, George; Higgins, Eddie; Shadows of Knight; Traut, Bill
Dylan, Bob 3, 10, 14, 55, 61, 80, 92, 100, 119, 144, 162, 164, 170, 197

Eagles, 113, 120
Earth, Wind & Fire 64, 213
The Ed Higgins Trio 95
The Ed Sullivan Show 25, 45, 60–61, 118, 137, 144, 147, 157
Eder, Bruce 147
Edwards, George 97, 99–101, 103, 116
E.J. Korvette 8–9, 28, 194–195, **196**, 197; *see also* Ferkauf, Eugene
El Dorados 46
"Eleanor Rigby" 192
Electric Prunes 92, 126, 133
Elliot, Cass 193

Elliott, Bobby 158
EMI Music Company 47, 158
Epic Records 202
Epitome Records 27, 183
Ertugen, Ahmet 96
Ertugen, Nesuhi 95–96
"Eve of Destruction" 81
Everett, Betty 46
Everly Brothers (Phil & Don) 19, 38, 116, 160
"Everybody's Talkin'" 21, 179
Exceptions 16, 111, 114, 138, 144
Executives 137
"Eye of the Tiger" 202–203

Fabulous Rhinetsones 113, 151
Fairs, James (Jim) 16, 154–155, 157, 161–163, 167, 169–170, *173*, 174, 176, 178, 180
Falcon Records 46
Fall Out Boy 214
Family Guy 204
Family Ties 151
Farfisa organ 2, 55, **63**, 65–66, 120
Farrow, Jesse Oris 177; *see also* "Get Together"; Powers, Chet; Valenti/Valente, Dino
Fender Stratocaster guitar 15, 138, 149
Ferkauf, Eugene 195–195, 225n11; *see also* E.J. Korvette
Fillmore Auditorium (San Francisco) 79, 101
Firesign Theatre (comedy troupe) 113
"First Train to California" 176–178
Fischer, André 128–129
Fisher, Fred 213
Five Americans 119
The Five Bucks (*also* Byzantine Empire) 102, 117
Five Emprees 16, 225n8
Flair Records 111
Flamingos 46
Fleming, Colin 85, 92
"Flip Side" 200
Flock 16, 112–114, 129–130, 142
The Flock 112–113
"Flower Power Cruise" 210
Flowers and Trees 201; *see also Silly Symphony*
Floyd, Eddie 21, 123, 128
Flying Burrito Brothers 177
Fogelberg, Dan 118–119, 192, 213
Foggy Notions 142
Foley, Red 34
Fontana Records 106–107
Ford, Jimmy 137
Ford, John 3, 5, 160
"Foreign Policy" 23, 146

Forgotten 45s ('60 music website/blog) 210
Forgotten Hits ('60s music website/blog) 45, 209
Fortson, Marty 14
Fortuna, Nick 15, 22, 24, 29, 134, **146**, 151, 208
Four Seasons 43, 46, 48; *see also* Valli, Frankie
Fowley, Kim 31
Franklin, Aretha 133, 192
Fratell, Ron 98
Frazier, Dallas 31
Freddie & the Dreamers 43, 62, 66–67
Free 81
Freed, Alan 52
Freedom Five 8
Freeport Records 16, 225n8
Friend and Lover (Post, Jim & Cathy) 44
"Friends of Feeling" 186, 188, 198
Frost, Max and the Troopers 103, 114
Furay, Richard 113, 179; *see also* Poco
Fuscaldo, Robert "Fuzzy" 122

Gallis, Paul 26, 28, 106
Gangi, Guy 8
garage rock 20, 85, 87, 92, 104, 111, 180
Gary and the Knight Lites (*also* Nite Lites) 15, 124, 140; *see also* American Breed; Loizzo, Gary
Gentry, Bobbie 133, 168, 192
Gentrys 111
"Georgia" 167, 171, 176
Gerry & the Pacemakers 60, 160
Gershwin, George 148
"Get It On" 136, 202
"Get Together" 21, 23, 100, 177–178; *see also* "Let's Get Together"
Get It Together (TV variety show) 193
Giammarese, Carl 19–20, 22, 27, 29, 31, 132, 134–135, 142–145, **146**, 149, 151, 207–208, 209–210; solo albums and autobiography of 210
Gibson guitar 15, 65, 149
Gimmer Shelter (film) 80
Ginnel, Cary 95
Ginny Records 142
girl groups 20, 115
Glass, Paul 140
Glen Records 106, 130
Glickstein, Fred 113–114
Gloria (album) 84–85, **86**, 102

Index

"Gloria" (song) 2, 13, 18, 21, 24, 56, 72, 74–76, 80–85, **86**–87, 89, 92–93, 98–99, 103, 109, 111, 116, 126, 204, 206, 209
"Gloria '69" 89
Goebel, George 34
Goffin, Gerry (*also* Goffin/King) (Carole) 21, 61, 118, 123, 125, 127, 134, 170
Golden, Jim 14, 27, 31, 96, 114, 130, 141, 143; *see also* Destination Records; MG Productions
Golden Voice Studio (Pekin, IL) 118
"Good Morning Starshine" 175
Goodman, Benny 213
Goodman, Jerry 113–114
Goodman, Steve 104, 213
"Goodnite, Sweetheart, Goodnite" 46
Gordy, Berry 46, 163
Gore, Lesley 43
Gotsch, Norm 75
Graffia, Ray, Jr. 24, 28, 55–**57**, 58–60, **63**–64, 66–68, 70–72
Graffia, Ray, Sr. 63
Graham, Bill 101
Grammy Awards/nominations 83, 113, 129, 138, 151, 167, 191, 203
The Grand Ole Opry 34
Grantham, George 113
Grass Roots 18, 34, 134, 152
Grateful Dead 101, 170, 193
Graziano, Lee 124, *127*, 128
Great Chicago Fire 172–*173*, 211
Great Lakes 4, 19
Great Society 141
"Great Train Robbery" 107
Grebb, Marty 102, 111, 114, 134, 144, *146*, 148, 150–151, 211
Greeley, Horace 58
"Green Tambourine" 90
"Greenburg, Glickstein, Charles, David Smith and Jones" 176, 178
Greenwich Village (New York City) 89, 166, 212
Grennan, Ed 36
Griner, Bill 189
Guercio, James William 23, 27, 112, 135–138, 144–149, 151, 187
Guess Who 18, 191
Guillory, Isaac 167, 169, **173**, 174, 176–178, 180, 211
The Guru (film) 150
Guthrie, Arlo 104

Hagar, Sammy 203
Haight-Ashbury (San Francisco) 198, 212
"Hair" 175

Hale, Bob 36–37, 51
Hamlin, V.T. 31; *see also* "Alley Oop"
"Hanky Panky" 183
Happening 42
Happening '68 42, 60
Happy Tiger Records 115, 130, 209
Happy Together Tour 152, 210
A Hard Day's Night 62, 99, 157
Hardy Boys 130
Harlem Avenue 6, 8, 194
Harrison, George 21, 45, 99, 150, 157–159, 161–162, 165, 193; *see also* Beatles
Hatch, Tony (*also* Nightingale, Fred) 21, 160
Hathaway, Henry 3, 5
Hayes, Isaac 122, 167
"Heat Wave" 21, 163
Hedgehoppers Anonymous 183
Heller, Steve 107
Help! 62, 99
Hemingway, Ernest 7
Hendrix, Jimi (*also* Jimi Hendrix Experience) 21, 48, 83, 87, 133, 148, 164, 193
Henke, James 83
"Here Comes My Baby" 32
Herman's Hermits 2, 18, 50, 62, 69, 78, 133, 152, 160
Hermes, Will 212
Herr, Ray 186, **190**, 193, 211
Herrera, Al 138
Herrera, Artie 138
"Hey Baby (They're Playing Our Song)" 68, 132, 136, 144–145, 149
"Hey Joe (Where You Gonna Go)" 16, 21, 87, 164, 178
"Hi-Heel Sneakers" 21, 128
Higgins, Eddie 93–97, 99, 117, 122, 125–126, 128, 130
"High Lonesome" 46
Hip Fables 41; *see also* Roberts, Art
Hold On 122–123
"Hold On, I'm Comin'" 21, 106, 122
Holder, Ron 120, 170–171, 176
Holland-Dozier-Holland (Brian, Lamont, Eddie) 150, 163
Hollies 9–11, 15, 18, 20–21, 50, 62, 67, 75, 105, 110, 118, 133, 140, 148, 152, 155, 158
Hollywood Argyles 31, *32*
Holman, Sam 34–36, 38
Holvay, Jim 20, 126, 132, 135–136, 138–139, 142, 145, 148; *see also* Buckinghams; The MOB
Holy Name Cathedral 204

"Home" 191–192
Hooker, John Lee 21, 46, 85
hop (*also* sock hop; record hop) 50–51, 57, 83, 142, 186
"House of the Rising Sun" 14
"How the Midwest Was Won" (ad) 3, 5, 17, 167
How the West Was Won (film) 3, 5, 172
Howlin' Wolf (Chester Arthur Burnett) 46
H.P. Lovecraft (band) 16, 23, 88, 96–97, 100–102, 115, 151
Huck, Bill 95
Hudson, Jennifer 214
Hulbert, Johnno 104–105
Hullabaloo 42, 60, 111, 175
Huns 16
Huxley, Aldous 114
"Hymn for Her" 198

"I Call My Baby STP" 109–110
"I Call Your Name"
"I Confess" 13, 24, 29, 55–56, 63–66, 72, 74, 206
"I Lie Awake" 66, 70
"I Wanna Meet You" 56, 162–163
"I Want to Hold Your Hand" 38, 47, 57
"I Was Lonely When" 168, 170–171
"I Will Always Think About You" 68–70, 191
Ian & Sylvia 169
Ides of March 3, 5, 7–8, 13, 16, 18–21, 24, 27, 31, 44, 56, 75, 79, 88, 124, 129, 136, 182, 184–189, **190**–191, 193–194, 197, 199, **205**–206, 209–211
The Ides of March Way **205**
Idle Few 16, 102, 119
"If I Needed Someone" 21, 99, 158, 161, 163, 165
Ifield, Frank 47–8
"I'll Be Back" 148
"I'll Go Crazy" 20, 140, 147
"Illinois" 119
Illinois Speed Press 44, 112–113; *see also* Rovin' Kind
"I'm a Believer" 17, 88, 134–132
"I'm a Man" 84, 112, 148
"I'm Gonna Make You Mine" 56, 74, 87–88, 128
"I'm Not Talkin'" 105–105, 109
"(I'm Not Your) Steppin' Stone" 88
Imperial Records 95
Impressions 46, 225n8
In One Ear and Gone Tomorrow 148–151, 206
"In the Café" 170
In the Woodland of Weir 107

Index

"Incense and Peppermints" 66, 133
Indiana 4, 16, 102, 104, 119, 121, 135; Fort Wayne 183; Gary 44, 46, 141; Hammond 120; Indianapolis 102, 119–120, 201; Munster 120; South Bend 14, 97, 141, 215; Valparaiso 80, 157
Inside Out 114
IRC Records 68, 106–107
Iron Butterfly 79
"It Could Be We're in Love" 13, 168, 170–171
"It Don't Matter to Me" 180
"It's All Right" 176–177
"It's Good News Week" 183
It's Happening 42
Ives, Burl 40
Ives, Charles 145
Ivory, James 150

Jackson, Michael 44
Jackson Five 44
Jagger, Mick 1, 3, 5, 122, 213
James, Chic 57, **63**, 67, 70–71
James, Tommy & the Shondells 44, 62, 134, 152, 183
Jamestown Massacre 202
Jan & Dean 99, 109
Jarema, Jeff 72, 87, 99, 107, 122, 209
Jay & the Americans 44
jazz 2, 19–21, 46, 59, 68–69, 82, 93, 95–96, 98, 100, 102, 104, 107, 113–115, 120–121, 125, **127**, 129–130, 136–138, 148–149, 159, 168, 170, 175–176, 187, 191, 193, 198, 202, 212–213; clubs in Chicago 95
Jazz Man Records 95
"Jean" 175
Jefferson Airplane 133
Jenney, William Le Baron 6
The Jerry Lewis Show 144
Jesters 104, 136
Jett, Joan 31
The Joey Bishop Show 144
John, Elton 151, 202
Jokers 16, 157
Jones, Brian 76
Jones, Davy 119; *see also* Monkees
Jones, Hoyt 69, 191
Joplin, Janis 78–79, 148, 162, 193, 208
"Journey to the Center of the Mind" 97
Joy and Fear: The Beatles, Chicago and the 1960s (Lyons) 22; *see also* Beatlemania; Beatles
jukebox 94–95, 108, 124, 200;

Audiophone 94; Rock-Ola 94; Selectophone 94; Wurlitzer 94; *see also* Seeburg Company
"July" 163

Kama Sutra Records 89
Kandy Kane Records 118
Kane & Abel 138
Kapp, David 186
Kapp Records 186
Kasem, Casey 49
Kasentz, Jerry 89–91; *see also* Super K Productions
Kass, Art 89
Kasuals 137
Kath, Terry 111, 137
Katz, Jeffrey 89–91; *see also* Super K Productions
Kaufman, "Murray the K" 45
Kaye, Lenny 189
Keen, John "Speedy" 7
"Keeper of the Keys" 101
Kelley, Joe 75, 79, 84, **86–88**
Kemp, Craig 57, **63**, 68, 71
Kemp, Wally 57, **63**, 66
Kerley, Lenny 169–170, **173–174**, 176–177, 179–180
Khan, Chaka (Stevens, Yvette Marie) 88, 129; *see also* Ask Rufus
Kidder, Bob 96
Kiddie A-Go-Go (also *Mulqueens Kiddie A-Go-Go*) 42, **43**, 44, 66, 160, 211; Sipple 43
"Kind of a Drag" (song) 13, 17, 20, 29, 56, 62, 72, 126, 132, 136, 142–147, 149, 209
Kind of a Drag (album) 135, 137, 147–148, 159
King, Carole 20, 61, 118, 123, 125, 134, 151, 170
Kingsmen 60, 81, 108, 116, 159
Kingston Trio 99, 178
Kinks 15, 24, 60, 62, 75, 89, 91, 105, 113, 133, 141, 161, 184, 200
Knaves 1, 15–16, 103–106, 211
Knight, Gladys & the Pips 44, 134
Kotal, Kent (*Forgotten Hits.com*) 45, 209
Krakow, Steve 209
Krein, Tommy 159
Kroc, Ray 7
Kummel, Les 68, 70–71, 211
Kunkel, Russ 103

"L.A. Goodbye" 3, 198–199, 206
Lake Michigan 3, 16, 19, 117, 135, 155, 168, 183
Lake Shore Drive (Chicago) 27, 94
"Lake Shore Drive" (song) 213

Lamm, Robert 111, 123, 138
The Lance Monthly 209
"Landlady" 201
Lane, Ronnie 200
Larson, John 187, **190**, 200, 211
"Last Time Around" 108–110
Lauer, Jim 108–109
Laurel Canyon (Los Angeles) 11, 166, 212
"Lawdy Miss Clawdy" 20, 132, 143–144, 148
"Lazy Day" 18
"Lead Me Home, Gently" 188, **190**–192
"Leave Me Alone" 105–106
Leaves 21, 87, 92, 164
Led Zeppelin 83, 115, 193
Ledger Records 118
Lee, Brenda 38, 137
Left Banke 20, 43, 70, 155, 171
Le Gros, George 134
Lehman, William 201
Leiber, Jerry 96, 160; *see also* Stoller, Mike
Lemon Pipers 90
Lennon, John 8, 14, 66, 202; *see also* Beatles; Lennon-McCartney (John & Paul)
Lennon-McCartney (John & Paul) 45, 99, 112, 148, 180, 183, 192, 200; *see also* Beatles
Lesley guitar 20, 55
Lester, Richard 99
"Let's Get Together" (*also* "Get Together") 23, 100, 177–178
Lewis, Gary & the Playboys 18, 50, 60, 62, 65, 89, 152, 160
Lewis, Ramsey 213
"Lies" 120
Life magazine 109
"Light My Fire" 55, 133, 168; *see also* Doors
Lighthouse 19, 129, 136, 191
"Like a Rolling Stone" 3, 55
Like Young (teen club) 27, 29, 58, 104, 156, 186; *see also* teen clubs
Lind, Jeff 210
Lindsay, Mark 59–62, 88
Little Artie & the Pharaohs (Herrera, Artie & Al) 138
"A Little Bit Me, A Little Bit You" 134
"Little Bit o' Soul" 133
Little Boy Blues 103, 106–107
"Little Latin Lupe Lu" 108
"Little Miss Sad" 16, 225n8
Little Richard 48, 87
Liverpool (England) 11, 71, 105, 137
Livers 137
Loizzo, Gary 23, 124–125, **127**–128, 211

Index

Lollapalooza Music Festival 214
London, Mark 150
London Records 71, 183
Lonely Side of the City 126, 128
"Long Cool Woman in a Red Dress"
"Look Through Any Window" 9, 158
Lord of the Flies 141
Los Angeles (CA) 10, 31, 42, 49, 58, 61, 84, 89, 110, 112, 115, 137–138, 145, 148, 156, 179, 193, 198, 212
Lost Agency 141
Loughnane. Lee 111, 128, 138
"Louie, Louie" 60–61, 81, 104, 157, 159, 161
Love, Darlene 32
"Love Me Do" 45, 69
"Love Potion No. 9" 160
Lovecraft, H.P. (author) 97–**98**
Lovin' Spoonful 18, 64, 76, 83, 89, 106, 112, 134, 150, 185
Lubin, Gene 1, 15, 104–106, 211
Lujack, Larry 25, 36, 38, 49, 70
Lulu 133, 150, 183
Luv'd Ones 16, 102–103, 115–117
Lyons, John F. 22

Madura 101
Magical Mystery Tour 134
Mahavishnu Orchestra 114
Majestic Hills Bandstand (Lake Geneva, WI) **78**
Malo, Ron 142–143, 157
Mamas & Papas 18, 134, 177, 186, 193
Mann, Barry 21, 61, 110, 114, 128, 163
Manson, Charles 61, 207
Manzarek, Ray 55, 66
Marina (City) Towers 50, 109
Marquette Piano Company 94
"Marrakesh Express" 201
Marsh, Dave 83
Marshall, George 3, 5
Martha and the Vanellas 21, 44, 115, 134, 163
Martin, Dewey 179
Martin, George 45, 158; *see also* Beatles
Masekela, Hugh 159
"A Master's Fool" 177–178
Mater Christi (school/church) 9, 10
Mathis, Johnny 151, 192
"Matthew and Son" 197
Mauds 16–17, 19–21, 27, 44, 79, 102, 106, 121–124, 131, 211
Max Frost & the Troopers 103, 114
Mayall, Monsignor Daniel 204

MayBees 136–137
Mayfield, Curtis 8, 21, 46, 122, 128, 136, 184, 187, 213
Maysles, Albert 80
Maysles, David 80
McBride, Pat 57–58, **63**, 66–68, 71
McCartney, Paul 171; *see also* Beatles; Lennon-McCartney (John & Paul)
McCormick, Robert "Colonel" 4
McCormick Place 27, 45, 169
McCoy, Van 21, 128
McFarlane, Elaine "Spanky" 18
McGeorge, Jerry 74–75, 83–85, **86**–88, 100–101, 120
McGuinn, Roger (Jim) 8, 151, 157, 162, 169, 213; *see also* Byrds
McGuire, Barry 81
McNeill, Don 35
McWilliams, Paulette 128–129
Meisner, Randy 113
Melcher, Terry 60–61
Memphis (TN) 94, 111, 166, 212
Mercury Records 18, 43, 68, 110, 122, 130, 160
"Mercy, Mercy, Mercy" 17, 20, 123, 132, 144–145, 148
Merseybeat 11, 60, 72, 75, 120, 160
Messengers 141
Messina, Jim 113, 179
MG Productions 13, 130, 143, 157, 166, **167**, 179; *see also* Golden, Jim; Monaco, Bob
MGM Records 68, 81, 89, 126, 139
Miccolis, Dennis 134, 144
Michigan 89, 102, 117, 135; Ann Arbor 102, 117; Benton Harbor 16, 51, 115; Detroit 97, 117, 195, 231n8; Holland 157; Niles 102, 115, 183; Saginaw 14, 141
Michigan Avenue (Chicago) 27, 35, 46, 50, 94, 95, 109, 136, 139, 141–142, 157, 180, 209, 213
Midnight Cowboy (film) 21, 179
"Midnight Hour" 141
Midnight Oil 200–201, 206
The Mike Douglas Show 67
Milano, Dean 209
Millas, Larry 182–183, **190**, 204
Miller, Mitch 60, 153, 162
Miller, Roger 43, 157
Miller Meadow 92
Milne, Jeff 185
Minneapolis (MN) 108, 212
Missing Links 137–138
"Mr. Unreliable" 4, 17, 167, 171–172, **173**

Mitchell, Joni 115, 193
The MOB 17, 88, 105, 136–137, 139, 142, 152
Modern Records 41
Mojo (UK music magazine) 85
Monaco, Bob 13, 27, 114, 130, 141, 143, 157; *see also* Destination Records; MG Productions
Monkees 17, 21, 50, 60–62, 66, 78, 87–88, 110, 112, 119, 125, 132–134, 177
Montana, Patsy 34
Monterey International Pop Festival 79, 162
Monterey Pop (film) 79
Montgomery Ward catalog 70, 162
Moody Blues 150, 178
Moonglows 46
Morden, Marili 95
Morrison, Jim 2, 168, 225n5; *see also* Doors
Morrison, Van 21, 44, 74, 85, 106, 133, 193; *see also* Them
Morton West High School (Berwyn, IL) 7, 182–183, 194, 202, **205**
"Mother America" 200
Motown Records 46, 48, 64, 115, 133, 138, 140–141, 163, 196
"Mrs. Grayson's Farm" 198
MTV 203
MTV Unplugged 8
Mulqueen, Elaine 42–**43**, 211; *see also* Kiddie A-Go-Go
Mulqueen, Jack 41, **43**, 211; *see also* Kiddie A-Go-Go
The Mulqueens 41
Murphy, Kevin 128, 137
Muscle Shoals (AL) 66, 118, 212
Music Explosion 133
"My Generation" 15, 112

Nash, Graham 23, 158, 226n21
Nashville (TN) 34, 118–119, 137, 157, 177, 212
The National Barn Dance 34
National Public Radio (NPR) 8
"The Nearest Faraway Place" 3, 225n6
Nedza, Tony 138
"Needles and Pins" 160
Neil, Fred 21, 100, 179
Nelson, Willie 104, 203
Nero Records 110
Nesmith, Michael 119, 125, 177; *see also* Monkees
Nestor, Larry 134
New Colony Six 13, 16–18, 20–24, 27–29, **38**, 43, 55–**57**, 58–59, 61–**63**, 64–74, 124, 134,

244 Index

153, 160–161, 164, 175, 186, 199, 204, 206, 211
Newman, Randy 100, 120, 193
New Orleans (LA) 36, 95, 104
"New York Mining Disaster 1941" 9
Next Album 159
Nico 10
Nietzsche, Jack 160
Nilsson, Harry 21, 179
1966: The Year the Decade Exploded (Savage) 92
1910 Fruitgum Company 68, 90
"96 Tears" 14, 66, 84, 90
Niven, David 128
No Way to Treat a Lady 126
Nordine, Ken 102–103, 228n20
"Norwegian Wood (This Bird Has Flown)" 99
Nuggets: Original Artyfacts from the First Psychedelic Era ((1965–1968) 180
Nuss, Otto 14, 66

O'Connor, Sinéad 38
Ode Records 151
"Ogre" 198
"Oh Yeah" 21, 56, 74, 84–85, **87**, 108–109, 116
Ohio Express 90
Old Town (district) 18, 27, 29, 58, 104, 109, 154, 156, 163, 186, 198
Old Town School of Folk Music 116, 214
O'Leary, Dick 42
Oliver (*also* Swafford, William) 175
Olmstead, Frederick Law 6
"On a Carousel" 9
Once Upon a Time in Hollywood 3
One Eyed Jacks 16
"One Tin Soldier" 179
"One Woman Man" 188, 191
"Ooh La La" 200
Opager, John 135
Orbison, Roy 45
Orkin, Dick 50
Orlando, Tony 64
Oscar & the Majestics 141
Ostroff, Paul 106–107
The Other Side 151
Outsiders 20, 84, 126–**127**, 209
"Over and Over" 10

"Painter Man" 177
Palmer, Bruce 179
Pankow, James (Jimmy) 111, 123, 138
"Paperback Writer" 170
Paragon Studio 94

Parazaider, Walt 11, 123, 137–138
Park Avenue Playground 141
Parker, Ross 165
Parlophone Records 47, 158
Parrot Records 27, 183–186
Parsons, Gram 177
Patsmen 56–57
Paytress, Mark 84–85
"People Get Ready" 8, 21, 187
Pennebaker, D.A. 14, 79–80
Pennell, Joe 14
Peoria, IL 18, 36, 102, 118, 157, 192, 213
Pet Sounds (Beach Boys) 92, 99, 171, 174
Peterik, Jim 3, 7–8, 19, 24, 31, 79, 124, 135, 182–192, 194, 197–198,; 204, 206, 210; *Don't Fight the Feeling* 202; Jim Peterik Band 202; memoir 203, 210; *see also* Survivor
Phair, Liz 214
Philips Records 48, 93, 97, 100, 102, 130
Phillips, Don 23, **26**, 36, 51–53
Phillips, Wally 49
Pilster, Jim (*also* J.C. Hooke) 1, 15, 19, 22–24, 76–77, 115, 154–156, 159, 163, 168–169, 172, **173**–174, 179, 181, 207–208
Pink Floyd 101, 113
Pip, Barney 25, 49
Piper's Alley 154, 163
"The Pizza Song" **40**
Plain White T's 214
"Pleasant Valley Sunday" 134
"Please Mr. Sullivan" 118
"Please Please Me" 45, 47
Poco 113, 179, 201
Polk Brothers 28, 195
"Polk Salad Annie" 193
Pollack, Neal 104–105
Pomeroy, Debi 116
Pomus, Doc 148, 159
Porgy and Bess 148
Portraits 148–149
Post, Cathy 44; *see also* Friend and Lover
Post, Jim 44; *see also* Friend and Lover
Poulas, John 134, 145–**146**, 151
Powers, Chet 23, 100, 177; *see also* Farris, Jesse Oris; Valenti/Valente, Dino
The Prairie Farmer (publisher) 33–36
Presley, Elvis 2, 20, 38, 44
"Pretty Ballerina" 70, 171
Pretty Things 105
Price, Alan 14, 66
Price, Lloyd 20, 132, 148
Priddy, Nancy 166, **167**

Pride & Joy 110
The Prime of Miss Jean Brodie 175
Prine, John 213
Procol Harum 133, 171
progressive rock 113, 198, 213
"Project Blue" 109, 121
Prowlers 154–155
Pryor, Richard 114
psych/psychedelia/psychedelic (music) 19, 20, 42, 44, 50, 66–67, 70, 72, 76, 84, 87–89, 92, 97, 99, 100–103, 107–108, 114–115, 125, 133, 142, 145, 148–149, 155, 157, 159, 161, 163–164, 166, 168–170, 174–175, 177–180, 186, 191, 201, 207, 209, 212
"Psychotic Reaction" 92, 108
Puckett, Gary & the Union Gap 18, 72, 152
Pulice, Pamela 211
Pulsations 15, 22, 116, 134, 154
Pumpkin, Powder, Scarlet & Green 126, 128
punk 8, 15, 66, 69, 71, 74, 83–85, 87, 90–93, 102–104, 106, 110, 115, 118–119, 121, 124–125, 129–130, 161, 164, 180, 184, 212
Pure Music 202
Purple, Dave "Grape" 154, 166–167, **173**, 211
Pursell, Wayne 75
Putnam, Bill 94

Queen 202
? and the Mysterians 14, 66, 84, 90, 92, 164
"Questions 67 and 68" 112
Quicksilver Messenger Service 177–178
Quill Records 68, 159–160
"Quit Your Low Down Ways" 100

R&B (rhythm & blues) 14, 19–21, 27, 32, 45–46, 59, 72, 74, 83–85, 87, 94–95, 122, 125, 128–129, 133, 136–138, 140, 142, 148, 152, 156, 167, 170, 175, 184, 187, 212–213
"Rain" 170
"Rainmaker" 21, 179
"Rainy Night in Georgia" 193
Raitt, Bonnie 151
Rand, Frank 187–188
Raymond John Michael Band 71
RCA Studio: Los Angeles 201; Nashville 177
RCA (Victor) Records 27, 68, 94, 119, 123, 178, 200, 201, 204
"Reach Out of the Darkness" 44

Record Row (South Michigan Avenue) 46, 94, 136
"Red Rubber Ball" 70, 162
Redding, Otis 122, 179
Reed, Jimmy 46, 87
Replica Studio/Records 95
Revelations 69
Revelles 68, 70, 167
Revere, Paul and the Raiders 2, 22, 58–62, **63**, 83, 88, 134, 144, 152, 162, 164
Revolver 92, 170, 192
Rhino Records 70, 87, 209
Ribas, Michael 48
Rice, Ronnie 17, 22–23, 28 ; 64, 68–71, 160; & the Gents 60
Richard, Cliff 75
Rickenbacker guitar 15, 157
Ricochettes 16, 157, 160
Riddles 16, 157, 159–161
Riley, Ron 25, **26**, 36–37, 41, 52, **54**, 56, 83, 184, 207
Riverside-Brookfield High School (RBHS; IL) 6–8
Riverview Amusement Park 184, 211
Rivieras 14, 16, 66, 97, 130, 140–141
Robbs 16, 44, 60
Roberts, Art 24–**26**, 36, 41, 43–45, 50, **53**, 56, 82, 189, 211; *see also* Hip Fables; *The Swingin' Majority*
Roberts, Billy 164; *see also* "Hey Joe (Where You Gonna Go)"
Roberts, Tony 178
Robinson, Smokey & the Miracles 44, 128, 133
Rock and Roll Hall of Fame 55, 83, 96, 151
Rock N' Roll Mass 111
Rock-Ola 94; *see also* jukebox
Rocky Horror Picture Show 151
Rocky III 203
Rodgers, Paul 81
Rogers, Jimy 19, 121–123, 131, 135, 211
Rogers, Kenny 160
Rogers, Warren 75, 84–**86**
"Roll On" 71
"Roller Coaster" 56, 184–185
Rolling Stone (magazine) 46, 83, 85
Rolling Stones 11, 15, 20, 22, 41, 50, 54, 62, 74, 76, 80, 85, 92, 102, 106, 116, 133, 142, 147, 155
Ronco Records 106, 107, 130
Roosters 154–155
Rotary Connection 16, 115
Rotondi, Cesar 109
Roulette Records 14, 111–112, 183

Rovin' Kind 16, 44, 103, 110–112; *see also* Illinois Speed Press
Rubber Soul 6, 99, 158
Rufus 129, 137, 208; *see also* Ask Rufus
Ruffino, Bobby 137–138
Runaways 31
Runyon, Jim 49
Russell, Leon 151
Ryder, Mitch & the Detroit Wheels 108, 116

"The Sailing Ship" 170
St. Mary's Church (Riverside) 8
Salowitz, Stew 52, 209
Sam & Dave 21, 106, 122, 133
Sam the Sham & the Pharaohs 66, 90
Sampson, Paul 79–80, 96, 122, 130–131; *see also* The Cellar
Sandburg, Carl 3
Saturday's Children 16, 79, 101, 103, 120, 170, 174, 176
Savage, Jon 92
Schiffour, Tom 75, **86**, 88, 101
Schmit, Timothy B. 113
Schollenberger, Jerry **63**, 67
A Scratch in the Sky 1, **2**, 4–5, 120, 153, 166, 168, 174, 176, 178–180, 199, 206
Searchers 21, 148, 159–161
Sears Roebuck & Company 33–34, 195
Sebastian, Joel 37, 49
Sebastian, John 64, 112
The Section 103
Seeburg (Sjöberg), Justus Percival (J.P.) 94
Seeburg, Noel 94
Seeburg Piano Company 93–96, 99–100, 108, 125
Seeds 66, 84, 92
Seeger, Pete 40, 165, 170
Seekers 3, 133, 162
Selectophone 94
Sentar Records 27, **63**, 67, 69–70; *see also* Centaur/Sentar
Seraphine, Danny 111, 137
Sgt. Pepper's Lonely Hearts' Club Band 60, 134, 145, 149, 171
Shadows 15, 75, 80
Shadows of Knight 4, 13, 16, 18, 20–22, 24, 27, 56, 74–76, 79–**86**, 87–89, 90–91
Shadows of Knight (album) 90–91
Shady Daze 141
"Shake" 90
Shannon, Del 118
"The Shape of Things to Come" 103, 114
"Sharing Christmas" 204

"She Don't Care About Time" 21, 158, 165
Shea, Stu 184–185
Sheffields 16, 157
Sheridan, Art 46
"Sherry" 46, 48
"She's About a Mover" 66
"She's Not There" 183
Shindig! 42, 111, 175
Shondell, Troy 183
Shondels (*also* Shon-dels, Shon Dels) 15, 75, 182–184; *see also* Ides of March
Shout Factory Records 48
Showcase '68 25, 67, 175, 177–178
Shuler, Dustin 194
Shulman, Irving 97
Shuman, Mort 148, 159
Shyette, Lowell 106–107
Siegel-Schwall Band 130
Signett Records 137
"Silence Is Golden" 32
Silly Symphony (Disney) 201
"Silverthumb" 96–97
Simmons, Rick 152
Simon, Paul 70, 162, 202
Simon & Garfunkel 92, 144, 162, 193, 198
Sinatra, Frank 65, 133, 213
Sinatra, Nancy 133
Singalong Series 162
Sipple, John 43
Sir Douglas Quintet 66
Sistak, Mike 137–138
16 Magazine 1, **2**, 52, 172, 225n5; *see also* Stavers, Gloria
"The Sky Is Falling" 188, 191
Sledge, Percy 66
Slick, Grace 168
Sloan, P.F. 81
Sly and the Family Stone 78, 124, 175
Small Faces (*also* Faces) 185, 200
Smash Records 110, 112
Smashing Pumpkins 214
Smith, Mike 14, 166; *see also* Dave Clark Five
Smith, Patti 83, 180
The Smothers Brothers Comedy Hour 25, 135, 144
Sohns, Jimy 1, 4, 19, 22, 24, 74–75, 80–81, 84–85, **86**, 88–91, 102, 122, 131, 135, 211, 213–214
Solid Gold Sixties Tour 210
"Solid Gold Sixties Tour" 210
"Someone Like Me" 88, 93
"Something in the Air" 7
"Song of the Breeze" 150–151
Sonny and Cher 44, 111, 160
"Soul Drippin'" 20, 123–124
Soul Train 42
Soulero 96

Soumar, Chuck 187, ***190***, 200–201
Sound Studios 94, 104, 142, 157, 161, 163
Sounds Unlimited 102, 119
Spaniels 46
Spanky and Our Gang 18, 133; *see also* McFarlane, Elaine
Spector, Phil 90, 115, 160, 185, 193
Spectra Sound Records 117, 159, 193
Spencer Davis Group 78, 110, 133
Spindle (sculpture) 194
"Spinning Wheel" 138, 188, 204
Squires 167, 174
SRI Records 8
Stagg, Jim 25, 49
Stallone, Sylvester 202
Standells 87, 92, 123, 164, 192
Staple Singers 46, 178, 211, 213
Starfire Records 103
Starr, Ringo 16
Stavers, Gloria 1, ***2***, 3, 5, 172, 225n5; *see also* 16 *Magazine*
Stax Records 46, 64, 106, 116, 122–123, 166
Steeltown Records (Memphis) 44
"Step Out of Your Mind" 125
Stereo-Sonic Studio 94
Sterling, Mindy 151
The Steve Hoffman Music Forum 197
Stevens, Cat 32, 197, 202
Stevens, Ray 32?
Stevens, Sufjan 231n8
Stills, Stephen 119
Stoller, Mike 96, 160; *see also* Leiber, Jerry
Stone, Gerry "Stonehenge" 154, 166–167, ***173***
Strawberry Alarm Clock 66, 133
Stroud, Bob 121
Styx 113, 129–130, 143, 213
Subterranean Circus 50; *see also* Britain, Ron
"Suburbs Seven" 16–18, 21, ***38***, 206, 209, 211–212
Sugar and Spice (album) 4, 21, 153, 163–165, 168–170, 172, 174, 179
"Sugar and Spice" (song) 13, 21, 56, 72, 142, 153, 160–163, 166–***167***, 180
Sullivan, Frankie 202
"Summer Sun" 202
"Summertime" 148
"Sun Within You" 73
"Sunday Will Never Be the Same" 18, 133

Sundazed Music (record label) 72, 80, 180, 209
Sunlight Records 27, 71, 199
Sunset Strip (Los Angeles) 3, 42, 145, 198
"Sunshine Palm" 171
Super K Productions/Records 89–91
"Superman" 197–198
Surfaris 16, 164
Survivor 202–203, 208, 211
"Susan" 20, 23, 67, 132, 136, 144–145, ***146***–149, 168
Swafford, William Oliver (also Oliver) 175
Swan Records 38
"Sweet Home Chicago" 3, 213
Sweet Tooth (candy shop) 163
"Sweets for My Sweet" 139, 148, 160
The Swingin' Majority 25, 43–45; *see also* Roberts, Art
Swinging Seven 17, 36, 54
"Symphony for Eleanor [Eleanor Rigby]" 21, 192
"Symphony of the Wind" 178
Synthesis 153, 176–179

"Take Me Back" 113, 142
"Take Me Home, Country Roads" 199
Talbot, John 119
Talbot, Terry 119
Tapestry 151
Tarantino, Quentin 3
Taylor, Chip 20, 100, 125, 128, 191
Taylor, Gene 36, 38, 52
Taylor, James 119, 170, 193
Team Records 90
Teen Beat (magazine) 52, 162
teen clubs 5, 8, 15–16, 27, 51, 76, 78–79, 93, 102, 104, 130, 166, 195, 208, 130; Black Orchid 112; Blue Moonbeam 77; Blue Village 27, 77, 141, 156, 169, 179, 186; Busters 112; Cellar 27, 77–78, 79–80, 82–83, 93, 96, 107, 120, 122–123, 130; Cheetah 27, 107; Deep End 79; Green Gorilla 27, 79; Jaguar Club 77; Kinetic Playground 27, 87, 107, 177; Like Young 27, 29, 58, 104, 156, 186; New Place 77, 176; Pink Fink 77; Pit 78; Rolling Stone 79; Wild Goose 27, 51, 77
Tegza, Mike 100–101
Tepper, Maurice 46
Ter-Mar Studio 27, 46, 142
Terissi, Tony 58
Tesinsky, Frank 143
Thaxton, Lloyd 25, 67, 175

Them 21, 72, 74, 80–81, 83, 106, 183, 206; *see also* Morrison, Van
"These Days" 10
"They're Coming to Take Me Away Ha-Haa!" 81
"Things I'd Like to Say" 13, 18, 69–70, 191
Things to Come 8, 103–105, 109
.38 Special 203
This Is Spinal Tap 194
Thomas, David Clayton 174–175, 187–188, 197, 204; *see also* Blood Sweat & Tears
Thomas, Rufus 103, 116
Thorogood, George & the Destroyers 32
Three Dog Night 18, 76, 78
Through the Eye of a Tiger: The Rock 'n' Roll Life of Survivor's Founding Member (Peterik) 203, 210
Thunderclap Newman 7; *see also* Keen, John "Speedy"
"Tie Dye Princess" 198
Tiger Beat (magazine) 52
"Tighten Up" 175
Time & Changes 147–149
"Time of the Season" 183
Tin Pan Alley 128, 176
Tiny Desk Concerts (National Public Radio) 8
"To Save My Soul" 8
To Sir, with Love (film) 150
"To Sir with Love" (song) 133
Tollie Records 48, 111
Tomek, Frederick F. 61
The Tooth Fairy (radio series) 50
Topanga Canyon (CA) 11, 212
Tork, Peter 66, 119; *see also* Monkees
"The Town I'd Like to Go Back To" 6, 170, 176, 199
Trafalgar Square 16, 141
Traut, Bill 27, 79–81, 84, 88, 91, 93–100, 102–103, 108–110, 114–115, 117, 120–122, 124–128, 130–131, 140, 143, 179, 187, 211
Traut, Dave 93, 121, 210; *see also* Classic Garage Rock Library
Travelers 15, 21, 75, 155–159, 181
Tremeloes 32
Trilling, Bob 105
Trilling, Geno 105
Troggs 62, 91, 100, 105–106, 191
Trolls 16
Tufano, Dennis 20, 134–135, 143–145, ***146***, 151, 210
Tufano & Giammarese 151
Tull, Jethro 78, 192
Turn! Turn! Turn! (album) 165

"Turn! Turn! Turn!" (song) 170
Turtles 7, 11, 18, 62, 68, 118, 133, 152
20/20 (Beach Boys album) 2131 South Michigan Avenue 139, 142; *see also* Record Row; U.S.A. Records
2131 South Michigan Avenue: 60s Garage & Psychedelia from U.S.A. & Destination Records 180, 209

"Uncle Wiggley's Airship" 91
Univacs 96
Universal (Recording) Studio 80, 93–96, 98, 106, 108, 117, 126
Unterberger, Richie 60, 72, 101, 178
"Up on the Roof" 21, 169–170, 174–175
"Up Where We Belong" 202
Upbeat 67
U.S.A. Records 14, 16, 27, 31, 64, 96, 117, 125, 130, 132, 137, 139, 144, 147, 157, 159, 162, 180, 209; *see also* Golden, Jim

Valenti/Valente, Dino 177–178; *see also* Farris, Jesse Oris; "Get Together"; Powers, Chet
Valli, Frankie & the Four Seasons 43, 46, 48, 133, 168, 186, 192
Vanilla Fudge 78, 192
Van Ronk, Dave & the Hudson Dusters 32
Van Steen, Ray 41
Varése Sarabande (record label) 209
Vaux, Calvert 6
Vee-Jay Records 27, 38, 46, 111, 136, 213; Beatles' debut 45, 47–48
Vehicle (album) 21, 192–194, 197–199, 201
"Vehicle" (song) 13, 18, 31, 44, 72, 126, 182, 187–189, **190**–192, 197–199, 203–**205**, 209
Ventures 15, 38, 107, 186
"Via Chicago" 6, 214
Vinnedge, Charlotte "Char" 115
Vinton, Bobby 133, 151, 175
Volt Records 94
Von Kollenberg, Gerry 55, 57, **63**, 65–67, 70–71
Voss, Ken 210
Vox Continental organ 14, 55, 65–66

Wadleigh, Michael 80
Wakefield, Dawn Lee 210

"Walk Away Renee" 70, 139, 171
"Walkin' the Dog" 103, 116
Walsh, Joe 91, 119
Wand Records 159
Wanderin' Kind 111
Warhol, Andy 10
"The Warm" 176
Warner Brothers (band) 102, 118, 157
Warner Bros. Records 18–19, 27, 81, 188–189, **190**–191, 193, 196–197, 199, 202, 205
Warnes, Jennifer 202
Waters, Muddy 46, 84
Watts, Charlie 10, 16
"Wayfaring Stranger" 100
Wayne, John 5, 160
WCFL AM-Radio 8, 25, 38, **40**, 49–51, 56, 71, 77, 103, 106, 112, 122, 129, 131, **146**, 153, 156, 158, 161, 16–168, 174, 199, 206; *Chickenman* 50; Sound 10 Survey 25, 49, **146**; *Subterranean Circus* 50
WCIU-TV 42
"We Are Pillows" 198
"We Could Be Happy" 56, 162–163
We Five 169, 178
"We Gotta Get Outta This Place" 21, 128, 163
Weavers 40
Weber, Bob 94
Weber, Clark 25, **26**, 36, 41, 51–**53**, 66, 80–82, 94, 96, 137, 161, 175, 211
Webster, Paul Francis 176
Weil, Cynthia 21, 61, 110, 114, 128, 163
Weintraub, Jerry 130, 143
Weird Tales 97
Weisberg, Tim 118
"We'll Meet Again" 165
Wells, H.G. 114
Wells Street 109, 156, 186
West, Sandy 31
Wexler, Jerry 95, 125
WGN-TV (Chicago) 22, 41–42, 135, 139
Wham Records **32**
When Chicago Rocked the '60s (documentary) 211
"When You Walk in the Room" 151
"Where Did You Come From" 150
Where the Action Is! 42, 58, 107, 110–111, 175; *see also* Clark, Dick; Revere, Paul and the Raiders
Whisky a Go Go (Hollywood club) 193
White, Tony Joe 193

"The White Ship" 97, 100–101
Whiteside, Bobby 114
Whitney 214
Who 15, 76, 78–79, 101, 112, 133
"Why Don't You Love Me" 148
Wilco 6, 214, 225n10
Wild Goose (teen club) 27, 51, 77; *see also* Card, Dex; teen clubs
Wild in the Streets 103, 114
Wildwood Records 115
Williams, Andy 34, 178
Williams, Paul 21
Williamson, Dick 49
Willamson, Sonny Boy 46
"Willie Jean" 88
Wilson, Brian 99, 168; *see also* Beach Boys
Wine and Roses (lounge) 58
Winwood, Steve 110
"Wipe Out" 16
Wisconsin 4, 16, 51, 60, 121, 135; Lake Geneva 51, **78**; Milwaukee 3, 36, 44, 138, 141, 157; Oconomowoc 44; Racine 141
Wisner, Jimmy 150, 160
Witchcraft Destroys Minds & Reaps Souls 179
"Without Us" 151 b
WLS AM-Radio 7, 17, 24–**26**, 31–**32**, **40**–42, 55, 64, 66, 71, 77, 93, 96, 103, 106, 109, 117, 122, 129, 131, 137, 140, 153, 156–158, 161–162, 167–168, 174–176, 178 184, 189, 199, 206–207, 209; airing "Gloria" 80–83; Beatles first U.S. radio airplay 45, 47; prairie to pop format transformation of 31–35; radio personalities 50–**53**, 54; rivalry with WCFL 49–50; Silver Dollar Survey 25, 37–**39**, 40, 47, 49, 55; "Swinging Seven" 17, 36, 54
Wolinski, Dave "Hawk" 75, 88, 101
Wonder, Stevie 44, 78, 124, 128, 133, 200
Wood, Ron 200
Wooden Nickel Records 130, 143
"Wooden Ships/Dharma for One" 27, 192
Woodley, Bruce 70, 162
Woodstock (film) 80
"Wooly Bully" 66
World Woven 200–201, 206
Wright, Frank Lloyd 6–7
Wright, Peter 63, 69, 159
Wrigley Field 45, 109, 204
WTTW-PBS TV 211
Wurlitzer 94

Yardbirds 20, 64, 66, 72, 76, 83–85, 102, 104, 108, 110, 121, 148, 155, 161
Yesterday and Today 158
"You Dove Deep into My Soul" 107
"You Make Me Feel So Good" 143
"You Were on My Mind" 169
"You Wouldn't Listen" 24, 56, 184–185

Young, Jesse Colin 178
Young, Neil 179, 193, 226n21
Young, Rusty 113, 201
"Young Birds Fly" 175, 178
Young Rascals 134
Youngbloods 23, 100–101, 178
"Your Love" 177
"You're Gonna Lose That Girl" 163, 180
"You've Made Me So Very Happy" 138, 188

Zawinul, Joe 123, 132
Zevon, Warren 213
Zombies 27, 81–82, 120, 143, 148, 160, 183
Zwillenberg, Joseph 194